Studies in
MALORY

Studies in
MALORY

edited by
James W. Spisak

Medieval Institute Publications
Western Michigan University
Kalamazoo, Michigan—1985

Copyright 1985 by the Board of the Medieval Institute
Western Michigan University
Kalamazoo, MI 49008

Library of Congress Cataloging in Publication Data
Main entry under title:

Studies in Malory.

   1. Malory, Thomas, Sir, 15th cent. Morte d'Arthur—
Addresses, essays, lectures.   2. Arthurian romances—
History and criticism—Addresses, essays, lectures.
I. Spisak, James W.
PR2045.S78   1985   823'.2   84-16542
ISBN: 0-918720-54-0 (hard)
ISBN: 0-918720-55-9 (paper)

Cover design by Elizabeth King

Printed in the United States of America

Preface

Five hundred years have passed since the publication by William Caxton of Sir Thomas Malory's *Le Morte Darthur*. The present volume has been compiled to mark that signal event in the history of English literature and printing. Critical studies of Malory's work are supplemented by essays that place his work in the larger context of Caxton's canon. The contributors to this volume are representative of an industrious and dedicated group of scholars who have vitalized Malory studies in our time. The differing approaches and methodologies in their essays reflect the variety of means through which an understanding of the *Morte* has been sought.

I am grateful to the following for permission to reproduce illustrations: The British Library, J. M. Dent & Sons, Ltd., Barbara Edwards, The Estate of Robert Gibbings, Michael Hornby, The Medici Society, Ltd., and The John Rylands University Library of Manchester.

I would like to thank Harry Damant and Margaret Schickel for their assistance in production; Scott Feathers for his help with the proofreading; and Juleen A. Eichinger and Thomas H. Seiler of Medieval Institute Publications for their valuable editorial advice.

J. W. S.

Table of Contents

Introduction:
Recent Trends in Malory Studies

James W. Spisak

Literary criticism on Malory has had a peculiar history. In a lecture on this topic published nearly twenty years ago, Larry Benson called *Le Morte Darthur* "a critical 'discovery' of the twentieth century."[1] Very shortly thereafter D. S. Brewer echoed Benson's statement: "The work of the last twenty years is greater than that of the preceding half millenium."[2] The burgeoning these statements describe was bounteous but localized—more like a rose bush than a rhododendron. Malory criticism since the time of these statements has grown in a more expansive way: scholars have reached beyond the questions of authorship and "unity" and are giving Malory the full literary treatment that other major (and minor) writers have long enjoyed. The aim of the present essay is to outline this new growth in hopes of suggesting a few topics for further research.[3]

Much of the work done on Malory before the discovery of the manuscript at Winchester was biographical. When the first edition of the *DNB* reported "there is no definite information respecting [Malory] outside his book,"[4] the hunt was on. In the following few decades documents from the Public Record Office and elsewhere were unearthed and fashioned into biographical sketches of Thomas Malorys. Two of the emerging candidates quickly gave

1

way to the third, Sir Thomas of Newbold Revel, Warwickshire, the only one whom we know to have been a knight. Following the energetic leadership of G. L. Kittredge,[5] scholars happily accepted the Warwickshire Malory as the author of England's classic romance.

The criticism boom of this century has allowed few hypotheses to go untested, as the subsequent investigations of this and other Malorys attest. In the 1920s some of Kittredge's followers—notably Edward Cobb, E. K. Chambers, and Edward Hicks—turned up information that seemed to taint the character of the Newbold Revel Malory. In only a few years the compatriot of Beauchamp also became a thief, a rapist, a ravager of convents, and the subject of a full-length biography.[6] The results of this scrutiny naturally raised many questions, including whether such a blackguard could have written the *Morte Darthur*. While most scholars accepted or attempted to resolve this "moral paradox," a few decades later William Matthews once again took up the hunt. He produced another Thomas Malory, from Yorkshire, who became the subject of the second full-length Malory biography.[7] As a prolegomenon to this man's life history, Matthews discredits the other Malorys—especially the Warwickshire knight—as serious candidates for authorship of the *Morte*. When Benson and Brewer wrote nearly twenty years ago, Matthews' work had just been published, but even then it was recognized as a landmark study.

Since the time of its publication, Matthews' work has itself been closely scrutinized, of course, and the lively exchange that has followed has been everything he could have hoped for. While many of his arguments, especially those based on dialect, have been challenged, the candidate he proposed cannot be readily dismissed. Perhaps more important is that the responses to several of Matthews' hypotheses produced some very thorough, if not conclusive, scholarship on the biographical issue. P. J. C. Field has promoted the candidacy of the Newbold Revel Malory, primarily on the grounds that he is the only one who was a knight. Field has meticulously removed many of the charges brought against this Warwickshireman and, more importantly, has shown that he was some twenty years younger than has been believed, thus answering the question of age that so troubled Matthews.[8] Age has also been an issue in the excavations of another scholar, Richard Griffith, who has returned to the Malory of Papworth St. Agnes that was edged out by Kittredge's candidate decades ago. But more important than this Malory's being in his forties at the time his work was allegedly completed is that he was a close friend of Anthony Wydville, the most likely patron of the *Morte,* and may have had access to his library.[9] The work of Griffith and Field has removed the glow Matthews' candidate had twenty years ago and has yielded a wealth of new information about all the candidates. But since no one has been able to establish a definite connection between any one of them and the *Morte Darthur,* the authorship question remains open to further research and debate.

An ancillary effect of Matthews' biographical study is that it focused attention on Malory's use of his English sources. Previous to that, most source studies treated his use of the French romances. The pioneer in that area was H. Oskar Sommer, who published the results of his researches in the third volume of his edition of Malory in 1891. Though Sommer's work has been greatly augmented and at times disputed, we remain grateful to him for the bold start he gave us. Another pioneer of source studies in Malory was Vida Scudder, who is credited with writing the first full-length critical study of *Le Morte Darthur.*[10] The most prominent scholar of Malory's handling of the French is, of course, Eugène Vinaver. Even before the Malory manuscript was discovered and turned over to him for editing, Vinaver had begun extensive studies on the sources for the Grail and especially the Tristram sections.[11] In the Commentary to his (1947) edition of the manuscript,[12] Vinaver gave us an extensive and rich account of Malory's handling of the French sources for all the sections of his work. His observations of Malory's practices and the conclusions he drew from them touched off the familiar "unity" debate, which resulted in even further readings of Malory against the French. The major opposition to Vinaver's theory of separate romances was presented in a series of essays by R. H. Wilson and in the two collections of essays edited by J. A. W. Bennett and R. M. Lumiansky.[13] But except for the alliterative *Morte Arthure* and stanzaic *Le Morte Arthur,* the sources scrutinized in these studies were predominantly French.

In the past twenty years, however, the study of Malory's English sources has grown. Matthews led the way in *The Ill-Framed Knight*, as well as in *The Tragedy of Arthur*,[14] his study of the alliterative *Morte Arthure*, by probing the boundaries of what Wilson and E. T. Donaldson had established. As a result we learned that Malory's use of the alliterative and stanzaic poems was more extensive than we had believed and, further, that his knowledge of the English chronicle and romance traditions was broader than we had supposed. Matthews suggested, for example, that Malory drew the triumphant conclusion to his Roman War episode from Hardyng's *Chronicle* and that he drew several of his minor figures from *The Avowynge of Arthur, Awntyrs of Arthur*, and *The Weddynge of Sir Gawen*. Supplementing Matthews' work, several scholars, notably Wilson and Edward D. Kennedy, have offered new evidence of Malory's familiarity with these and yet other English works.

Among the major proponents of Malory's English heritage is Larry Benson. In his *Critical Approaches* survey, Benson found it "curious that Malory has never been studied as an English romancer."[15] Pointing to Arthur Ferguson's study of chivalric idealism,[16] Benson suggested that Malory was anglicizing, rather than simply translating or modernizing, the French sources he used and that his method was characteristically that of an English romancer. We can now see that this survey offered only a sampling of what was to come ten years later. In *Malory's Morte Darthur*[17] Benson offers a full treatment of Malory's work in the context of his English sources. After discussing the nature of the continental prose cycles and their influence on Malory, he amply demonstrates that prose romance continued to flourish in the fifteenth century, both on the continent and in England. Benson then examines the specific characteristics of English romance, drawing upon many examples to give us a sense of their "typical" form and content. In this context Benson discusses Malory's technique, showing his adherence to some conventions and his modification of others. While we may quibble with some of Benson's assumptions about Malory's progress as a writer, we come away from this book with a much better understanding of the literary and social world in which he worked.

We are fortunate that the recent interest in Malory as an English romancer has invigorated rather than detracted from the study of his use of the French sources. We have a clearer sense now than we did twenty years ago of Malory's literary context, and as a result we can more accurately evaluate his work with the French. Rather than accuse Malory of translating or adapting *La Queste del Saint Graal*, for example, we can appreciate him as an English writer producing a Grail story for an English audience. His emphasis on chivalry, then, does not indicate a tendency to secularize so much as it reveals the author's sensitivity to his readership as well as to the larger construct of his narrative. Such an enlightened perspective has informed recent scholarship on Malory's use of the French, notably that by Mary Hynes-Berry, Dhira Mahoney, and Jill Mann.

Scholarship on Malory's language and style has grown so much in the past twenty years that the few studies which came earlier are often forgotten. The first was C. S. Baldwin's methodical study of Malory's morphology and syntax.[18] Over thirty years later Vinaver devoted a chapter in *Malory* to style, which is a useful if limited comparison of a few specific passages in Malory with their French sources. Nearly another twenty years later Jan Simko compared the word order of the two versions of Malory's work,[19] but again his study was rather narrowly defined: he limited his discussion to the Roman War episodes, where there was the most drastic change, but where, as a result, we are able to see all the fewer aspects of syntax that can with certainty be called Malorian. In 1968 A. O. Sandved published a more broadly based comparison of the two versions,[20] concluding that there is a marked difference between Caxton's own language and that which appears in his edition of *Le Morte Darthur.*

Linguistic studies in Malory have been greatly enhanced by the appearance of Tomomi Kato's *Concordance* in 1974.[21] This massive volume, while listing the linguistic forms as they appear in Vinaver's edition of the manuscript, does include cross references to the book and chapter numbers in Caxton, so that one who wanted to use it for linguistic comparison of the two texts could, with some effort, do so. Kato's work signals the burst of linguistic study in Malory that has been going on in Japan for the past two decades. Yuji Nakao, Kunio Nakashima, and Shunichi Noguchi have been the most prolific of an impressive syndicate of philologists.

When Benson and Brewer wrote nearly twenty years ago, Malory's style had been praised much more often than it had been probed. Since then, however, two fine full-length studies on the subject have been published, independent of the more straightforward linguistic analyses being done in Japan. The first of these, *Romance and Chronicle: A Study of Malory's Prose Style*,[22] by P. J. C. Field, appeared in 1971. In this thorough study, Field places Malory in the tradition of chronicle writers of the fifteenth century, thus explaining the lack of ornateness and self-consciousness in his style. Field sees Malory as being far from the omniscient narrator that we see in other medieval romances, but rather more like an innocent, naive narrator whose only concern was the simple truth of his story. Such a view of the narrator is attested, Field claims, by the simple vocabulary and very straightforward syntax that characterize Malory's prose. Field supports his theory by examining both the descriptive passages in the *Morte*, which he shows to consist primarily of stock phrases taken either from Malory's sources or from the common language of his day, and his dialogue, which is characterized as direct and familiar, though not without variety. Field succeeds in convincing us of Malory's colloquial style without lowering our estimation of the fifteenth-century author, perhaps because the examples he cites also show us that Malory was, in fact, in control of his narrative.

The second full-length study of Malory's style, *Malory: Style and Vision in Le Morte Darthur* by Mark Lambert,[23] appeared four years later. As his title indicates, Lambert regards Malory as a more conscious stylist than does Field. While Lambert acknowledges his indebtedness to Field's study, he suggests that some of the devices Field regards as colloquial could also be seen as self-conscious. Lambert begins by neatly describing some of the features of narration and dialogue that characterize fifteenth-century prose, thus providing a backdrop against which he then outlines Malory's technique. Asserting from the outset that Malory's style is an "impure, inconsistent" one, Lambert reveals the various patterns he used throughout the narrative. Malory reduces the number of physical comparisons, the amount of description given to setting, the details associated with the mechanical aspects of chivalry, and most overt expressions of emotion. Lambert sees the historical style that results from these changes as essential in conveying the sense of the tragedy inherent in the closing tales: only by keeping us separate from these events could Malory show us their tragic impact. The value of Lambert's work, and of Field's, is that both scholars study style as a means of further understanding the meaning of Malory's work. Such an approach nicely complements the purely linguistic one.

Two decades ago studies of the structure of Malory's work had been dominated, following the discovery of the manuscript version, by the question of unity, a debate sufficiently familiar that it need not be rehearsed here. Since then other types of structural criticism have been written. Stephen Knight was among the first to break away from the unity debate in *The Structure of Sir Thomas Malory's Arthuriad*.[24] He argues that Malory's work is neither a unified whole nor a series of discrete tales, in the senses scholars have suggested. Knight suggests that Malory changed the structure of his work midstream: that the first half is episodic, consisting of independent tales only loosely connected by their setting, and the second half is a continuous narrative, moving with a single vision and the same basic set of characters toward a clearly defined end. While Knight's answer to the unity debate is often very insightful, the structure he offers seems only slightly less artificial than the ones it is trying to replace, and he seems no more able to refrain from trying to establish Malory's intentions than those whom he criticizes for doing so by relying too heavily upon source study.

A concern with Malory's structure also underlies other recent studies whose focus is fixed on other critical approaches. In *Malory's Morte Darthur* Benson demonstrates how the structure of English romance, which he calls "bracketing," differs from the *entrelacement* that characterizes the French prose romances. Benson further shows how both historical and thematic structures are important to the impact of the entire work and how one works alongside the other to exhibit the stories of Arthur and his knights and to exemplify Malory's ideas of chivalry. Structural concerns also underly an essay in which Murray J. Evans closely examines the explicits, decoration, and layout of the manuscript to conclude that Malory's work, as represented here, falls into five parts, not the eight tales to which we have grown accustomed.[25] Most recently,

Sandra Ness Ihle, in *Malory's Grail Quest*,[26] uses poetical and architectural terminology as a basis for discussing the structures of *La Queste del Saint Graal* and Malory's careful adaptation of it.

A thorough consideration of the style and structure of a work needs to take another factor into account, the order in which the various parts of the work were composed. In this aspect Malory scholarship has been somewhat spare. We are fortunate, with Malory, that both extant versions of the texts present the tales in the same order, which has prevented the wholesale rearranging that, say, the *Canterbury Tales* have suffered; there has never been any doubt that the whole of the *Morte* should be read in the order in which its various parts appear. But this has allowed us, all too easily, to assume that they were written in that order. When Vinaver published his first edition of the manuscript, he became the first to question Malory's order of composition, contending that the Roman War episode, because of the unpolished state in which it exists in the manuscript, was an early work, composed before the tales that precede it. But the reasons for this argument were soon turned against it, and it now receives little support. Aside from the debate over the early tales, the major challenge to the conventional assumptions about sequence have come from Terence McCarthy. In his first essay on the topic,[27] McCarthy suggested, on the basis of stylistic evidence and a few allusions, the following order: Grail, Roman War, Tristram, Merlin, Lancelot, Gareth, and Morte (both sections). He has reaffirmed this order in a sequel,[28] citing forward and backward allusions within the *Morte*, the clustering of minor characters, and recurring words and phrases for further support. Though he warns that such details cannot stand alone as evidence for ordering the tales, he shows that their cumulative effect indicates that Malory began *in medias res*.

Though this is certainly not the place to tackle the question of order, a bit of speculation on the Tale of Gareth may illustrate the complexity of the issue. There is no known single source for this tale, though recent contributions by P. J. C. Field and T. L. Wright[29] bring us closer to one than we have been so far. The final position of the tale, also traditionally thought to be the position of its sequence in composition, is after the Tale of Lancelot. But we cannot accept this without question: there is no connection at the beginning of the Tale of Gareth to the previous tale, and the character of Lancelot—particularly his age or level of maturity—is drastically different in the two tales. If they were written in the order they now occupy, something else was probably written during the intervening time. The Tale of Gareth is generally regarded as a highly polished, "mature" tale, which may be why McCarthy places it near the end of Malory's canon. But for all its pleasures and charms, this tale is no more refined than the Tale of Balin, and in fact it betrays certain aspects of a neophyte redactor. There is a relatively large amount of inverted word order, which suggests early work with the French sources, and a notable number of Gallic words remain as well. Furthermore, the heavy use of alliteration in the Tale of Gareth, as well as the appearance of vocabulary found elsewhere in Malory only in the Roman War episode, suggests that these two were written during the same period. Finally, we ought not to assume that the Tale of Gareth was written all at once: it does fall rather neatly into two parts, the division marked by the arrival of the Queen of Orkeney. This suggests the possibility of two major sources and, consequently, of two separate "sittings" for the writer. If the sources of this tale are ever discovered, its rudimentary construction may become more apparent; but like the Tale of Balin, it will be none the less enjoyable for the wear.

Questions of language and style—and even of the order of composition—are complicated by the presence of two versions of the text. Since the discovery of the manuscript was one of the motive forces of the criticism boom in Malory, it is only natural that the scholarship of the past fifty years has centered around that witness to the text. When the manuscript was discovered, Vinaver set aside the edition of Caxton he was working on so that he could edit the newer version. This edition, familiar to us now as *Works*, has provided a solid foundation for Malory studies since its publication. But around that foundation have grown two assumptions which are less solid: that the manuscript version is somehow closer to Malory's holograph than Caxton's edition, and therefore more "authentic"; and that Caxton exercised a heavy editorial hand in producing his Malory. Both of these assumptions have been challenged recently— a task made easier by the appearance of facsimile editions of the two texts[30]—and scholars have come to realize that the manuscript has no better claims to authenticity than does its incunabular counterpart. Since Caxton's version is now available in a scholarly edition,[31] future studies in Malory may consider both witnesses to the text.

Virginia Polytechnic Institute
and State University

NOTES

[1]"Sir Thomas Malory's *Le Morte Darthur*," in *Critical Approaches to Six Major English Works*, ed. R. M. Lumiansky and Herschel Baker (Philadelphia: University of Pennsylvania Press, 1968), p. 81.

[2]"The Present Study of Malory," in *Arthurian Romance: Seven Essays*, ed. D. D. R. Owen (1970; rpt. New York: Barnes and Noble, 1971), p. 83.

[3]Such an essay is, in Brewer's words, "necessarily impressionistic." In what follows full bibliographic references are given only for those works that have been drawn from directly. For a complete chronological listing of Malory scholarship through 1977, see Page West Life, *Sir Thomas Malory and the Morte Darthur* (Charlottesville: University Press of Virginia, 1980).

[4]Sidney Lee, "Sir Thomas Malory," *Dictionary of National Biography* (1893; rpt. 1917).

[5]"Sir Thomas Malory, or Maleore," *Johnson's Universal Cyclopedia*, 5 (1894), p. 498, and *Sir Thomas Malory* (1925; rpt. Folcroft, Penn.: Folcroft Press, 1974).

[6]Edward Hicks, *Sir Thomas Malory: His Turbulent Career* (1928; rpt. New York: Octagon Books, 1970).

[7]*The Ill-Framed Knight* (Berkeley and Los Angeles: University of California Press, 1966).

[8]"Thomas Malory: The Hutton Documents," *Medium Aevum*, 48 (1979), 213-39; "Thomas Malory and the Warwick Retinue Roll," *Midland History*, 5 (1979-80), 20-30; "The Last Years of Sir Thomas Malory," *Bulletin of the John Rylands Library*, 64 (1982), 433-56.

[9]"Arthur's Author: The Mystery of Sir Thomas Malory," *Ventures in Research*, 1 (1972), 7-43; "The Authorship Question Reconsidered: A Case for Thomas Malory of Papworth St. Agnes, Cambridgeshire," in *Aspects of Malory*, ed. T. Takamiya and D. S. Brewer (Cambridge: D. S. Brewer, 1981), pp. 159-77.

[10]*Le Morte Darthur of Sir Thomas Malory: A Study of the Book and its Sources* (1917; rpt. London: J. M. Dent, 1921).

[11]*Le Roman de Tristan et Iseut dans l'oeuvre de Thomas Malory*

(Paris: H Champion, 1925), and *Malory* (1929; rpt. Oxford: Oxford University Press, 1970).

[12] *The Works of Sir Thomas Malory*, 3 vols. (Oxford: Oxford University Press, 1947; 2nd ed. 1967).

[13] J. A. W. Bennett, ed., *Essays on Malory* (Oxford: Oxford University Press, 1963); R. M. Lumiansky, ed., *Malory's Originality* (Baltimore: John Hopkins Press, 1964).

[14] Berkeley and Los Angeles: University of California Press, 1960.

[15] *Critical Approaches*, p. 107.

[16] *The Indian Summer of English Chivalry: Studies in the Decline and Transformation of Chivalric Idealism* (Durham, N. C.: Duke University Press, 1960). For an interpretation quite different from Benson's, see Elizabeth T. Pochoda, *Arthurian Propaganda* (Chapel Hill: University of North Carolina Press, 1971).

[17] Cambridge, Mass.: Harvard University Press, 1976.

[18] *The Inflections and Syntax of the Morte D'Arthur of Sir Thomas Malory: A Study in Fifteenth-Century English* (Boston: Ginn and Co., 1894).

[19] *Word-Order in the Winchester Manuscript and in William Caxton's Edition of Thomas Malory's 'Morte Darthur' (1485)—A Comparison* (Halle: Niemeyer, 1957).

[20] *Studies in the Language of Caxton's Malory and that of the Winchester Manuscript* (Oslo: Norwegian University Press, 1968).

[21] *Concordance to the Works of Sir Thomas Malory* (Tokyo: University of Tokyo Press, 1974).

[22] Bloomington: Indiana University Press, 1971.

[23] New Haven: Yale University Press, 1975.

[24] Sydney: Sydney University Press, 1969.

[25] "The Explicits and Narrative Division in the Winchester MS: A Critique of Vinaver's Malory," *Philological Quarterly*, 58 (1979), 263-81.

[26] Madison: University of Wisconsin Press, 1983.

[27] "Order of Composition in the 'Morte Darthur'," *Yearbook of English Studies*, 1 (1971), 18-29.

[28] "The Sequence of Malory's Tales," in *Aspects of Malory*.

[29] P. J. C. Field, "The Source of Malory's *Tale of Gareth*," in *Aspects of Malory*; T. L. Wright, "On the Genesis of Malory's *Gareth*," *Speculum*, 57 (1982), 569-82.

[30] *The Winchester Malory: A Facsimile Edition*, E.E.T.S. S.S. 4 (Oxford: Oxford University Press, 1976); Sir Thomas Malory, *Le Morte Darthur* [facsimile of Caxton's edition] (London: Scolar Press, 1976).

[31] James W. Spisak, ed., *Caxton's Malory. A New Edition of Sir Thomas Malory's Le Morte Darthur Based on the Pierpont Morgan Copy of*

INTRODUCTION

William Caxton's Edition of 1485, 2 vols. (Berkeley and Los Angeles: University of California Press, 1983). Several contributors to this volume have kindly used this edition for citations to Malory's text; they should be seen as indulging an editor, not giving tacit approval to an edition. Vinaver's *Works* will continue to be cited by many long after this volume goes to press.

Malory's Identification of Camelot as Winchester[1]

Sue Ellen Holbrook

In Sir Thomas Malory's *Morte Darthur*, Arthur, a peripatetic monarch, has courts at several of the work's 110 cities, castles, and other secular dwellings: notably, at London, Caerleon, Carlisle, Kinkenadon, Westminster, Winchester, and Camelot.[2] Most of these courts are known sites. Specifically, London, Westminster, Winchester, Caerleon, and Carlisle had existed under those names for hundreds of years before Malory finished his book in 1470 and have remained under those names until this very day. But such is not the case with Camelot, now the most famous Arthurian city of them all. Although Malory is not the first author to mention Camelot, he is the first to identify it, to tell us where it is. His identification is not only first but also unique. Malory alone has said that Camelot is Winchester. What led Malory to this identification? The answer turns on a piece of furniture that he connected with the Grail legend: the Round Table at Winchester.[3] To discover how Malory made this connection, we shall look at his references to Camelot and to Winchester, at his sources for those references, and at what made Winchester appropriate as Camelot, particularly the Round Table there. We shall see that Malory may have associated Winchester with Camelot because he had read in

John Hardyng's *Chronicle* of a link between the knight who achieved the Holy Grail and the table at Winchester.

As the scene of court or an important activity, not just a passing reference, Camelot occurs in fourteen of the twenty-one books in Caxton's version of *Le Morte Darthur.* Malory first brings in Camelot at the start of Book II, the Tale of Balin: Arthur, who is at London, calls a council-general and great jousts at a castle "called Camelot in tho dayes" (62.11). As the story develops, Malory refers to Camelot another four times. In the last reference, which occurs within the final fifteen sentences of this book, Malory glosses Camelot as Winchester. After burying Balin and Balan on the island where they killed each other, Merlin takes from Balin a certain sword, which he says is destined for Sir Lancelot or Galahad his son, and he puts the sword in a "marbel stone," which, we then hear, eventually "swam doun the streme to the Cyte of Camelot, that is in Englysshe Wynchestre," where Galahad withdrew the sword (78.33-38).

In the ten books that follow, the name Camelot comes up another thirty-one times. When Malory reaches Chapter 10 of Book XII, he glosses the name again: Lancelot and his brother Ector leave the Joyous Isle, where Lancelot has lived in banishment with Elaine, the mother of Galahad, and they come to "Camelot, that is called in Englyssh Wynchester" (422.26-27). In the final four chapters of Book XII and in the Quest of the Holy Grail, which comprises Books XIII-XVII, Camelot is mentioned several more times, though not glossed as Winchester. Camelot makes its last appearance in the second half of Book XVIII, which tells the story of another Elaine, the Fair Maid of Astolat. There Malory brings in Camelot by name three times, glossing it the first two times as Winchester. Arthur calls "a grete iustes and a turnement that shold be at that daye att Camelot, that is Wynchester" (515.4-5), and a bit later Sir Lancelot and Sir Lavayne "rode soo long til that they came to Camelot, that tyme called Wynchestre" (517.8-9).

Apart from the four Camelot glosses, Winchester itself appears three times in *Le Morte Darthur*, first as the place where Pedivere finds Guenevere and Arthur towards the end of the tale of Lancelot (156); later as the place of the trial by combat between Mador and Guenevere's defender in the story of the Poisoned Apple (509, 512);[4]

14

and finally as the place where the usurping Mordred, who has had himself crowned at Canterbury, "drewe him . . . And there he took the Quene Gueneuer and sayd playnly that he wold wedde hyr" and prepares for the wedding (584.6-7).

Malory owes many of these references to Camelot and Winchester to the works out of which he made his Arthuriad. Camelot he found in certain French works that form the thirteenth-century Vulgate Cycle.[5] Specifically, all but one of Malory's five references to Camelot in the Tale of Balin also exist in the *Suite du Merlin* (which includes Camelot as one of Arthur's courts along with Cardoel and Caerleon). Malory adds that the dwarf who finds Balin after he has slain Launceor comes from the city of Camelot (67), and he provides the phrase "called . . . in tho dayes" to the first reference (62.11) and the gloss "that is in Englysshe Wynchestre" to the last (78.35). For Books III and IV, which begin with Arthur's marriage to Guenevere and cover several adventures, Malory retains five references to Camelot that the *Suite du Merlin* has, omits at least four others, and adds another eleven not in the *Suite*. A look at E. Löseth's synopsis of the prose *Tristan* (which sets Arthur primarily at Camelot) suggests that Malory found in that romance all fifteen of the references to Camelot that his Tristram section has. For the Quest of the Holy Grail, Malory carries over seven references from the French version (in which Camelot alone is Arthur's court), adds another four, and evidently leaves out a good many others. For Book XVIII, where Malory mentions Camelot three times in conjunction with the tournament at Winchester, he transfers the *Mort Artu* references to Winchester from that city to Camelot— presumably doing so because earlier he has identified the two cities with each other—whereas the *Mort Artu* treats them as separate places. Malory changes or deletes all the other, numerous references to Camelot that the *Mort Artu* (which emphasizes Camelot as Arthur's court) has both in the story of the tournament and throughout the rest of the narrative. As for Winchester in *Le Morte Darthur*, only the tournament at Winchester comes to Malory from a French source.[6] He himself contributes the glosses, the reference in Book VI, where Winchester is Arthur's court, and that in Book XVIII, where the trial by combat takes place in the meadow beside Winchester. Malory finds the third Winchester reference, as the place Mordred prepares to marry Guenevere, in one of his English sources, the stanzaic *Morte Arthur*.

Camelot, then, comes to Malory as an inheritance from the Vulgate cycle,[7] but its identification with Winchester does not. What led Malory to make that identification? One possibility is that he did not expect his readers to recognize Camelot as a current place name—for so the phrase "in tho dayes" implies—and therefore looked around for a suitable English city that they would recognize. Winchester certainly was suitable, for, as a royal city, it carried a reputation in both medieval literature and history. Within specifically Arthurian literature, Winchester is introduced by Geoffrey of Monmouth's *Historia Regum Britanniae*. There Winchester is a residence not of Arthur but of Aurelius Ambrosius, Arthur's uncle; moreover, Arthur besieges his usurping nephew Mordred at Winchester, and not long after Arthur's death, the new king, Constantine, kills one of Mordred's sons at Winchester. Wace and Layamon perpetuate Geoffrey's use of Winchester as the place where Aurelius dies of poison and as the place where Arthur besieges the retreating traitor Mordred. Chrétien de Troyes, in his tale *Cligés*, gives Winchester as the court where Alexander, Cligés' father, finds King Arthur. In various other French verse and prose Arthurian stories, Winchester comes in, usually as the place of a tournament or a battle against Mordred or his sons.[8] In English, the stanzaic *Morte Arthur*, as we have seen, places Mordred at Winchester when he announces his intention to wed Guenevere; the alliterative *Morte Arthure* has Gawain buried at Winchester; and John Hardyng's *Chronicle*, begun in 1436 and in a final revision by 1465, mentions Winchester three times, once as the place that Uther set the Round Table, once in a list of Arthur's courts, and finally as the site of Arthur's siege of Mordred. Furthermore, in *Sir Orfeo*, a non-Arthurian English verse romance of the fourteenth century, King Orfeo lives in England at Winchester, which was then called, says the poet, Traciens, "a cite of noble defens."[9]

Winchester had, indeed, been a city of noble defense for a long time in British history, as Martin Biddle's recent excavations make especially clear.[10] In the pre-Roman Iron Age, the Belgae built a defended enclosure on the spur of the west side of the valley. By the end of the first century A. D., a Roman fort and town had been established in the valley bottom, Venta Belgarum, which was refortified in the fourth century and still occupied around the walls and probably within from ca. 500 through the seventh century. From about 675 on, Winchester was the seat of a bishop and probably an occasional residence of the West Saxon Kings as well as the site of secular, private dwellings and a street market. By the ninth century, Winchester had definitely become a royal city, a ceremonial center that existed in complement to the urban community of Southampton. From Alfred's refoundation of Winchester as a fortified city in the late ninth century to William's residence there within four months after the battle of Hastings, Winchester grew into the principal royal city of England. It reached its peak of size and wealth about the mid-twelfth century, but even during its gradual decline after the civil war, royalty visited and were crowned or born there and—until the mid-seventeenth century—kept the royal castle in use. In the later fifteenth century, Winchester's mayor and citizens, who wanted lighter taxes, referred to it as one of the kingdom's ancient cities, which in times past had been chosen over others for royal coronations and burials.

Winchester, then, though not a significant royal city since losing its treasury to Westminster in the 1180s, was known in Malory's day to trail a long and venerable history as a city of kings. Malory himself had Winchester's legendary past before him in some of the very books that he drew upon: *Sir Orfeo*, [11] the stanzaic *Morte Arthur*, the alliterative *Morte Arthure*, the French *Mort Artu*, and probably Hardyng's *Chronicle*, from which Malory seems to have taken, among other details, Arthur's coronation at Rome.[12]

Given Winchester's reputation in literature and history, we see easily why Winchester might seem fitting to Malory as one of Arthur's courts. Yet, to be fitting as one of Arthur's courts is not inevitably to be identified as Camelot; after all, the author of the French *Mort Artu* treats Camelot and Winchester as separate entities within the same story. Furthermore, Camelot is not the only one of Arthur's courts in *Le Morte Darthur* that bears a name apparently unfamiliar to fifteenth-century readers. At the beginning of the Tale of Gareth, Malory locates Arthur at "a cyte and a castel, the whiche in tho dayes was called Kynkekenadonne, vpon the sondes that marched nyghe Walys" (158.2-4). He does not, however, go on here, or at the end of the tale when Arthur is again at Kinkenadon, to explain what this place is called in his day and tongue as he does with Camelot. Therefore, it was not a search for a plausible city with a current and well known name that brought Malory to identify Camelot as Winchester. Rather, he lighted upon a specific link of identification between the two cities, a round table. And what led him to this link was not any Wincastrian claim to having been an Arthurian capital with relics of the king, for Winchester itself does not appear to have made such a boast. Rather, Malory made the connection through the Grail legend in which young Galahad arrives at Camelot to take his seat at the Round Table, a type of round table to be found in Malory's day only at Winchester.

Malory's first two identifications of Camelot show this connection with the Grail legend, while his third, during the Fair Maid of Astolat story, surely results from the first two. In the first identification, the Balin passage, Malory amplifies the forecast his source gives, explaining that "that same day Galahad the Haute Prynce came with Kyng Arthur" and pulled "the swerde that was there in the marbel stone houynge vpon the water" (78.35-38). Malory mentions the Table as an object in the chapter that immediately follows the Balin story (80) and three chapters later (83) refers to the Siege Perilous, i. e., the seat reserved for Galahad at the Table. The next identification of Camelot comes at the end of the Lancelot and Elaine of Corbenic story in which Lancelot begets Galahad. After Ector has persuaded Lancelot to return to Arthur from his exile, Elaine tells Launcelot that "at this same feest of Pentecost shall your sone and myn Galahalt be made knyghte, for he is fully now xv wynter old" (422.25-27). Within a few lines we read that Ector and Lancelot "departed and within fyue dayes iourney they came to Camelot, that is called in Englyssh Wynchester" (422.30-31),[13] where Arthur mentions Galahad, "and men saye he shalle doo merueylles" (423.1). Four short chapters later, which end with Palomides and Tristram having come to Camelot for the "same feeste [at which] came Galahad and sat in the sege perillous" (426.31), Malory opens his Grail story at Camelot. In chapter two he describes the inscription that appears on this Siege Perilous and the two actions he had forecast in Book II—the arrival of Galahad and the pulling of the sword in the stone "here bynethe

at the ryuer" (429.4-5). In both instances in which Malory identifies
Camelot, then, the context is Galahad's arrival at court, which
within a few continuous passages in each case involves the physical
Round Table and its Siege Perilous.

To find out why Malory connected the table used in his Grail
story with the physical table at Winchester, we must unravel both
the history of the "round table" that he inherited from literature
and the history of the table that Winchester still houses. For Malory,
the "Round Table" is the name of both a special order of knights
and a physical feasting table that the knights of that order use. He
found this association of an order with a piece of furniture in the
Vulgate cycle, which in turn drew upon a notion of the Round
Table that had developed during the twelfth century from two
distinct traditions, both with obscure origins. In the first, the
Round Table is a secular feasting table associated with a special
band of warriors. In the second, it is a religious feasting table
associated with the Grail.

The first of these traditions comes to us through Wace and
Layamon in their versions of Geoffrey of Monmouth.[14] There
Arthur has a round table made so that at royal feasts his
companions will not vie for privileged seating. The idea in twelfth-
century romances that Arthur headed a special order of knights
associated with a round table probably results, indirectly, from the
passage in Wace or the British sources Wace himself refers to.[15] The
first instance that we have of the idea of the special order occurs in
Erec et Enide (ca. 1170s or 1180s), where Chrétien refers to Erec,
"who belonged to the Round Table."[16] Chrétien does not, however,
bring the Round Table in as a piece of furniture in any of his extant
romances, including the *Conte del Graal.*

In the second tradition, Merlin makes the Round Table as a
successor to the table at Christ's Last Supper and its symbolic
progeny, the table that Joseph of Arimathea used when he came to
Logres with the Grail. The earliest reference we have to the Round
Table's having been built to resemble that made by Joseph of
Arimathea comes in a prose *Merlin* that precedes the Didot *Perceval,*
which was probably composed as early as 1191-1215. This prose
Merlin is thought to be a redaction of the now fragmentary verse
Merlin of Robert de Boron, which follows Robert's *Joseph*

19

d'Arimathea, in which Joseph makes the Grail table in the image of the Last Supper table.[17] The idea of linking Arthur's Round Table with these two other tables is, according to Alexandre Micha, Robert's own "daring and felicitous conception."[18] The inspiration of Robert de Boron or otherwise, this second tradition of the Round Table, in which it is associated with the Grail, clearly picks up the secular feasting table that Wace introduced and conflates it with the belief that the table of the Last Supper was round, a belief that pilgrims back from the Holy Land attested to and that illustrators of the Last Supper observed.[19]

Malory, then, receives from sources blended in the late twelfth to thirteenth centuries the idea of the Round Table as a piece of furniture that has places inscribed with the names of knights of a special fellowship for them to sit at during ceremonial feasts and that has a special seat for the achiever of the Grail. He also inherits directly from the *Suite du Merlin* and *Queste del Saint Graal* this Round Table's location at Camelot.[20] And, this location of the Grail Round Table at Camelot is what leads Malory to identify Camelot as Winchester. For, although physical round tables were fairly rare in medieval Europe, it so happens that at Winchester one has existed for centuries—an Arthur's Round Table.[21]

The Winchester Round Table is an enormous oaken object, eighteen feet in diameter, perfectly round. Since 1522 when Henry VIII brought the Emperor Charles V to see it as part of a splendid celebration, it has been painted, showing twenty-four spokes of green and white with the Tudor white rose upon red rose at the center, names of Arthurian knights around the rim, and in a canopied seat at the top a King Arthur in full regalia whose sweet face is an eighteenth-century repainting of the original one to be found underneath—that of Henry VIII himself.[22] Since at least the fifteenth century, the table has been hanging, like a hatchment— now normally on the west wall, earlier on the east wall—of the Great Hall of the erstwhile castle. But, as the mortices on its back show, it was designed to be a table standing on legs when it was first built, probably during the 1270s.[23] Although we can suppose that the patron responsible for the building of this table was Edward I, a king known for Arthurian interests,[24] we do not yet know why the table was built or whether its original sponsor was influenced by the

Grail tradition as well as the secular tradition, both evidently in existence before the Winchester table was.

In whatever way the Winchester Table came into being, in Malory's day it was hanging, unpainted, in the Great Hall of Winchester Castle and associated with Arthur.[25] Might Malory have concluded that Camelot was Winchester because he knew of the Winchester Round Table in general or even knew Winchester itself well enough to have seen the table there? Clearly, Malory was familiar with the frequently travelled route from London to Winchester via Guildford, for he is specific and accurate beyond his sources about it in Book XVIII, in which he identifies Astolat, where Arthur and later Lancelot stop overnight, as Guildford ("a towne called Astolot, that is now in Englyssh called Gylford" [515.21-22], and "Astolat, that is Gylford" [515.40]). Moreover, although he does not describe Camelot/Winchester extensively, the details that he gives here and there are—with one crucial exception—details that Winchester itself did have, i. e., a location in the south, a forest, a meadowland for a tilting ground, a river, a major road, a royal castle, and a great minster. Malory's French sources, however, also provide these details about Camelot (although Malory is more emphatic about its southern location), and besides, except for the southern location, they are details one expects of any royal city. Furthermore, there is a crucial detail that makes Malory's knowledge of Winchester unlikely to be more than casual: the name he gives for the great minster in the stories of Balin and of Arthur's marriage is St. Stephen's (71.8, 83.20). This name occurs in his French sources for the minster in Camelot, but had Malory known Winchester at all well, he would not have retained it without at least a comment like his earlier aside about St. Paul's in London (37.6-7), for Winchester has never had a St. Stephen's as minster, church, or chapel.[26] Thus, although Malory may have been aware of Winchester's table, it is not likely to have been an acquaintance with Winchester itself that led him to conclude that Camelot was Winchester.

Malory may well have come to this conclusion, however, because he had read in Hardyng's *Chronicle* that the Round Table of the Grail Quest was at Winchester, not at Camelot as the French source said. In a passage before Arthur's coronation in Rome—the description of which Malory seems to have used for the end of his War with Lucius—Hardyng records the story of Uther's marriage to Igrayne and his commission of the Round Table:

> To comfort her he sette the table rounde
> At Wynchester, of worthiest knightes alone
> Approved best in knighthode of their foone;
> Which table rounde Ioseph of Arimathie,
> For brether made of the seynt Grall onely.
> In which he made the seege perelouse,
> Where none shulde sytte without great mischiefe;
> But one that should be moste religious
> Of knights all, and of the round table chiefe,
> The saynt Graal that shuld recouer and acheue
> By aduenture of his fortunitee,
> And at his death a virgyne shulde bee.[27]

Although Hardyng does not name Galahad here, by the fifteenth century, the Siege Perilous and the achievement of the Holy Grail were linked exclusively to Galahad, and in fact Hardyng begins the story of the Grail Quest in another eleven pages with Galahad at fifteen coming to court.

In the dozen lines of his account of the Round Table, Hardyng compresses the two traditions about the Round Table that had developed by the beginning of the thirteenth century, the secular feasting table for a special fellowship and the table of the Grail Quest. A few pages later, Hardyng, who never mentions Camelot anywhere, lists Winchester as one of the twenty cities where Arthur "held his household and the Round Table" (p. 126). Then shortly after Arthur's coronation at Rome, we read of Arthur's battle with Mordred at Winchester, at which point Hardyng adds that "The round table at Wynchester beganne,/ And there it ended, and there it hangeth yet" (p. 146).

In short, Malory probably would not have attempted to identify Camelot at all had he not made the connection between the round tables of the Grail legend and Winchester. Since Hardyng, like Malory, associates the Winchester Round Table with the Grail Quest, his *Chronicle* seems to be a more likely source for Malory's identification than anything else we know of.[28] It is probable, then, that the passage in which Hardyng links the Round Table at Winchester with the Grail achiever gave Malory the idea that Camelot, a name he did not recognize as current for an English locality, must be Winchester because it was to Camelot that the Grail achiever came to sit at the table that Hardyng says is at Winchester. But, even if Malory did not identify Camelot as Winchester because he had read Hardyng, he surely did make this identification because he associated the round table of the Grail legend with the round table of Winchester.[29] And so came "the Cyte of Camelot, that is in Englysshe Wynchestre."

Franklin and Marshall College

NOTES

[1] This essay derives from earlier versions that I have given at the Thirteenth Congress of the International Arthurian Society, Glasgow, 11-19 August 1981; the Lilly-Pennsylvania Colloquium on Town and Country in Medieval Europe, University of Pennsylvania, Philadelphia, 22 March 1980; and the symposium on Medieval and Renaissance Studies sponsored by the Central Pennsylvania Consortium, Gettysburg College, 9 February 1980. I wish to thank A. T. E. Matonis for her advice on an earlier phase of this essay.

[2] Arthur also has his lords pay him homage at the Castle of Bedegrayne, which Malory says "was one of the castels that stondyn in the Forest of Sherwood" (52.7-8). Furthermore, Arthur is found once at Cardoylle (94.19), a name that appears in Malory's French source for this book (IV), the *Suite du Merlin*, but that Malory elsewhere regularly alters to Caerleon. All references to Malory's text are to *Caxton's Malory*, ed. James W. Spisak (Berkeley and Los Angeles: University of California Press, 1983).

[3] George Stewart mentions in passing that local tradition about the round table is likely to be behind Malory's identification of Camelot with Winchester; see "English Geography in Malory's 'MORTE D'ARTHUR'," *Modern Language Review*, 30 (1935), 204. Stewart does not develop this observation, however, nor does he suggest that the connection is embedded in the Grail Quest.

[4] Spisak correctly emended Caxton's "westmynster" at 509.39.

[5] The following editions print the analogous material for the stories in which Malory's Camelot figures: *Merlin*, ed. Gaston Paris and Jacob Ulrich (Paris: Didot, 1886); *Le Roman en prose de Tristan*, ed. E. Löseth (1891; rpt. New York: Burt Franklin, 1970); *La Queste del Saint Graal*, ed. Albert Pauphilet (Paris: H. Champion, 1923); and *Le Mort le Rois Artu*, 2nd rev. ed., ed. Jean Frappier (Paris: Droz, 1956). Malory does not mention the name Camelot in his Tale of Lancelot (Book VI), but it is interesting to note that apparently two cities named Camelot exist in one of his sources for that

tale, the *Perlesvaus* (*Le Haut Livre du Graal: Perlesvaus*, ed. William A. Nitze and T. Atkinson Jenkins [1937; rpt. New York: Phaeton, 1972]); on Malory's use of *Perlesevaus*, see Eugène Vinaver, *The Works of Sir Thomas Malory*, 3 vols., 2nd ed. (Oxford: Oxford University Press, 1967; rpt. 1973), p. 1410.

[6] For the Fair Maid of Astolat story, Malory used not only the *Mort Artu* but also the English stanzaic *Morte Arthur*; both works specify that the tournament is at Winchester.

[7] Cedric Pickford argues that it is particularly the *Lancelot, Queste del Saint Graal*, and *Mort Artu* that promoted Camelot as the chief Arthurian city and made "Camelot" a well known name; see "Camelot," in *Mélanges le langue et de littérature médiévales offerts à Pierre Le Gentil*, ed. J. Dufournet and D. Porion (Paris: Société d'Editions d'Enseignement Supérieur, 1973), pp. 635-36. The conduit through which Camelot reached the authors of the Vulgate cycle has long been acknowledged as *Lancelot* by Chrétien de Troyes, composed in the 1180s. There Chrétien names Camelot once as well as Caerleon. Elsewhere Chrétien sets Arthur's court at Carduel, Winchester, or Caerleon. How Chrétien came upon the name Camelot has yet to be confirmed. For one hypothesis, see Urban T. Holmes, "Old French: Camelot," *Romanic Review*, 20 (July-September, 1929), 235-36.

[8] For a few other French allusions to Winchester, both in and out of Arthurian tradition, see P. Rickard, *Britain in Medieval French Literature: 1100-1500* (Cambridge: Cambridge University Press, 1956), p. 67.

[9] *Middle English Verse Romances*, ed. Donald B. Sands (New York: Holt, Rinehart and Winston, 1966), ll. 23-26.

[10] Among Martin Biddle's reports on Winchester's history, the most useful for the synopsis given here are "Excavations at Winchester, 1971: Tenth and Final Interim Report," *The Antiquaries Journal*, 55 (1975), 96-127, 295-337; *Winchester in the Early Middle Ages* (Oxford: Oxford University Press, 1976); and "Winchester: the development of an early capital," in *Vor-und Frühformen der europäischen stadt im Mittelalter*, ed. Herbert Jankuhn, Walter Schlesinger, and Heiko Steuer (Gottingen: Vandenhoeck and Ruprecht, 1973), pp. 229-61.

[11] Vinaver notes that *Sir Orfeo*, ll. 267-80, may have suggested to Malory two elements of his account of Tristram's madness (*Works*, p. 1473).

[12] Edward D. Kennedy gathers up and extends the similarities between Hardyng's *Chronicle* and Malory's *Morte Darthur* that have led him and others to believe that Hardyng is among Malory's English sources; see "Malory and His English Sources," in *Aspects of Malory*, ed. Toshiyuki Takamiya and Derek Brewer (Totowa, N. J.: Rowman and Littlefield, 1981), esp. pp. 42-48.

[13] The Winchester MS. gives fifteen days (*Works*, p. 832).

[14] See *Le Roman de Brut de Wace*, ed. Ivor Arnold (Paris: S.A.T.F., 1935), II, ll. 9747-60, and *Layamon's Brut*, ed. Joseph Hall (Oxford: Oxford

University Press, 1924), ll. 1173-95. Wace writes about 1155 and Layamon, who translates Wace, about 1200.

[15] Beate Schmolke-Hasselman has put forward a fresh view on the origin of this special order, implicating Henry II, in "La Table Ronde: Idéal, Fiction, Réalité," paper presented at the Thirteenth Congress of the International Arthurian Society, Glasgow, 11-19 August 1981; an abstract of this paper is in *Bibliographical Bulletin of the International Arthurian Society*, 32 (1981), pp. 310-11.

[16] "Aprés les siut a esperon / Uns chevaliers, Erec ot non. / De la Table Reonde estoil, / Mout grant los an la cort avoit," *Erec und Enide*, ed. Wendelin Foerster (Halle: Romanische Bibliothek, 1896), ll. 81-84.

[17] See *The Didot Perceval*, ed. William Roach (Philadelphia: American Philosophical Society, 1941), esp. pp. 11-17; and Pierre Le Gentil, "The Work of Robert de Boron and the Didot *Perceval*," in *Arthurian Literature in the Middle Ages*, ed. Roger Sherman Loomis (Oxford: Oxford University Press, 1959), pp. 251-62.

[18] "The Vulgate *Merlin*," in *Arthurian Literature in the Middle Ages*, p. 321.

[19] See Laura Hibbard Loomis, "The Table of the Last Supper in Religious and Secular Iconography," *Art Studies*, 5 (1927), 71-88; and A. A. Barb, "Mensa Sacra: The Round Table and the Holy Grail," *Journal of the Warburg and Courtauld Institutes*, 19 (1956), 40-67, esp. 45.

[20] Within both the Grail tradition and the secular tradition the site of the court where Arthur uses the Table varies. In Wace, Layamon, and the *Merlin* preceding the Didot *Perceval*, the court remains unnamed. In Beroul, Arthur is at Isneldoune in Wales (probably Snowdonia, meaning the uplands of Wales north of Glamorgan: see E. M. R. Ditmas, "The Round Table at Stirling," *Bibliographical Bulletin of the International Arthurian Society*, 26 [1974], p. 196). In the *Suite du Merlin* (a redaction of Robert de Boron's poem), Merlin makes the Round Table at Carduel, receives it from Guenevere at London, and then apparently removes it to Camelot where the wedding takes place. In the *Queste del Saint Graal*, the Round Table is at Camelot.

[21] Other places in Britain are said to have Arthur's Round Tables—for example, the ruins of the Roman amphitheater at Caerleon; the old tiltyard at Stirling Castle—but only Winchester has a piece of furniture known as Arthur's Round Table. On medieval tables in general, see, for instance, Mark Girouard, *Life in the English Country House* (New Haven: Yale University Press, 1978), pp. 30-60, and Eric Mercer, *Furniture: 700-1700* (London: Weidenfeld and Nicolson, 1969), pp. 79-81.

[22] We owe a better understanding of both the construction of the Table and the painting on its surface (particularly the existence of Henry VIII's portrait) to Martin Biddle's recent excavation of the Table, the findings of which Biddle has reported in various talks as well as in a letter to me of 7

March 1980 and the final volume of his Winchester report (Oxford). The iconography of the painted Table bears further looking into. P. J. C. Field, for instance, points out that Malory's work was probably the main source of the names on the Table ("The Winchester Round Table," *Notes and Queries*, 25 [1978], 204). Also interesting is the fact that the half dozen names to the right of Arthur on the Winchester Round Table (Galahallt, Lancelot deu Lake, Gaweyn, Percyvale, Lyonelle, Tristram de Lyenss) appear together (with French spellings), almost in that order, in the work called "La form quon tenoit des tournoys et assembles au temps du roy uterpendragon et du roy artus," ca. 1452-75, which lists the names and illustrates the arms of the knights of the Round Table when they gathered at Camelot on Pentecost for the Quest of the Holy Grail; in two manuscripts this group begins the list, while in another it comes after the thirty-third knight (on this work, see Edouard Sandoz, "Tourneys in the Arthurian Tradition," *Speculum*, 19 [1944], 389-420). None of Malory's catalogues groups these six (and Arthur). Interestingly, however, Caxton, in his Prologue to *Godfrey of Boloyne* (November, 1481) does give this list—precisely in the order on the Round Table—in conjunction with "the great and many volumes of Saint Graal." Apart from the possibility that "La form quon tenoit des tournoys" is related to Caxton, to Malory, or to the Winchester Round Table, this coincidence in grouping suggests that the Grail story with its initial tournament or gathering at Camelot may lie somewhere behind the painting on the Winchester Round Table.

[23] Biddle, using radio carbon and tree ring dating and being mindful of political conditions, argues that the 1270s are the most plausible date.

[24] On Edward's enthusiasm for the entertainments already known as "Round Tables," see Roger Sherman Loomis, "Arthurian Influence on Sport and Spectacle," in *Arthurian Literature in the Middle Ages*, pp. 552-59, and "Edward I, Arthurian Enthusiast," *Speculum*, 28 (1953), 114-27. One should note, however, that no record of a Round Table entertainment exists for Winchester; for that matter, no record of Round Table entertainments that anyone held anywhere mentions the use of a round feasting table. On Edward's use of Arthurian legend as an inspirational force for the men who fought wars for him and as propaganda to quell Welsh resistance to coming under his crown, see F. M. Powicke, *King Henry III and the Lord Edward* (Oxford: Oxford University Press, 1947), II, p. 724; and Michael Prestwich, *War, Politics and Finance under Edward I* (London: Faber and Faber, 1972), pp. 241-43. N. Denholm-Young says that Edward's wife Eleanor "encouraged her husband to emulate" Arthurian heroes; see *History and Heraldry, 1254-1310* (Oxford: Oxford University Press, 1965), pp. 47-54.

[25] The Winchester Table's fifteenth-century association with Arthur is found both in Hardyng (before 1465) and in Caxton (1485). Caxton mentions "at Wynchester, the Rounde Table" in his Prologue to *Morte Darthur* in a passage where he reports the evidence of Arthur's existence

cited to him by a certain one of the gentlemen who asked him to print an Arthuriad (2.13-14). This gentleman does not connect Winchester with Camelot; rather, several lines later, Caxton reports that he says, "And yet of record remayne in wytnesse of hym in Wales, in the toune of Camelot, the grete stones and meruayllous werkys of yron lyeng vnder the grounde, and ryal vautes, which dyuers now lyuyng hath seen" (2.20-22).

[26] Winchester's old minster was dedicated to St. Swithun and its new minster to Sts. Peter and Paul; not one of Winchester's three hundred or so other churches was ever dedicated to St. Stephen, nor does any record exist of any chapel there dedicated to that saint.

[27] *The Chronicle of John Hardyng*, ed. Henry Ellis (1812; rpt. New York: AMS Press, 1974), p. 120.

[28] Kennedy, though not mentioning the round tables or the Winchester/Camelot connection, has argued recently that Hardyng's account of the Grail influenced Malory's in a number of ways (see "Malory and His English Sources," pp. 44-47); his argument strengthens the probability that Hardyng led Malory to the identification of Camelot as Winchester.

[29] Although writers after Malory have not perpetuated the identification of Camelot as Winchester, Malory's association may have had something to do with the fact that in 1486, the year following Caxton's publication of *Morte Darthur*, Henry VII's son was born at Winchester and named Arthur after the legendary king. Scholars interested in Henry's use of Arthurian propaganda refer to the Winchester Round Table and to Hardyng's mention of it, but so far Malory's contribution to the status of Winchester as Arthur's chief court has been overlooked. (See, for instance, Charles Bowie Millican, *Spenser and the Table Round* [1932; rpt. New York: Octagon Books, 1967], pp. 17-21; and Sydney Anglo, "The *British History* in Early Tudor Propaganda," *Bulletin of the John Rylands Library*, 44 [1961], 28-33.) It also seems likely that Malory's use of Winchester has something to do with the existence of a manuscript of his Arthuriad at Winchester College. See, for instance, N. R. Ker, *The Winchester Malory: A Facsimile*, E.E.T.S. S.S. 4 (London: Oxford University Press, 1976), p. xx; Walter Oakeshott, "The Matter of Malory," *Times Literary Supplement*, February 18, 1977, p. 193; Lotte Hellinga and Hilton Kelliher, "The Malory Manuscript," *British Library Journal*, 3 (1977), 105-06; and Hilton Kelliher, "The Early History of the Malory Manuscript," in *Aspects of Malory*, pp. 151, 153.

Ordinatio and Narrative Links: The Impact of Malory's Tales as a "hoole book"

Murray J. Evans

In the past, Malory critics have basically divided into two camps concerning narrative links and the structure of *Le Morte Darthur*. In keeping with his theory that Malory wrote eight separate romances, not a unified whole, Eugène Vinaver argues that such links give "the *feeling* . . . of a larger story" without contributing to any "structural unification of the material"; most of them, he adds, are merely survivals from Malory's sources. Thomas Wright and Wilfred Guerin, in contrast, argue that narrative links have both thematic and structural importance for what they see as the "organic unity" of the *Morte*, including self-consistent, developing characters, and a thorough linear time-scheme.[1] The present essay proposes another view of narrative links in Malory, which rests neither on Vinaver's theory of discrete tales nor his critics' anachronistic paradigm of organic unity. After briefly examining the data on Malory's narrative links, I shall discuss three sets of links which suggest how Malory means us to experience his tales as a whole book.

The layout of the Malory MS. indicates five linked narrative units in the *Morte Darthur*: 1) the tale of King Arthur; 2) the tales of Arthur and Lucius, Lancelot, and Gareth; 3) the Tristram section;

4) the Grail Quest; and 5) more tales of Lancelot and the Morte proper. This division of narrative into parts is what medieval commentators call *forma tractatus* or *ordinatio*. My essay focuses on links between, but not within, these five narrative units and on how these links dispose the parts of Malory's *ordinatio*.[2]

Some allusions in Malory's narrative may at first sight appear to be narrative links, but really are not. When Malory, for example, forecasts Arthur's conquest of "the North, Scotland, and alle that were under their obeissaunce, also Walys" (16.38-39), Vinaver (xlvii) points out that the forecast indicates no event that takes place anywhere in Malory. Another sort of non-link is in Lyonet's remark that if Beaumains were Lancelot, Tristram, or Lamerok, he still could not survive a dangerous adventure (308). This passage is not an allusion to later or earlier sections of Malory in which these three characters appear, but a drawing on the common matter of Arthurian story: this apparent thrust to unity of Malory's tales is in fact, in the words of C. S. Lewis, the unity of "a matter (historical or legendary) previous and external to the author's activity." Since my analysis explores the lines of correspondence between Malory's five narrative units, it will not focus on links involving material within a single unit of narrative.[3]

The narrative links themselves fall into four categories (see Table 1). Category I includes enigmatic prophecies such as no. 3, in the Tale of Balin, which associates the death of Garlon's victim with Gawain's future revenge on Pellinore for the death of Gawain's father. The lack of clear rationale in this and the other links in this category makes them vague; only three out of the seven, moreover, show signs of Malory's originality.

Category II includes twelve passages which link one general context with another in Malory. One example, in the Tale of Arthur and Lucius, alludes to the central love triangle of the Tristram section, and another links Pellinore's pursuit of the Questing Beast with Palomides' later pursuit of the same beast. Both links are Malory's own. This sort of link lacks the mystery of those in Category I and thus establishes a stronger correspondence between two narrative contexts. What adds further cogency to this category is the fact that ten out of the twelve links are original to Malory.

The links in Category III provide even stronger evidence

because they clearly bind each of the narrative sections of Malory one to another by either forward or backward links. The Tristram section, for example, ends with mention of several events to follow at the beginning of the Grail Quest: Galahad's arrival in court and sitting in the Siege Perilous, and the dispersal of the Round Table knights on the Quest; the Tristram *explicit* also announces the Tale of the Sankgreal to follow. This and the other four links in this category, all significantly Malory's, not only join the five units of narrative one to another, but also in the process of linkage establish a sequence of the units, in the order in which they appear in the Malory MS.

Category IV includes sixteen links which interconnect particular events in different parts of Malory's narrative. The greater specificity of these links in relation to those of the other three categories, and the fact that fifteen out of sixteen are significantly Malory's, make this evidence the most convincing of all four categories. In the Tale of Balin, for example, a prophecy appears on Launceor's tomb concerning Lancelot's and Tristram's future combat at that place. In the Tale of Tristram, when that combat occurs and the earlier prophecy is recalled, Malory actually copies his earlier phrasing in the later allusion (1483). Such detailed connections between particular events in different sections of Malory's narrative betray a writer who sees specific links between events in his own version of the stories he retells.[4]

Table 2 illustrates the relative preponderance of links among the five units of narrative. The table does not take into account whether links are prospective or retrospective: out of a total of forty links, thirty are prospective and ten are retrospective. The focus of attention is rather on the degree of connection between particular units of narrative. In each case, the totals indicate links significantly original to Malory and those already present in his sources. For Category I, for example, the "1+1" under "Narrative Units Linked," "1&4," means that in a total of two links between units 1 and 4, "1" link is original to Malory and "1" he reproduces from his sources. Link 16 is not included in these totals because of uncertainty regarding its source. The table counts links such as no. 10 twice: once as a link between units 1 and 3, and once as a link between units 1 and 4.

On the most general level of consideration, the table shows that the narrative units of Malory *are* linked together. In only two out of a possible ten combinations are there no links: between units 2 and 4, and units 2 and 5. But unit 2 is linked to units 1 and 3; unit 4 to units 1, 3, and 5; and unit 5 to units 1, 3, and 4: so none of units 2, 4, or 5 is a discrete narrative section. Links are most prevalent between units 1 and 3, 1 and 4, and 3 and 4, i. e., between the Tale of King Arthur and the Tale of Tristram, the Tale of Arthur and the Grail Quest, and the Tristram section and the Grail Quest.

These four categories of narrative links, then, establish beyond all doubt the connectedness of Malory's five larger tales. The links are not merely survivals from Malory's sources, as Vinaver argues, for only six of the forty links does Malory simply reproduce from his sources. Twenty-five of the forty are his own invention, and eight more are markedly original.[5] In other words, over 4/5 of the links are significantly original to Malory. He means us to contemplate his tales as a whole. What is the significance, then, of these narrative links for Malory's "whole story"?

Two sets of links[6] begin to suggest an answer to this question. The first group occurs in the last section of Malory's Tristram, where five links, four of them original to Malory, predict Galahad's surpassing greatness and his achievement of the Grail. This preoccupation with Galahad is underscored by four more links, all Malory's, which connect Merlin's early preparation of Balin's sword in a stone after the Dolorous Blow with Galahad's drawing out the same sword at his arrival in Camelot, when all other Round Table knights have failed to do so. In Malory's source there are two swords and two prophecies: Balin's sword Lancelot will use to kill Gawain; another sword, the second one, is placed in the stone for Galahad in the future. Malory combines these two swords into one (1322), to be handled, in the first link by "sir Launcelot other ellis Galahad, hys sonne" (91.23), but in the other links, simply by Galahad. Intriguingly, Malory never comments further on the mythic suggestiveness of this connection which bears a little more consideration.

Close to the beginning of Malory's narrative, Balin alone among Arthur's knights is able to draw from its sheath a noble sword brought by a damsel to court. In the subsequent dialogue, the damsel praises Balin as the best and most virtuous knight she has ever encountered and asks for the sword back. Balin refuses, even when the damsel predicts that the sword will destroy his best friend as well as himself. Balin counters with a stock chivalric response: "I shall take the aventure . . . that God woll ordayne for me." Of Balin's destruction to come, the maiden replies: "that ys grete pité" (64.12-19). These four motifs—Balin as greatest knight in the world, his impending fate and the pity of it, and his typical knightly responses in crises—are continually repeated in combination throughout the tale.

This recurrence goes far beyond the rhetorical dazzle of ironic themes, for it helps to call forth that sense of strangeness which accumulates in the tale like a gradually thickening fog: strangeness which, in Owen Barfield's words, "arouses wonder when we do not understand."[7] Shortly after Balin leaves court, Merlin praises him in the highest terms and foretells his pitiful doom (67-68), again a combination of the praise, pity, and fate themes. In Merlin's rebuke of Balin for allowing Launceor's lover to kill herself (72.19-22), the fate and romance ethic themes, although both present, are becoming more disjunctive. Merlin tells Balin that he might have saved her; Balin retorts that he could not, for she slew herself quickly. The narrator's version of the suicide in part agrees with Balin's defence of himself; "And he [Balin] wente unto hir for to have tane the swerde oute of hir honde; but she helde hit so faste he myght nat take hit oute of hir honde but yf he sholde have hurte hir. And suddeynly she sette the pomell to the grounde, and rove hirselff thorowoute the body" 69.27-31). Not only does Merlin judge Balin culpable, but because of Lady Columbe's death, Balin will strike a blow second only to that against Christ, thereby giving a protracted wound to the noblest man alive and laying waste three kingdoms for a dozen years. In Malory's source, the dolorous stroke is punishment for breaking a commandment, probably violating the Grail sanctuary (1309). Malory substitutes for this rationale his own mysterious cause-and-effect relationship between the death of Columbe and the stroke, with powerful literary effect. Balin has done the typical knightly thing in trying to save a lady, but he fails, apparently through no fault of his own. A supernatural seer nevertheless accounts him guilty and predicts staggering consequences to his act. Balin is clearly out of his depth. In his adventure, typical romance responses will not do. But what is more, even the reader is left in the dark, for he cannot see what Merlin apparently sees and knows.

Shortly hereafter, when Royns surrenders to Arthur, Malory adds to his source (B)[8] details which enhance Merlin's reiteration of Balin's greatness and imminent fate. In place of B's comment by Arthur that Balin "a plus fait pour moi que chevaliers morteus peust faire" (B, 40), Malory's Merlin speaks of Balin and Balan as "two mervayles knyghtes of prouesse"; "there lyvith nat a bettir of proues, nother of worthynesse" (75.5, 10-11). In the French Source, Merlin assures Arthur that he will never see Balin again: "Vous ne l'averés em piece mais en vostre compaignie, non par aventure ja mais."[9] Malory's version emphasizes more explicitly Balin's pathetic and fated end: "And hit shall be the grettist dole of hym that ever y knew of knyght; for he shall nat longe endure" (75.11-12). Similar combinations of themes, reminiscent of the Columbe episode, follow. Balin agrees to be a warrant for a knight whom Arthur wants to see and pledges his life to that effect (80). This action of Balin's is typical enough for romance. Arthur, for example, exclaims to Balin after he has beheaded the Lady of the Lake that she had come to court under his safe conduct (66); and later in the Tristram section a strange knight promises himself as King Mark's warrant against a pursuer (588-89). In Balin's case, however, even a pledge of his life does not go far enough, for Garlon, the invisible knight, murders the knight under Balin's nose. What follows (80-81) is an *expolitio* (repetition, refinement) of this incident, in which Peryn de Mounte Beliard offers himself as a life-long companion to Balin, in a way similar to Lavayne's desire never to leave Lancelot later in Malory (1090). Again, Garlon invisibly slays Peryn in spite of Balin's presence (81). In these two incidents, normal romance motifs—the warrant and friendship of knights—are again undercut by a supernatural fate; for not only are Garlon's crimes supernatural, but they also arouse that strange sense of a fated Balin whose great prowess cannot cope with the mystery of events in which he is caught up.

This *expolitio* pattern continues and intensifies as the tale moves to an end. Balin shows Garnyssh his lover in bed with another knight "that ye myght see and knowe her falshede, and to cause yow to leve love of suche a lady." By this action, Balin believes he is doing Garnyssh a favor: "God knoweth I dyd none other but as I wold ye dyd to me" (87.32-34). But in response to Balin's courtesy, Garnyssh replies that he wishes he had never seen the pair together, and, having murdered them both, he drives himself through with his own sword. The subsequent incident of the horn blowing undergoes an important adaptation in Malory's version. In *B* (99), when the hunting horn blows, Balin smiles and says to himself: "Qu'es che? Me tiennent il a pris, qui cornent de prise?" For Malory's Balin, the horn blowing is more emphatically a sign of his bitter fate—"That blast . . . is blowen for me, for I am the pryse, and yet am I not dede" (88.11-12). This *sermo* is the *sforzando* of the mood of strangeness so far, and from then on, Balin moves as if in a dream into the multitude of ladies and knights who tell him of his fate: he must do battle with the knight of the castle with a shield which no one will recognize. Malory adds in a damsel's speech the familiar note of superlative praise for Balin's prowess, a detail not in his source (*B*, 101), and its ironic counterpart, Balin's ineffectual courtly response, follows: "'Me repenteth,' said Balyn, 'that ever I cam within this countrey; but I maye not torne now ageyne for shame, and *what aventure shalle falle to me*, be it lyf or dethe, *I wille take the adventure that shalle come to me*'" (89.1-4). Malory converts his source material here into a dialogue, and the italicized phrases are his own addition to *B*. Balin, the greatest of knights, approaches an evil fate, but he cannot turn back for shame; he will take his adventure. And in the last conversation between Balin and Balan, during which Balan at first "myght not knowe hym [Balin] by the vysage, it was so ful hewen and bledde" (90.6-7), two of the themes again reappear. The two brothers realize the evil fate which has brought them together. Through "myshap" Balan did not know his brother; it was an "unhappy" knight who made Balin exchange his familiar shield for another; once "it happed" Balan to slay the knight of the island, he "had never grace" to leave the island which a custom forced him to guard. The wording of the fate theme is Malory's own; for *B* does not blend the notion of fate so organically with the flow of events, but more abstractly asserts: "sans faille che poons nous bien dire que onques si grant mesqueanche n'avint a deus freres coume il nous est avenue" (108). Here also the stock romance motif, which Malory transplants from an earlier context in *B* (102), makes its last appearance. Recalling the knight who gave him the strange shield, Balin says "And yf I myght lyve I wold destroye that castel for ylle customes" (90.17-18).

It is the essence of the great knight, as Auerbach, Finlayson, and others remind us, to take the adventure God sends him, coming out of it with greater self-awareness and "worship."[10] These accumulating events across the Tale of Balin, however, and the brooding tone of strangeness which attends them like a fog, underline that Balin's supreme chivalry is out of joint with a hostile world in which the adventure ethic is utterly beside the point. This is, I think, the significance of Balin's sword as it comes into Galahad's hands.

The parallels in plot between Balin's and Galahad's careers via the sword are obvious enough. Balin is repeatedly called the greatest knight in the world; the stone from which Galahad pulls the sword announces that only "the beste knyght of the worlde" will wield it. King Pellam, to whom Balin gives the Dolorous Blow, will only be healed after many years by Galahad in the Grail Quest. But the specifics of the two linked contexts invite a much more complex view.

The terminus of the four links we are discussing is the opening episode of the Grail section which raises a number of issues typical of Malory's whole treatment of Galahad (853-72). The pervasive note is praise for Galahad, for what he will ultimately achieve, and curiously from Guenevere, for the nobility which he has inherited from Lancelot. Galahad, in fact, goes on that day to beat every knight in the field (save Percival and Lancelot), having refused the use of a shield, and a roving damsel informs Lancelot of his instant demotion to best *sinful* knight in the world. In a burst of grief, Arthur already realizes that the coming of Galahad and inception of the Quest will mean the sundering of the Round Table. These details already cast considerable doubt on some critics' view of Galahad as "a supernatural object lesson in heavenly chivalry," abstracted from the real life of Camelot.[11] True, Galahad's similarities to Christ are undeniable—the healing of the cripple (1033), his judgement of Gawain and to an extent Lancelot by example, the division of the Round Table at his coming. But in the larger tale, they co-exist with passages, some original to Malory, presenting Galahad as supreme Arthurian knight.

One group of dialogues, for example, presents a Galahad whose knighthood enters into the chivalric life of Camelot. Guenevere tells Galahad that as Lancelot's son, "ye ought of ryght to be of youre dedys a passyng good man" (869.13-14): in this case, not Galahad's saintliness, but his derivation from Camelot's greatest knight, guarantees his knightly excellence. Later, a squire wishes Galahad to knight him (881), and the knight, Sir Melyas, subsequently regards Galahad as "myne owne lorde" (883). Shortly thereafter, Galahad destroys the evil custom of the Castle of Maidens and delivers all imprisoned within (888-90). When Percival is waylaid by twenty knights, Galahad rescues him (909); and after Percival's sister girds Galahad with his sword in the ship "Faith," Galahad pledges himself her knight all the days of his life (995). The emphasis of these dialogues stressing Galahad's greatness as son to Lancelot, knight-maker and lord, deliverer of distressed maidens, victor against great odds, and devoté of his lady, and the nature of the actions which provide their context, clearly reveal that Galahad, however holy, is involved in the chivalric activity of Camelot: in some ways he is quite like other Arthurian knights, only better.

Malory's departures from his source heighten this sense of Galahad as superlative Arthurian, as well as holy, knight. Some of these changes are relatively modest. Malory, for example, turns indirect speech in his source (Q, 3)[12] into dialogue from Lancelot's lips at Galahad's dubbing: "God make you a good man, for of beauté faylith you none as ony that ys now lyvynge" (854.29-30). Subsequently, Malory extends a page's praise for Galahad in Q (10), giving the speech to Guenevere, thereby doubly increasing the focus on Galahad's nobility (862.2-7). In another case, Malory singles out Galahad as an object of praise in dialogue where Q leaves the worthy knight anonymous (986; cf. Q, 204). Others of Malory's alterations are more telling. After Galahad unhorses both Lancelot and Percival, who do not recognize him, a recluse exclaims: "God be with the, beste knyght of the worlde!" (893.7; not in Q, 56). Much later, when Lancelot hears of the death of Elaine from Pelles,

Malory both creates a dialogue and also includes praise for Galahad not in his source: "And well I wote she bare the beste knyght that ys now on erthe, or that ever was syn God was borne" (1018.23-25; cf. Q, 259). Malory creates another dialogue where Guenevere states that because Galahad resembles Lancelot, "hit ys no mervayle thoughe he be of grete proues" (865.2-3). Guenevere goes on in more detail than Q (14-15) to elaborate on Galahad's high lineage: "sir Launcelot ys com but of the eyghth degré frome oure Lorde Jesu Cryst, and thys sir Galahad ys the nyneth degré frome oure Lorde Jesu Cryst." This comment would make Malory's rendering more religious than Q's "'il est de totes parz estrez des meillors chevaliers dou monde et dou plus haut lignage que len sache'" except for Malory's own subsequent remark: "Therefore I dare sey they be the grettist jantillmen of the worlde." Again, Malory ultimately singles Galahad out for his nobility rather than his holiness. Finally, when Galahad is about to leave a wounded Melyas behind in an abbey, Malory adds a speech by Melyas, the devotion of which reminds us of Galahad as knight-maker and lord: "My lorde, syr Galahad, as sone as I may ryde I shall seke you" (886.33-34; cf. Q, 46). This "secular" comment balances the religious overtones of the hermit's praise for Galahad as being without deadly sin. The constant note, throughout these dialogues, is of Galahad's universal, rather than merely religious, knightly superiority, a theme Malory emphasizes by departures from his source.

For a time, then, Galahad combines the best of Camelot and Corbenic, of secular and religious chivalry; and in this light, his being linked with Balin becomes clearer. For if Balin, early in Malory's story, is the best of Camelot who still goes badly wrong, then the figure of Galahad who bears his sword is a redemption and transformation of the chivalry Balin represented. Galahad uses Balin's sword in a new key, by modelling a supreme Arthurian chivalry caught up into a higher spiritual plane: Camelot transfigured by Corbenic.[13] The sword links thus suggest what Charles Williams says of Galahad in his relation to Camelot: the knight is "as much of a union and a redemption as of a division and a destruction."[14]

You will notice that I use the word "suggest" of the significance of this set of links. Is their interpretation so tentative a venture that we can speak with no more certainty? To answer this question, I turn to another narrative link, this time between the Grail Quest and Malory's final tales of Lancelot and the Morte. The link occurs when a hermit, after disqualifying Gawain from the Quest, further comments on Lancelot's place in it:

> For I dare sey, as synfull as ever sir Launcelot hath byn, sith that he wente into the queste of the Sankgreal he slew never man nother nought shall, tylle that he com to Camelot agayne; for he hath takyn upon hym to forsake synne. And nere were that he ys nat stable, but by hys thoughte he ys lyckly to turne agayne, he sholde be nexte to encheve hit sauff sir Galahad, hys sonne; but God knowith hys thought and hys unstablenesse. And yett shall he dye ryght an holy man, and no doute he hath no felow of none erthly synfull man lyvyng.   (948.20-29)

I have elsewhere argued that here Malory hovers from assessment to assessment of Lancelot in an ironic vision which spans his many strengths and his weaknesses.[15] What is also significant is that the dialogue contains a narrative link, a forecast of Lancelot's good end ("And yett shall he dye ryght an holy man . . ."), as well as an anticipation of Ector's lament for Lancelot at the end of *Le Morte Darthur* ("no doute he hath no felow of none erthly synfull man lyvyng").

Any consideration of Lancelot's death as "an holy man" must take account of his decision to take holy orders; the motives for his decision have been the focus for heated literary critical debate. Vinaver comments concerning Lancelot's penance: "To share her fate he becomes a hermit; not for the love of God, but for the love of the Queen. . . . He repents not of the sins he has committed against God, but of the griefs he has caused his lady and King Arthur" (*Works*, xcviii-xcix). In "Lancelot's Penance," F. Whitehead argues that the passage makes a "strangely profane impression." Whereas in Malory's source only earthly mutability remains while the sinner undergoes penance to be admitted to heaven, Malory's version allows for two other elements in the ruin of the Round Table: "the power of human affection and the remembrance of the past."[16] C. S. Lewis finds too harsh Vinaver's opinion that Lancelot repents of ruining those he loves, not of his sins: "It is in such a tragic glass that most men, especially Englishmen, first see their sins with clarity."[17] Wilfred L. Guerin goes so far as to assert that "Malory heightens the degree of holiness in the last years of both Lancelot and Guenevere."[18] Benson bridges the religious/non-religious poles of the argument by calling Lancelot's following Guenevere into orders "a curiously worldly way of renouncing the world."[19]

Each of these critics concentrates on the religious status of the content of Lancelot's and Guenevere's leavetaking; meanwhile the style of the passage begs further attention. Especially significant is part of a speech of Lancelot's which Malory adds to the material in his source.[20] After Guenevere expresses doubt that Lancelot will enter a monastery as he has just promised, Lancelot replies:

> "Well, madame," seyde he, "ye say as hit pleasith you, for yet wyste ye me never false of my promyse. And God deffende but that I shulde forsake the worlde as ye have done! For in the queste of the Sankgreall I had that tyme forsakyn the vanytees of the worlde, had nat youre love bene. And if I had done so at that tyme with my harte, wylle, and thought, I had passed all the knyghtes that ever were in the Sankgreall excepte syr Galahad, my sone. And therfore, lady, sythen ye have taken you to perfeccion, I must nedys take me to perfection, of ryght. For I take recorde of God, in you I have had myn erthly joye, and yf I had founden you now so dysposed, I had caste me to have had you into myn owne royame. But sythen I fynde you thus desposed, I ensure you faythfully, I wyl ever take me to penaunce and praye whyle my lyf lasteth." (1253.10-24)

Lancelot's comments on his being second only to Galahad in the Grail Quest clearly link the speech with the hermit's similar comment to Gawain in the Grail section. But the heuristic quality of the speech is quite curious: it seems to feel its way around a hidden center, crossing and recrossing the *locus* of the irony of his character explored in Malory's version of the Grail Quest, an irony involving Lancelot's honor, his love for Guenevere, and his relative failure in the Grail Quest. Lancelot says, in effect, "I have never gone back on my word; if I had forsaken your love in the Grail Quest, I would have been second only to Galahad; I must follow you in forsaking the world; if you hadn't, I would have taken you as my lady; but since you have, I will also." There is a hint here of Malory's irony in the hermit's speech during the Quest, for we see Lancelot from several angles, all at once: a Lancelot faithful to his word, potentially more faithful to God in the Quest, faithful to his beloved in her vow but willing to have been faithful to her as

40

mistress if she had so chosen. The parataxis of the passage almost embodies Lancelot's own conflict over these potential contradictions, a conflict rendered even more vivid by his and Guenevere's subsequent lamentation and swooning. In these ways, not only is the content of the speech linked to the earlier hermit's speech, but so is the speech's style, in its multifaceted presentation of Lancelot the great. And in the latter dialogue, a sense of conflict and loss also intrudes.

The pathos deepens in one of Lancelot's last speeches, in response to the hermit who rebukes him for his sorrow at Guenevere's funeral, "for ye dysplese God with suche maner of sorow-makyng":

> "Truly," sayd syr Launcelot, "I trust I do not dysplese God, for He knoweth myn entente: for my sorow was not, nor is not, for ony rejoysyng of synne, but my sorow may never have ende. For whan I remembre of hir beaulté and of hir noblesse, that was bothe wyth hyr kyng and wyth hyr, so whan I sawe his corps and hir corps so lye togyders, truly myn herte wold not serve to susteyne my careful body. Also whan I remembre me how by my defaute and myn orgule and my pryde that they were bothe layed ful lowe, that were pereles that ever was lyvyng of Cristen people, wyt you wel," sayd syr Launcelot, "this remembred, of their kyndenes and myn unkyndenes, sanke so to myn herte that I myght not susteyne myself." (1256.24-38; 1659)

Lancelot mourns for the king and queen when he remembers their past glory and sees their corpses lying before him, remembers his pride and unkindness which brought down those who had been so kind to him. The syntax of the speech thus draws us into Lancelot's way of seeing the dissonances which torture him—of past glory and present death, his pride, and Arthur's and Guenevere's kindness— rather than positing a "cause" of the fall of the Round Table. A number of other details are also significant in this connection. Lancelot cries that his sorrow "may never have ende," and twice that his heart cannot sustain his body for grief. Malory amplifies bare hints from his sources (*Works*, p. 1659) to deepen the image of Lancelot's grief in the narrative following his complaint:

> Thenne syr Launcelot never after ete but lytel mete, nor dranke, tyl he was dede, for than he seekened more and more and dryed and dwyned awaye. For the Bysshop nor none of his felowes myght not make hym to ete and lytel he dranke, that he was

> waxen by a kybbet shorter than he was, that the peple coude not
> knowe hym. For evermore, day and nyght, he prayed, but
> somtyme he slombred a broken slepe. Ever he was lyeng
> grovelyng on the tombe of kyng Arthur and quene Guenever,
> and there was no comforte that the Bysshop, nor syr Bors, nor
> none of his felowes coude make hym, it avaylled not.
>
> (1257.1-11)

These details taken together certainly confirm Mark Lambert's
view that the sense of loss conveyed in Malory's last tales "is far
deeper and clearer than his sense of the reason for that loss, or its
lesson."[21] What both this speech and Lancelot's previous farewell to
Guenevere do as well, moreover, is attempt to arouse the reader,
draw him into an ambiance of the conflict and grief which is
Lancelot's.

What follows in the account of Lancelot's death is strangely
anticlimactic by comparison. Lancelot rather straightforwardly
requests the last rites and his burial at Joyous Garde in fulfillment of
a vow, and his actual death is reported secondhand by the bishop,
awakened from a joyful vision of Lancelot's angelic escort to
heaven; the corpse, discovered, seems to smile, surrounded by "the
swettest savour . . . that ever they felte" (1258.17). The events
themselves are certainly climactic, but the method of their
presentation lacks the sustained vividness of Lancelot's previous
dialogues of conflict and grief. It is not only that the hero is now
"offstage," but also that Malory's dialogues which have absorbed us
into Lancelot's sense of loss are also gone.[22] As readers we are in that
regard rhetorically "unemployed"; both the image and means of
our emotional engagement are no longer before us. The same
rhetorical dynamic holds for the last terminus of the link in the
Grail hermit's speech, Ector's lament, which includes an echo of the
hermit's earlier comment ("no doute he hath no felow of none
erthly synfull man lyvyng"): "and thou were the trewest lover, *of a
synful man*, that ever loved woman" (1259.14-15; emphasis added.)
Although the threnody is vividly flanked by Ector's swoon and
"wepyng and dolour out of mesure," there is that same curious
sense of vacuum, as Ector addresses Lancelot's corpse in a string of
apostrophes which are (again) directed at someone no longer there,
someone whose greatness is now in the past: "A, Launcelot! . . .
thou were hede of al Crysten knyghtes! And now I dare say . . . thou

sir Launcelot, there thou lyest, that thou were never matched of erthely knyghtes hande."

The hermit's speech in the Quest, then, has sent us to the end of Malory's tales to find more than the holy death of Lancelot and another's estimate of him as admittedly sinful. For at Lancelot's death, Malory uses dialogue to draw us into his hero's conflict and grief, then leaves us looking back with Ector at a knightly greatness withdrawn from sight and our emotional involvement—but not quite. For Ector's response is elegiac: his apostrophes, eulogistic superlatives, and past tenses hint that Lancelot is the more precious for being lost and in the past. The hermit's dialogue invited a multifaceted critique of Lancelot, the knight's own last speeches aroused our emotional identification; the withdrawal of both Lancelot and the rhetorical pull of those speeches, by the time of Ector's threnody, invites our nostalgia, our retrospective praise and longing for an ideal knight now alive only in memory.

Malory's links thus not only suggest deeper correspondences between figures such as Balin and Galahad, but also rhetorically manipulate our involvement with, and estimate of, his main character Lancelot. The fuller dimensions of such rhetorical manipulation become evident in a consideration of one further example in which Malory himself appears to be reflecting on the significance of a narrative link.

The pertinent passage is Malory's own digression on "virtuous love" before the Knight of the Cart episode in his final set of tales (1119-20). Here Malory contrasts the "winter" of fickle "unstable love" "nowadays" with the burgeoning "Maytime" of what he calls "vertuouse love" in which "every man of worshyp" should "firste reserve the honoure to God"; "secundely thy quarell muste com of thy lady." The arresting lyricism of the passage culminates in a final apostrophe: "And therefore all ye that be lovers, calle unto youre remembraunce the monethe of May, lyke as ded quene Gwenyver, for whom I make here a lytyll mencion, that whyle she lyved she was a trew lover, and therefor she had a good ende" (1120.9-13). Malory's link in this context thus foreshadows Guenevere's "good ende," which encompasses her becoming a nun and her subsequent death. How does this connection, though, enhance Malory's presenting her as an *exemplum* of the "true lover"? He *has* altered his sources so that Guenevere enters a monastery, not for fear of Mordred or Arthur, but in penance, *after* their deaths.[23] Yet in her final parting with Lancelot, her resolution to do penance for the tragic effects of their relationship and commanding him to leave her forever is qualified by more oblique signs of her love: "there was never so harde an herted man but he wold have wepte to see the dolour that they made, for there was lamentacyon as they had be stungyn wyth sperys, and many tymes they swouned. And the ladyes bare the quene to hir chambre" (1253.29-33). These details imply a Guenevere who has not fallen out of love with her Lancelot. We have similarly to dig below the literal level of the narrative, to speculate on significance, at Guenevere's death and funeral, another episode quite original to Malory. Here Guenevere's prayer, "I beseche Almyghty God that I may never have power to see syr Launcelot wyth my worldly eyen!" (1255.36-37) appears to hide a tangle of emotional undercurrents and motives which the surface of the text hints at obliquely and leaves us to speculate upon.[24] In the eyes of Malory who has set up the link, Guenevere must be the exemplary "trew lover" at her "good ende" because she does at the last "firste reserve the honoure to God," while other details I have mentioned also hint at the emotional conflict between her decision and her ongoing "true love" for Lancelot.

This "hinting" medieval rhetorical treatises call *significatio* ["emphasis"], by which, in Geoffrey of Vinsauf's words in the *Poetria Nova* "sententia . . . / Non detecta venit, sed se per signa revelat./ Lucet ab obliquo, non vult procedere recte/ In lucem" ["thought . . . does not appear unveiled but makes itself known by signs. It shines with an oblique ray and chooses not to advance directly into the light"].[25] Geoffrey's descriptions of the various figures of *significatio*, moreover, can remarkably illuminate this narrative link as well as the Balin-Galahad one. Guenevere's speeches at her parting with Lancelot and at her death are, for example, instances of "consequence," a device for revealing a character's emotions obliquely "by signs." Malory's repeated use of superlatives throughout his story, as of Balin and Galahad as "the greatest knight in the world," corresponds to Geoffrey's "hyperbole" by which "Sermo . . . nimius in re minus innuit esse" ["excessive language does suggest that there is less excess in the fact itself"].[26] The undeveloped suggestiveness of Malory's links reminds us of two other figures of *significatio.* "Understatement," Geoffrey tells us, figures "plus . . . in se quam sermo sit in re" ["more consequence in the actual fact than the expression of it indicates"].[27] (How *is* Guenevere's "good end" that of a "true lover"?) The use of truncated analogy leaves "part to the ears" and "part to the understanding." By this "a skilled speaker" manages "Dimidio verbo totam vim claudere verbi" ["to include the whole force of a remark in half a remark"].[28] (What *is* the "whole force" of Malory's link between Balin's fatal career and Galahad's achieving the Grail with the help of Balin's sword?)

The correspondence, then, between Geoffrey's prescriptions for *significatio* and the impact of Malory's narrative links illuminates his method. In a narrative whose fabric is often understatement, Malory's links function as dropped analogies which invite the reader to complete structuring the story, discerning its *significatio.* What is more, Malory's own comments in the "virtuous love" digression suggest some guidelines for our interpretation. As we have noticed, he sees his material lyrically, as a matter which should engage our emotions. Guenevere as "true lover" is an exemplary character whom we are to "call into our remembrance," "nowadays," having fallen away from a nobler past. Other glimpses of Malory in his own additions to his sources fill out this picture. Earlier when he describes Tristram as originator of the terms and customs of the hunt, he concludes on the note of praise which pervades his narrative: "all maner jantylmen hath cause to the worldes ende to prayse sir Trystram and to pray for his soule. Amen, sayde sir Thomas Malleorré" (683.2-4).[29] His later parallel between the fickle English who leave Arthur's side to support Mordred and "us Englysshemen" today (1229.6-14) suggests an approach which judges his contemporaries in terms of an exemplary past. Finally, we see Malory's reminder at Gawain's death that we may still view Gawain's skull, with Lancelot's wound thereon, at Dover (1232.18-20); as well as Malory's protracted and meticulous weighing of the evidence for Arthur's actual death and possible return (1242)— passages which betray his care for the verifiable historical accuracy of his material.[30] Taken together, these glimpses of Malory at work on the *significatio* of his own story provide a kind of scaffolding upon which we can scale and order the edifice of his Arthuriad. He means us, as imaginary medieval readers, to remember, praise, and be drawn into emotional empathy with his exemplary characters, to see our "nowadays" in the light of the virtuous love and noble deeds of a better, and lost, historical Arthurian past. But he does this, in his links and elsewhere, not by outright didacticism, but through figures of *significatio,* by letting us work out the "whole force" of his analogies. The service is his; the ball is in our court.

Malory's narrative links thus remind us that the exact nature of the unity of Malory's "whole book" remains an open question: because at least some of that unity is "participatory," depending on our pursuing the often intriguing correspondences which his narrative links suggest. C. S. Lewis has compared the Arthurian matter to a cathedral to which Malory has made a limited contribution in his book, an edifice "on which many generations laboured, which no man foresaw or intended as it now is."[31] In the ways I have described, Malory's narrative links include us as readers, too, in this labor of structuring his story and discerning the *significatio* of his "hoole book."

University of Winnipeg

NOTES

[1] Eugène Vinaver, ed., *The Works of Sir Thomas Malory,* 2nd ed., 3 vols. (Oxford: Oxford University Press, 1967; rpt. 1973), xlvi-vii (all references to Malory's text are to this edition); Robert M. Lumiansky, ed., *Malory's Originality: A Critical Study of "Le Morte Darthur"* (Baltimore: Johns Hopkins Press, 1964), passim.

[2] This argument is put forth in my "The Explicits and Narrative Division in the Winchester MS.: A Critique of Vinaver's Malory," *Philological Quarterly,* 58 (1979), 263-81; also see M. B. Parkes, "The Influence of the Concepts of *Ordinatio* and *Compilatio* on the Development of the Book," in *Medieval Learning and Literature: Essays Presented to R. W. Hunt,* ed. J. J. G. Alexander & M. Gibson (Oxford: Oxford University Press, 1975), pp. 115-41.

[3] C. S. Lewis, "The English Prose *Morte,*" in J. A. W. Bennett, ed., *Essays on Malory* (Oxford: Oxford University Press, 1963), p. 21. I do discuss one link within a tale, an exception to my method, because the "true love" digression illuminates Malory's broader use of links.

[4] Arguments that Malory's "Tristram" was composed before the tale of Balin would alter the sequence in, but not the substance of, my point. See for example Terence McCarthy, "The Sequence of Malory's Tales," in *Aspects of Malory*, ed. Toshiyuki Takamiya and Derek Brewer (Cambridge: D. S. Brewer, 1981), esp. p. 119.

[5] In Table 1, under the heading "Malory's," all links but the following eight are of Malory's invention: Nos. 4, 6, 7, 12, 13, 20, 24, and 33.

[6] Category IV, nos. 31 to 35, and nos. 27-29 and 38.

[7] Owen Barfield, *Poetic Diction: A Study in Meaning* (London: Faber, 1928; rpt. 1962), p. 177.

[8] *Le Roman de Balain: A Prose Romance of the Thirteenth Century*, ed. M. Dominica Legge (Manchester: Manchester University Press, 1942).

[9] *Merlin: Roman en Prose du XIIIe Siècle*, ed. Gaston Paris and Jacob Ulrich, 2 vols. (Paris: Didot, 1886), I, 245.

[10] See Erich Auerbach, *Mimesis: The Representation of Reality in Western Literature*, tr. Willard R. Trask (Princeton: Princeton University Press, 1953; rpt. 1974), pp. 133 ff.; John Finlayson, "Definitions of Middle English Romance," Parts I & II, *Chaucer Review*, 15 (1980), 44-62, 168-81.

[11] Charles Moorman, "'The Tale of the Sankgreall': Human Frailty," in Lumiansky, pp. 196-97. See also Larry D. Benson, *Malory's Morte Darthur* (Cambridge, Mass.: Harvard University Press, 1976), pp. 216, 219; Mary Hynes-Berry, "Malory's Translation of Meaning: 'The Tale of the Sankgreal,'" *Studies in Philology*, 74 (1977), 252.

[12] For the "Grail Quest," Q is *La Queste del Saint Graal . . .* , ed. Albert Pauphilet (Paris: Champion, 1961).

[13] See Murray J. Evans, "Camelot or Corbenic?: Malory's New Blend of Secular and Religious Chivalry in the 'Tale of the Holy Grail,'" *English Studies in Canada*, 8 (1982), 249-61.

[14] Charles Williams, *Arthurian Torso*, in C. S. Lewis and Charles Williams, *Taliessin through Logres, The Region of the Summer Stars and Arthurian Torso* (Grand Rapids, Mich.: Eerdmans, 1974), p. 278.

[15] Evans, "Camelot or Corbenic?", 258-59.

[16] F. Whitehead, "Lancelot's Penance," in *Essays on Malory*, pp. 112-13.

[17] "The *Morte Darthur*," in C. S. Lewis, *Studies in Medieval and Renaissance Literature*, ed. Walter Hooper (Cambridge: Cambridge University Press, 1966), p. 110.

[18] Wilfred L. Guerin, "'The Tale of the Death of Arthur': Catastrophe and Resolution," in Lumiansky, p. 247.

[19] Benson, pp. 44-45.

[20] Cf. Edmund Brock, ed., *Morte Arthure*, E.E.T.S. O.S.8 (London: Oxford University Press, 1871; rpt. 1967), ll. 3696-3709.

[21] Mark Lambert, *Malory: Style and Vision in Le Morte Darthur* (New Haven: Yale University Press, 1975), p. 176.

[22] I borrow "absorption" here from Judson Boyce Allen, *The Ethical Poetic of the Later Middle Ages: A Decorum of Convenient Distinction* (Toronto: University of Toronto Press, 1982), pp. 29-31, and 293.

[23] Benson, p. 242.

[24] See, for example, Benson, pp. 242-43.

[25] Geoffrey of Vinsauf, *Poetria Nova* in Edmond Faral, ed., *Les Arts Poétiques du XIIe et du XIIIe Siècle* (Paris: H. Champion, 1923), p. 245, ll. 1580-83; Geoffrey of Vinsauf, *Poetria Nova*, tr. Margaret F. Nims (Toronto: Pontifical Institute of Medieval Studies, 1967), p. 72.

[26] Faral, p. 244, l. 1544; Nims, p. 71.

[27] Faral, p. 244, l. 1537; Nims, p. 70.

[28] Faral, p. 245, l. 1579; Nims, p. 72.

[29] "Amen, sayde sir Thomas Malleorré" (all in capitals in Vinaver's text) is not in Caxton, an omission consistent with the absence of Malory's name in Caxton's version of *explicits* for the tales of King Arthur, tale of Gareth, Tristram section, Grail Quest, and later tales of Lancelot (preceding the Morte). In the Malory MS., these *explicits* all include mention of Malory's name.

[30] Lambert, pp. 128-29.

[31] Lewis, in Hooper, ed., p. 110.

APPENDIX

Table 1
Narrative Links between the Five Narrative Units of *Le Morte Darthur*

KEY: Unit 1—Tale of King Arthur
Unit 2—Tales of Arthur & Lucius, Lancelot, and Gareth
Unit 3—Tale of Tristram
Unit 4—Tale of the Sankgreal
Unit 5—Tales of Lancelot, and the Morte Arthure

Reference	Topic	Malory's	Source's	Units Linked
	CATEGORY I			
1. II, 8, 72	Launceor's tomb & Tristram's & Launcelot's future combat		V, 1308	1 & 3
2. II, 8, 72	Merlin to Mark on Tristram's future affair with Isode		V, 1309	1 & 3

48

Table 1, continued

Reference	Topic	Malory's	Source's	Units Linked
3. II, 13, 81	on tomb of Garlon's victim concerning Gawain's revenge on Pellinor		V, 1313	1 & 3
4. III, 1, 97	Merlin warns Arthur about Lancelot's future affair with Guenevere	V, 1323-24		1 & 3
5. II, 11, 78	Merlin to Arthur on the future Grail adventures		Paris, I, 264	1 & 4
6. III, 1, 97	Merlin prophesies the Grail adventures	Paris, II, 61		1 & 4
7. II, 11, 79	Merlin prophesies Mordred's battle against Arthur at Salisbury	V, 1312		1 & 5

CATEGORY II

8. IV, 29, 180	Nynyve keeps Pelleas away from Lancelot at jousts	V, 1364		1 & 2 (& beyond)
9. I, 19, 43	Palomides to follow the Questing Beast after Pellinor	V, 1298		1 & 3
10. I, 24, 51-52	Lamorak & Percival to be great knights	V, 1301		1 & 3, 4
11. II, 10, 77	at Lot's death, Gawain to be revenged on Pellinor		Paris, I, 261	1 & 3
12. IV, 26, 175	Fergus, afterwards Tristram's knight	V, 1363		1 & 3
13. II, 13, 82	after Balin's maiden is bled, allusion to death of Percival's sister in the Sankgreall	V, 1314		1 & 4
14. IV, 29, 180	Pelleas one of the four who achieved the Grail	V, 1364		1 & 4
15. V, 3, 195	Lancelot angry when Tristram leaves with Mark out of love for Isode	V, 1377		2 & 3
16. VII, 2, 295	when Kay mocks Beaumains, Lancelot recalls outcome of his mocking La Cote Mal Taille	source unknown		2 & 4

49

Table 1, continued

Reference	Topic	Malory's	Source's	Units Linked
17. VI, 11, 272	Tintagel castel, with allusions to Igrain, Uther, and Arthur	V, 1423		2 & 1
18. X, 24, 612	Lamerok protests Balin, not Pellinor, killed Lot	V, 1493-94		3 & 1
19. XVIII, 8, 1059	Nynyve, wife of Pelleas & supporter of the Round Table, exposes Pynell	V, 1599-1600		5 & 1

CATEGORY III

Reference	Topic	Malory's	Source's	Units Linked
20. V, 1, 185	beginning of 2: allusions to Arthur's marriage, the Round Table, victory over his enemies, & the coming of Tristram & Lancelot to court	V, 1372		2 & 1
21. VIII, 1, 371	beginning of 3: on Arthur's lordship over the realms of other kings	V, 1456		3 & 1, 2
22. XII, 14, 845	end of 3: on Galahad's arrival & sitting in the Siege, & the dispersal of the Round Table knights		Löseth, 277-78	3 & 4
23. XII, 14, 845-46	7th *explicit*: announcement of the tale of the Sankgreal to follow		VT, 219, n.2	3 & 4
24. XVIII, 1, 1045	beginning of 5: allusion to "the BOOKE OF THE SANKGREALL" & joy at the return of Bors & Lancelot	cf. *LMA*, 1-4; V, 1596		5 & 4

CATEGORY IV

Reference	Topic	Malory's	Source's	Units Linked
25. IV, 26, 175	Taulard's brother, Taulas, later slain by Tristram in his madness		Wright, in Lumiansky, 54	1 & 3
26. IV, 29, 180 in battle	Tristram to kill Marhalt	V, 1364		1 & 3
27. II, 19, 91	Lancelot or Galahad to handle Balin's sword	V, 1322		1 & 4
28. II, 19, 91	Merlin leaves scabbard for Galahad to find		Wright, in Lumiansky, 47	1 & 4

Table 1, continued

Reference	Topic	Malory's	Source's	Units Linked
29. II, 19, 91-92	Merlin places Balin's sword in the stone to be claimed by Galahad on a future Whitsunday	cf. Paris, II, 59-60		1 & 4
30. XI, 2, 793	the Grail to break the Round Table for a season	V, 1524		3 & 4
31. XI, 2, 794	Pelles knows the union of Lancelot & Elaine, Galahad, will achieve the Grail	V, 1524		3 & 4
32. XI, 3, 796	Elaine predicts that Galahad will be the noblest knight in the world	V, 1525		3 & 4
33. XI, 4, 798	prophecy that Galahad will sit in the Siege, achieve the Grail, and surpass Lancelot	cf. Sommer, 70-71		3 & 4
34. XII, 9, 832	Elaine predicts Galahad's dubbing at Pentecost & future greatness	V, 1454		3 & 4
35. XII, 5, 832	Arthur predicts that Galahad will do marvelous deeds	V, 1531		3 & 4
36. XVI, 5, 948	Lancelot to die a holy man	V, 1564		4 & 5
37. X, 5, 568	Tristram to battle at Launceor's tomb as Merlin earlier prophesied	V, 1483		3 & 1
38. XIII, 5, 863	Galahad now wields Balin's sword	V, 1547		4 & 1
39. XVI, 2, 906-07	recollection of Merlin's institution of the Round Table & the Siege and prophecy concerning the quest		Q, 77-78	4 & 1
40. XX, 6, 1172-73	Bors advises Lancelot & Guinevere to take refuge at Joyous Gard as Tristram and Isode did	V, 1631-32		5 & 3

Key for Works Cited in Table 1

Q	*La Queste del Saint Graal: Roman du XIIIe Siècle,* ed. Albert Pauphilet (Paris: Champion, 1967).
LMA	*La Mort le Roi Artu,* ed. Jean Frappier, 3rd ed. (Genève: Droz, Paris: Minard, 1964).
Löseth	Löseth, E., *Le Roman en Prose de Tristan . . .: Analyse Critique d'après les Manuscrits de Paris* (1891; rpt. New York: Burt Franklin, 1970).
Paris	Paris, Gaston & Jacob Ulrich, eds. *Merlin, Roman en Prose du XIIIe Siècle.* 2 vols. (Paris: Didot, 1886).
Sommer	Sommer, H. Oskar. "Galahad and Perceval." *Modern Philology,* 5 (1907-08): 55-84, 181-200, 291-341.
V	Vinaver, *Works.*
VT	Vinaver, Eugène. *Le Roman de Tristan et Iseut dans l'Oeuvre de Thomas Malory* (Paris: Champion, 1925).

Table 2

Category	Narrative Units Linked										Totals/Category
	1&2	1&3	1&4	1&5	2&3	2&4	2&5	3&4	3&5	4&5	
I		1+3	1+1	1+0							3 + 4 = 7
II	2+0	4+1	3+0	1+0	1+0						11 + 1 = 12
III	1+0	1+0			1+0			2+0		1+0	6 + 0 = 6
IV		3+0	4+1					6+1	1+0	1+0	15 + 1 = 16
	3	13	10	2	2	0	0	8	1	2	35 = 6 = 41
	(3+0)	(9+4)	(8+2)	(2+0)	(2+0)			(8+0)	(1+0)	(2+0)	

KEY: Unit 1—Tale of King Arthur
Unit 2—Tales of Arthur & Lucius, Lancelot, and Gareth
Unit 3—Tale of Tristram
Unit 4—Tale of The Sankgreal
Unit 5—Tales of Lancelot, and the Morte Arthure

Malory and the
Alliterative Tradition

Terence McCarthy

Two quotations will illustrate the controversy with which I wish to begin. C. S. Lewis said that when Caxton revised Malory's Tale of Arthur and Lucius he made it "more Malorian, more like the best and most typical parts of Malory."[1] N. F. Blake's verdict on the same work of revision is that "all Malory's particular quality has been lost."[2]

On the one hand, Book Two is seen as the least representative of Malory's tales, and as such is speedily dismissed. We can learn little of Malory's method since the prose is constantly, and obviously, disrupted by an alien poetic influence. Malory's own style is not to be found here but should be traced back to his French originals, from which he copied "as closely as English can, the style of the French prose romances."[3] On the other hand, comparisons have been made between Malory and his French books to show just how closely he copied the text of his sources. William Matthews goes so far as to argue that Malory's method was so typical of fifteenth-century translations, where the English follows the French at every turn, that "it would be a confident judge who could be sure that any short sample of the anonymous [prose *Merlin*] translation was not Malory's work."[4]

Matthews' position, I would suggest, is basically unfair. He backs up his assertion by taking an example from the one book, Book Six, where Malory does follow his source faithfully, and offers it as being typical of Malory's style and method. I am not sure that much confidence is required to distinguish Malory from the prose *Merlin*—unless one takes care to choose a particularly literal rendering from the Grail book and an unusually competent one from the prose *Merlin*. Indeed, the anonymous translation is enlightening in this respect. If its method is not unlike Malory's, and if the two books could even—in short samples—be confused, why is it that the prose *Merlin* has fallen into total oblivion? One reason could be that Malory's abridged anthology appeals more readily to modern taste, as it has appealed more readily to cultured taste for the last five hundred years. But we must admit that the *Morte Darthur* is a book more often dipped into than read, and there is nothing to stop us from dipping into the prose *Merlin* in the same way. But the *Merlin* remains no more than a translation[5]—and an incompetent one at that—whereas Malory achieves a degree of independence even when he is translating faithfully. His is an individual literary contribution; he has raised his material beyond the level of anonymity and given it a personal stamp. From the point of view of style, few would pick out Book Six as Malory's finest work, but it seems unwise to say that "the forms of the sentences and their continuing even rhythms . . . are . . . indebted to the French sources."[6] Eugène Vinaver has pointed out with great authority that "the vast tradition of French Arthurian prose romances is . . . irrelevant to Malory's handling of his native prose,"[7] but adds that "as long as [the] French sources maintain their status of the 'Great Unread'"[8] critics will tend to trace Malory's sentences with their basic structure of coordination back to French models that use complex levels of subordination.

Having dismissed the possible French origins of Malory's style, it then becomes possible to assert that the alliterative *Morte Arthure*, far from having a merely passing and isolated influence on Malory, was the initial inspiration of his work and that Book Two reveals the bases of Malory's style. This is the position Vinaver adopts. It is true that Malory takes lines wholesale from the poem and that his prose is accordingly heavily loaded with alliteration, but he "never abandons his real task for more than a brief spell. With a persistence amounting to genius he manufactures out of a somewhat commonplace web of alliterative verse a language endowed with a simplicity and power all its own."[9] By means of genuine abridgment, judicious choice, and the exclusion of tags, Malory produces "the most astonishing tissue of pure and straightforward prose."[10] Blake follows Vinaver in this view. He sees Malory abridging with care "much that was decorative or repetitive in the poem,"[11] thoughtfully choosing the alliterative words he retains, and giving full weight to what were mere tags in the poem. Malory, he states plainly, writes alliterative prose, and Caxton's revision robs the text of its essential character.

Blake's analysis is rather puzzling in that he never makes it quite plain to what extent he is discussing Malory's style as a whole or merely that of Book Two, and the basic weakness of his argument (and Vinaver's) is that whatever may be singled out as the real merits of Malory's style in Book Two, they certainly seem to have had no lasting effect. Not only did the reviser undo all of Malory's work, but Malory himself made little use in later books of what he had learned in adapting the *Morte Arthure*. It is not enough to show how Malory's style in Book Two is forged; if we wish to claim the alliterative poem as the basis of Malory's prose, we must go on to deal with the other books. Vinaver admits that his analysis deals only with Malory's first attempts at handling English prose; he has nothing to say about later developments. What he calls "the unexpounded miracle of style"[12] is a fine phrase, but it also sounds like an excuse.

I would suggest that the conflicting opinions concerning Book Two—at once the least Malorian of the tales and yet full of Malory's "particular quality"—are the result of an incomplete investigation of Malory's method. Those who favor the French origins of Malory's style see no more than the direct borrowings from the *Morte Arthure* that corrupt the prose, while those who see the influence of the poem as seminal tend to overlook the fact that at times Malory does not dispel the poetic effect but positively increases it. A reexamination of Malory's method in Book Two will help clarify the issue.

Malory's handling of the *Morte Arthure* shows that he was

entirely at home in the alliterative genre and quite prepared to be as faithful to his model as he was (or was to be) with his French Grail book. His working method in Book Two may well be immature in that he rarely strays far from the poetic text and allows himself to be submerged in its style, but his readiness to do so is a clear measure of his admiration. Even an apprentice would surely not have worked in this way if he had had the slightest disdain for the "rum, ram, ruf" of alliterative meter.

Obviously a great admirer of the poem's style and spirit, Malory abridges his source by picking out and reproducing its most vivid phrases. Frequently this amounts to lifting whole lines from the poem, but more often he disrupts its structure. So, at the very opening of Book Two, he summarizes a speech of the messengers. In the poem it reads:

> Kynge coroundede of kynd, curtays and noble,
> Misdoo no messangere for menske of thi seluyne, . . .
> We come at his commaundment; haue vs excusede.[13]

Malory adapts this and writes: "Crowned kynge, myssedo no messyngers, for we be com at his commaundemente" (185.17-18). His version is, apart from its alliteration, not unlike his general style. The vocabulary and syntax are quite normal. He simplifies the meaning, but he does not give a careless reading of the poem; he merely selects what is most important. He cuts out the courtly politeness and substitutes a more direct—though no less polite— speech. What happens to the style is what we might expect would happen to a prose version of an alliterative poem when the translator was not eager to avoid the alliteration. It seems to be alliterative prose. I shall come back to this.[14]

Now, since the writer of the *Morte Arthure* tended to group together lines alliterating on the same letter, we should not be surprised to find that Malory, by using the same process of selecting the most vivid phrases, produces a sentence or clause which, as it stands, could be more than alliterative prose, even an acceptable alliterative line. Such a line could come about quite by accident. His desire to stick closely to his original means that his prose to that extent must suffer, must at times appear not to be prose at all. So, where the *Morte Arthure* has:

> He graythes to sir Gawayne graythely to wyrche,
> For grefe of sir Gayous, that es one grounde leuede.
>
> (1384-85)

Malory's version, "he gurde to sir Gawayne for greff of sir Gayus" (208.20), remains admissible verse.

Matthews seems to credit Malory with this creation of lines rather than accuse him of it. He says that "Malory took elements from two lines of the poem and combined them into one shorter alliterating phrase," and "Malory was familiar enough with alliterative verse to be able to produce good lines even when abbreviating and simplifying his source."[15] Matthews seems to be looking at the question from the wrong side. He seems to be suggesting that Malory was making a conscious effort to write verse. Surely the opposite is true. His very method of reduction, and his attitude toward his source, simply meant that he was bound to fall into verse. Malory has entered into the spirit and the rhythm of the poem so completely that he surrenders his own style; without any conscious effort (presumably) he wrote lines of verse. Captivated by his source, Malory forgot (if he ever thought about) the task of writing prose and rewrote the poem in the poem's own poetic style. On a simple level he borrowed and reproduced its words, but the more significant sign of its influence is that, unprompted, he answers the very requirements of the verse himself. The examples multiply. He borrows whole lines, and while changing one or more of the unusual words, nonetheless does not damage the alliteration.[16] Often, too, when Malory is freely paraphrasing the poem, what he produces has its own alliteration and rhythm. A glance at Vinaver's edition in which the alliterative lines are marked will show that Book Two is almost as much poetry as prose; Malory is falling in and out of verse.

There are short passages, of course, which are quite without any alliterative lines, but there are also passages which could qualify for being called pure verse. Towards the end of Book Two Malory follows his source fairly closely and the number of lines directly borrowed increases. But so does his own production of alliterative lines from the substance of the poem. A good example of this tendency to write verse is Malory's version of 35 lines of the poem which could be printed as 25 lines itself.[17] Malory's 242.1-26 contains only two lines directly borrowed from the *Morte Arthure* (3057-67 and 3084-109), and while the rest is still very close to the poem the wording is substantially recast. Malory's version is not a perfect reconstruction of the poetic style and it must be admitted that some of the lines are a little overlong, yet alliterative verse often had defective lines, and its unwieldy length did not disqualify Malory's "Than was he ware of a man armed walkynge a paase by a woodis ease" (228.21-22) from being marked by Vinaver as an alliterative line. But the style of the passage does show that Malory's preoccupation with his source made him deaf to the requirements of his own work.

I said a moment ago that Malory seemed to be writing alliterative prose, and the sentence I quoted would certainly suggest this. N. F. Blake reached the same conclusion—apparently about Malory's style in general, but at least as far as Book Two is concerned. And yet I would suggest that there is little in Book Two that resembles the alliterative prose of, say, Rolle—a writer Blake makes passing reference to in his discussion of Malory—and I wonder to what extent we can call it alliterative prose at all. Alliteration there certainly is, and in abundance, but its role is difficult to determine. It has no clear or regular structural basis; it does not—or does not consistently—increase in quantity at moments of high intensity; nor is it merely decorative. Quite simply it is everywhere, and everywhere combined with a rhythmical pattern which is neither prose nor verse. Not everyone would agree that "throughout the prose version Malory maintains a rhythm and balance which owe little to his source,"[18] for the alliterative *poetic* effect is overwhelming. John Lawlor's opinion that Book Two is "a kind of half-strangled alliterative poem"[19] will seem to many far nearer the mark.

Of course we must take care. In certain periods distinctions between prose and verse have been fairly straightforward, but twentieth-century readers should be well aware of the confusions that can exist. When Oscar Wilde said that Meredith was a prose Browning, and so was Browning, there was perhaps as much wit as wisdom in the judgment, but Noel Coward's jibe that T.S. Eliot did not mean to write poetry at all, that he merely had a narrow typewriter, may well arouse a sympathetic response in the more traditionally minded. Blake himself has written persuasively on the confusion in early medieval times between poetry and prose in the alliterative mode, and coins the useful term "rhythmical alliteration.''[20] Perhaps it would be wiser not to classify Malory's Book Two as alliterative prose, but to see it in a category by itself, on an uneasy borderline between verse and prose, an incomplete prosification or an imperfect poetic recasting.

In this context Vinaver's marking of the alliterative lines in Book Two is a good guide, but somewhat misleading. There are many more lines which could qualify but which he does not mark. We could not raise this objection if Vinaver had marked only those lines which are direct borrowings from the poem. Omissions would not then be a matter of opinion but the result of lack of care. As it is, Vinaver does overlook four lines directly borrowed from the poem.[21]

Vinaver goes beyond marking merely direct borrowings, however, and marks those lines that Malory manufactures from the text (where he makes two lines one), those that are paraphrases of lines in the poem, and also those which Malory adds himself and which have no parallel in the poem. The range suggests that Vinaver was aiming at completeness. In fact, he understates his case and fails to mark a good many lines—no doubt because his criteria were too strict. The vast majority of the lines Vinaver marks have the standard aa/ax pattern, and he may well have been reluctant to single out lines which appeared dubious. But it should be noted that not all the lines marked have the standard pattern, that some of them are indeed dubious, and that the rules for alliterative verse were not absolutely rigid: some extant poems contain lines which are far from satisfactory. No doubt Vinaver did not wish to go too far, but for my purpose it is essential to see just how many alliterative lines (good and bad) crop up in Book Two. There are dozens that could be added, and when we take into account lines which might be called "corrupt"—those without binding alliteration[22]—and lines without alliteration at all,[23] the poetic structure of Book Two becomes fully apparent. Of course "corrupt" lines, and those which lack alliteration, though they do occur in alliterative verse, no doubt seemed sufficiently imperfect for Vinaver not to single them out. Yet I would argue that the important thing to note is not that Malory was a writer who could produce superb examples of alliterative lines, but one who in writing a prose version of an alliterative poem almost wrote verse himself. If some of the examples are weak, we must remember that we are not searching for alliterative lines with which to credit Malory and display his stylistic skill; rather the examples we find are more of a reproach, a sign of his failure to achieve his proper task.

With often only the minimum of change, Malory reproduced his original. His reorganization of the syntax was fitful, and if passages could be assimilated intact (apparently) so much the better. If there are a good many "corrupt" lines in Book Two, it is because Malory's process of composition was never a thorough transformation of a poem into prose; at times he did little more than "corrupt" the poetry. This is why I hesitate to follow Blake's verdict that Malory was writing alliterative prose, even in Book Two. Often we might call it prose merely because it fails to be verse.

And yet if we are seeking the full impact of the *Morte Arthure* on Malory's style, we must not stop at the alliterative line, for Malory's involvement in the poem led him to respond creatively to more than the rhythm. The whole nature of the alliterative line exerted an influence. English syntax will not always fit very easily into the alliterative scheme, and so certain tendencies establish themselves. Other things—beyond alliteration and rhythm—typify alliterative verse, and these become prominent in Malory as he responds to the basic nature of the verse technique.

Unlike in Old English verse, where new material was often introduced in the second half of a line, the second part of the Middle English alliterative long-line tended to be subordinate to the first, and the poet generally drew the sense out through the whole line. A single line elaborated a single concept. Several things resulted. There was a strong tendency towards repetition—particularly in the duplication of nouns. Often the whole of the second half-line is mere padding; the poet has said what he wants to say but still has to fill the requirements of the verse. The temptation is to say nothing in a conventional phrase, or to expand upon some aspect of the first half-line rather than to carry on the meaning. Redundancy was common and tags abound.

Inversion of the syntax also resulted. It was rare in the first half-line, since the sense could dictate the pattern, but common in the second where the pattern was already established. If the poet wanted to conclude a line already alliterating on "l" with a mention of "noble ladies," he would have no second thoughts about inverting his tag and writing "ladies noble." The syntax is changed to fit the line.

Features like these are clearly present in the *Morte Arthure,* and since Malory took whole lines from the poem without change we ought not to be surprised to find that his version is also full of inverted syntax, tags, redundant phrases, and sentences which tend to fall off towards the end. However, since Malory was also abridging his source, many of these line fillers disappear because they were the easiest things for him to omit. Some do remain, however, especially when the line filler was in the form of a tag. It is not unlikely that these appealed to his sense of grandeur and decorum. Perhaps to him they were not mere fillers but did add something.

But these features of the alliterative line that he carried across to his own version in direct borrowings also exerted a more subtle influence. Vinaver and Blake point out how Malory eliminates tags and "nerveless phrases,"[24] but what they fail to notice is that, responding to the basic technique of the line structure, Malory produced these features in his own book *without* the prompting of the original. We can see this not only in passages which are original to Malory, but also where he is following the poem. At times he inverts the word order when the poem does not. It is as though he had found certain features of style in the poem and determined to accentuate them. In these parts Malory's version reads more like an alliterative poem than the poem itself. Again there are scores of examples—tags, inversions, and weak endings—that give the impression that the requirements of alliterative verse are being considered even though no trace of them can be found in the poem. So, for example, Malory's inversion "I make myne avow unto the vernacle noble" (190.7) improves on the poem's "I make myne a-vowe to Gode, and to the holy vernacle" (386); the "nerveless phrase" "ten thousand be tale of bolde men" (212.17-18) has no basis in the poem (cf. 1611-17), while

> Than this doughtty duke dubbyd his knyghttez,
> Ioneke and Askanere, Aladuke and other,
> That ayerez were of Esexe, and alle thase este marchez
>
> (1738-40)

is adapted by Malory with alliteration, tags, and inversions that the
poem does not justify:

> tho two myghty dukis, dubbed knyghtys worshyp to wynne.
> Joneke was the fyrste, a juster full noble; sir Hectimer and sir
> Alyduke, both of Inglonde borne.

(214.13-16)[25]

As he worked with the *Morte Arthure*, and as the features of its
style and construction became second nature to him, Malory began
to reproduce these features at random—perhaps even intentionally.
While we might dislike the overabundant use of alliteration in Book
Two, we cannot deny the effect of the other features. The inversions
give a stateliness to the style, a sense of quaintness which is not out
of place. The weak endings, which appear so often to be redundant
phrases in Malory, may well be the basis of some of the rhythms and
cadences of the book—the steady rise and fall of the prose, the gentle
but stately flow.

This, then, is something of the influence of the alliterative
Morte Arthure. It is, I would argue, deeper and more complex than
has generally been admitted, certainly deeper than Vinaver's
marking of alliterative lines would suggest. For the real test of
Malory's debt is not that he borrows but that he imitates. He
abandons his own style, or begins to forge his own, by writing in
that of another man.

I have so far totally ignored a theory which was put forward
some time ago, and which would tend to undermine much of what I
have been saying. E. V. Gordon and Vinaver, examining the
corruptions in the text of the *Morte Arthure* with the help of the
(then) newly discovered Winchester manuscript, came to the
conclusion that the poem exists today only in a very corrupt state,
and that Malory quite clearly used a superior version.[26] Fortunately
Malory's adaptation of his source is so faithful that we can use it to
repair obvious damage in the Thornton text, and can get an idea of
what the poem must have been like as we realize that, although
there is much which cannot be traced back to the poem, there is no
doubt that it did have an alliterative source. The first part of their
argument is convincing, the second open to debate.

It is true that when the alliterative pattern in the poem is
defective we are able to make amends thanks to Malory's faithful

translation.[27] Occasionally whole lines are missing from the poem and Malory has happily followed his source in such a way that the lost line can be retrieved.[28] The examples Vinaver and Gordon give are persuasive and few would wish to take exception. However, when they go on to point out that Book Two contains many alliterative lines which are absent from the poem but which cannot merely be inserted mechanically into the Thornton text to repair a corruption because the text shows no trace of being corrupt at the corresponding point, we can only conclude that Malory used a far superior version of the poem, much fuller and occasionally with a different arrangement of the material. Although they resist the idea (no doubt because they wish to use Malory to emend the Thornton text and would not be able to do so if they took their arguments to the logical limit), Malory's source must be as different from Thornton as the A and B texts of *Piers Plowman*.

I have made a point of discussing at (too) great length Malory's handling of the *Morte Arthure* to make it quite clear what I believe of this theory. Minor repair work on the Thornton text can well be undertaken by using the Winchester manuscript, but we should go no further. The evidence of Malory's text in syntax, vocabulary, alliteration, rhythm, and phraseology is that if Malory was not responsible for the changes, his version of the poem was a radically different one. We cannot just add bits and pieces to Thornton, we must change substantially, and there is little point in using Malory to tamper with Thornton at all.[29] Malory's alliterative lines are frequently and obviously his own. When he makes a single line out of two in the poem, why should we believe his single line existed in that form in a lost version of the poem? The line is Malory's own creation, part of the natural process of his reduction. Indeed any single line that Vinaver and Gordon would care to fit back into the poem may well not have been a single line at all in the superior version they postulate. And when we add up all the alliterative lines, the perfect ones, the passable, the "corrupt," and the non-alliterating, there is just too much that we need to fit in. On top of this we must presumably try to rehouse all the tags, inversions, and weak endings that are imitated but not taken directly from the poem. Vinaver and Gordon are forced to admit too often that Malory's phraseology suggests a pre-Malory state of the text but that the words cannot be fitted in.

It seems much more plausible to believe that Malory's working method brought about a vast number of changes to the alliterative poem and that, although he is at times faithful enough to his original to warrant a slight emendation occasionally, the idea that anything original to Malory and tainted with alliteration is a remnant of some Ur-*Morte Arthure* is unacceptable.

Vinaver and Gordon's theory was taken further by J. L. N. O'Loughlin when he stated categorically what they resisted: the Thornton text is a very poor representative of the original text. Its corruption is a severe drawback in any discussion of the poem: "whole passages . . . have been transposed, half-lines have been substituted from other contexts, names altered or introduced from other romances, words and phrases changed to the detriment of metre and sense, passages omitted or clumsily patched over."[30] He bases this judgment on internal evidence (though he offers none) and on a comparison with Malory's Winchester redaction. Someone, before Thornton got hold of the poem, had handled it in such a way that our surviving copy is but a pale shadow of the original. He offers the interesting suggestion that there is "clear evidence that . . . the *Morte Arthure* has been reconstructed from memory."[31] But I fail to see why we must postulate a lost reviser of the poem when we have Malory. If Malory offers evidence that the poem has been tampered with, the evidence that he offers is that, more often than not, he is to blame.

Indeed, it might be tempting to take O'Loughlin's suggestion further, or rather, to invert it. If the poem has been reconstructed from memory, might we not propose that it was Malory who was working in this way? The idea will seem ludicrous, of course, and it is hardly susceptible of proof. Moreover, for twentieth-century readers the feat of memory involved seems excessive. Yet memorial reconstruction is accepted in other fields: corrupt versions of Shakespeare's plays were apparently produced in this way.[32] Even in recent times we have examples of men with prodigious memories for verse. C. S. Lewis was able "given any line in *Paradise Lost* [to] continue with the next line."[33] Lewis' familiarity with Milton was due, of course, to a lifetime of close study, but ours is not a culture which encourages the exercise of memory.[34] Medieval men were not able to rely on readily available printed matter, and a good part of their individual libraries may well have been stocked in their heads.

The theory of a reconstruction from memory seems to me an interesting possibility in that it might explain Malory's working method more fully. In a precise effort to recall the words of the poem he was constantly obsessed by the words. Any movement away from the text would be—as it were—an inducement to forget. Naturally he copies whole lines, and inevitably he changes others, at times because he is abridging, at times because his memory lets him down. Certain changes show that he did not realize that his memory was faulty since by using a different alliterating word, or by making a single line out of two, for example, he seems to be following his original strictly. If lines are occasionally transposed or speeches assigned to the wrong characters,[35] this could well be a further sign of imperfect recall rather than an indication that the Thornton manuscript is a bad copy of the poem.

Frequently Malory neither copies nor translates words of the poem, but chooses others which have similar sounds.[36] Is this a symptom of the fact that those words were not on the page in front of Malory, but rather ringing in his head? Certainly if Malory were writing his version of the *Morte Arthure* from memory this would explain why he was so submissive to its style and apparently blind to his task of producing a prose adaptation. He was not in a position to stray away into his own style since the style of the poem was a condition of his recalling the text. Charles Moorman suggested that if Malory had found time he would have revised the Roman War episode, and Matthews suggests that he did find time.[37] But one is still left with the question of why Malory should have been so intoxicated in the first place. If he had been aware of the niceties of style he would perhaps have been sensitive enough to notice the faults of Book Two (and they are hardly small ones) as he wrote it. For it is not a book with occasional sylistic blemishes; it is, as it were, all blemish. But whatever his interest in style might have been, if Malory were working from memory he would simply not be in a position to exercise the required freedom. That would have to come later. Tennyson once remarked to his son: "People sometimes say how 'studiedly alliterative' Tennyson's verse is. Why, when I spout my lines first, they come out so alliteratively that I have sometimes no end of trouble to get rid of the alliteration."[38] Malory may well have found himself in a similar position, and have been similarly forced to take trouble to revise.

At the end of Book Two Malory abandons his source and substitutes his own victorious conclusion to the episode. Naturally the alliterative content drops considerably, but it does not entirely disappear, since the poem was still ringing in his head. It has been suggested that Malory did not substitute the victorious ending himself but that he followed a version of the poem which ended in this way. The alliteration found at the end of Malory's text reveals a lost souce.[39] I prefer to see the alliteration as an indirect result of an alliterative source and to give Malory the credit or the blame; and that for a simple reason. If Malory were following a lost version of the poem which contained the victorious conclusion, why should he, after following his source faithfully till then, suddenly work with such freedom at the end that only a little alliteration remains? The coincidence that it is just that part that Malory handled so freely that has since been lost is perhaps too much to accept.

That Malory might have worked from memory in Book Two is suggested here as no more than a useful idea. Perhaps, too, it might be useful in a biographical context if ever we try to identify the library Malory used. If we feel that the *Morte Arthure* was hardly likely to be found on the same shelves as the noble French volumes, we now no longer need to make that suggestion. Perhaps Sir Thomas, whoever he was, came across the poem during his travels (or in his native region) and admired it so much that it (but not the volume containing it) remained with him. If the idea seems far-fetched it is worth recalling that at the end of his whole book Malory remembers the poem well enough to make several references back to it—and indeed to passages he did not adapt in Book Two. It seems far more likely that these allusions *are* from memory rather than a sign that Malory went back through the poem to find suitable material to add.

But whether or not the memorial reconstruction theory is feasible, Malory's handling of the poem shows just how familiar with the genre he was. Nor is the *Morte Arthure* the only poem he knew, and the list of English works Malory seems to show a debt to is long. I am not sure we can always claim these to be sources, or rather I am not always sure what we mean by the word "source," but the various works suggested do help to fill out the cultural background against which Malory should be judged. I do not always believe that Malory used a given book as a source, or had read it, or that he even knew it as such; but what he certainly did know was the tradition. We have all heard of more books than we have read. Few readers can claim these days that they read *Oliver Twist* before ever having heard of the hero asking for more or of Fagin and his band of pickpockets. Names and even narrative details can be common knowledge—and for obvious reasons today. In the Middle Ages the general situation must have been, in certain cases, very similar. Malory's inclusion of such and such a knight's name (even a minor one) or such and such a detail does not necessarily prove that he had *read* or consulted a particular work. He may refer to them because he had picked up a knowledge of them in a much more general way, as part of a shared, oral culture.

In Book Two Malory's admiration for the alliterative tradition is patent, but the matter does not stop there, and there are traces throughout the *Morte Darthur* of an affinity with the tradition both at a linguistic level and from the point of view of the spirit of the book. Stylistically Malory may have lived to regret the exaggerated alliteration of Book Two—if Caxton did not edit the work, or have it edited, or *force* Malory to edit it—but the same basic traits appear elsewhere, as though Malory's initial impulse was to the alliterative mode. I would not suggest that Malory consistently writes alliterative prose, since the alliteration is too sporadic; it is not a guiding principle, although it is regularly there ready to break the surface, a question of spirit rather than technique. We must not forget, of course, that alliteration comes naturally to English writers and to the English language. An English king is doomed to alliterate every time he comes to court, and matters are even worse if he brings his queen with him, but authors writing about kings coming to court are not necessarily working in an alliterative tradition. Malory, however, continually resorts to alliteration and to phrases typical of the alliterative mode even when the language itself makes no demands and when he is under other strong influences.

The quantity of alliteration in Malory has often been commented on and has been used to provide evidence of other aspects of Malory's method. Helen Wroten argues that we might try to isolate the order of composition of Malory's tales by noting the alliterative content of the different books. The tale composed directly after Book Two is likely to contain a higher proportion of alliterative phrases.[40] But there is a great deal of alliteration throughout Malory, even well into the middle of long books, and my own opinion is that Malory did not, when he adapted the *Morte Arthure,* undergo a momentary influence which eventually wore off. Rather his debt to the alliterative tradition was a permanent matter—seen in heightened form in Book Two—and the traces of that debt can be found throughout.

The Grail book is particularly interesting here. Malory is translating a French source with great fidelity; he abridges but to a large extent *translates* the parts he keeps. Nonetheless the same alliterative habits can be seen. Vinaver comments, for example: "the phrase *crakynge and cryynge of thunder,* which characteristically combines rich alliteration with onomatopoeic effect, was, like so many of [Malory's] descriptive phrases, suggested to him by the words he found in his source" (note to 865.17). The French version is "escrois de tonnere," and one would be tempted to suggest that Malory's phrase is far more characteristic of the poetry of the alliterative tradition than of the French. Similarly, the expression "than founde they be tale an hondred and fyffty" (871.17-872.1) contains an expression ("be tale") which Malory only uses elsewhere in Book Two, where it comes directly from the *Morte Arthure.* In another passage early in Book Six Malory translates the French "venu au mostier et il orent oi le servise"[41] by the words "to go to the monastery to hyre their masse and servyse" (871.15), automatically augmenting the alliterative pattern as he translates word for word. At times of course the alliteration may be no more than accidental; even so it remains of interest. So, in a description of Galahad, the French "que a peines trovast len son pareil ou monde" (2.23-24) becomes "men myght nat fynde hys macche" (854.12) and "si bele forme d'ome" (2.32) becomes "so fayre a fourme of a man" (854.20-21). But when Malory writes that Lancelot "saw hym semely and demure as a dove" (854.18-19) we can trace nothing corresponding to this in the French text. Malory may well have used a manuscript which did contain the detail, but if so, the alliterative pattern of his translation is surely from another source. The alliteration in Book Six is not systematic or intrusive, but a sign no doubt that Malory was, even when translating faithfully from French, trying to give (or unconsciously giving) a native ring to his prose.

Malory was not, of course, alone in this. Even the anonymous translator of the prose *Merlin* can occasionally break free from his source to write with an energy which has a particularly English coloring.[42] But the examples are rare, and they scarcely stand out from his indiscriminate and unimaginative word-for-word translation. In Malory they are a constant feature, less frequent in Book Six (but present even there) and typical of his style throughout. For Malory's basically paratactic structures owe little to the involved periods of his French originals. He writes in brief units and is far more ready to rely on the repetition of key words than on any complex organization of the thought. Perhaps Malory wrote as he spoke, since we all use a limited amount of structural subordination in speech, but although Malory has a fine ear for natural colloquial idioms, his prose is not consistently conversational in style. It is formal and stately too, and one is tempted to suggest that Malory could have learned this aspect of his art—its simple formality—from his knowledge of alliterative verse. G. T. Shepherd, speaking of alliterative verse, singles out the "paratactic, itemizing constructions, sometimes dependent for cohesion only upon the phonemic signal; the selection of words with a view to 'alliterative rank'; the use of variation and of epithets with a high level of predictability," and describes the alliterative style as one that "simplifies as well as intensifies, it produces the effect of idealization under the appearance of realism, the sense of a high style hoisted up out of colloquialism."[43] Malory's prose is surely not far away.

In alliterative poetry certain words inevitably occur together as a result of both the context and the alliterative scheme. Set phrases, lines, or half-lines become so common that they can be found in the same form in more than one poem. Other expressions may not occur in alliterating patterns in such a regular form, but tend to crop up in similar surroundings. Alliterative clusters of this kind occur, of course, in Malory's Book Two, but elsewhere we can also find Malory using the same (limited) set of expressions for the same situations, especially combat and knightly encounter. From one angle it can be argued that this is a sign of Malory's linguistic poverty, that he was only too ready to roll out the same old expressions for the same kind of descriptions. On the other hand we could argue that Malory uses these repetitions, these verbal clusters, because in the context they form the proper vocabulary of warfare and impose a pattern on the scenes he is narrating. We might grow impatient as we feel that the scores of encounters in Malory all look alike, but he may not have been trying to characterize them, to individualize them at all. Just as the alliterative poets used a language that was suitable for a certain kind of narrative, so Malory uses verbal repetition or clusters. Jill Mann has commented on Malory's use of repeated key words to direct our attention to the basic concepts of his book,[44] and even at a local level Malory prefers to repeat words rather than express himself through complex syntactical and logical organizations. The famous passage on the month of May (1119.1-1120.13) functions in this way. The key words are repeated; there is no attempt to manipulate thought; and even the whole passage is later repeated in brief (1161.1-8).

Perhaps Malory's tendency to use repetitive patterns is part of his debt to a tradition, and when the expressions used reveal traces of alliteration we should not necessarily rush to identify a specific source. Some of the verbal aspects of Malory's Tale of Gareth could perhaps be seen in this way—Malory using a traditional style. P. J. C. Field, however, has recently suggested that Book Four is more than that, that it is an abridgement of an English alliterative poem now lost. The theory is attractive, but the linguistic evidence he presents is slight and requires one or two precisions.

Field quotes the following words: *kempys, warly* walls, *hale and how, wylsom* way, *gysarne, shafftemonde, bye, luske, ladyllwayssher,* and *shondeshyp,* pointing out that only *bye* occurs elsewhere (in a passage from which it was borrowed from *Le Morte Arthur),* and that these words are not part of Malory's usual vocabulary. They are all distinctly English, most are characteristic of English verse romance, some were apparently confined to that genre by the late fifteenth century, and the alliterative context of some is noticeable.[45]

Gysarne should be omitted from the list, perhaps, because it is not distinctly English; the word is of French origin. More important

70

is the fact that the word is not unique in Malory to Book Four. It appears in Book One (175.35). A single reference is not much, but it does weaken Field's point a little.

Shondeshyp is English right enough, but it too appears elsewhere, in a modified form. 843.9 mentions "senshyp and shame," a reference quoted in *OED* where *shondeshyp* is mentioned as an alternative form of the word. G. L. Brook in his glossary to Vinaver's edition lists the words separately.

Ladyll-wayssher is unique to Book Four and may well be from the lost source, but it is by no means surprising that it is not part of Malory's general vocabulary. The context of knightly adventures gives little scope for this kind of word. Only in the Gareth story is there a narrative element which could give rise to its use. In the same way, the Gareth story is the only one in which we find the word "kychyn" (30 times). That too may well come from the source, but it may just as well come from the story.

Its absence elsewhere from the *Morte Darthur* suggests indeed that *shafftemonde* was not an item of Malory's active vocabulary, and he may well have taken it directly from an English source here, but the word is clearly one he knew. He translates "the brede of an hande" (229.20-21). The fact that he felt obliged to translate it here might show how unfamiliar Malory felt the word to be, but in that case it is odd that he should use the word in Book Four when, even if his source is English, he is clearly not following it at all slavishly. We could say, of course, that since he knew the word well enough to translate it accurately in Book Two, then the word did not seem unusual to him and that he would not hesitate to borrow it from his source in Book Four. But in that case we can also say that the word was familiar to him and that it is present in Book Four as an indirect result of his knowledge of the *Morte Arthure*. After all, alliterative vocabulary appears in Malory in passages which have no English source. I have already mentioned *be tale* in Book Six. There is a *foule carle* in Book Three. The only other *foule carle* is in Book Two and its corresponding passage in the *Morte Arthure*.

And yet having made these remarks, I must add that I do not wish to weaken Field's theory, which I find attractive and convincing—so much that one wishes to be as critical as possible towards the evidence in order to support it. Indeed I would like to mention other items which might give further weight to the theory.

Words like *shafftemonde* and (despite 175.35) *gysarne* are rare in Malory, and so is *ladyll-wayssher*. But this last example is rare for a clear reason. The strangeness of certain words that appear once is that they are the kind of word which, given Malory's subject, could occur repeatedly. Wounds and weapons abound in the *Morte Darthur*, and yet Malory's vocabulary of warfare, of the things that happen and the equipment that knights have, is both reduced and general. Of course there are scores of helmets, swords, armor, etc., but why should certain other items be so scarce? Perhaps, precisely, because Malory was on particular occasions taking those details from his source.

So, for example, in Book Four we find references to three items of armor for horses—*paytrels, sursynglys* and *crowpers* (322.26-27). They occur nowhere else. They are not, it is true, English in origin, but they were, nonetheless, common words in lists of armor and knightly exploits in verse romance. *Paytrels* and *crowpers* appear together in *Sir Gawain and the Green Knight* (e.g., 168, 601-2). If Malory used them here in Book Four, when he had ample opportunity to use them throughout his work, it may well be because he found a reference to them in his English source.

When knights engage in single combat in Malory, the effects of their blows and the resulting fatigue are expressed in a certain number of ways. And yet despite all the fighting that goes on, only once, in Book Four, do we find knights "waggyng, stagerynge, pantynge, blowynge, and bledyng" (323.9-10). There is profuse bleeding throughout the *Morte*, but the other four words are unique, and all, this time, are distinctly English. To "wag" occurs at 1138.31 in the sense of wagging the head; it is unique in Book Four in the sense of tottering, a word *OED* quotes from Langland, for example. To "blowe" appears throughout Malory in the sense of blowing a horn, to the field, etc., but this is its only occurence with the sense of panting. Also unique to the Gareth book is the phrase to "blowe suche a boste" (312.6), for which *OED* quotes a reference to the *Avowing of Arthur*. A third unique sense of "blowe" is found at 1190.21 in another book where Malory had an English source in his head.

There are further examples unique to Book Four. The only *"waytis* uppon the wallys" (352.29) are in Book Four. Gareth and his mistress are unique in exchanging "many a goodly *loke* and goodly wordys" (359.21); the noun occurs nowhere else in Malory. At 352.30 there is a *barbycan* of the castle. Two others appear in Malory, both in the alliterative section of Book Two. In "nothir of wylde nor tame" (358.32) the final word is not unique to the Gareth book, but it is used in that sense only in books which bear the influence of an English source. Elsewhere the word is a verb with the (now dialectal) meaning of "injure," "cut through." Only in the Tale of Gareth do we find the word *borowys* in the sense of pledges. There are only two drawbridges in Malory, both in Book Four. *Wrake* in "worche you wrake" (329.33) is a word Malory only uses elsewhere in passages directly from an English source (1162.4, 1252.23). *Gobbettis*—admittedly of French origin—and *bawdy* (six times) are unique to Book Four, and only in books with English sources and Book Four do we find ladies giving vent to their emotion in a very English verb and "shrieking"!

Book Four contains a good number of expressions with a proverbial ring,[46] which might denote the easy rhythms and easy philosophy of a poetic source. The book also contains a high proportion of phrases with a four-beat rhythm, and Field gives one example of a poetic couplet. Perhaps it is worth adding an example of an unusual rhyme which might suggest another couplet although the rhythm of the verse has been totally disrupted: "the Grene Knyght rode unto an horne that was grene, and hit hynge uppon a thorne" (305.21-22). There are not many thorns in Malory—at 750.22 a knight is sitting under a thorn (hawthorn); elsewhere the word is connected with beating and pain—and it is only in Book Four that we find anything hanging from a thorn. That it should be a horn is interesting. Elsewhere shields hang on trees or shoulders, truncheons of spears over gates, etc., but there are no horns on thorns. The only other hanging horn is also in Book Four (320.31). It is hanging from a sycamore tree, and there are no other sycamores in Malory either.

Definite proof for the existence of an alliterative source for the Tale of Gareth is still lacking, but the accumulation of details is interesting. My own view is that the native alliterative tradition had a general influence on Malory and that he regularly drew on its resources, but it may well be that in Book Four a precise source is involved. If this is the case, Malory was adapting that source with great freedom, as traces of the poem are not obtrusive. Since adapting Book Two, Malory has gained in maturity—unless he has the text in front of him this time and finds it easier to adapt his source than when he was striving to remember the *Morte Arthure*. But the source of Book Four is still in doubt. If a French source were discovered tomorrow, my basic point would still stand: the alliterative and poetic traces in Book Four are part of the wider impact of the alliterative tradition; and if the English source came to light, we would probably find that Malory adapted it with such freedom that the specific influence of the poem would merely be heightening the general impact that the tradition had on Malory elsewhere. For when Malory chose an alliterative source for his Tale of Arthur and Lucius he was placing himself alongside, if not within, a native tradition of English literature, a tradition which helped to give both a personal and an English stamp to his work. He was not merely striving to imitate French elegance; rather he was ready to enrich his writing with the virtues of a tradition which was in many ways considered "rude and brood"[47] and provincial. (Happily, of course, all the Malory candidates are from the provinces.)

The alliterative tradition was "closer to his consciousness"[48] than that of his French originals, but it is not only at a linguistic level that we can trace Malory's debt. So, for example, his reading of English texts may well be the guiding principle behind his structural simplifications of the Arthurian tales, since the English romances have none of the involved interlacement so typical of Malory's French books. In a more general way, much of the tone or spirit of the *Morte Darthur* seems more in keeping with the world of the alliterative poets than with that of the French prose sources.

Of course it is one thing to speak of the alliterative corpus in matters of language, since the poems, for all their metrical diversity, stand as a group as far as form is concerned. That they represent a "school" in any other sense is quite another matter, for there are enormous differences among them in matters of date, genre, and subject, not to mention quality. Had they not displayed common characteristics of versification, would we necessarily have been tempted to discuss, say, *Morte Arthure* and *Mum and the*

Sothsegger, or *The Parlement of the Thre Ages* and *Sir Gawain and the Green Knight* together at all? Recent research, however, has gone a long way to isolating common features, and it is now conceded that there is a certain unity.[49] The alliterative poets are sober, didactic in spirit, and concerned for truth. Their moralizing can be lightly handled, as in *Sir Gawain and the Green Knight,* but they are nonetheless basically serious. The culture they represent, like the language they use, is regional (but not provincial) rather than metropolitan. They are not concerned with the shallow elegancies of life and they avoid "corrupting topics; after *William of Palerne* the only sustained love scenes in the entire corpus occur in *Gawain,* and of course they are anti-love scenes."[50] What they write is profitable as well as pleasing, designed to be worth remembering, even at a local level. The "persistence of the mnemonic habit"[51] can be seen in the delight they take in composing lists—Arthur's domains at the opening of *Morte Arthure,* the naming of the apostles in *The Siege of Jerusalem,* the account of Alexander's conquests at the end of *The Wars of Alexander,* etc. "Such lists even through print, manage to suggest that they were well-remembered by the poet and worth remembering by his audience."[52] Similarly, they excel in composing set-piece descriptions designed, no doubt, to stay in the memory—battles, feasts, storms, pageants, and ceremony—and some of the most outstanding passages in alliterative verse deal with the martial spirit. Battle scenes incompetently handled can descend into noisy rant; in the hands of a gifted poet they give fine expression to the sturdy, manly virtues of active heroism.

Derek Pearsall has suggested a possible link between the writers of the alliterative tradition and the monastic houses of the South West Midlands that so often played the role of "four-star hotels" to travelling members of the nobility and court.[53] The alliterative poems may well have been composed to provide "sophisticated but uplifting entertainments, with perhaps a historical and moral bias," and the absence of love as a theme could be due to "the kind of monastic context . . . from which women of course were rigorously excluded." The clerics may later have had occasion to practice their talents as they moved out into the secular world, but the initial impulse seems to have been that of a community in which the civilizing or sentimentalizing role of women was reduced.

Whatever the origins of the alliterative poems, their spirit must surely have appealed to a writer like Malory, who was not interested in imposing patterns of love and courtesy on the sentimental plane, but who creates a world in which women have a reduced role, a world of soldiers, the military world of uniforms, rank, and duty, where a man has a proper role to play more than an individual identity. No one is likely to deny the masculine aspects of the *Morte Darthur*, which has always made—if in simplified and illustrated form—a fine Christmas present for boys.

Malory is interested in action, not analysis of feeling, in "problems of human heroism, not . . . the subtle issues of courtly behaviour,"[54] and his *Morte Darthur* is very much a picture of a masculine world of military campaign and honor. The importance of the bond of loyalty between Arthur and his men, which is so apparent in the *Morte Arthure*, is one of the key themes of Malory's book. The passage where Arthur grieves more over the disbanding of the Round Table than over the loss of his wife is often, and rightly, quoted. Even when Malory writes a tender love scene—the final meeting of Lancelot and the Queen—the lovers regret the havoc that their love has caused in terms of the breakdown of a whole society in which unity and faithfulness had been so important.

Malory's attitude toward love is not one which he could find mirrored in his French sources. Vinaver rightly remarks concerning the Tristram book:

> nor is love ever allowed to interfere with the customs of knight-errantry. Tristram devotes his whole life to knightly adventures which take him far away from Isolde, and never regards this as a hardship. For, as a true knight-errant what he really values is not the presence of his beloved, nor the joy of sharing every moment of his life with her, but the high privilege of fighting in her name. It is this aspect of the story that Malory endeavours to emphasize: he wants Tristram to be more consistently and more deliberately concerned with knighthood than was his French prototype, and to look upon the "service of love" as yet another form of his self-assertion as a champion of the "high order."[55]

Malory has no time for dallying with sentiment. Love, faithful love, is a proper motivating force for a knight because it is one aspect of the concept of loyalty that is so important for Malory. A modern writer could hardly hope to get away with a statement such as "whether they were abed other at other maner of disportis, me lyste nat thereof make no mencion, for love that tyme was nat as love ys nowadayes" (1165.11-13), or "whyle she lyved she was a trew lover, and therefor she had a good ende" (1120.12-13). But Malory refuses to go into the matter; the subject is not open to debate or analysis. There is no *luf-talkyng* in Malory. He reveals a soldierly lack of fuss about sexual relations. Women appear in the *Morte Darthur* not in order to bring emotional refinement or courtly manners, but to bear offspring or further the intrigue in the social and sexual context of a clear hierarchy. There are no stray women and few pictures of contented domestic bliss. Women serve a purpose, otherwise they are absent. If in Chaucer's day Arthurian tales were on the decline because they had become trivial, suitable according to the Nun's Priest for the lightheaded female community,[56] Malory has taken an important step by writing his Arthuriad under the guidance of the alliterative tradition. The concentration on the more masculine virtues of loyalty and honor and the rejection of any French-influenced analyses of refined behavior have given his story a moral seriousness that had—at least according to the Nun's Priest—hitherto been lacking.

Another important point that Pearsall's theory helps to explain is the essentially didactic spirit of the alliterative tradition. Malory is perhaps not didactic as such, but his book throughout is characterized by its moral earnestness. In the spiritual field, in the Grail book, this moral earnestness owes little to the French source. Malory consistently rejects the French interpretation and refuses to admit that earthly chivalry is inferior to heavenly chivalry. His Grail book does not show up the shortcomings of an essentially earthly code because "spiritual knighthood is placed on an equal footing with secular knighthood. The Quest becomes one knightly adventure among many others."[57] Malory refuses to reject this world in favor of higher ideals, and his book regularly deals with the moral difficulties and conflicts that exist in this world. To this extent he is very much in line with the works of the alliterative tradition, and in particular the *Morte Arthure*. The alliterative poem is based on the tension between the contradictory attitudes of praise and condemnation. The prologue to the poem lays emphasis on the heroism and splendor of Arthur and the knightly world, while the philosopher interpreting the dream of fortune speaks of doom. The story is one of a hero "brought low for his misdeeds and at the same time exalted for his heroism and in which the tensions created by these conflicting themes are finally unresolved."[58] Valerie Krishna's words describe the alliterative poem; they could well be taken from an essay on Malory.

The alliterative poet "protests that he is to be counted, above all else, as a truth teller,"[59] and Malory's moral commitment is seen in the way he presents his material with the urgent concern of an historian, not a mere romancer. He has read his sources with a critical eye and refers to them frequently; he has made use only of "bokis that bene auctorysed" (1242.3-4); he rejects hearsay or the "favour of makers" (1260.7); and at times he goes so far as to assert the authority of what he writes to conceal his own invention, his own higher vision of the truth. Similarly, although Malory's love of lists no longer springs from the "mnemonic habit," it nonetheless reveals a desire to give memorable, historical weight to the facts he is chronicling. Throughout the *Morte Darthur* he regularly expands lists taken from his sources, adds others, and even adds one whole section, the healing of Sir Urry, which is in essence a dramatized list, a long catalogue of knights trying to heal Urry's chronic wounds. The event is constructed around a repetition, and if Malory's set-piece battle descriptions strike us in the same way by their repetitive, "traditional" character, it may well be because they reveal little of the literary author's desire to render lively and individual, but much of the military historian's urge to record.

The same earnest commitment is seen in Malory's portrayal of a society based on stability, cohesion, and proper codes of conduct. Bravery, loyalty, and chastity (not abstinence) are essential ingredients of a moral outlook eloquently expressed in the famous knighthood oath. The tragedy of Malory's book is that this world cannot survive; within it—however ideal it may be—are the seeds of its own destruction. Basically Malory's book takes a conservative stand. There is no statement that the old order was perfect, but it was better than the new. Derek Brewer sums it up well when he writes: "The tragedy for Malory is indeed the advent of the modern world."[60] And one is perhaps reminded of another English author—

ô combien différent—whose outlook in this respect shares much with Malory's: Jane Austen. They are of course worlds apart, but both write with similar moral concern. She is feminine, perhaps, as he is a masculine writer. He is a gentleman, as she is a gentleman's daughter. Both take a stand for a society which is passing and under attack from a modern world. Both admire order, uprightness, and proper behavior. Both were Christian, but neither was an enthusiast. Even in a novel like *Mansfield Park*, with its supposed subject of ordination, Jane Austen makes no attempt to contrast the moral decay of (her) modern society with the spiritual values of a higher world. The kingdom of heaven has no place in her novels; her other world is old England. In *Mansfield Park* the answer provided is not spiritual. No one is brought to God, they are brought together. For the key concept is (family) unity, and the novel is a comedy because that unity is finally achieved as the characters who represent the threat of the modern world are banished. Malory's book is a tragedy because the unity is not achieved. Instead, and properly, the characters are brought to God, but that in itself was not the ideal. The final words speak of knights dying on a Good Friday for God's sake, but we cannot feel that they have at last reached a higher aim. Others take to a holy life and abandon their horses, but what is a *chevalier* without his *cheval*? The religious ending is the proper ending, but the price paid has been very high. The sense of loss and waste is overwhelming. The conflicting themes are left unresolved.

For Malory is not interested in explaining, or setting up systems, and even less in spiritual propaganda. He concentrates on the conflicts involved in trying to reconcile the knightly code with life on this earth. If he takes out from his sources the explanations and interpretations it is because he lays the emphasis on the hazardous nature of life[61] and on the virtues of manly acceptance. He concentrates on action because his interests are in conduct, in a genuine sense, in morals. His is a serious book, and if the Arthurian legend is no longer favorite reading matter for frivolous ladies Malory is surely responsible. The earnest spirit of the alliterative tradition has raised the level of the *matière*, or stopped further decline. The importance of profit and pleasure in the alliterative poems has recently been stressed,[62] and surely the same features can be traced in the *Morte Darthur*. Malory has no axe to grind, but was Caxton so wrong in his prologue to draw attention to the fact that:

> And for to passe the tyme thys book shal be pleasaunte to rede in, but for to gyue fayth and byleue that al is trewe that is conteyned herin, ye be at your lyberte. But al is wryton for our doctryne and for to beware that we falle not to vyce ne synne, but t'excersyse and folowe vertu, by whyche we may come and atteyne to good fame and renomme in thys lyf, and after thys shorte and transytorye lyf to come vnto euerlastyng blysse in heuen. [63]

If the sentiment is conventional it is not out of keeping with the moral convention of alliterative poetry. The writer of the *Morte Arthure* writes in similar terms; he hopes his words will be "Plesande and profitabille to the popule that them heres" (11).

It is not easy to explain the particular coloring or tone of an individual work, but some attempt must be made in Malory's case to explain, quite simply, why his book among so many fifteenth-century prose works has survived. A renewed interest in Arthurian matters in the fifteenth century can explain his contemporary popularity but not his continuing reputation today. Nobody reads the prose *Merlin* anymore. But Malory has enriched his material by his individual approach. We may not know (yet) who Sir Thomas Malory was, but his book is not anonymous, and rightly so. He has made it a part of English literature because he has brought native English elements to it. Of course, beyond the merely local examples we cannot trace direct borrowings. We can only see parallels and, recognizing Malory's knowledge of and sympathy for the alliterative tradition, draw conclusions.

Caxton seems to have had little affection for this native tradition of English unadorned by the courtly embellishments brought in from France, and he published nothing from that tradition—there is not even a Caxton Langland. By the fifteenth century the alliterative movement was in decline or travelling north. In the south there was one last major moment of rejuvenation when Malory took up the *Morte Arthure* and fitted it in to his own anthology, and when inevitably he gave that anthology a coloring it could never have had if it had been imported directly from France. It is ironic therefore—but to his credit nonetheless—that it should have been Caxton who was responsible for launching a book which has lasted five centuries. His noble patrons had asked for a version of the Arthurian histories in English; perhaps it would be more fitting to say that by printing Malory's text he was giving them an English version of the Arthurian histories.

Université de Dijon

NOTES

[1]C. S. Lewis, "The English Prose *Morte*," *Essays on Malory*, ed. J. A. W. Bennett (Oxford: Oxford University Press, 1963), p. 26.

[2]N. F. Blake, "Late Medieval Prose," *The Middle Ages*, ed. W. F. Bolton (London: Barrie and Jenkins, 1970), p. 400.

[3]Lewis, p. 23.

[4]W. Matthews, *Later Medieval English Prose* (New York: Appleton-Century-Crofts, 1963), p. 20.

[5]*Merlin*, or *The Early History of King Arthur*, ed. H. B. Wheatley, E.E.T.S. o.s. 10 (London: Oxford University Press, 1899). Wheatley does not identify the manuscript the English translator used but writes, "I am firmly convinced that the English version is a slavish translation of a fourteenth-century manuscript, now lost, and that a careful collation of all the extant MSS. might enable us to find a French equivalent for almost every word" (p. clxxxiv).

[6]Matthews, p. 20.

[7]E. Vinaver, "A Note on Malory's Prose," *Aspects of Malory*, ed. T. Takamiya and D. S. Brewer (Cambridge: D. S. Brewer, 1981), p. 9.

[8]*Aspects*, p. 11.

[9]*The Works of Sir Thomas Malory*, ed. E. Vinaver, 2nd ed., 3 vols. (Oxford: Oxford University Press, 1973), p. lxiii. All citations to Malory's text are to this edition.

[10]*Works*, p. lxii.

[11]Blake, p. 398.

[12]*Works*, p. lxiv.

[13]*Morte Arthure*, ed. E. Brock, E.E.T.S. o.s. 8 (London: Oxford University Press, 1871), ll. 125-26 and 131. Future line references will be quoted in the text.

[14]It is worth noting, however, that Malory has not totally disrupted the poetic impact of the passage. He has (instinctively?) chosen from the three adjectives offered in the poem ("crowned," "courteous," "noble") the one which forms an alliterative unit. "Courteous" would, of course, alliterate, but "crowned king" is a phrase used elsewhere in the *Morte Arthure* with

poetic force. On this phrase see T. Turville-Petre, *The Alliterative Revival* (Cambridge: D.S. Brewer, 1977), p. 85.

[15] W. Matthews, *The Ill-Framed Knight* (Berkeley and Los Angeles: University of California Press, 1966), pp. 228, 229. P. J. C. Field has suggested that Malory may well be the author of *The Wedding of Sir Gawain and Dame Ragnell.* If the poem is incompetent verse, the poetic fragments in the *Morte Darthur* suggest that Malory, a great prose writer, had little talent as a versifier. Perhaps Malory's instinctive competence in Book Two might undermine that theory somewhat. See "Malory and *The Wedding of Sir Gawain and Dame Ragnell*," *Archiv,* 219 (1982), 374-81.

[16] Compare, for example, Malory's versions (198.16 and 202.17-18) of *Morte Arthure* 856 and 1061.

[17] See T. McCarthy, "Order of Composition in the *Morte Darthur*," *The Yearbook of English Studies,* 1 (1971), p. 20, where the lines are printed as verse.

[18] Blake, p. 399.

[19] Sir Thomas Malory, *Le Morte D'Arthur,* ed. J. Cowen, introd. J. Lawlor, 2 vols. (Harmondsworth: Penguin, 1969), p. xxv.

[20] N. F. Blake, "Rhythmical Alliteration," *Modern Philology,* 67 (1969), 118-24.

[21] Malory's 188.8, 204.18, 205.1-2, and 240.26 are direct borrowings from *Morte Arthure* 278, 1180, 1175, 3020.

[22] Vinaver marks two lines which are "corrupt": 213.29-30 and 244.1-2. I have found over seventy others. Examples can be found at 232.2-3, 185.17-18, 222.30-31, 225.2, 194.4-5, 201.3, 208.23-24, and 214.17-18.

[23] Four-stress "lines" without alliteration can be found throughout Book Two; the following are a few examples from the opening pages: 192.8-9, 192.11-12, 192.23, 193.17-18, 194.13-14, 194.16, 194.18, 194.20, 195.16.

[24] The phrase is Vinaver's (*Works,* p. lxi).

[25] I have traced over a hundred tags, weak endings, and inversions that Malory has not taken from his source. A few examples are 188.7, 207.18-19, 213.4, 213.5-6, 213.17-18, 214.14-15, and 225.2.

[26] E. V. Gordon and E. Vinaver, "New Light on the Text of the Alliterative *Morte Arthure*," *Medium Aevum,* 6 (1937), 81-98.

[27] Gordon and Vinaver, pp. 94-98, give examples.

[28] Gordon and Vinaver, pp. 86-87.

[29] The example already discussed, *Works* 214.13-16 and *Morte Arthure* 1738-40, is a case in point.

[30] J. L. N. O'Loughlin, "The English Alliterative Romances," *Arthurian Literature in the Middle Ages,* ed. R. S. Loomis (Oxford: Oxford University Press, 1959), pp. 520-27, 522-23.

[31] O'Loughlin, p. 522.

[32]Corrupt texts of Shakespeare provide textual difficulties of quite the same kind that O'Loughlin mentions. Nor is the text reconstructed from memory always obviously inferior.

[33]See R. L. Green and W. Hooper, *C. S. Lewis: A Biography* (London: Collins, 1974), p. 144.

[34]On the role of memory in Western European thought see F. Yates, *The Art of Memory* (Chicago: University of Chicago Press, 1966). For the question of memory in the alliterative tradition see G. T. Shepherd, "The Nature of Alliterative Poetry in Late Medieval England," Sir Israel Gollancz Memorial Lecture, British Academy, 1970.

[35]One obvious objection is that critics feel that Malory occasionally assigns speeches to the right character where the *Morte Arthure* (Thornton MS.) is in error. (See, for example, Gordon and Vinaver, pp. 88-89.) For an example of where a reading from a bad (memorially constructed) quarto of Shakespeare has, by some, been considered to have a better arrangement of speeches, see *Romeo and Juliet*, III.iii.85-86.

[36]Consider the following examples. In each case the *Morte Arthure* is quoted first: "rauyschett oure wyfes" (294), "raffte us of oure lyves" (188.20); "wagge" (333), "wagis" (189.19); "Wyghte" (334), "wyghteste" (189.19); "ryotous" (432), "royallyst" (190.21); "graythede" (602), "gadirde" (193.15). A full list will always be a very personal matter; not everyone will agree on what sounds like what. I traced almost a hundred examples.

[37]C. Moorman, *The Book of Kyng Arthur* (Lexington: University of Kentucky Press, 1965), p. xxix, and Matthews, "Who Revised the Roman War Episode in Malory's *Morte Darthur*?", read posthumously at the Eleventh International Arthurian Congress, Exeter, 1975.

[38]H. Tennyson, *Alfred Lord Tennyson, a Memoir, by His Son*, 2 vols. (1897; rpt. New York: Macmillan, 1905), I, 428.

[39]O'Loughlin, p. 526.

[40]H. I. Wroten, *Malory's Tale of King Arthur and the Emperor Lucius compared with its Source, The Alliterative Morte Arthure*, Diss. Illinois 1950, p. 39. If the influence of the *Morte Arthure* was so weak that it could wear off quickly under the influence of another source, it could also wear off between books. If Malory took a break after writing Book Two there would be no particular alliterative influence to trace. Wroten is forced to assume that Malory was working non-stop.

[41]*La Queste del Saint Graal*, ed. A. Pauphilet (Paris: Champion, 1967), 22.30. Future citations will be to this text. The "escrois de tonnere" quoted by Vinaver above is "escroiz de tonoire" (15.9) in this edition.

[42]Wheatley, the editor, singles out—though not for praise—the sentence "and stour and ffull grete crakke, and noyse ther was of brekynge of speres, and stif strokes of swerdes vpon helmes" (p. ccxlii).

[43]Shepherd, pp. 7-8.

[44] J. Mann, "Malory: Knightly Combat in *Le Morte D'Arthur*," *The New Pelican Guide to English Literature*, ed. B. Ford, I, 1 (Harmondsworth: Penguin, 1982), p. 332.

[45] P. J. C. Field, "The Source of Malory's *Tale of Gareth*," *Aspects*, p. 67.

[46] Consider: "but as he is, so he askyth" 295.2-3; "be as fatte at the twelve-monthe ende as a porke hog" 295.7; "as the wede growyth over the corne" 306.2; "styke a swyne" 301.22-23; "fed hym like a hog" 339.17-18; "Be as be may" 294.20, 312.22, 329.34; "dedys that be done . . . undone" 325.19; "as hevyn and erthe sholde go togydir" 352.23-24; "by fylde other by strete" 353.20; "nothir of wylde nor tame" 358.32; "he is my fyrste love and he shall be the laste" 359.36-360.1; "is the wynde in that dore" 360.6-7.

[47] The phrase is Caxton's of course. See *Prologues and Epilogues of William Caxton*, ed. W. J. B. Crotch, E.E.T.S. o.s. 176 (London: Oxford University Press, 1928), p. 108.

[48] L. D. Benson, *Malory's Morte Darthur* (Cambridge, Mass.: Harvard University Press, 1976), p. 42.

[49] See Shepherd, Turville-Petre, and D. Pearsall, *Old and Middle English Poetry* (London: Routledge and Kegan Paul, 1977).

[50] D. A. Lawton, "Middle English Alliterative Poetry," *Speculum*, 58 (1983), 80.

[51] Shepherd, p. 5.

[52] Shepherd, p. 6.

[53] D. Pearsall, "The Origins of the Alliterative Revival," *The Alliterative Tradition in the Fourteenth Century*, ed. B. S. Levy and P. E. Szarmach (Kent, Ohio: Kent State University Press, 1981), pp. 15, 16.

[54] *Works*, p. 1370.

[55] *Works*, p. 1447.

[56] See lines 446-47 of the *Nun's Priest's Tale*, and, of course, the Arthurian tale of the Wife of Bath.

[57] K. H. Göller, "From Logres to Carbonek: The Arthuriad of Charles Williams," *Arthurian Literature I*, ed. R. Barber (Cambridge: D. S. Brewer, 1981), p. 130.

[58] V. Krishna, review of *The Alliterative "Morte Arthure": A Reassessment of the Poem*, ed. K. H. Göller (Cambridge: D. S. Brewer, 1981), in *Speculum*, 58 (1983), 179.

[59] Shepherd, p. 11.

[60] D. S. Brewer, "Malory: The Traditional Writer and the Archaic Mind," *Arthurian Literature I*, p. 118.

[61] See J. Mann, "'Taking the Adventure': Malory and the *Suite du Merlin*," *Aspects*, pp. 71-91.

[62] See, for example, Shepherd, Lawton (note 50), and J. Wurster, "The

Audience," *The Alliterative "Morte Arthure": A Reassessment of the Poem,* pp. 44-56.

[63] *Caxton's Malory,* ed. J. W. Spisak (Berkeley and Los Angeles: University of California Press, 1983), 3.5-10.

Indiscreet Objects of Desire: Malory's "Tristram" and the Necessity of Deceit[1]

Maureen Fries

Before Malory was to incorporate the tale of Tristan into his complex, many-storied *Morte Darthur*, that narrative passed through several centuries of development. At its center was, first, the conflict in one man of two opposing loyalties: that of the warrior to his feudal lord and his society and that of the lover to his lady. Unlike the parallel story of Lancelot and Guenevere,[2] the Tristan story from its beginning exhibited three indissolubly linked motifs: the love potion, the multiple relationship to Mark, and the *liebestod.* Both potion and *liebestod,* in their insistence upon the inseparability of the illicit lovers, precluded any such reform as Lancelot and Guenevere pursue, and Mark's status both as lord and as uncle of Tristan led, in the triangular desire of the story, to a double mediation. He possesses Isolt, the desired object, both as king and as elder male relative, and, as both nephew and vassal, Tristan violates clan and *comites* loyalty in trying to wrest her from him. The chief trait needed for such wresting, and the other element at the center of the legend, is deceit.[3] To understand Malory's use of this archetype of conflict and dissimulation, we must examine its development in the early versions of the Tristan story, with their emphasis upon a fated love, and its transformation in the *Tristan en prose,* in which a newly Arthurianized hero discovers different, but also indiscreet, objects of desire.

- I -

Deceit in Tristan is adjunct to desire, for his competitor, Mark, is within rather than beyond his sphere of action. But as Tristan's actions, in all versions of the story, become more and more audacious, as his affair with Isolt is no longer a secret to Mark or to Cornish society, he is pushed into increasingly desperate (though often unsuccessful) expedients. Tristan risks more, for ultimately less, than any other medieval lover. The Arthurian heroes into whose ambiance he was eventually drawn use their loves as a motivation toward socially approved action. As formulated by Chrétien de Troyes, Erec, Yvain, and—for a time—Lancelot perform recognizably and culturally beneficial deeds while they sublimate their obsessive loves for their respective ladies. That Lancelot performs so superbly as a representative of his culture emboldens him to break into Meleagant's castle to sleep with Guenevere, an ultimate *lack* of sublimation Chrétien perhaps found so distressing that he did not finish his poem. A similar and constant unwillingness to sublimate his desire leads Tristan to deceive a whole society.

Yet wherever his pre-potion career is part of the story, Tristan displays social responsibility similar to that of the successful Arthurian hero. To end the evil custom of the truage of Cornwall, he defeats the Irish Marhalt; to free the Irish people from a dragon, in the course of his bride-quest on behalf of Mark, he slays it. Such selfless, widely beneficial action ceases once he drinks the love potion. This famous symbol masks the real character of his triangular desire, in which the preciousness of the beloved object is measured by its value to the Other, the Third who mediates that desire. Significantly, in the early versions based on the presumably archetypal Tristan, but not in the *Tristan en prose* or in Malory, Isolt becomes overwhelmingly, irresistibly attractive after she becomes the betrothed of Tristan's uncle and king. From its inception Tristan's love, like that of all triangular desire, is self-absorbed, as Denis de Rougemont has shown: Tristan and Isolt love each other "from the standpoint of self and not from the other's standpoint," with a "false reciprocity, which disguises a twin narcissism."[4] This implicit narcissism emerges paradoxically in a seeming conjunction of selves which is as deceptive as Tristan's actions thereafter, no matter how beautifully—say in the memorable couplets of Marie de France and Gottfried von Strassburg—the poets may crystallize the covering emotion.[5]

That emotion, inner- rather than other-directed, requires deceit for the fulfillment of its desire. The cultural champion who loves his aunt and queen not only ceases to be an asset to his society, but must resort constantly to tricking it. From Béroul and Thomas on, and in spite of alleged differences in "courtly" versus "common" versions, Tristan's love is intimately tied to dissimulation. In the early works, this trickery is justified, principally by two deliberate narrative devices, one auctorial and one within the plot itself. Because of the authors' intervention—whether Béroul's sympathy for the lovers and antipathy for the barons, or Thomas's and Brother Robert's tendency to blame Tristan's flaws upon the women in the story, or Gottfried's ambiguous insistence upon the sanctity of the love in spite of itself—dissimulation seems justified. And because of the unique nature of the love potion—whether for three years or forever tying two hearts indissolubly together in the face of medieval marital and feudal values—it seems inevitable.

Even alteration of narrative emphasis does not change the formula which ties Tristan's love to deceit. In the only early work which stresses the heroic—the epic rather than the romantic side of Tristan—Eilhart von Oberge expands on the traditional tendency toward disguise. Nor does the overlaid image of Tristan as artist allow transcendence of this basic characteristic. Marie de France's brief coda to her brief narrative, ascribing the authorship of her *lai* to Tristan himself, in no way obviates the central events of the poem, the deceit of the hazel wand and the secret meeting in the forest. Thomas's and Robert's use of the Hall of Statues as motif introduces a new level of trickery: far from Tristan's turning "the destructive force of love to a creative end . . . when physically free of the woman who inspired him," as some critics would have it,[6] his caressing and talking to a statue of Isolt is surely the greatest narcissism of all. This moves beyond deceit of a hostile world into self-deceit, the most insidious side-effect of unrecognized or unacknowledged triangular desire. It is the idea of his loving Isolt and not his love for Isolt with which Tristan is obsessed. The very talents with which he is traditionally credited—his playing upon the harp, his singing, his invention of the training of dogs and the calls of the hunt—seem to accumulate as if by encomium to conceal his introversion and his narrow world of dissimulation.

Such dissimulation assumes various forms in the early works. Besides the episodes in Marie de France which involve simple hiding or the presentation of the obviously symbolic object, different forms of disguise appear in different works. In the two fragments of the *Folie Tristan*, the hero makes a secret return to Mark's court after banishment, disguised as a fool. Fuller versions of the story—in Eilhart, Gottfried, and Brother Robert—show the gradual growth of deception as a weapon for self-aggrandizement. The simple incognito of the first Irish visit, to effect the wound-cure, gives way to the deliberate assumption of the pseudonym of Tantris during the bride-quest for Mark. Of all episodes, that of Isolt's trial by ordeal mandates a convincing disguise for Tristan— as pilgrim, as madman, even as leper—so that she may convincingly (and blasphemously) swear that no man but Mark and this stranger has been held in her arms. Elsewhere, the dissimulation of the sword that separates the lovers cannot but contrast with Mark's generous misinterpretation of it. Nor does Tristan's deceit cease once he has left Isolt of Ireland and married Isolt White Hands: he manages to trick the latter over the matter of the consummation of their marriage (except in Eilhart, where he finally ratifies it in anger at the first Isolt).

Isolt of Ireland is only the first associate of Tristan to catch the contagion of his deceit. Her substitution (in some versions) of Brangwayn in the bridal bed with Mark and her subsequent attempt to murder her cousin are only a beginning. She participates in the duplicitous tryst-under-the-tree and flour-under-the-bed episodes recounted by Béroul, Thomas, Eilhart, and Gottfried. Brangwayn and Governail eventually catch the contagion of deceit as well, but it reaches a tragic pitch in the actions of Isolt of Brittany. Caught up in Tristan's triangular desire, striving to wrest him finally from Isolt of Ireland, she lies about the sail on the Queen of Cornwall's ship and precipitates the *liebestod*. Prophetically for Tristan's future as a hero, especially in the *Tristan en prose* and Malory, the chief representatives of Arthurian society catch this disease of deceit and bear witness to the lover's unearned virtue during the trial by ordeal.

Deceit and disguise become an essential part of the reality, not just the pretense of Tristan's situation. Tristan's various masks—as fool, merchant, pilgrim, madman, leper, and (even more obviously, in Eilhart) player—reflect his moral situation. Madness and leprosy were considered punishment for sexual sin in the Middle Ages, and leprosy could also be a divine rebuke for blasphemy.[7] Tristan's expertise at illusion emerges in his masks of merchant, which epitomizes his cupidiousness; of pilgrim, his need for repentance; and of player and fool, his penchant for charade. Tristan is trickster in all these early works;[8] but as long as his deceit is tied to an apparently ideal love, it is more or less justified, even by authors who condemn that love for its danger to society.[9] Only when his dissimulation ceases to be a necessary concomitant of his desire and becomes a blind political force in its own right, or in some cause less sympathetic than a fated and irresistible love, does a different judgment become possible.

Precisely those circumstances precipitate the major change in Tristan's literary history which occurs in the *Tristan en prose* and in Malory. In the remainder of this essay, we will see the process by which an Arthurianized Tristan evolves from a necessarily deceitful lover into an heroic, indeed a counter-heroic, champion of the Round Table—but still a dissimulator. This new role begins when he is swept from his own, essentially private world of the earlier works into the *Tristan en prose*, which consists of the essentially public world of the Arthurian prose Vulgate; cast of characters, settings, and themes are all but identical. There we may begin to discover the developments which undermined his status as a lover, emphasized his standing as a warrior, and utilized his fully developed role as deceiver toward new ends. Finally, in Malory's masterly melding of the prose *Tristan* with parts of the Vulgate we will see the ultimate split between lover and trickster, and find Tristan himself supplied with new mediation and a triangular desire far different from that of his beginnings.

- II -

Although the date of the early or "First" Version of the *Tristan en prose* is roughly contemporaneous with the works of Gottfried and Brother Robert, its world differs irrevocably from theirs and the earlier twelfth-century poems. At its center is the court of Arthur and those proven knights of the Round Table against whom the individual hero must take his martial measurement. Like Lancelot, the greatest champion in the Vulgate as well as the prose *Tristan*, Tristan must have been drawn into the full involvement of the huge prose romance because of his early fringe connection with Arthur's court—and because of his French ancestry (the Gaelic fringe heroes, such as Welsh Culhwch, remained forever beyond the pale). Tristan had appeared as a minor character in *Der Lanzelet*, a Swiss translation of an Anglo-Norman poem, as the hero of a lost poem cited by Chrétien, and as benefactee of the Arthurian witness to the trial by ordeal in Béroul. The immense appetite of Arthurian romance for devouring originally independent heroes explains this growth.[10] And the focus of his new milieu was to change the triangular desire, if not the deceit, of the archetypal Tristan.

After the conventional recitals of the hero's ancestry and *enfances*, the *Tristan en prose* follows the traditional Tristan narrative up to the hero's marriage to Isolt White Hands. Already in this first section, and even more in the freely invented narremes which follow, both mediator and object of desire suffer such profound alterations that their triangular relationship with Tristan totters. Mark, avuncular and kingly Other from whom his nephew had previously repeatedly wrested Isolt only to lose her again, is no longer sympathetic. Gone are his affection for Tristan and his spousal protectiveness, symbolized respectively, in the discovery in the forest, by his reaction to the separating sword and his placing his glove to protect Isolt from the sun.[11] Now he is a dangerous and treacherous opponent, not only Tristan's enemy but the enemy of all good knights: a sort of nonmagical male equivalent of Morgan la Fée, unworthy of being either a king or an uncle. As was customary with the adversary in late medieval romance, as happened finally with Gawain in the same genre, the opponent's character is blackened so that the hero's may shine the brighter.

But what Mark loses as uncle and as king he also loses as mediator to Tristan's desire, and this necessarily changed the configuration of the original plot.[12] With no mediator between them, Tristan's constant returns to Isolt, which unify his adventures both before and after her marriage to Mark in the previous works, assume that diffuse quality characteristic of Arthurian romance generally. The love potion's symbolic value vanishes along with Mark's mediation: witness the ease and frequency with which Tristan now rides away for long periods from Isolt, from whom in earlier works he could not remain separated without death or at least unbearable longing. Retained as an ineffective function of the plot, the potion ceases to impel adventure.

Adventure nevertheless continues in a different set of circumstances: the presence of a new mediator, the striving for a new object of desire, but with the same mode of dissimulation. Like Lancelot—on whose career, by a strange paradox, the prose *Tristan* is modeled, rather than vice-versa as in the earlier poems—Tristan must now sublimate what remains of his love in constant questing. To remain top-seated, the Arthurian knight must never stay long from the quest: he must match or, better, surpass not only the exploits of others but even his own earlier exploits in order to keep his worship. This necessarily ceaseless activity in the *Tristan*, and especially in two long series of adventures (one after the hero's shipwreck with Isolt White Hands and her brother Kahedin, the other after his own final banishment from Cornwall), results in the virtual disappearance of the Irish Isolt from most of the work. Only the various discoveries of their affair, and Isolt's restorations of Tristan to health, retain some semblance of the old relationship, some remnant of tragically intense desire.

Rather than Isolt as object of desire for which Mark is mediator, Tristan now has a new ambition—his longing for a seat at the Round Table, and a new mediator—its knights, particularly Lancelot. So obsessed is Tristan with Arthur's court that he refuses to appear there until he has repeatedly, brutally, and—most notably—with considerable deceit, conquered or matched all of its worthy knights. The sanctity which seemed to accrue formerly to the figure of Isolt now accrues to the Round Table. Witness the detail of a successful Tristan's finally taking the *siège* formerly belonging to Marhalt, but now miraculously bearing his name—a secularized parody of Galahad's taking the Siege Perilous and a (perhaps unintentional) blasphemy of the whole story of the Grail.

Secular blasphemy of the core narrative attaches to the new version of the lovers' deaths. Instead of insatiable and repeated triangular desire (in which Isolt of Ireland had also become a mediator, for the longing of Isolt White Hands) reaching for its inevitably tragic issue, both principals die of forces other than their own wills. Tristan, living in semi-retirement with Isolt, obviously has no more need of mediation either by Lancelot and other Arthurian knights, or by Mark's now vestigial opposition. So the favored ending in most manuscripts of the *Tristan en prose* is anticlimactic: not the double death in Brittany resulting ostensibly from the treachery of Isolt White Hands yet ultimately from the love potion, but the slaying of Tristan by King Mark and the inadvertent, almost ludicrous slaying of Isolt by Tristan. Once the discarded mediator has killed his nephew with a poisoned lance (interrupting his playing and singing for Isolt), Tristan's new priorities emerge unmistakably. He thinks not of Isolt but of his honor as a knight of the Table Round, asking Sagramor to give his last greetings to his fellow knights Palamède, Dinadan, and Lancelot, and to take his armor to King Arthur. Then he kisses his sword with an ardor reserved in other times and places for Isolt alone. She, meanwhile, dies not of his love but of his strength. As Eugène Vinaver reminds us, "according to the majority of manuscripts it is Tristan's last embrace which causes Iseult's death: Tristan 'estraint la royne de tant de force que il li fist le cuer partir.'" But Vinaver's assertion that they thus died *par amour* and that the author(s) restored "to the scene its genuine meaning" cannot be validated.[13] What the scene proves instead is that the new desired object, his seat at the Round Table, and the new mediators, Arthur's knights, particularly Lancelot, are verifiable in the text. Like the love potion, the *liebestod* is a relic without viable function in the *Tristan en prose*.

In love as in adventure and death, the new mediation weakens the original motifs. Tristan's faithful love for Isolt, which in the early versions survives eventual perpetual exile and marriage to the other Isolt, all but vanishes—after as well as before the love potion.

Immediately upon his first return from Ireland, potionless but having promised himself to Isolt as her knight and defeated his rival Palamède, he undertakes a blatantly adulterous affair with the wife of Ségurade, Palamède's brother. Since Mark also craves this flirtatious lady's affections, this incident could have been a foreshadowing of the former major triangular desire, had the old love any real function in this new version of the story. As it stands, it only illustrates Tristan's fickleness, as does his other brief affair with the daughter of King Pharamont (whom he at first repulses, by whom he is then caressed, and through whom he is at last accused of attempted rape). Such treason in love would be unthinkable to the old Tristan who, banished forever from Isolt, could not even consummate his marriage except in Eilhart's version, and even then only out of revenge. That the betrayal with Ségurade's wife precedes the drinking of the love potion is irrelevant since, in the prose version, the love between Tristan and Isolt antedates that draught (in itself an indication of the old symbol's atrophy).

The ineffectiveness of old elements of the legend is not the only evidence of the changes that evolved in it. New characters, particularly Palamède and Dinadan, are introduced and alter the relations between the major actors of the story. Palamède enters the *Tristan en prose* as a temporary mediator for Tristan's desire for Isolt upon his first visit to Ireland; Tristan's belief that the Saracen already has the princess's heart arouses his own desire for her. But in spite of Palamède's many laments, Isolt never returns his affection, and so his behavior becomes a parody of amorous intent rather than that kind of effective mediation resulting in triangular desire. Vinaver's contention that this rival introduces a "sombre (*sic*) note" into the story of Iristan and Isolt is curious,[14] since Palamède's unfulfilled longing is never tragic in its dimensions and more often borders upon the comic, like the actions of his narrative shadow, the love- and war-mocker, Dinadan.

Dinadan is a new and special companion of Tristan, who takes for his target the total mystique of Arthurian romance, with its visored encounters in which friend is as liable to wounding as foe, and especially with its cultivation of tormenting rather than fulfilling love. However, his perceptive appraisal of "courtly love" as folly—something he prays God to keep him from—does not prevent his own role in the chivalric system from being both a noble and admired one. Although he demonstrates a courage he blithely denies in himself, this Cyrano de Bergerac of the prose *Tristan* shows none of the new triangular desire that has consumed his friend Tristan, any more than he gives his heart to an obsessive and doomed passion for a lady. In articulating his contrapuntal code, Dinadan questions the emotional force which underlay the original Tristan story and undermines its vestiges with his wit and insouciance.

The *Tristan en prose*, therefore, offers a variety of changes in character and situation, in themes of desire, adventure, and death, which alter (whether consciously or subconsciously) the structure presented by the earlier works. Tristan's loss of fealty to Mark and fidelity to Isolt combine with his ubiquitous "Arthurianization" to destroy the original triangular desire except for ineffective vestiges. Comic rivalry with Palamède mocks the original love sentiment, and companionship with a critically acute Dinadan, the prime chivalric impetus. Above all, the emergence of a compelling Arthurian competition for the desired object of a Round Table seat, with Lancelot and other "good" knights as mediator, draws Tristan into a new and public orbit. Only the element of deceit persists from the original to the succeeding mediation in a fully articulated form: the matter of Ségurade's wife and the deceit and disguise in his battles with Arthur's knights are examples of new dissimulation; Tristan's name change in Ireland, his cuckolding of Mark in Cornwall, his deception of his wife Isolt White Hands in Brittany, of old dissimulation carried into a new context—the prose romance—and without the force of the old desire. This persistent deceit, this new triangular desire, was to be carried to its full synthesis and narrative development by Sir Thomas Malory in his Tale of Sir Tristram.

- III -

As emerged years ago from the voluminous and learned researches of Eilhart Löseth and Eugène Vinaver, Malory's source for his Tristram was some version of the *Tristan en prose* with elements now extant only in four separate French MSS. Any conjectures about his originality must therefore recognize that he probably used a more comprehensive original, but also that—like Marie, Chrétien, Gottfried, and even Chaucer in other contexts—Malory was recasting his material according to the tenor of his own theme. Some of Malory's changes in the *Tristan en prose* were designed to contrast the values of the English Tristram with those of Lancelot and Arthurian society generally.[15] But in this large book, thought to have been reduced to about one-sixth the size of its source(s), Malory had much room for other development. Taking his clues from his French books and, at times it seems, from other earlier versions of the Tristan legend, such as the *Folie Tristan*, Malory carried the old technique of deceit and the new triangular desire to their most complete union, and further demonstrated the failure of the original love and its decayed mediation.

The original Tristan legend in Malory emerges only in the first stage of Tristram's career: his sad birth, his conquering of Marhalt to win his knighthood, his two journeys to Ireland, his affair with Isolt (Isolde in Malory), his exiles because of it, his marriage to Isolt White Hands, all fill comparatively few pages, and even these are interrupted with knightly encounters—mainly with Lamerok—such as make up the bulk of the second and third stages. In the second, Tristram rises by many (and appropriately deceitful) chivalric adventures to claim his seat at the Round Table; in the third, his temporary eclipse of even Lancelot in fame (as not in the French) ends in his subsequent virtual retirement and death at the hands of Mark. Malory's handling of the prose *Tristan* is strikingly different from his way with the Vulgate prose *Lancelot*, and perhaps illustrates the differences he found between the two heroes and their careers.

In the Tale of Lancelot, Malory had encapsulated many hundreds of pages from the French into a short and unified narrative of triangular desire. Lancelot, whose love for the queen is mediated by her husband, Arthur, appropriately the victorious hero of the earlier pages of the *Morte*, undertakes a multiple quest in which he demonstrates the virtues enunciated by his liege lord on the occasion of his wedding, briefly conflated as justice and mercy. Resisting three sexual temptations (one quadruple!) by other women, succeeding in three successively more important knightly combats with members of the Round Table, thrice giving mercy and thrice solving dilemmas between justice and mercy, Lancelot arrives at court to the acclamation of his vanquished opponents and grateful rescuees alike. His is the most apt and concise example of the uses of sublimation of triangular desire to Arthurian knighthood. While his standard is ratified by the somewhat longer and similarly structured Tale of Gareth, Lancelot will always be the prime champion at whose chivalrous record all others will aim. Especially Tristram.

For if Lancleot's rise is short and (seemingly) simple, Tristram's is long and difficult. Not even a partisan of Malory's art can deny the relative diffuseness and exaggerated length of this tale. On the other hand, we must admire the comparative order Malory manages to bring to his *matière*, recognizing important narrative elements either expressed or latent in the French and reorganizing them into thematic units. Chief among these is the new triangular desire, centering upon the Round Table, and not upon Isolde. Malory's special contribution is his making Lancelot a new mediator who is as influential as Mark was, by adding references (unknown to the French sources familiar to us) to Tristram's story from its beginning until after its end. Cumulatively, these references to Lancelot produce still another transformation in the character of Tristram, extending his role from mediatee to mediator in an external rather than internal world of action.

Even before Tristram takes up the fight against Marhalt, Malory's Cornish barons counsel Mark to insure defeat of the Irish champion by sending for "Syre Launcelot du Lake, that was that tyme named for the merueilloust knyght of alle the worlde" (203.10-11).[16] As he begins to gain upon Marhalt, Tristram cries to him, "A, sir knyght of the Round Table, why withdrawest thou the? . . . I promyse the thy suerd and thy sheld shal be myn, and thy sheld shalle I were in al places where I ryde on myn aduentures, and in the syghte of Kyng Arthur and alle the Round Table" (206.17-23). After defeating Palomides in Ireland, Tristram meets a damsel who both asks after Lancelot and then praises Tristram, "for she demyd that there was no knyght in the world myghte do suche dedes of armes but yf it were Launcelot" (209.37-39). Tristram's reply is that, if God wills it, he may yet become "as good a knyght as the good knyght

Sir Launcelot" (209.40-41). Perhaps the most blatant indication of his new desire and its new mediation comes as Tristram escorts Isolde home after successfully completing Mark's bride quest and *after* having drunk the magic potion. Hearing of Lancelot's victory over Carados of Scotland, he exclaims, "and I had not this message in hand with this fayre lady, truly I wold neuer stynte or I had fonde Syre Launcelot" (227.23-24). So much for the love potion and its death-dealing separation; so much for Isolde.

Correlative to this new mediation and longing is a concomitant loss of consuming interest in the former triangular desire for the Irish princess that extends far beyond the similar effect in the prose *Tristan*. Malory has his hero fall in love with Isolde, not from jealousy of Palomides but because of her beauty alone—a reduction of triangular desire by one-third. He also adds to the first Irish adventure their plighting their troth with an exchange of rings. Tristram nevertheless betrays his love, as in the French, with Segwarides' wife, and also displays a lust for her which is new: "in his ragyng he took no kepe of his grene wound [from Mark, who also wanted the lady] . . . And soo Syr Tristram bebled both the ouer shete, and the nether, and pelowes, and hede shete" (213.14-16). A more profound alteration is Malory's treatment of his hero's marriage to Isolde White Hands: with her, Tristram "had suche chere and rychesse and alle other plesaunce that he hadde, allmoost he hadde forsaken La Beale Isould" (235.28-29). Malory thus weakens and distorts that episode which, in the French versions, had been meant to show the inability of a literary double—no matter how beautiful, and even with the same name—to replace the original object of desire. Even more significantly, Tristram's excuses for his marriage are sent not to Isolde, but to his new mediator, Lancelot (248).

Tristram's desire may have changed, but his method of obtaining it—deceit—has not. A method of fighting he will display over and over in Malory appears as early as the tournament in which he defeats Palomides during the first Irish visit, and in the episode of Lancelot's cousin Bleoberis's abduction of the (here ubiquitous) Segwarides' wife. This method may be patterned as follows: a pretended initial reluctance to fight; an encounter with the opponent only after the latter has beaten at least one other strong knight; a victory; a revelation of identity concealed until the battle has been decided; and a quick departure.[17] As far as I can discover, this pattern in all its parts is peculiar to Tristram in Malory. It appears in truncated form earlier, in the Tale of Gareth, where "Syr Lamerak and Syr Trystram departed sodenly, and wold not be knowen, for the whiche Kyng Arthur and all the court were sore displeasyd" (198.3-5). It appears in its most extended form very late in the Tale of Tristram, where its hero finally encounters Lancelot, an engagement to which I shall return.

Verbal as well as physical encounters elicit a deceitfully defensive style from Tristram. Usually these are either not in the French or, if there, are spoken by Tristram's admirers rather than himself. Examples of verbal defensiveness include his exhortation to the Irish barons and his departure speech to the Cornish barons. In the first, he offers to make amends for any wrongs he has done, and then challenges anyone who has wronged him. In the second, after being taken "naked abedde with La Beale Isoud," he reminds his captors of his victory over Marhalt, adding that "I neuer met with no knyght but I was as good as he or better" (234.1-2)—hardly an "amends" for adultery but a persuasive argument against attempting to punish it. In the French, moreover, not Tristan but the admiring Cornish populace defends him.[18] Evasive or deceitful speech also marks his relationship with the second Isolt, who (in a variant on the "bold water" motif of earlier *Tristans*) thinks there is nothing to married love except "kyssynge and clyppynge" (235.36).[19] Both old motifs and new reinforce the consistency of Tristram's trickery.

Trickery shades into behavior which violates the "troth" of the very knightly group to which Tristram aspires. In the long series of encounters and adventures he shares with Lamerok, taken over from the French, Malory repeatedly emphasizes his hero's lack of knightly manners—manners exemplified by the very Lancelot who is his new mediator and hallowed by the very Table which is his new desire. Lamerok had earlier rerouted the horn of Morgan la Fée (a chastity test) from the British to the Cornish court, a burst of patriotism with dire results for Isolde; Tristram has earlier, supposedly, forgiven him; but now the Cornish hero wishes to fight Lamerok for the old cause. "Sire, said Sir Lamerak, remember that we were togyders in the Yle of Seruage, and at that tyme ye promysed me grete frendship" (254.22-23). Yet Tristram rejects the "gentylnesse" of Lamerok as surely as he had earlier rejected the "gentylnesse" of Bleoberis, one of the ubiquitous relatives of Lancelot he repeatedly encounters before his engagement with the chief of the clan much later in the romance. In the case of Blamour, another of Lancelot's clan, Tristram leaves the "gentylnesse" to the Irish judges of their combat rather than taking the proper (and suggested) knightly perogative of implementing it himself.

Even more serious a violation of knightly conduct is his (literal) ladykilling. While this is by no means unknown in Arthurian romance—Gawain mars his first quest, early in the *Morte*, with a blatantly brutal example—it is fairly rare, and always condemned. Significantly, in Malory's earlier Tale of Lancelot, the hero's most heartfelt reproaches of himself are for allowing Sir Pedivere to distract his attention in order that he may kill his own wife—an action Lancelot assumes the blame for, saying it will shame him forever. Tristram, on the other hand, beheads Sir Brewnor's lady without a qualm, once she loses to Isolde the grisly contest of the Castle Pleure. In the *Tristan en prose*, the hero performed the act reluctantly and, like Lancelot, said it would shame him forever; but Malory's man has no such scruples: "with an auke stroke he smote of her hede clene" (225.7-8). The casual and offhand stroke alone betrays the insouciance with which he violates Round Table mores. Malory's later treatment of Tristram's madness, in which Tristram consorts with a band of rural louts and fights dwarfs and giants, traditional knightly enemies, in decidedly unknightly fashion, is it itself a burlesque of Tristram's aspirations.

Such aspirations emerge in a series of individual encounters and tournaments, presented in rapid succession and culminating in Tristram's seating at the Round Table, in which deceit and disregard of chivalric values predominate. Tristram's departure from the Tournament at the Castle of Maidens rather than have Lancelot give him the prize he has won (and which in Malory's French source Tristan wins fairly) leads to his imprisonment, first by Sir Darras and then, more disastrously, by Morgan la Fée. To obtain his release from her, he agrees to carry before King Arthur at the tournament of Harde Roche a shield designed to reveal Lancelot and Guenevere's affair to all: it has "a kynge and a quene therin paynted, and a knyght standynge aboue them, with hys one foote standynge vpon the kynges hede and the other vpon the quenes" (289.32-34). Morgan glosses the shield for him (as she does not in the French) by identifying Arthur and Guenevere, but not the dominant figure of Lancelot; and Tristram (who, one should note, is not too bright in Malory) cannot complete the triad, even though several previous incidents point to his understanding of Lancelot's relations with the queen—his letter excusing himself of fleshly ado with the second Isolde, for instance, or the first Isolde's letter to Guenevere proclaiming that there are but four lovers in the world.

Tristram's deceit in this episode of the shield is threefold. First, by taking it at all he violates an earlier declaration that he would never abandon Isolde's shield "for her sake that gaf it me" (267.9). Second, by his ignorance (real or feigned) of Lancelot's place in the crude diagram, he fails to comprehend that Lancelot's Arthurian arrangement with Guenevere is analogous to his own with Isolde, and that both relationships bring shame to all concerned. Third, his refusal to explain his new shield to Arthur—"I can not descryue these armes, for it is no poynt of my charge" (293.3-4)—is not only unknightly and illogical but deceitful, since Morgan has clarified the king's and queen's figures to him, and he could at least explain this part of the emblem. Obviously he does not because his own culpability in flaunting a semiotic comment upon the unmentionable affair might hinder him in his desire to gain a seat at Arthur's table. Hence, perhaps, Malory's addition to the French of his denial of his own identity: "I knowe not Sire Tristram, said Tristram" (291.11).

Concealment of identity coeval with immoderate and wrong force spreads to Tristram's new mediator, Lancelot, in the sequel to these main tournaments. Arthur, now able to be enchanted with strength rather than knightly conduct, bluntly orders Lancelot to obtain Tristram for the Round Table. Vowing to perform this deed with "fayreness or foulnesse" (282.28)—a phrase found nowhere in the French where, moreover, Lancelot does not know whom he is pursuing—Arthur's chief knight then violates his own code as earlier illustrated in Malory's Tale of Lancelot. In a burlesque of his former career, Lancelot slanders the queen whom he had earlier defended, sorely wounds fellow knights he had earlier helped (such as Kay), kills an innocent stranger knight rather than helping him (as with an earlier counterpart) to membership in the Table—in short, behaves like an enemy of Arthurian society rather than its chief exemplar. Since the original protaganist of this narreme was anonymous in the French, whatever can Malory be doing in assigning his misdeeds to Lancelot?

What Malory is doing goes beyond Vinaver's suggestion that the transformation of the "anonymous champion" into Lancelot "detracts from [the latter's] character"; but was "a lesser evil than leaving a character unidentified" and thus not "solving the mystery."[20] As we have seen of earlier works on Tristan, deceit is catching; not even Lancelot is immune. While he had earlier and would later indulge in typical, harmless Arthurian disguise, nowhere else in Malory—not even in the final books where mishap causes him to sorely wound and/or kill some of his best friends— does Arthur's prime knight so violate his own ideals. Exposure to Tristram's dissimulation and the violence (Malory's repeated "grete force") that accompanies it has affected him. Thus there is great irony is his remark to an Arthur who has already recognized him (by his fighting style) as the anonymous knight, "bycause I wold not be knowen that I was of your courte, I said no worship of your hows" (300.1-2).

Malory's addition of welcoming speeches to Tristram as he takes his Round Table seat, after he and Lancelot have fought to a draw, formalizes the change most obvious in Lancelot. Tristram has now achieved his new object of desire, and, along the way, has changed his mediator into an entity somewhat like himself—at least for the present. It is perhaps no accident that the decay of Gawain and his brethren (except for Gareth) in their feud with the house of Pellinore, as well as their concomitant personal decline, occur in the Tale of Tristram, where Malory intensifies those relevant elements he already had found in the French. Thus, in the earlier Tristan poems Isolt, Brangwayn, Governail, and the second Isolt had all decayed through contact with Tristan. But the greatest decay is still Lancelot's, and it incorporates some striking motifs from the Tristan legend. The love potion is used twice, to slake Elaine's lust as well as for her begetting of Galahad, and Lancelot ends by running mad, by reason of his lady's displeasure, as Tristan had. Since these episodes, although inspired originally by Tristan's story, were first used in the prose *Lancelot* and only later in the prose *Tristan*, and since from internal evidence we know how well Malory knew both works, that he chose his Tale of Tristram as the most striking illustration of decay both in the Round Table and especially in Lancelot indicates his deliberate use of deceit linked with desire.

Further, after some uneventful tournament activity following upon his reception into the Table, Tristram surpasses his ultimate goal: in possession and in power he all but *becomes* his mediator, as the original Tristan never had. "But thus . . . Sir Tristram encheued many grete batails, wherethorough alle the noyse felle to Syr Tristram and it seaced of Sir Launcelot" (398.4-6). Implicit in all stories of triangular desire is not only the possession of the contested object but the status of its possessor as well; it is the wellspring of the fairy tale's king's daughter *and* the kingdom as surely as it is of Julien Sorel's successive mistresses *and* the power their husband/father represents. Lancelot's innate generosity, which limits his own triangular desire for Guenevere as compared to the unlimited appetite of his rival's, appears in his angry reaction to his kinsmen's determination to slay Tristram "bycause of his fame." "Allas, fy for shame, shold ye for his noble dedes awayte vpon hym to slee hym" (398.11), he cries, the mediator unmediated, and apparently unaware of the difference between Tristram and himself.

Yet Malory certainly understands that difference, as the denouement of his Tale of Tristram demonstrates. Once Malory, unlike the author of any other *Tristan*, presents his hero as the most famous knight of the Round Table, he then has him go into semi-retirement. "And euer bitwene, Sir Tristram resorted vnto Ioyous Gard, whereas La Beale Isoud was that loued hym as her lyf" (398.17-18). His home, significantly, is that place most lastingly identified with his displaced mediator Lancelot—"Joyus Garde that was his own castell, and he had wonne hit with his owne hondis"— who has installed Tristram and the now permanently won Isolde in it "to welde for their owne" (350.15). Tristram has succeeded, as Tristan never did, in his old as well as his new desire; and although he never achieves Mark's status (which has been so degraded as to be no longer desirable), he has at least temporarily won Lancelot's—a victory for which the fortress Joyous Garde is an objective correlative. One wonders what Malory might have done with his formidable character had he allowed him to live.

But of course he does not, and invents instead an apparently completely original ending for Tristram's adventures before his undramatized death. Here the hero encounters for the last time his first rival (in the *Tristan en prose* and the *Morte*) Palomides, fights him, sees him baptized as a result, and goes in his company to Camelot. "And so the kynge and alle the court were glad that Syre Palomydes was crystened" (426.30-31). This Christian mediation would seem to be capable of serving as a nice bridge to the Grail adventures which follow. But Malory not only chooses not to send his Tristram on the Quest, but emphatically reminds us that he is not doing so: "Here endeth the second book of Syr Tristram . . . but here is no rehersal of the thyrd book" (426.35-36). His omission of the French prose version of Tristan's holy adventures is thus deliberate and probably due to the nature of his hero himself as much as to the prior decision to make Lancelot (after the Arthur of the early books) the prime hero. Even the final contest with Palomides is less religious than chivalric; had Tristram not offered Palomides the final *battle* to complete his vow, the baptism might never have taken place. The crusade mentality in Malory, plus his use of the concept of the Good Pagan, remain to be discussed elsewhere. What is pertinent here is that, outside of the conventional pieties, Tristram remains a remarkably secular hero, capable of the already self-vowed conversion of a Palomides but incapable of the thaumaturgical grace of Lancelot's healing of Sir Urry. With the Quest and the repentance/conversions at the end of his *Morte*, when Lancelot—after being briefly and somewhat unconvincingly superseded by his son Galahad—becomes once again the unquestioned mediator of the Arthurian world, Malory has no further use for Tristram. Even his death is offstage, mentioned only three times, the first a considerable distance from the end of his tale.

In the first two of these post mortems, the narrator couples his name with Lamerok's, first as examples of valor, "for and Syr Tristram de Lyones outher Syr Lamorak de Galys had been alyue,

Syr Launcelot wold haue demed he [Gareth] had ben one of them tweyne" (535.25-26), and then as victims of treachery, "for they were traytoursly slayne: Syr Trystram by Kynge Marke, and Syr Lamorak by Syr Gawayne and his bretheren" (551.41-552.1). Additionally, from the last two mentions we learn the details of Tristram's death, and of Isolde's, but not in logical order. Rather Tristram has now become analogical.[21] Malory is reminded of him by his mention of "Syre Bellangere le Beuse" in the long catalogue of knights who try to heal Sir Urry's three wounds and fail (until Lancelot succeeds). This knight's father, Alysander le Orphelyn, was slain by the treason of Mark, who also "slewe the noble knyghte Syre Trystram, as he sat harpyng afore his lady La Beale Isoud, with a trenchaunt glayue . . . And La Beale Isoud dyed swounyng vpon the crosse of Syr Tristram" (551.38-552-4). What preceded their deaths is only told some time later, as Bors and Lancelot's other kinsmen and friends advise him on what to do to rescue Guenevere. Lancelot is urged by Bors to follow Tristram's example with Isolde, and keep the queen at Joyous Garde. Lancelot at first objects: "for by Sir Tristram I maye haue a warnynge. For whanne by meanes of treatyce Syr Tristram brought ageyne La Beale Isoud vnto Kynge Mark from Ioyous Gard, loke what befelle on the ende, how shamefully that fals traitour Kyng Marke slewe hym . . . Hit greueth me . . . to speke of his dethe, for alle the world may not fynde suche a knyghte" (562.8-13).

This speech, original with Malory, gives us circumstances surrounding Tristram's death which are strikingly analogous to events awaiting Lancelot. Although, as Bors reminds his cousin, Arthur is not Mark and therefore presumably will not break his promise, Lancelot too will surrender his desired object from Joyous Garde and thereby begin the slow movement toward his own very different death. Lancelot's speech is also a recognition of Tristram's new position as analogical in a quasi-Christian sense (as opposed to an authentically Christian one, as Chaucer intends for the dead Troilus). No longer the internal mediator he had become in briefly eclipsing the greatest Arthurian knight, Tristram through death has become an external mediator, beyond rather than within Lancelot's sphere of action—and beyond the deceit he once needed to obtain his triangular desire, whether Isolde or Round Table championship.

In this apotheosis, however far from the potion-induced, anti-social, and fatal love of his archetypal beginnings, Tristran/ Tristram may be said finally to triumph.

State University College
at Fredonia

NOTES

[1] This paper was given, in a very different form, at the Twelfth International Congress of the Société Internationale Arthurienne, Universität Regensburg, West Germany, August 7-15, 1979, under the title, "Tristan, Trickster: The Decline of the Ideal Lover in the *Tristan en prose* and Malory's *Morte Darthur."*

[2] For a full discussion of the parallels between these couples, see my "Malory's Tristram as Counter-Hero to the *Morte Darthur,"* *Neuphilologische Mitteilungen,* 76 (1975), 605-13.

[3] For full discussion of triangular desire and mediation, mostly in later literature, see René Girard, *Deceit, Desire and the Novel: Self and Other in Literary Structure,* tr. Yvonne Freccero (Baltimore: Johns Hopkins Press, 1965).

[4] *Love in the Western World,* tr. Montgomery Belgion, rev. and aug. ed. (New York: Harper & Row, 1974), p. 44.

[5] That these authors' and nearly all early treatments of the story are either fragmentary or unfinished is perhaps as much a comment upon the essential insolubility of the lovers' situation as it is upon the existence of so much medieval literature in shards.

[6] See, for example, Joan Ferrante, *The Conflict of Love and Honor: The Medieval Tristan Legend in France, Germany and Italy* (The Hague: Mouton, 1973), pp. 75-87.

[7] See Penelope Doob, *Nebuchadnezzar's Children: Conventions of Madness in Middle English Literature* (New Haven: Yale University Press, 1974). Leprosy appears in this character in, for instance, the Middle English romance *Amis and Amiloun,* and the Middle Scots poem by Robert Henryson, *The Testament of Crisseid.*

[8] Merritt Blakeslee, "Mythic Structures in the Old French Verse Versions of the Tristan Legend," Diss. Tulane 1979, discusses Tristan as Trickster.

[9] If sympathetic to the love, like Thomas and Gottfried, writers leave the society around the lovers in doubt about their guilt and eventually vindicate them through the ordeal; if condemnatory, like Béroul and Eilhart, they allow the society to sentence the lovers to execution. See Ferrante, p. 46. Even sympathetic authors may show distress at deceit,

though: the blasphemous ordeal of Isolt rouses Gottfried to his famous aside on using God as a sleeve for selfish reasons.

[10] And not only Arthurian romance: for one aspect of this tendency, see my *"Dux/Rex* Pattern in the Matters of France, Britain and Spain,"* [Papers of the] *VIII Congreso International de la Société Rencesvals,* ed. Carlos Alvár and Victoria Cirlot (Pamplona: Diputación Foral de Navarra, 1981), pp. 149-57.

[11] While it is true that Mark does, once, deliver Isolt to lepers as punishment for her adultery, this is an anomaly in a portrait of an otherwise good man.

[12] Eilhart Löseth's theory, generally accepted, that there are only two versions of the prose *Tristan,* a short and superior one (ca. 1225-35) and a longer, cyclic one (ca. latter 13th c.), has recently been challenged by Emmanuèle Baumgartner in her book, *Le "Tristan en prose": Essai d'interpretation d'un roman médiéval* (Genève: Droz, 1975). She feels there are five or six different adaptations, and the prose *Tristan* was "un texte en perpetuel devenir," p. 330, a theory which ties in with the transformations in the narrative suggested in the present paper.

[13] Eugène Vinaver, "The Prose *Tristan,"* in *Arthurian Literature in The Middle Ages,* ed. Roger Sherman Loomis (Oxford: Oxford University Press, 1959), pp. 342-43.

[14] Vinaver, "The Prose *Tristan,"* p. 343.

[15] See my "Tragic Pattern in Malory's *Morte Darthur:* Medieval Narrative as Literary Myth," *ACTA,* 5 (1978), 81-99.

[16] All references to Malory's text are to *Caxton's Malory,* ed. James W. Spisak (Berkeley and Los Angeles: University of California Press, 1983), by page and line number.

[17] For full discussion of this method, see my "Sir Launcelot and Sir Tristram: Characterization and *Sens* in Malory's *Morte Darthur,"* Diss. State University of New York at Buffalo 1969, pp. 40-249 passim.

[18] Other such speeches occur before Tristram's exile (265-84), and, surprisingly, in a reproach to Isolde in which he laments the "many landes and rychesse" he has forsaken for her (260.17). A study remains to be done of Tristram's rhetoric in Malory.

[19] The "bold water" episode in the archetypal *Tristan*s revealed that he had not consummated his marriage to Isolt White Hands, when her brother Kahedin(s) learned that some water in a stream had splashed higher upon her leg than her husband had yet reached.

[20] Eugène Vinaver, *The Works of Sir Thomas Malory,* 3 vols., 2nd ed. (Oxford: Oxford University Press, 1967), p. 1484.

[21] For a different discussion of Tristan's analogic status, especially with Lancelot but with little of the *sens* here adduced, see T. C. Rumble, "'The Tale of Tristram': Development by Analogy," in *Malory's Originality,* ed. R. M. Lumiansky (Baltimore: Johns Hopkins Press, 1964), pp. 118-83.

The Truest and Holiest Tale: Malory's Transformation of *La Queste del Saint Graal*

Dhira B. Mahoney

Sir Thomas Malory tells us that his Tale of the Sankgreal, "breffly drawyn oute of Freynshe . . . ys a tale cronycled for one of the trewyst and of the holyest that ys in thys worlde."[1] Despite the reverence of this assertion, there has been much disagreement among scholars about Malory's fidelity to his French source, the thirteenth-century *La Queste del Saint Graal.* Although no critic denies that he reduced it considerably, with many omissions and small alterations, many insist that what remains is still a close translation of the source romance. Eugène Vinaver calls the Tale "the least original of his works" (*Works*, p. 1534), and Terence McCarthy describes it as "slavishly, indeed thoughtlessly faithful."[2] Yet Mary Hynes-Berry has shown in her recent studies that Malory's simpler paratactic style has resulted in a very different kind of prose from the patterned, rational French of the *Queste*: Malory translated "his French book not just into another language but into another idiom."[3] The chief argument, however, has been not over style, but *sens*: to what extent did Malory understand the theology of his source, and did he successfully transmit its message or meaning? Hynes-Berry claims that he did not: "the *Sankgreal* is a case study in how one man read the *Queste del Saint Graal* two centuries and a culture later." She also endorses P. E. Tucker's view that Malory did not understand its theology. Vinaver also maintained that, despite his fidelity to the original *matière*, Malory's "one desire seems to be to secularize the Grail theme as much as the story will allow" (*Works*, p. 1535), and Larry D. Benson agrees that "he drastically alters its thematic meaning." On the other hand, Charles Moorman asserts that Malory "always preserves the core of the French book's doctrinal statements, no matter how great his deletions," and Charles Whitworth, while taking issue with many of Moorman's points, claims that Malory did understand the Grail legend and was "able to adapt it without denaturing it."[4] I propose to thread my way through this thicket of conflicting opinions by suggesting that what Malory does to his source is not so much secularize it as anglicize it. He faithfully transmits the central dichotomy of the *Queste* between worldly and spiritual chivalry, whereby the traditional chivalric standards are reinterpreted in the light of spiritual values. However, at the same time, by cutting much of the doctrinal exegesis of the French he shows that he is not sympathetic to its typological method. The result is the expression of the thirteenth-century spiritual message in language and thought that is characteristic of the religious temper of fifteenth-century England, where secular and spiritual pursuits could be considered complementary rather than competitive elements of a knightly life.

That Malory belongs firmly in the fifteenth century has been demonstrated effectively by the criticism of the past two decades. His choice of chivalric subjects was not, as once was thought, an exercise in nostalgia. Arthur B. Ferguson and Benson have shown that chivalric ideals were taken extremely seriously in fifteenth-century England, even if they were beginning to have little relationship to the actual facts of political and social life.[5] The line between romance and reality was shifting and faint; real tournaments and passages of arms imitated literary ones, and literary descriptions echoed the rules and rituals of real ones. Kings and knights consciously reenacted the vows, battles, and disguises of romance heroes, the actual deeds becoming interchangeable with those of romance as models of knightly behavior.[6] The audience for these exploits, fictional or actual, was, of course, aristocratic, the comparatively limited agrarian and military class for whom jousting, hunting and the rules of war were not merely leisure activities but living and urgent concerns. When young John Paston III writes to his mother in 1468, describing the nuptials in Bruges of Princess Margaret and Charles, Duke of Burgundy, he falls easily into the language of romance:

> And as for the Dwykys coort, as of lordys, ladys, and gentylwomen, knytys, sqwyirs, and gentyllmen, I herd never of non lyek to it save Kyng Artourys cort. By my trowthe, I have no wyt nor remembrans to wryte to yow halfe the worchep that is her.[7]

Yet it was not John III but his elder brother John II who loved tournaments and chivalric romance, and was sometimes rebuked for it.[8] Though the main preoccupations of the Paston family were the acquisition and administration of property, the language of romance was neither remote nor unfamiliar to them. Like John II, Malory must have delighted in chivalric literature, and considered tournaments and knightly training significant and worthwhile activities. The world of his Arthurian knights is one in which horses and armor are not only the trappings but also the symbols of knightly life. When Palomides falls "oute of his wytt," the mark of his changed state is that he has put his horse out to pasture (423.19-23), and during the Quest, when the Grail knights disembark from the Ship of Solomon, Malory is quick to remind his readers that "they had no horse in that contrey, for they lefft their horsys whan they toke their shippe" (996.27-29). At the end of the *Morte* a tiny detail suffices to indicate renunciation of the knightly life by Lancelot's seven companions when they follow him into the cloister: "And soo their horses wente where they wolde, for they toke no regarde of no worldly rychesses" (1255.8-9).

The significance of the outward trappings lies in the fact that the primary motivation for action in the world of the *Morte Darthur* is the search for earthly glory, for "worshyp" and a name. "Name" comes to mean, in this context, not only a knight's identity and rank, but also his lineage and past exploits. "Worshyp" is more than reputation; it is a man's worth-ship, his self-worth, captured in his "name," or what is publicly known about him—the battles he has won, the great knights he has defeated. For this is a society in which self-worth is exclusively bound up with the public recognition of it. Action is validated by public recognition, and values are externally apprehended. A great knight has a role to maintain, and it is his duty to maintain it. In the episode of the Poisoned Apple, when the Queen has banished Lancelot from the court in a jealous fury, he considers returning to his own country, but is counseled not to do so by Bors: "ye muste remembir you what ye ar, and renomed the moste nobelyst knyght of the worlde, and many grete maters ye have in honde" (1047.16-18). Similarly Isolde urges Tristram not to stay away for her sake from the great tournament and feast at Pentecost: "ye that ar called one of the nobelyste knyghtys of the worlde and a knyght of the Rounde Table, how may ye be myssed at that feste?" (839.31-33). The pursuit of worship is essentially agonistic, and the desire for it informs the actions of Malory's knights. "Hit is oure kynde to haunte armys and noble dedys" (810.6-7), says young Percival to his mother when she begs him to stay at home.

Given such chivalric predilections, it would not be surprising to find Malory secularizing the Grail story when he came to translate what is, after all, primarily a theological treatise on salvation, in which innumerable hermits and recluses explicate the visions and adventures "in [the] bitterest detail," as E. K. Chambers puts it.[9] Yet Malory's colophon shows that he held the story in great reverence, and he seems to have chosen the Vulgate version in preference to the more secular version that he is likely to have known from the prose *Tristan*, his source for the Tale of Tristram.[10] The prose *Tristan* contains a post-Vulgate version of the *Queste* in which the adventures of non-Grail knights such as Tristan, Erec, Kaherdin, and Palamède are so interlaced with the traditional ones that the spiritual message of the *Queste* is entirely dissipated.[11] One might argue, if one were following McCarthy's contention that the Tale of the Sankgreal was the first to be written, that Malory had not yet come upon the prose *Tristan* version of the Grail, but Edward D. Kennedy has shown that it is very likely that Malory knew other secular versions as well, such as that in Hardyng's *Chronicle*.[12] Apparently Malory's choice of the Vulgate *Queste* was deliberate, perhaps because this earlier version of the story was purer, less adulterated by the wider chivalric narrative of the prose *Tristan*.

La Queste del Saint Graal is a tightly woven interlaced romance, which progresses by a series of deepening revelations. The controlling metaphors of the narrative are finding one's way and seeing. At the first appearance of the Grail at the Arthurian court, there is only mystery and marvel. It is Gauvain's oath not to give up till he sees the Grail more openly that precipitates the Quest, and the knights set out on individual paths which converge and diverge until the narrative narrows its focus to the three Grail knights and Lancelot.[13] The Grail knights achieve the highest stage of revelation, but even they have to progress by stages. In the first half of the romance they are purified by trial and temptation, until they come together on Solomon's ship, where they are brought in touch with the whole range of Old Testament tradition that has prefigured the Quest. Arriving at the castle of Corbenic, they celebrate a Mass in which Josephus, the son of Joseph of Arimathea and the first Bishop of Christendom, descends from Heaven to conduct the service, and the crucified Christ himself issues from the Grail to administer the sacrament to the knights. Yet, marvellous though this is, it is not the ultimate revelation. Galaad does not see as openly as he will see. The three knights must take the Grail, with its table and bleeding lance, to the holy city of Sarras. Here, after imprisonment and further tribulation, Galaad is granted the supreme Vision: celebrating Mass, he looks into the Grail, and, trembling with ecstasy, asks to pass over into the next world. Perceval also dies in holy orders, and only Boort returns to tell the court the story of the *Queste*.

Albert Pauphilet was the first to identify the religious order featured in the *Queste* as Cistercian, and to study its narrative technique. "Sous l'apparence chevaleresque," writes Pauphilet, "c'est la grande adventure de l'homme qui est ici exposée: c'est un tableau de la vie chrétienne telle que pouvait l'observer ou la rêver une conscience du treizième siècle."[14] Throughout the narrative a constant dichotomy is built up between the worldly, chivalric values of the Arthurian knights and the spiritual values by which their actions must now be interpreted. What each knight has to learn is that this is a totally new order of adventure: to succeed in this quest, unlike so many previous ones, it is not enough that a knight should improve his life; he must learn to think in a new way, to abandon his traditional values and adopt a new ethic. The different levels of achievement among the knights reflect their capacity to understand this, or to act upon it once understood. Gauvain never does understand it; he gets bored and discouraged, and finally returns to the court. Lancelot is the repentant sinner who is granted a partial, corporeal vision of the Grail: at the castle of Corbenic, he looks into the room where Mass is being celebrated. However, his impulsive entrance to help the celebrant apparently struggling to raise a human figure above the altar shows that he is still, in Pauline Matarasso's words, "interpret[ing] in physical terms an experience purely mystical."[15] His punishment is to be knocked down by a burning wind and lie unconscious for twenty-four days. The three Grail knights do achieve the penitential vision, but even among them there is a heirarchy: Boort is the deliberate saint, the type of those who win salvation by the sweat of their brows; Perceval is the innocent, ingenuous type, saving himself by instinct rather than conscious thought; and Galaad is the perfect hero, the figure of Christ, redeemer and deliverer.[16]

It is not surprising that the lesser knights take so long to understand the nature of the new quest, for the language in which the adventures are announced is the traditional chivalric language. Galaad is "cil qui metra a fin les aventures de la Grant Bretaigne" (he who will bring the adventures of Britain to a close, p. 10), and he will prove by his achievements that Lancelot is no longer "li mieldres chevaliers dou monde" (the best knight of the world, p. 12). In his first adventure, the new-made knight Melyans chooses the left-hand fork to prove his courage because of a warning sign that forbids entry to all except one who considers himself a "preudome" (p. 41). This term can mean an exceptionally wise or a valiant man, and Melyans is clearly interpreting it as the latter. After he has narrowly escaped death, his error is explained to him: "li escriz parloit de la chevalerie celestiel, et tu entendoies de la seculer" (the writing referred to spiritual chivalry, and you understood it as worldly chivalry, p. 45).

This constant tension between the familiar chivalric terms and their new meanings, the usurpation of the old values by the new, is best exemplified in the temptations of Boort and Percevel. Perceval's major test occurs when he is alone on a rocky island and told in a dream:

114

demain te covendra combatre encontre le champion dou monde
qui plus fet a redouter. Et se tu ies vaincuz, tu ne seras pas
quites por un de tes membres perdre, ainz te menra len si mal
que tu en seras honiz a toz jorz mes.   (p. 97)[17]

When a beautiful lady arrives on a barge and asks his help to regain
her lost inheritance, invoking his duty as a companion of the
Round Table, Perceval is easily deceived. She persuades him to
come into her silken pavilion to eat and drink, and almost entices
him into her bed, but just in time he catches sight of the pommel of
his sword and instinctively crosses himself. There is a cloud of black
smoke and the lady and barge vanish in flames on the water. Only
later does Perceval learn the full significance of the encounter: the
lady was the devil and this was the battle with the champion that he
was due to fight. Boort's major test forces him to choose between
saving his brother Lyonel from certain death and a virgin from
equally certain dishonor. It is a terrible dilemma: by traditional
chivalric standards, his first duty should be to his brother, but he is
also aware of his duty to save defenseless virgins. In anguish, he
calls on God to look after his brother and saves the virgin. Although
his torment is increased when he is shown what appears to be
Lyonel's corpse, he later discovers that his choice was the correct
one, for he had put behind him "toute naturel amor por amor de
Jhesucrist" (p. 187). Brotherly love has no place in the *Queste*. Its
doctrine demands total absorption, total detachment from worldly
ties. "L'attachement au monde est chose d'enfer," explains
Pauphilet.[18] Not surprisingly, Lyonel does not see it that way, and
when next he meets Boort he accuses him of treachery and tries to
kill him.

The technique of the *Queste* is not allegorical so much as
typological, or, as Erich Auerbach would call it, figurative. Whereas
modern history views events chronologically, interpreting their
significance according to cause and effect, the figurative approach
interprets an event by projecting it vertically onto the plane of
providential design. The victory of Joshua, for instance, prefigures
Christ's, and the victory of Christ is a fulfillment of Joshua's. "Both
entities in the figurative relationship are equally real and equally
concrete," explains Auerbach; "the figurative sense does not destroy
the literal, nor does the literal deprive the figured fact of its status as
a real historical event."[19] Tournaments in the *Queste* are real, but

115

when Lancelot goes to help the weaker party he is also proving his kinship with those who cannot shake off worldly values;[20] the city of Sarras is real, concrete, but at the same time it prefigures the city of God, Jerusalem. The Table of the Last Supper, the Table of the Grail, and the Round Table are all linked: each is a figure of the next or an echo of the last, yet each is a separate table, belonging to a different occasion and era. The whole patristic exegetical tradition is evoked in these links and correspondences, which use an imagery always public, not secret, yet which flows from abstract to concrete and back, never quite identifiable by a charted system. The Grail itself appears sometimes as a cup, sometimes a dish, sometimes on the table, sometimes without it, sometimes carried by an unseen agency, sometimes accompanied by angels. As Frederick Locke observes, "at the end of the *Queste* we cannot define the Grail with any greater precision than when we first saw it or when we continued to see it in the development of the narrative."[21]

In conventional allegory one event is pure sign, but in the figurative technique neither the prefigured nor the prefiguring event loses its literary and historical reality. As Locke explains, Galaad does not "stand for" Christ, but acts like Christ at times, reminds priest and hearers of Christ, then "emerges from his temporary analogical immersion and stands alone once more—a knight confined by time and space to the fifth century" (p. 35). Thus the *Queste* is not a *Pilgrim's Progress*. Bunyan uses allegory to present a concrete realization of what is actually a spiritual and moral journey. The *Queste* is also a journey, but one which takes place on different planes of experience simultaneously. It is a journey back to the primal innocence, or its recreation in the Divine Union. Virginity is extolled as a primal virtue because it denotes a state as far removed as possible from the corruption of the flesh. The narrator, or rather "li contes," even distinguishes between "virginitez" and "pucelages." "Pucelages" is the condition of those who have never experienced carnal companionship, but virginity is the condition of those who would never desire it, who have no knowledge of its existence—the state of absolute purity before the Fall.[22] Thus the "archetypal movement" of the *Queste*, as Locke puts it, is "from obscurity and darkness to light and vision" (p. 9), and, because obscurity is the condition of the flesh, from the carnal to the spiritual. The vision of the Host is a reward for Lancelot, but one in accord with his stage of development, his limited capacity for seeing. The ultimate achievement is Galaad's—he looks into the vessel of the Grail and is translated.[23] After his apotheosis the Grail is removed from Logres, from England, because most men are not capable of the search. Galaad's vision, however, foretells the Beatific Vision at the end of time, the face-to-face vision of God which St. Paul tells us will be granted to the whole Church.

It is this theological view, the doctrinal significance of the Quest in the context of the history of the human race, that Malory chooses not to transmit, perhaps because it is alien to the temper of his time. He cuts long sections of doctrinal explication, as in the Ship of Solomon episode,[24] and, above all, he cuts the "senefiances"—the cobweb of doctrinal significance that structures the *Queste*, the subtle and beautiful correspondences that link disparate elements and show the action taking place on many planes at once. He omits, for instance, the explanation of the link between the three Tables, of the Last Supper, the Grail, and the Round Table (pp. 74-78); and while he retains the heat which provides an excuse for the devilish lady to invite Percival into her pavilion (917.32), he cuts the subsequent explanation that the sun is a figure of Christ's grace, which would have melted the ice of the fiend, and which she therefore feared and tried to avoid (p. 114). Similarly, Malory modifies the figurative imagery of the *Queste*. The ambiguous, shifting image of the French Grail becomes in his hands a constant image of a miraculous vessel filled with Christ's blood, though it still has the power to heal, to feed, to beautify, to make happy. His treatment of Gawain's dream points up the difference most clearly. The French Gauvain dreams of a meadow full of bulls, all but three of whom have stained and speckled skins (p. 149). The bulls represent the Arthurian knights, whose mortal sin and carnal enslavement appear outwardly, as stains on the skin (p. 156). The French author uses the image once only. Malory turns the scene of the dream into a meadow full of proud black bulls, among whom are three white ones, one with a black spot (942, and 946). He has also used the image previously. Where the French author categorized the three companions who would achieve the Grail as "li dui virge et li tierz chastes" (p. 77), Malory shows that he is already thinking of the dream: "There sholde be three whyght bullis sholde encheve hit, and the two sholde be maydyns and the thirde sholde be chaste" (906.31-33). The single, delicate image of the French has become for Malory a recurrent moral sign to distinguish the Grail knights from the rest of the Questers.

Yet, though he may eliminate much of the doctrine, Malory does not fail to understand or to transmit the central dichotomy of the *Queste* between worldly and spiritual values. Apart from a few minor details he translates Perceval's temptations and Boort's dilemma faithfully and effectively,[25] though one can imagine that he sympathized strongly with Boort's anguish at having to abandon his brother. He even adds a passage to the Tale of Tristram, which is not authorized by the source, warning Lancelot that, although "of all worldly adventures he passyth in manhode and proues all othir, . . . in this spyrytuall maters he shall have many hys bettyrs" (801.31-33).

Indeed, Lancelot is the key figure in both French and English Quests. Though he is not the hero, he is the doctrinal pivot, for it is in his partial success or partial failure that the Quest is defined. Most of the critical discussion has been over Malory's treatment of Lancelot's role, and whether it is classed as a success or a failure seems to depend on each critic's attitude to the *Morte Darthur* as a whole. Vinaver claims that Malory, in accord with his desire to secularize the story, attempts to "rehabilitate" his favorite knight, by underlining that he is the best of all earthly knights (*Works*, pp. 1536-37). Tucker and Moorman maintain that Malory emphasizes Lancelot's failure, because of his adulterous relationship with the Queen.[26] It is true that Malory does accentuate Lancelot's superiority among earthly knights more than the French text, but he is always careful to qualify that praise. On the other hand, those critics who are obsessed with the theme of adultery do not seem to notice that neither in the French nor in the English Quests is adultery the main issue.

The French Lancelot is told by a hermit that he had, initially, five great virtues: virginity, humility, patience, rectitude, and charity. The devil, casting about for a means to destroy him, hit on the idea of woman and, entering into the Queen Guenievre, caused her to eye Lancelot with desire. Through her seduction of him his virtues were corrupted and transformed into lust and pride, "luxure" and "orgeuil." The description of the effect on Lancelot shows the intimate relationship between these two vices:

> Car si tost come tu eus tes eulz eschaufez de l'ardor de luxure, maintenant enchaças humilité et atresis orgeuil et vousis aler teste levee ausi fierement come un lyon, et deis en ton cuer que tu ne devoies riens prisier ne ne priseroies ja mes, se tu n'avoies ta volenté de cele que tu veoies si bele.   (p. 126)[27]

Pauline Matarasso's exhaustive discussion of the passage shows that the desire for possession is linked with the desire for self-aggrandizement: both are forms of concupiscence in which the main object is self-gratification instead of the service of God. Lancelot's love for Guenievre is indeed idolatrous; he has seen her as the source of his prowess and must learn that the true source is God.[28] Idolatry rather than adultery is the issue. When Lancelot confesses his sin to a hermit in the early stages of the romance, he is told to promise never again to offend his Maker "en fesant pechié mortel de la reine ne d'autre dame ne d'autre chose dont vos le doiez corrocier" (in committing mortal sin with the queen nor with another lady nor doing anything else by which you are bound to anger Him, p. 67). It is not the extra-marital relationship but the abandonment to the flesh, the enslavement by the world, that is the sin by Cistercian standards. The devil tempted Lancelot through woman, as he did Adam, Solomon, Samson, and Absolom (p. 125). Lancelot thus becomes a figure of Adam, the fallen sinner; Guenievre is also a type, of "Eve la pecheresse." Her opposite and redeemer is Perceval's sister, the virgin who gives her blood to save another, the figure of Mary, the new Eve.[29] Although Malory modifies the interpretation of Lancelot's character, cutting out the long description of the provenance of Lancelot's sins, he does not travel far from the implications of the French. Since the figurative view is foreign to him, he refashions Lancelot's imperfections. Lust and pride, which in the French are the result of Lancelot's initial corruption by the flesh, become in Malory's version Lancelot's main sins. In his confession to the hermit Lancelot admits that all his battles in the past were motivated by the desire to win worship and be better loved, "and litill or nought I thanked never God of hit" (897.21-22). Whereas the French Lancelot erred in thinking the source of his valor was the Queen, Malory's Lancelot errs in believing that the source of his valor is himself; both Lancelots have to learn that the true source is God.

Indeed, this is Lancelot's chief lesson throughout the Tale of the Sankgreal. In one of his dreams, God appears to him in the form of an accusing old man: "thou hast ruled the ayenste me as a warryoure and used wronge warris with vayneglory for the pleasure of the worlde more than to please me" (928.34-929.1). Much has been made of the "wronge warris,"[30] but they are surely just an attempt to render the idea of the French: "tu ne m'as mie esté comme sergans, mais comme guerroiers; tu ne m'as mie esté comme fieulx, mais comme fillastre" (You have not acted towards me like my soldier, but like my opponent; you have not been to me like a son, but like a stepson).[31] The wars were wrong because of their motivation by personal pride rather than the desire to serve God. When Lancelot instinctively joins the weaker party in the tournament, thinking to "[increse] his shevalry" (931.25), he is again in error; he is told later that he "enclyned to that party for bobbaunce and pryde of the worlde, and all that muste be leffte in that queste" (933.31-934.1). Even after many sermons, penances, and humiliations, when he comes to the castle gate of Corbenic and finds it guarded by lions, Lancelot still instinctively draws his sword, and has it struck from his hand while a voice from above rebukes him: "O, man of evylle feyth and poure byleve! Wherefore trustist thou more on thy harneyse than in thy Maker?" (1014.21-22). The source of his strength is God, not himself, and that Malory considers he has finally learned the lesson is proved by the episode of the healing of Sir Urry, after the Quest is over. When all the Arthurian knights at court have failed to heal the wounded knight, Lancelot succeeds, because he prays secretly to be given the power to do so "by the grete vertu and grace of The, but, Good Lorde, never of myselff" (1152.23-25).

Though pride is his major sin, lust is a close second. Lancelot never denies to others or to himself that it is his love for Guenevere that prevents him from achieving the full vision of the Grail, as he tells her at their last meeting: "in the queste of the Sankgreall I had that tyme forsakyn the vanytees of the worlde, had nat youre love bene" (1253.13-14). As in the French, the fault is not so much that the love is adulterous, as that it exists at all. It is enslavement by the flesh that prevents Lancelot from forsaking the vanities of this world and pursuing perfection.

The central issue to most arguments by the critics who emphasize Lancelot's failure is Malory's introduction of the concept of stability in connection with the evaluation of Lancelot's achievement. In a speech that has no parallel in the French, a hermit explains to Gawain, using the familiar opposition between worldly and spiritual values, why Gawain will see no adventures in this Quest. He is a sinner, but Lancelot

> hath takyn upon hym to forsake synne. And nere were that he
> nys nat stable, but by hys thoughte he ys lyckly to turne agayne,
> he sholde be nexte to encheve hit sauff sir Galahad, hys sonne;
> but God knowith hys thought and hys unstablenesse.
>
> (948.23-27)

"Stable" is usually glossed as steadfast, constant, and it is certainly a common doublet with "steadfast" in Middle English. Tucker interprets Lancelot's instability as emotional weakness, a fault of character that prevents him, despite his best resolve, from pulling free of the adulterous liaison (pp. 87-89). However, I believe Tucker, and those who follow him, are missing the specific context the term is being given in this tale. Malory uses the adjective form of the word a few pages later, in connection with Bors: "And thys good man founde hym in so mervales a lyffe and so stable that he felte he was never gretly correpte in fleyshhly lustes but in one tyme that he begat Elyan le Blanke" (956.1-4). Bors is so stable that he only once yielded to the desires of the flesh (he was the bull with one spot in Gawain's dream). The corresponding term in the source passage is "religieuse" (p. 166), which meant pious, honest, good, and was frequently used as a doublet with "bone" or "sainte" in Old French.[32] Malory's translation of the adjective by "stable" suggests that the latter term had a significant religious connotation at the time. The suggestion is confirmed by reference to other Middle English works and to the *OED*. A person is "stable" in faith or virtue, and stability is frequently invoked in the context of perseverance in the religious or monastic life.[33] A novice promises "de stabilitate sua perseverantia" in the first stage of acceptance into the Benedictine Order.[34] Caxton's translation of this phrase in his

Abstract of the *Rule* reads: "And yf he promyse to contynwe and to be stable in his purpoos, thenne after two monethes the rule shall be red hole by ordre unto hym."[35] In similar vein, the writer of the devotional treatise *The Pilgrimage of Perfection*, printed in 1526, urges his readers to be strong on the difficult journey to the heavenly Jerusalem: "Therfore let us be stable and never loke backwarde agayne to the worlde, lest it happen to us as it fortuned to the wyfe of Loth, whiche (as scripture sheweth) for ones lokynge backwarde was turned into a salte stone."[36]

Thus Malory is not simply confusing stability with holiness, as Vinaver suggests (*Works*, p. 1536, n. 5). In the context of his Sankgreal, stability means perseverance in the pursuit of holiness, and connotes withdrawal from the world. It is not surprising, then, that Lancelot should forget his promise to take himself to perfection after the Quest. For when he returns to the Authurian world, he returns to public life, and, moreover, to his role in it: the best of all earthly knights, and the lover of the Queen. "Ye muste remembir you what ye ar" (1047.16), Bors had told him when he was thinking of returning to his own country. Lancelot's fault is less a weakness of character than a failure of his whole being, his self-integrity. He cannot renounce the world because his love is too great; and he cannot remain in the world and not love. Only when Guenevere herself renounces it is he free to do so. As he says to her at their last meeting, "I take recorde of God, in you I have had myn erthly joye" (1253.19-20). Arthur's death and Guenevere's rejection release him from his final ties to his old life. Public values are no longer given shape in action: there is no longer any necessity to maintain his "name"—indeed, once the world in which he had a name is gone, there is no longer any meaning to that name. Lancelot turns hermit and dies of grief, but at his death his corpse lies smiling. His relatives go to fight in the Holy Land, where they die "upon a Good Fryday for Goddes sake" (1260.15). When the public world which gave their lives meaning has gone, they too can turn to private redemption.

Benson and Ferguson have shown us that withdrawal from the world was an acceptable alternative to the knightly life in fifteenth-century England.[37] The two avenues of action were equally valid, but not to be led concurrently; one was a recognized successor to the other. Malory's hermit Sir Bawdwyn of Bretayn tells us, "sometyme

I was one of the felyship, but now I thanke God I am othirwyse disposed" (1075.22-23). Real as well as literary knights turned hermit in their old age. Malory's contemporary, Sir Stephen Scrope, suggests that knights whose physical strength has failed them because of old age should occupy their time "in gostly chevallrie off dedes of armes spirituall."[38] The attitude is not unlike the Hindu view of life, which teaches that a man's duties are divided into four stages: first childhood and education, then marriage and procreation, then establishment in world affairs, and finally renunciation of the world and retreat into asceticism. The last stage does not invalidate the others.

Here, then, lies the essential difference between the two Quests. For the French author the "chevalerie celestiel" was to replace the "terriene," to invalidate and supersede it. For Malory it is a separate pursuit, of equal validity, in which success is fully achievable only by withdrawal from the world, either into the reclusive life, like Percival and the hermits at the end of the *Morte*, or into death, like Galahad. The contrast is pointed up most clearly in the two scenes of Galahad's death. Malory's Galahad, seeing the Grail openly at last, prays, "Now, my Blyssed Lorde, I wold nat lyve in this wrecched worlde no lenger" (1034.25-26), and asks Bors to greet his father Lancelot and "bydde hym remembir of this worlde unstable" (1035.11-12). "Wrecched worlde," "worlde unstable," "thys unsyker worlde" (1036.28)—these phrases ring of the homiletic tradition which surfaces so often in late medieval English literature, that particularly Boethian contrast between this fickle, unreliable, "corrumpable" world with the perfection and "perdurability" of the next.[39] It is a note which is not struck in the French. When the French Galaad finally sees the full mystery of the Grail, he sends greetings but no message to his father and prays that he be allowed to "trespasse de ceste terriene vie en la celestiel" (p. 278). He is not asking to be released from this wretched world, or what Chaucer would call "this foule prisoun of this lyf" (A 3061), for he has already achieved on this earth the highest kind of vision, that which the heart cannot conceive nor the tongue describe, the intellectual vision of God. He prays for death simply to sustain that vision forever. In Charlotte Morse's words, "he passes from the shadow of the heavenly banquet, the sacrament of the Mass, to the reality of its eternal celebration, a passage from time to eternity without any division between the two conditions."[40]

The controlling image of Galaad's journey in the *Queste* is a progression into more and more refined revelation, till the vision of the ineffable in this world shades imperceptibly into union in the next. The controlling image of the journey of Malory's Galahad is also a progression into greater spirituality, but one which culminates in his translation from one world into the next, with a sharp awareness of the division between them. Malory presents the spiritual pursuit of perfection as complementary to rather than competitive with the pursuit of earthly glory. Matarasso has shown that the function of the *Queste del Saint Graal* in the Vulgate Cycle as a whole is to redeem earthly chivalry by presenting a new way of life that negates and exposes the old one.[41] To Malory, however, the Grail Quest is a digression rather than an exposure: "the Rounde Table shall be brokyn for a season" (799.33-34).[42] For his knights the "ghostly chivalry" is an alternative that is only emotionally available after the earthly chivalry has been relinquished, after the fellowship that gave it meaning has gone. Malory is not, therefore, turning the Grail Quest into just another earthly adventure, as Vinaver averred (*Works*, p. 1535); it is still the truest and holiest tale in the world. However, he is, inevitably, transforming it in the light of his own culture and his native literary tradition. Just as the Boethian ending of *Troilus and Criseyde* does not negate the passionate earthly drama that precedes it, but puts it in perspective, so the Tale of the Sankgreal does not negate the heroic-chivalric values of the *Morte Darthur* as a whole. Only in the perspective of eternity is the greatest of all earthly institutions seen as fragile and finite, doomed inevitably to fall.

University of Arizona

NOTES

[1] *The Works of Sir Thomas Malory*, ed. Eugène Vinaver, 2nd ed., 3 vols. (Oxford: Oxford University Press, 1967), 1037.9-11. All quotations and references are to this edition.

[2] Terence McCarthy, "The Sequence of Malory's Tales," in *Aspects of Malory*, ed. Toshiyuki Takamiya and Derek Brewer (Cambridge: D.S. Brewer; Totowa, N.J.: Rowman and Littlefield, 1981), p. 117.

[3] Mary Hynes-Berry, "Language and Meaning: Malory's Translation of the Grail Story," *Neophilologus*, 60 (1976), 318.

[4] Hynes-Berry, "Malory's Translation of Meaning: *The Tale of the Sankgreal*," *Studies in Philology*, 74 (1975), 257; P. E. Tucker, "Chivalry in the *Morte*," in *Essays on Malory*, ed. J. A. W. Bennett (Oxford: Oxford University Press, 1963), p. 83; Larry D. Benson, *Malory's Morte Darthur* (Cambridge, Mass: Harvard University Press, 1976), p. 210; Charles Moorman, *The Book of Kyng Arthur: The Unity of Malory's Morte Darthur* (Lexington, Ky.: University of Kentucky Press, 1965), p. 33; Charles Whitworth, "The Sacred and the Secular in Malory's *Tale of the Sankgreal*," *Yearbook of English Studies*, 5 (1975), 19.

[5] Arthur B. Ferguson, *The Indian Summer of English Chivalry* (Durham, N. C.: Duke University Press, 1960), p. 222; Benson, p. 201, and Chs. 7-9 generally; see also *Chivalric Literature: Essays on Relations between Literature and Life in the Later Middle Ages*, ed. Larry D. Benson and John Leyerle, Studies in Medieval Culture, 14 (Kalamazoo: Medieval Institute Publications, 1980).

[6] Benson, pp. 196-97.

[7] *Paston Letters*, ed. Norman Davis (Oxford: Oxford University Press, 1958), no. 50, p. 66.

[8] See, e.g., *Paston Letters*, no. 49.

[9] E. K. Chambers, *Sir Thomas Wyatt and Some Collected Studies* (London: Sidgewick and Jackson, 1933), p. 32.

[10] Fanni Bogdanow has shown that the *Queste* section of the prose *Tristan* is derived from the First redaction of the post-Vulgate *Queste*, which, together with an extended *Suite du Merlin* and a post-Vulgate *Mort Artu*, formed what may be called the Roman du Graal; see *The Romance of the Grail: A Study of the Structure and Genesis of a Thirteenth Century Arthurian Prose Romance* (Manchester: Manchester University Press; New York: Barnes and Noble, 1966), Ch. 4. Since the *Suite du Merlin* was Malory's source for his opening Tale, it is likely he knew this version of the *Queste*. Furthermore, a reference in Malory's colophon to the "Tristram" to a division between a second and third book of the French work is reflected in certain MSS of the prose *Tristan* (see *Works*, pp. 1531-32), which suggests that Malory's source MS contained the *Queste*.

[11] See Emmanuèle Baumgartner, *Le "Tristan en Prose": Essai d'interprétation d'un roman médiéval* (Geneva: Droz, 1975), pp. 199-200.

[12] Terence McCarthy, "Order of Composition in the *Morte Darthur*," *Yearbook of English Studies*, 1 (1971), 18-29; also "The Sequence of Malory's Tales," in *Aspects of Malory*, pp. 107-24; Edward D. Kennedy, "Malory and His English Sources," in *Aspects*, pp. 44-47.

[13] Suzanne Greer Fein discusses this aspect in "Thomas Malory and the Pictorial Interlace of *La Queste del Saint Graal,*" *University of Toronto Quarterly,* 46 (1977), 214-40.

[14] Albert Pauphilet, *Etudes sur la Queste del Saint Graal attribué à Gautier Map* (Paris: H. Champion, 1921), p. 26.

[15] Pauline Matarasso, trans. *The Quest of the Holy Grail* (Harmondsworth: Penguin Books, 1969), p. 301, n. 73.

[16] Albert Pauphilet, ed., *La Queste del Saint Graal, roman du XIIIe siècle,* CFMA 33 (Paris: H. Champion, 1921, rpt. 1967), p. xi. Subsequent quotations from the *Queste* are from this edition; the glosses are my own.

[17] "Tomorrow you must fight against the most dreaded champion of the world. And if you are vanquished, you will not escape with the loss of a limb, but it will go so badly with you that you will be shamed for ever after."

[18] *Etudes,* p. 44. Love between spiritual "brothers," those who are united in the common pursuit of the mysteries of the Grail, is a very different matter. The Grail questers frequently show affection to one another, embracing joyfully in welcome and tearfully in farewell, e.g., pp. 194, 245-46, 250, 252. It is, however, an exclusive brotherhood, limited to those who are "compainz de la Queste" (p. 268).

[19] Erich Auerbach, "Typological Symbolism in Medieval Literature," *Yale French Studies,* 9 (1952), 4.

[20] See *Queste,* p. 143; also see Eugène Vinaver, *Malory* (Oxford: Oxford University Press, 1929; rpt. 1970), p. 185,. for a partial edition of MS. B.N. fr. 120, which is in some respects closer to Malory's translation than Pauphilet's base text (see Vinaver's explanation in *Works,* pp. 1534-35).

[21] Frederick Locke, *The Quest for the Holy Grail: A Literary Study of a Thirteenth Century Romance* (Stanford: Stanford University Press, 1960), p. 95. See also Pauline Matarasso, *The Redemption of Chivalry: A Study of the Queste del Saint Graal* (Geneva: Droz, 1979), pp. 182-83.

[22] *Queste,* p. 213, and Pauphilet, *Etudes,* pp. 39-40.

[23] Locke explains this very persuasively, pp. 95-100.

[24] Hynes-Berry discusses some of the major alterations to the *Queste* in "Malory's Translation of Meaning," especially pp. 245-48.

[25] Malory does expand the virgin's appeal to Bors with a reference to King Arthur and "the hyghe Ordre of Knyghthode" (961.7-11), and adds the sentence "he ys a murtherer and doth contrary to the Order of Knyghthode" (968.11-12) to the hermit's description of Lionel's character. However, this particular criticism may well have been suggested by the French text, where Lyonel represents the "type" of anger, just as Hector does of pride. See Pauphilet, *Etudes,* pp. 125-27.

[26] Tucker, p. 85, and Moorman, pp. 36-37.

[27] "For as soon as your eyes were inflamed by the fever of lust you chased away humility and welcomed pride and wished to carry your head as proudly as a lion, and said in your heart that you should not nor never would value anything unless you had your desire of her whom you saw as so beautiful." Cf. the corresponding passage in Vinaver's *Malory*, pp. 165-66.

[28] Matarasso, *Redemption of Chivalry*, pp. 145-49.

[29] See Locke, pp. 74-77.

[30] Tucker, for instance, argues that Lancelot's love for Guenevere has obscured his sense of right and wrong, p. 85; Hynes-Berry endorses his view in "Malory's Translation of Meaning," pp. 248-50.

[31] *Malory*, p. 171, which is closer here; cf. *Queste*, 131:14-15.

[32] See *religïos, Altfranzösisches Wörterbuch*, ed. Tobler-Lommatzch, 9 vols. (Wiesbaden: Franz Steiner Verlag, 1969-73), which cites "mout sainz hon et religïeus," *Perceval*, H. 1912; also *religios, Dictionnaire de l'ancienne lange française*, ed. F. Godefroy, 10 vols. (Paris, 1881, 1902), which cites "saint homme et de religieuse vie," *Livre du Chevalier de la Tour Landry*.

[33] See *OED, stable*, 6. a, b; *stability*, 3. a, b.

[34] See *RB 1980: The Rule of St. Benedict, in Latin and English with Notes*, ed. Timothy Fry, OSB (Collegeville, Minn.: Liturgical Press, 1981), p. 266, 58:9. "Stability" is usually taken to mean a vow of loyalty to the house in which the novice is professed, but in his Commentary on the passage Fry shows that the early promise, made either after a few days or after two months, "simply means that the candidate . . . has decided to stay and wants to persevere through the novitiate to profession. The second promise, at the end of the year, means that he wants to make profession and bind himself permanently to all the obligations of the monastic life" (p. 445); see also pp. 463-65.

[35] *Three Middle English Versions of the Rule of St. Benet*, ed. Ernst A. Kock, E.E.T.S., 120 (1902), 135:28-30; see also the Lansdowne ritual for the ordination of nuns, 141:27-142:3.

[36] William Bonde, *A Devout Treatyse in Englysshe Called the Pilgrymage of Perfeccyon*, printed by Wynkyn de Worde (1531), STC 3278, fol. 86b (my own punctuation); for the earlier printing by Richard Pynson (1526), STC 3277, see fol. 24b (repaginated from Book 3 onwards).

[37] Ferguson, pp. 52-56, and Benson, pp. 194-95.

[38] Stephen Scrope, Preface to Sir John Fastolf, *The Epistle of Othea, trans. from the French Text of Christine de Pisan*, ed. Curt F. Bühler, E.E.T.S. 264 (1970), p. 121.

[39] The *locus classicus* is Theseus' speech in Chaucer, *Knight's Tale*, A 2994-3010, *The Complete Works of Geoffrey Chaucer*, ed. F. N. Robinson, 2nd ed. (Boston: Houghton Mifflin, 1957); but see also the Balade, "Lak of

Stedfastnesse" (p. 537), and *Boece*, 2, m3, lines 16-23, and 4, p6, lines 42-47; also *OED, unstable*, 3, *unstableness*, 1.b. As in the *Knight's Tale*, 2995, "wrecched" is frequently associated with the sinfulness of this temporal world. For evidence that the association persists through the fifteenth century, see *OED, wretched*, 2.*y wretchedly*, 2, *wretchedness*, 1.a, 2: a good example is the citation, c. 1450, of Lovelich, "For more they loven wrechednesse Thanne hevenely thing," *Grail*, xliii, 413. Note also that the alliterative *Morte Arthure*, which is Malory's source for the Tale of Arthur and Lucius, begins with a prayer to God to guide us "here / In this wrechyd werld, thorowe vertuous lywynge," *The Alliterative Morte Arthure*, ed. Valerie Krishna (New York: Burt Franklin, 1976), ll. 4-5.

[40] Charlotte Morse, *The Pattern of Judgment in the Queste and Cleanness* (Columbia and London: University of Missouri Press, 1978), p. 128.

[41] *Redemption*, pp. 92-95.

[42] "For a season" is not in Caxton's edition.

Malory's Lancelot and the Quest of the Grail

Stephen C. B. Atkinson

The most basic difference between Malory's account of the Grail Quest and its source, the French *Queste del Saint Graal*, is not one of content but of context. The *Queste* is doubtless its author's sole contribution to Arthurian literature, an essentially self-contained work, while Malory's Grail narrative is part of a complete history of Arthur's kingdom. Thus Malory's Tale of the Sankgreal cannot be isolated from its context in the *Morte Darthur* as the *Queste* can be from the other branches of the Vulgate cycle. In particular, Malory's treatment of Lancelot during the Grail adventures derives from his depiction in earlier episodes and proves crucial to his role in later ones. Accordingly, a discussion of Lancelot's role in the Grail Quest must begin with two features of his life and character emphasized especially in the material of Caxton's Book VI: first, the strict dichotomy between his public career as the Round Table's preeminent knight and his private relationship with the queen, and second, his profound attraction to a religious ideal.

We can be sure that Malory was familiar with virtually the entire Vulgate *Lancelot* since he extracted material from widely separated sections of the French work, and thus he certainly knew of the Lancelot-Guenevere adultery as he composed his own Tale of

Lancelot. Yet he contrives to leave stubbornly unanswerable the question of whether the adultery has already begun. Had Malory wished to establish the adultery, there was no lack of material in his source with which to do so; nor, had he wished to deny it, was he averse to injecting authorial comments. Instead, he manipulates his material in what appears to be a conscious strategy to frustrate the reader's curiosity. By holding back episodes which show the private lives of Lancelot and the queen and using only those episodes which show their public lives at court or Lancelot's pursuit of adventures, Malory has made it impossible for us to know the precise state of their love before it emerges in the Tale of Tristram as common knowledge.[1] At the same time, he insures that the question itself remains a prominent concern.[2] In particular Malory sustains our curiosity by adding three original episodes in which Lancelot is accused of the adultery. The accusers, however, seem hardly trustworthy. Two are sorceresses—the first, Morgan le Fay, has already been established, through the Accolon episode, as a vicious enemy of Arthur and his court; the second, Hellawes, suffers from mad jealousy and, apparently, from necrophilia—while the third cites popular rumor and accuses Guenevere herself of sorcery. Each accusation raises the question; none allows us to answer it. Thus Malory involves us in the sort of tension that a dichotomy of public and private creates.

In the world of the Grail Quest, however, public reputation is of no consequence, and private secrets cannot be kept. The adventures by which the various knights are tested in the Quest are specifically designed to probe their inner lives, to assay their spiritual conditions, and to expose their most deeply hidden weaknesses. They prove, therefore, especially disorienting for Lancelot. At the same time, Lancelot is neither so disabled by past wickedness nor so indifferent to spiritual matters that, like Gawain, he can easily resign himself to failure and abandon the Quest without regret; in fact, Book VI reveals a side to Lancelot's character which leads him, despite the spiritual handicap of the adultery, to pursue the Quest with special determination. The damsel who suggests that Lancelot is under the queen's enchantment opens her speech by regretting that Lancelot is "a knyghte wyueles." Lancelot brushes the rumor about Guenevere aside and then proceeds to

130

disagree emphatically with the proposition that knights should marry or devote themselves to love:

> But for to be a wedded man, I thynke hit not, for thenne I must couche with her, and leue armes and turnementys, batayls, and aduentures. And as for to say for to take my plesaunce with peramours, that wylle I refuse, in pryncypal for drede of God. For knyghtes that ben auouturous or lecherous shal not be happy ne fortunate vnto the werrys, for outher they shalle be ouercome with a symplyer knyghte than they be hemself, outher els they shal by vnhap and her cursydnes slee better men than they ben hemself, and soo who that vseth peramours shalle be vnhappy, and all thyng is vnhappy that is aboute hem. (147.15-22)[3]

This speech is both original on Malory's part and daring. Only the fact that we cannot be sure when the adultery begins keeps us from immediately branding Lancelot a hypocrite. Malory takes the risk, however, because regardless of Lancelot's conduct, these are deeply held beliefs, essential to his character and closely similar to those that emerge as the demands of the Grail Quest. The combination of what we might call Lancelot's Grail-world leanings with the public-private dichotomy which governs his life forms the uniquely Malorian background for Lancelot's quest.

That quest is a turbulent affair, in which spiritual progress alternates with sudden backsliding. In tracing this irregular career, Malory follows the French source closely, although he makes countless alterations, many of them subtle but most, significant. However, the underlying rationale for Lancelot's uneven progress which emerges from the context of the *Morte Darthur* differs somewhat from the rationale in the *Queste*. For the French monastic author, it is essential, as Jean Frappier points out, that Lancelot be condemned as "the ideal of worldly chivalry and romantic passion" but that "as the father of the messianic Galaad he be treated with sympathy."[4] By developing the dichotomy of public and private as the distinguishing feature of Lancelot's career, Malory has accounted in his own terms for the condemnation of Lancelot on the Quest, adding to the doctrinal stance of the French author a more tangible consideration. As justification for Lancelot's partial success, Malory depends less on Lancelot's position as Galahad's father than on his deep-seated belief in a spiritual basis for true knighthood. By means of these preparations in Book VI,

Malory makes the Grail Quest a part of Lancelot's career, a no less rigorous and at times degrading part than it is in the French, but a part which is consistent with what we already know of Lancelot's character and one which influences strongly the role he plays after the Grail Quest is completed.

Malory found Lancelot's accustomed status challenged for the first time in the *Queste*'s account of the coming of the Grail to Camelot, and his response was neither to abandon his hero nor struggle to defend him, but simply to exploit material already present in the *Queste* and to add a few crucial lines of his own, in order to develop a meticulously balanced portrayal. On the one hand, Lancelot speaks with authority on the subject of the Grail. When the new writing appears on the sieges at Pentecost, it is Lancelot who calculates that the Siege Perilous will be filled that day and who suggests that it be covered (429.17-18). On the other hand, Lancelot recognizes his true status in these affairs. When Galahad has drawn the sword from the floating stone, a damsel arrives to announce that Lancelot should no longer consider himself the best knight in the world. The *Queste*'s Lancelot agrees not to think of himself in that light any longer,[5] but Malory's hero gives a very different answer: "As touchynge vnto that, said Launcelot, I knowe wel I was neuer the best" (431.24-25). Lancelot seems to refer here not to prowess or to chivalric courtesy, in both of which his excellence is established, but to the new demands of the Grail adventures. We should remember that Bors has passed on to Lancelot the words of the old man at King Pelles' castle: "And telle thou Sir Launcelot, of alle worldly aduentures he passeth in manhode and prowesse al other, but in this spyrytuel maters he shalle haue many his better" (405.8-10).[6] Lancelot echoes the old man's words, and his awareness of the new standards raises him above his Round Table fellows at the same time that he is giving up his former preeminence.

In this passage we can find the key to Malory's handling of his hero in the Tale of the Sankgreal. The humiliation of Lancelot is an integral part of the story Malory inherited, and he makes no consistent attempt, here or elsewhere, to eliminate evidence of Lancelot's failure or soften the blow to his prestige. Malory does, however, allow us to retain our respect for Lancelot through careful

132

portrayal of Lancelot's reaction to these developments. Any hint of resentment on his part, now or later, the least suggestion of jealousy towards Galahad or the other Grail knights, or of deliberate resistance against this new order, would be fatal. Lancelot's survival as Malory's hero requires that he openly accept the consequences of the Grail's appearance, agree to the justice of the humiliations visited upon him, and be grateful in the end for what has been given him, not bitter over what has been withheld. Thus, in the adventure of the sword Malory makes no attempt to evade the fact that Lancelot is no longer the best knight in the world; the words of the maiden are clear. Instead, he has Lancelot not only agree with the maiden (as Lancelot does in the French), but exceed her in accusing himself. Having altered Lancelot's reaction, Malory can then add, in response to Lancelot's denial that he was ever the best, an original sentence in which the maiden says, "Yes . . . that were ye and are yet of ony synful man of the world" (431.25-26). Thus Malory allows us to maintain our respect for Lancelot as a human hero without in the least vitiating the impact of the coming of the new order.

This approach to characterizing his hero persists throughout Malory's account of the Grail adventures. His aim is a consistent balance, and he achieves it by a variety of means. Nowhere else in his work, for example, does Malory adhere to the structure of his source as closely as he does in the Grail material, but that structure itself reflects the balance he seeks. Following the *Queste*, Malory interweaves Lancelot's adventures with those of Gawain and his fellows on the one hand and the Grail knights on the other, inviting us to compare his quest with those doomed to failure and those assured of success. Thus, Lancelot's first appearance after the departure from Camelot comes after we have witnessed both the initial humiliations of Bagdemagus, Melyas, and Gawain and the first achievements of Galahad. Lancelot's attitude in this section contrasts sharply with Gawain's; he is quite prepared to repent his past life. But his fortunes contrast equally with Galahad's; at one chapel, Galahad is sent to cleanse the Castle of Maidens by a mysterious voice, while at another, the voice rebukes Lancelot and drives him away into the wilderness.

Where Malory departs from his source—by altering details or

inserting original material, even by the omissions or condensations which are his most overt revisions of the *Queste*—he does so again to emphasize the balance in his portrayal of Lancelot. That balance derives in part from the sharp contrast between Lancelot's failures on the Quest and his achievements. As a result, Malory's hero on occasion fares worse than his French original. When we first see him engaged in the Quest, he is little more than an extra, one of those knights whom a young hero, in proving his prowess, unhorses and leaves in his wake: "and Galahad smote hym so ageyne that he smote doune hors and man" (443.27-28). This is a shattering reversal for Lancelot, who has thus far in the work never been defeated, but Malory intensifies its impact. First, he has Lancelot and Percival recognize Galahad. In the *Queste* Lancelot is desperate to learn his conqueror's name and immediately sets off after him; in Malory's account Lancelot is forced to confront the facts of the new order more directly. Second, Malory adds to the speech of the recluse who witnesses the fight a crucial phrase: "and when she sawe Syr Galahad ryde she said, God be with the, *best knyghte of the world.*" (443.32-33; emphasis mine).[7] The damsel at Camelot has, of course, prepared us for this development, but to any reader who has shared Malory's concern with the ranking of knights—particularly clear in the Tristram material—this episode is a shock.

The next episode demonstrates the obstacles facing Lancelot at the beginning of his quest, but it is also, in Malory's balanced approach, the beginning of his spiritual growth. Lancelot comes to a chapel whose altar is brightly lit, "but he coude fynde no place where he myghte entre; thenne was he passynge heuy and desmayed" (444.14-15). Here, Lancelot appears on the edge of the spiritual world of the Quest but unable to penetrate to its center. In what follows, Lancelot is neither utterly barred from witnessing the miracles of the Grail nor able to see them completely: "half wakynge and slepyng" (444.18), he watches as the sick knight is healed by the Grail, but—as Malory explicitly states—"he had no power to ryse ageyne the Holy Vessel" (444.35). A further step in his humiliation follows when the healed knight takes his horse and his sword and helmet, the trappings of his chivalry.[8]

This loss begins a series of episodes where the Malorian technique of heightening contrasts in the interests of a final balance is clearly visible. When the account of Lancelot's quest resumes after the testing of Percival and immediately before the section which brings the quest of Gawain to its miserable climax, Lancelot comes as before to a chapel, where he is again an onlooker at marvels. Here, however, he is awake and able to understand and take part in events; the episode is not a setback for him, as the earlier one was, but a step forward. Lancelot's progress peaks when he wins back his horse from the knight who took it at the ruined chapel. Lancelot shows more initiative in this scene than he does in the *Queste*. Malory's Lancelot challenges his opponent, rather than being challenged, as in the French, and after defeating him takes his own original horse, leaving the one he had been riding. In the French version Lancelot overthrows his opponent, but does not reclaim the horse that had been his. Malory seized the opportunity to exchange the horses in order to make this scene a more complete reversal of the earlier episode: the horse Lancelot had lost during his first night sleeping by a cross he has now recovered after confession and penance, again sleeping by a cross. The pairing is more complete in Malory's account, and the episode correspondingly more encouraging.[9]

The third episode in this sequence follows Lancelot's defeat in the tournament of the black and white knights and offers again a careful balance of elements. Lancelot's wandering brings him to the river Mortayse and we know from the previous section that he is following Percival's course. In the *Queste*, when he reaches the bank of the river a black knight appears and kills his horse, leaving him stranded in a particularly desolate landscape.[10] In Malory's version, Lancelot crosses the river before meeting the black knight, and the grim description of the terrain is omitted. In one sense, Malory has lightened the atmosphere; however, since in his version the horse killed is the one Lancelot lost originally at the ruined chapel and later regained, this closing episode becomes a more dramatic indication of his backsliding than it is in the French—the pattern of humiliation, recovery, and relapse is clearer. Nonetheless, Lancelot's reaction to this setback is encouraging: "And thenne he

took his helme and his shelde and thanked God of his aduenture"
(463.36-37).

The attitude reflected by Lancelot's words here is another
element in Malory's complex balancing of the facets of Lancelot's
character and experience. After the loss of horse and arms at the
ruined chapel, Malory adds to the *Queste* account the statement,
"but he took repentaunce after that" (444.36).[11] Malory is
anticipating at this point the attitude which allows Lancelot to
survive the Quest as the hero of the whole work—his readiness to
accept the Grail world and his sincere attempt to meet its demands.
The lesson of the ruined chapel is not lost on him. In abbreviating
the *Queste's* passage describing Lancelot's lamentation, Malory has
altered the emphasis so as to give Lancelot an insight that he lacks
in the French version. This is a fine example of how Malory
combines the roles of translator, editor, and independent author in
the service of his own view of his hero. The *Queste* reads:

> Et quant il ot ceste parole, si est tant dolenz qu'il ne set que il
> doit fere. Si se part maintenant d'iluec sospirant dou cuer et
> lermoiant des eulz, si maudit l'ore qu'il fue nez, car ce set il bien
> qu'il est venuz au point qu'il n'avra ja mes honor, puis qu'il a
> failli a savoir la verité del Saint Graal. Mes les trois paroles dont
> il a esté apelez n'a il pas oubliees ne n'oubliera ja mes tant come
> il veve, ne se sera granment aeise devant que il sache por quoi il
> fu einsi apelez.[12]

Malory reduces the passage to only two clauses: "for the wordes
went to his herte tyl that he knewe wherfor he was called soo"
(445.15). This abbreviation fundamentally changes the meaning;
Malory's Lancelot deciphers for himself the message of the voice, a
fact Malory underlines by having him state his conclusion in
another speech, entirely different from its counterpart in the French:

> my synne and my wyckednes haue brought me vnto grete
> dishonour. For whanne I soughte worldly aduentures for
> worldly desyres, I euer encheued them and had the better in
> euery place, and neuer was I discomfyt in no quarel, were it
> ryght or wronge. And now I take vpon me the aduentures of
> holy thynges, and now I see and vnderstande that myn olde
> synne hyndereth me and shameth me, so that I had no power to
> stere nor speke whan the holy blood appiered afore me.
>
> (445.19-24)[13]

Again, Launcelot recalls the message (itself largely original with

Malory) of the old man at Corbenic, whose prediction of his fortunes in the Grail Quest first distinguished between worldly and spiritual adventures. It is in those terms that Lancelot is coming to understand his position.

The same distinction underlies the scene with the hermit which follows. Malory's version is less than a tenth the length of the corresponding scene in the *Queste*; Malory omits, for example, the lengthy explication of the parable of the talents around which the French hermit organizes his discourse, and preserves a closer focus on Lancelot's experience at the chapel. The basic thrust of the hermit's message is retained, however—that from Lancelot, to whom much has been given, much is demanded:

> And ther is no knyght lyuynge now that ought to kenne God soo grete thanke as ye, for He hath yeuen yow beaute, semelynes, and grete strengthe aboue all other knyghtes. And therfor ye are the more beholdyng vnto God than ony other man, to loue Hym and drede Hym, for your strength and manhode wille lytel auaylle yow and God be ageynst yow.
>
> (446.1-5)

The hermit urges Lancelot to confess. The *Queste* dwells at some length on Lancelot's hesitation at this point;[14] Malory's Lancelot is also reluctant to admit his sins, but he sees clearly that they are to blame for his recent "disauentur" and proceeds freely to confess them (446.11-15). Lancelot's confession differs somewhat from its French counterpart: in the *Queste*, Lancelot cites Guenevere's gifts to him, while Malory's Lancelot concentrates on the now familiar distinction between worldly chivalry—fighting for the queen in both right and wrong causes to gain her love—and heavenly chivalry, fighting "alle only for Goddes sake."[15] After listening to a brief explication of the words which drove him away from the chapel, Lancelot accepts "suche penaunce as he myghte doo" (447.10), and the hermit absolves him. The section closes: "And thenne Syr Launcelot repented hym gretely" (447.13-14).

Even from this quick survey, the sense of a distinctly Malorian balance emerges. From his defeat by Galahad to his overthrow by the river Mortayse, Lancelot's humiliation is painfully clear. Yet at the same time, Malory shows him deeply concerned by the events which befall him and committed to understanding their significance—an attitude thrown into sharp focus by his willingness to undertake penance. In earlier alterations of the *Queste*, especially in Nacyen's message to the Round Table and in the hermit's interpretation of Melyas' adventures, Malory stresses the importance of the individual decision to repent,[16] and he creates a vivid contrast between Lancelot's attitude towards penance and Gawain's: "Nay, said Syre Gawayne, I may doo no penaunce, for we knyghtes aduenturous ofte suffren grete woo and payne" (443.15-17). This notion, plausible as it is for worldly quests, is entirely inappropriate in a quest whose whole foundation is spiritual, and our sense of Lancelot's promise is enhanced by the memory of Gawain's recalcitrance. Finally, in the words of the hermit, Malory shows us Lancelot's worldly chivalry as both the cause or context of his sin and as evidence of God's special favor which now entails new demands: "And now our Lord wille suffre the no lenger, but that thow shalte knowe Hym whether thow wilt or nylt" (446.32-33).

Other episodes reinforce each of the elements of this complex picture. Lancelot's most remarkable defeat, for example, comes in the tournament of the black and white knights. Here, Lancelot faces a test calculated to arouse and then confound his Round Table principles and to depict in the most vivid terms the conflict between earthly and heavenly chivalry. That Lancelot should join the weaker party "in encrecynge of his chyualry" (462.6) is entirely normal, and would not have disturbed us in the least a hundred pages earlier. But the phrase is Malory's own addition and an ominous one in this context. For the first time in his life Lancelot is captured by force of arms. It is important, too, that he is taken by a tactic designed "for to tyere hym and wynde hym" (462.11-12); earlier in the work, Malory told us that "Sir Trystram . . . was called byggar than Sir Launcelot, but Sir Launcelot was better brethed" (225.23-25). Lancelot is captured in spite of his greatest strength, a dramatic illustration of the hermit's earlier warning: "your strength and manhode wille lytel auaylle yow and God be ageynst yow" (446.4-5). In the Quest of the Grail, increasing of chivalry is simply what the recluse calls (in another Malorian addition) "bobaunce and pryde of the world, and alle that must be lefte in that quest" (463.13-14).

Yet Lancelot's concern with understanding the meaning of what befalls him is also clear here. As he did after the adventure of the ruined chapel, Lancelot leaves the scene of his humiliation with some sense of its meaning; he is the only knight engaged in the Grail Quest who begins to interpret events before they are explicated by an expert: "for neuer or now was I neuer at turnement nor iustes but I had the best, and now I am shamed. And thenne he sayd, now I am sure that I am more synfuller than euer I was" (462.20-22). The interpretation which Malory's recluse offers for these events confirms Lancelot's judgment and differs considerably from that of her French counterpart. In the French, Lancelot's adventure is primarily an allegorical recapitulation of his earlier experiences in the quest, from his encounter with Galahad to his dream of the night before.[17] Malory omits this material, and retains only the more general identification of the black and white knights as the earthly knights engaged in the Quest—he attributes their black trappings to unconfessed sins, dwelling again on confession—and the heavenly knights, virginal or chaste. Malory continues to focus our attention on the contrast between the two sorts of chivalry and on the dilemma of Lancelot, required to abandon the habits and attitudes of a lifetime.

The other elements noted above are also reiterated in later episodes. At Lancelot's request, the hermit at the second chapel imposes a fresh penance on him: that he wear the hair shirt of the dead hermit-knight (whose story is itself a model of heavenly chivalry offered for Lancelot's emulation) and that he abstain from meat and wine—precisely the sort of privation that Gawain, pleading the exigencies of knight-errantry, refused. Similarly, the judgment passed on Lancelot by the hermit who first confesses him is repeated by a series of religious figures until it becomes virtually a formula. The good man at the second chapel gives in capsule form the same balanced evaluation of Lancelot and of his prospects in the Grail Quest as was given in the earlier section:

> Wel, sayd he, seke it ye may wel, but though it were here, ye shalle haue noo power to see hit no more than a blynd man shold see a bryghte suerd; and that is longe on your synne, and els ye were more abeler than ony man lyuynge. (459.27-30)

The metaphor of blindness suggests what will befall Lancelot at the end of his quest. But again, there is the balancing assertion: "and els ye were more abeler. . . ." The hermit who interprets the dream of the nine knights for Lancelot offers the same stock evaluation in a speech original with Malory (461.18-21),[18] and the recluse who explains the nature of the tournament renders the same judgment, warning Lancelot of the burden of his sinful past but adding, to preserve the now standard balance, a Malorian conclusion: "For of alle erthely knyghtes I haue moost pyte of the, for I knowe wel thow hast not thy pyere of ony erthely synful man" (463.28-29).

The most comprehensive and complex view of Lancelot offered in Malory's tale comes in a section where Lancelot himself does not appear, the section focused on Gawain and Ector. In Gawain's view, Lancelot is grouped with the Grail knights: "they foure haue no pyeres" (464.13). Yet Gawain is as aware as any hermit of Lancelot's flaw; in Malory's original addition to the French, he goes on to say, "And yf one thyng were not in Syr Launcelot, he had no felawe of none erthely man, but he is as we be, but yf he took more payne vpon hym" (464.13-16). That "but yf" is crucial; as we have seen, Lancelot does take "more payne vpon hym." Another view of Lancelot appears in Ector's dream. Here, paired with Ector and setting out to "seke that we shal not fynde" (465.17), Lancelot faces what seems to be repeated humiliation and ultimate failure. However, when Nacyen interprets Ector's dream, the events bear very different meanings from those we imagined. The ass on which Lancelot is forced to ride seems an ignoble substitute for a horse, but Nacyen points out that it is the animal that Christ rode and it "betokeneth mekenes" (468.2). Likewise Lancelot's knotted garment sounds like an indignity, but when Nacyen interprets it as corresponding to the hair shirt, we see it as precisely the sort of "payne" that sets him apart from Gawain and Ector.

Nacyen also foretells the climax of Lancelot's Grail Quest and the twenty-four days of unconsciousness which follow his attempt to enter the forbidden chapel. The prose of the message is somewhat confusing, but again what sounded in the dream like failure—"And whan he stouped to drynke of the water, the water sanke from hym" (465.21)—sounds like a triumph in Nacyen's account, where Malory adds the statement that Lancelot "sawe grete preuydence of the Sancgreal" (468.10). The statement is true of course, both to the account Malory gives of Lancelot at Corbenic and to his French original, but Malory introduces it here because he is especially concerned with carrying the balanced picture he has developed of Lancelot through to the end of his quest.

Finally, in a passage which has no counterpart whatsoever in the *Queste*, Malory has Nacyen anticipate Lancelot's career after the Grail quest:

> For I dar saye, as synful as Syre Launcelot hath ben, sythe that he wente into the quest of the Sancgreal he slewe neuer man, nor nought shalle tyll that he come vnto Camelot ageyne, for he hath taken vpon hym for to forsake synne. And nere were that he nys not stable, but by his thoughte he is lykely to torne ageyne, he shold be nexte to encheue it, sauf Galahad, his sone; but God knoweth his thoughte and his vnstabylness. And yet shalle he dye ryght an holy man, and no doubte he hath no felawe of no erthely synful man.   (468.28-34)

The full importance of this passage emerges only gradually through the remainder of Malory's work, but the suggestion is plainly made here that while the Grail Quest is an isolated period of the Round Table's history, it is not an inconsequential one. As we learn in the final tales, the Arthurian world cannot return to its pre-Grail condition. When the Quest is over, the issues which appeared as remote threats in the earlier tales will be greatly intensified, and the consequences of Lancelot's turning again, disastrous.[19] Yet the Malorian balance persists: Nacyen adds that Lancelot will "dye ryght an holy man."

Within a few pages, then, we have heard Gawain group Lancelot with the Grail knights and also say that he is "as we be"; we have seen Lancelot apparently humiliated in Ector's dream but praised by Nacyen in the interpretation of that dream, although his failure in the Quest is at the same time foretold; we have heard him commended for forsaking sin but condemned for "vnstabylness"; and we have been told that he will die a holy man. These juxtapositions, some original with Malory, others made more striking by his condensation, epitomize both Malory's view of his hero and his technique in depicting him.

Following the Gawain-Ector episodes, the story of the Grail Quest turns to the Grail knights. Only when they have been prepared for their achievement do we return to Lancelot and witness the climax and culmination of his quest. Here, Lancelot largely achieves the heavenly chivalry to which we first saw him drawn in his speech to the damsel in Book VI. Yet even in these final events, Malory preserves the ambivalence which he has cultivated since the opening pages of the Grail story.

The section opens by the river Mortayse, where Lancelot had thanked God for his adventure when his horse was slain by the black knight; now, we are told, he "leyd hym doune and slepte, and toke the aduenture that God wold sende hym" (494.9-11).[20] That adventure leads him into the world of mystical experience, of "grete clerenes," miraculous food, and joy which "passeth alle erthely ioyes" (494.19). When Lancelot finds the body of Percival's sister on board the ship and reads the letter in her hand telling "all the aduentures" of the previous section "and of what lygnage she was come" (494.24), he appears at last to have joined the chosen knights of the Grail Quest.

Galahad's appearance sets the seal on Lancelot's new status. As the first figures of their respective worlds, Lancelot and Galahad have thus far embodied the conflict between earthly and heavenly chivalry; Galahad drew the sword which Lancelot refused to touch, and Galahad, in their first encounter, won an easy victory and vanished. Here, for the first time since Galahad's knighting, they are together as father and son, and the clear evidence of their love for each other replaces our earlier sense of them as rivals.

Malory has tended throughout the Grail Quest to pare down Galahad's speeches and thus make him a more remote and inaccessible figure than he is in the French. It is easy to remember what Galahad does in the Grail Quest but difficult to remember anything he says. Yet in the reunion scene, Malory shows a new element in Galahad's character. When he appears, Lancelot abandons his play by the water's side:

> And thenne Launcelot dressid vnto hym and said, ye be welcome. And he ansuerd and salewed hym ageyne, and asked hym, what is your name? For moche my hert gyueth vnto yow. Truly, sayd he, my name is Launcelot du Lake. Sir, saide he, thenne be ye welcome, for ye were the begynner of me in this world. A, sayd he, ar ye Galahad? Ye, forsothe, sayd he. And so he kneled doune and asked hym his blessynge.   (494.32-37)

The kneeling is original with Malory, and it is not at first clear who is kneeling to whom; given Malory's general carelessness with pronouns, the ambiguity may not be intentional, but in any case the effect is interesting, for it raises the issue of the respective standing of father and son. It would not be unreasonable for Lancelot to kneel to Galahad. The next sentence resolves the problem: "and after toke of his helme and kyssed hym" (494.37). Galahad has just arrived on horseback; the helm must be his, so it was he who kneeled. It is a small detail but significant, because it establishes that the human hierarchy of father and son, as well as the spiritual one of sinner and saint, is still valid. The same amalgamation is seen in the repetition of "ioye"; the mystical joy that Lancelot feels on board the ship is matched with the personal joy felt here: "and there was grete ioye bitwene them. For there is no tonge can telle the ioye that they made eyther of other" (494.37-39).

The exchange between father and son at their parting shows us Galahad at his most human and Lancelot at his most spiritual. The dialogue is closely modeled on its counterpart in the *Queste*,[21] but Malory has, through minor alterations, given the scene a wholly different tone. Having heard the summons of the white knight, Galahad

> wente to his fader and kyst hym swetely and sayd, fair swete fader, I wote not whan I shal see you more tyl I see the body of Ihesu Cryst. I praye yow, sayd Launcelot, praye ye to the Hyghe Fader that He hold me in His seruyse.   (495.22-25)

Galahad's evident affection for his earthly father is balanced by Lancelot's concern with serving his heavenly Father. Further, Lancelot, in asking his son to pray for him, emphasizes Galahad's spiritual standing at the same time that we are admiring Galahad's humanity. No such balance exists in the French, where only Galahad speaks at this point, himself commending Lancelot to Christ's service. After the voice is heard warning them that they will not meet again "before the dredeful Day of Dome" (495.27), Lancelot himself offers a prayer, and Galahad closes the dialogue with a striking statement:

> Now sone Galahad, said Launcelot, syn we shal departe and neuer see other, I pray to the Hygh Fader to conserue me and yow bothe. Sire, said Galahad, noo prayer auaylleth soo moche as yours.   (495.27-29)

Lancelot's speech here is Malory's invention; in the *Queste*, it is at this point that Lancelot asks Galahad to pray for him. Not only does this change enhance Lancelot's stature—in the *Queste* he seems unwilling to petition the Almighty directly—but it radically alters the force of Galahad's reply. In Malory's version, that reply is a gracious compliment and stamps Galahad's *imprimatur* on Lancelot's own prayer. In the French version, as a reply to Lancelot's request for Galahad's prayers, it is a pointed reminder that Lancelot's spiritual condition is in his own hands. The *Queste*'s dialogue thus ends on a moralizing note which exalts Galahad at Lancelot's expense; Malory's version closes in a complex interplay of piety and love which exalts Lancelot and Galahad together.

After Galahad's departure, Lancelot is swept on for another month during which he "prayed to God that he myght see some tydynges of the Sancgreal" (495.32-33). The restraint of Lancelot's prayer is a key feature of this section. Throughout the tale, there have plainly been two ways of looking at Lancelot. On the one hand, he and the Grail knights together are separable from the remainder of the Round Table—"they foure," Gawain calls them; on the other hand, we can as easily separate only the three Grail knights, leaving Lancelot behind—"he is," Gawain also says, "as we be."[22] As the climax of the Grail Quest approaches, the French author, while concerned that Lancelot receive some reward for his efforts as a penitent, is far more anxious that the outcome of his quest be clearly separated from the high destiny awaiting the Grail knights. The *Queste* accordingly focuses on how much less Lancelot is granted than are Percival, Bors, and Galahad. Malory seems to aim at something more complex, an approach designed to exploit the ambivalence inherent in the separate outcome of Lancelot's quest. To retain this balance, Malory needs to emphasize the element of success in Lancelot's experience at Corbenic, not to the exclusion of the element of failure but in conjunction with it. His approach is not to alter events, such as Lancelot's blunder at the gate (495.36-40), but to show Lancelot as satisfied with, and profoundly grateful for, the achievement he is allowed.

When Lancelot enters the Castle of Corbenic and comes to the closed door of the Grail's chamber, he prays as before and with the same restraint: "fair swete Fader Ihesu Cryst, yf euer I dyd thyng that pleasyd The, Lord, for Thy pyte ne haue me not in despyte for my synnes done aforetyme, and that Thou shewe me somethynge of

144

that I seke" (496.16-18). The prayer is a concise summary of Lancelot's spiritual position, with its emphasis—not found in the French—on his past misdeeds; it is a testimonial to the self-knowledge he has gained, but also a clear admission that he is making no claim to merit. The prayer could not be more quickly answered: "And with that he sawe the chamber dore open" (496.18-19).

Lancelot's attempt to help the aged priest raises two questions. The first concerns Lancelot's immediate motive for the action which draws down upon him the twenty-four days' punishment. When the door to the chamber opens, Lancelot steps forward to enter, but the voice warns him not to. Forbidden to enter but not ordered to leave, he is left occupying a middle ground between departure from the sacred precinct, a command associated with Gawain and his fellows, and approach, associated with the Grail knights.[23] The French account says that Lancelot forgot the command, though in the French version as in Malory's, Lancelot asks to be pardoned for going to the old man's aid.[24] Malory eliminates what must have struck him as a contradiction; in his account, Lancelot knows perfectly well that he is violating the voice's order, but he claims extenuating circumstances: "faire Fader Ihesu Cryst, ne take hit for no synne though I helpe the good man whiche hath grete nede of help" (496.34-35). At first, Lancelot's desire to come to the aid of the weak seems unexceptionable; in fact, this is a final instance of his resorting to traditional chivalric values: to feel that his help is needed in the presence of such visible omnipotence is absurd.

The second question concerns the significance of Lancelot's twenty-four days of unconsciousness. Nacyen's explanation that Lancelot is refused full participation in the Grail mysteries because of his future backsliding and not because of his behavior in the Quest itself removes some immediate suggestion of failure from Lancelot's incomplete vision of the Grail and prepares us for the continuation of his and the Round Table's history in the tales to come. His present contrition and penance are not questioned, only his perseverance once the Quest is completed. In the long run—a Malorian perspective irrelevant to the *Queste*—he proves too weak to meet the highest demands but not too callow to perceive them.

After his humiliations at the ruined chapel and at the tournament of the black and white knights, Lancelot immediately set himself to consider the reasons for his failure. He does the same here when the inhabitants of Corbenic tell him "how he had layne there four and twenty dayes and nyghtes" (497.21-22). But in this case no hermit is required to complete the explication; Lancelot immediately grasps the full significance of the experience: "Thenne hym thoughte hit was punysshement for the four and twenty yeres that he had ben a synner, wherfore our Lord put hym in penaunce four and twenty dayes and nyghtes" (497.22-24). We, of course, have heard Nacyen interpret this episode to Gawain and Ector, but Lancelot has not; thus Malory's version, by means of that earlier insertion, emphasizes Lancelot's perspicacity. But Lancelot does not take even this enforced penance as final; he immediately resumes the hair shirt. The suggestion that Lancelot intends to persist in the penitential practice he undertook in the Grail Quest even after the Quest, for him, is over, has a special importance in Malory's continuing history that it cannot have in the essentially self-contained *Queste*.

To more than one modern critic, preoccupied with Malory's alterations of his source, it has seemed as if Malory was struggling to overcome the obviously incomplete vision granted Lancelot at Corbenic and to put Lancelot's achievement on a more equal footing with that of the Grail knights.[25] To Malory, the problem must have seemed very different. The ultimate qualification on Lancelot's achievement is that the tale now turns to the far greater achievement of the Grail knights. Malory's concern, then, was not to exalt Lancelot's accomplishments in defiance of what were to him the facts of the case, but to prevent the legitimate accomplishments of his hero from fading out next to the greater glory of Galahad and his companions, to preserve to the very end of Lancelot's quest the balance he had so carefully cultivated in his treatment of it.

Thus, when the bystanders at Corbenic tell Lancelot in the *Queste* that he need not put his hair shirt back on since he has seen all that he can of the Grail, and then make it clear that they can hardly wait for the arrival of those who will see more,[26] Malory deletes both the beginning and the end of their speech. There is no reason, he must have thought, that Lancelot should abandon his penance as if its only value was as a ticket of admission to Corbenic, and the wonders that the Grail knights witness on their later arrival surely speak for themselves. Malory retains only the bystanders' announcement that Lancelot's quest is over, and follows it with a completely original speech in which Lancelot assesses his own accomplishment:

> Now I thanke God, said Launcelot, of His grete mercy of that I haue sene, for it suffyseth me. For as I suppose, no man in this world hath lyued better than I haue done to encheue that I haue done.   (497.33-36)

Lancelot's last sentence is a syntactic puzzle, but what precedes it is clear enough. He clearly believes that he has been given more than he earned. "It suffyseth me" cannot be made to imply, as Eugène Vinaver claims, that "it matters little to him . . . that the supreme reward of the Grail is denied him."[27] When he awakens in Corbenic after the twenty-four days, his first thought is of that supreme reward: "O Ihesu Cryst, who myghte be soo blessid that myght see openly Thy grete merueyls of secretenes there where no synnar may be?" (497.17-19). But Lancelot is too thankful for what has been allowed him by God's mercy to dwell on what could never have been his. What Vinaver takes for complacency is gratitude.

The puzzle of Lancelot's last sentence, on which scholars, including Vinaver, have been generally silent,[28] can be resolved if we look ahead to the scene, also original, of Lancelot's return to Camelot. There, he resumes the role he played during the preliminaries for the Quest, that of intermediary between the Round Table and the Grail mysteries:

> And ther Launcelot told the kynge of his aduentures that had befallen hym syn he departed, and also he told hym of the aduentures of Galahad, Percyuale, and Bors, whiche that he knewe by the letter of the dede damoysel and as Galahad had told hym. Now God wold, sayd the kynge, that they were all thre here. That shalle neuer be, said Launcelot, for two of hem shalle ye neuer see, but one of hem shalle come ageyne.
>
> (499.10-15)

The news of the Grail knights which Lancelot offers at court, and especially his knowledge of their destinies, helps us to understand his speech at Corbenic. He plainly knows that they will receive a greater reward. He has known since before the Quest began that by the standards of the Grail world he "was neuer the best." Thus, his statement that "no man in this world hath lyued better than I haue done to encheue that I haue done" is testimony to the special mercy he has been shown. The Grail knights are understood to be in a separate category, but no one—not even men who may have lived better lives—has shared the achievement of Lancelot; though not the highest achievement of the Quest, it is by God's grace nonetheless his.

Lancelot's career does not end with the Quest, as his son's does. Just as the earlier portrayal of Lancelot lays an essential foundation for his depiction in the Grail story, so his experience in the world of the Grail is itself prologue to the yet more complex picture Malory gives us of his hero in the final tales of the work. In adapting the account he inherited, Malory has, through the cumulative effect of comparatively minor changes, transformed Lancelot. Malory's Lancelot has a past and a future, and his conduct in the Grail Quest is determined less by his place on a moral or religious spectrum than by the nature of his own continuing biography. In the course of Lancelot's quest, the dichotomy of public and private which dominated his earlier career is replaced by the more fundamental dichotomy of earthly and heavenly chivalry. Within this new dichotomy, which Lancelot—in Malory's balanced depiction—comes gradually to understand and appreciate, both his public reputation and his private life are included in the earthly chivalry which he must struggle to abandon, the "worldly aduentures" which the old man at Corbenic, speaking to Bors, first contrasted with "this spyrytuel maters" (405.9-10).

From Nacyen's speech to Gawain we learned of Lancelot's instability and were warned that he would "torne ageyne." Though he does, the experience of the Grail Quest, as he tells Guenevere, cannot be "lyghtely forgeten" (507.11). This declaration, made immediately after the Tale of the Sankgreal, may be seen as a warning to the reader that although the narrative has reverted to the familiar setting of Camelot and to its courtly and chivalric concerns, the perspective offered by the Grail Quest must not be dismissed as we read on. Before the Grail's appearance, Lancelot was capable of maintaining the public-private dichotomy; after the Grail Quest the potential dangers of such a life become suddenly real and the moral questions it raises, far more insistent. Lancelot can no longer preserve his and Guenevere's public reputation, maintain their private love, and at the same time tolerate the knowledge that he has abandoned the world of the Grail and "the hygh seruyse in whome I dyd my dylygent laboure" (507.11-12). That knowledge haunts the last tales, undercutting Lancelot's heroism in the Melyagaunt affair, reducing him to tears at the healing of Sir Urry.[29] And when, after the last battle, he turns away from Guenevere at the nunnery, he turns toward the Grail world, preparing to fulfill the last of Nacyen's prophecies: "And God defende but I shold forsake the world as ye haue do, for in the quest of the Sankgreal I had fosaken the vanytees of the world, had not your loue ben" (595.16-18).

Missouri Southern State College

NOTES

[1] Malory's selection completely ignores the chronology of the French, where, for example, the *charrette* episode adapted in Book XIX precedes material used in Book VI; this free use of his source suggests how careful and deliberate is Malory's adaptation here.

[2] It is testimony to the urgency Malory imparts to the question that critics feel obliged to answer it, though there is no definite evidence in the text to support them. The most forceful position has been taken by R. M. Lumiansky, who attempts to show that Lancelot is in love with Guenevere but that his love has not yet been returned ("'The Tale of Lancelot': Prelude to Adultery, *Malory's Originality* [Baltimore: John Hopkins Press, 1964], pp. 95-98). The evidence does not contradict such a view but is still not sufficient to prove it. See also Eugène Vinaver, ed., *The Works of Sir Thomas Malory*, 2nd ed. (Oxford: Oxford University Press, 1967; rpt. 1973), pp. 1413-14 (hereafter cited as *Works*), where Vinaver gives his view, conditioned by his isolation of each of the tales; and Beverly Kennedy, "Malory's Lancelot: 'Trewest Lover, of a Synful Man,'" *Viator*, 12 (1981), 417-19.

[3] All references to Malory's text are to *Caxton's Malory*, ed. James W. Spisak (Berkeley and Los Angeles: University of California Press, 1983).

[4] "The Vulgate Cycle," *Arthurian Literature in the Middle Ages*, ed. R. S. Loomis (Oxford: Oxford University Press, 1959), p. 305.

[5] Albert Pauphilet, ed., *La Queste del Saint Graal* (Paris: H. Champion, 1921; rpt. 1967), p. 13. All references to and quotations from the *Queste del*

Saint Graal are taken from this edition, hereafter cited as *Queste*. However, all such references must be offered with a clear reservation: we do not know the precise contents of the text Malory used and can only hope to approximate it by citing a modern edition such as Pauphilet's.

[6] Malory is careful to show that this message is delivered: "And there [Bors] fonde Sire Launcelot du Lake and told hym of the aduentures that he had sene with Kynge Pelles at Corbyn" (404.20-21).

[7] See *Queste*, pp. 56-57. Additions such as these do little to support Vinaver's claim that Malory's adaptation is governed by "his confidence in the unfailing merits of Arthurian chivalry and in the undisputed greatness of its protagonist" *(Works*, p. 1537).

[8] Larry Benson, in *Malory's Morte Darthur* (Cambridge, Mass.: Harvard University Press, 1976), pp. 212-15, offers an interesting discussion of the role of armor in the Grail Quest, though he is wrong in saying that Galahad gives Lancelot the horse on which he rides to Corbenic.

[9] Benson sees this scene not as the high point of the section but as the beginning of Lancelot's relapse, leading directly to the episode of the tournament (p. 214). See also Charles Moorman, *The Book of Kyng Arthur* (Lexington: University of Kentucky Press, 1965), p. 40. It seems to me that Malory's careful pairing of this scene with that of Lancelot's humiliation at the ruined chapel in order to bracket the two scenes of confession and penance, a feature of Malorian narrative to which Benson is usually sensitive, makes a positive reading more plausible.

[10] *Queste*, p. 146.

[11] See *Queste*, p. 59.

[12] "And when he hears this speech, he is so sorrowful that he does not know what he should do. Now he departs thence, sighing from his heart and weeping from his eyes; he curses the day when he was born, because he knows he has come to the point where he will never have honor, since he has failed to know the truth of the Holy Grail. But he has not forgotten the three words which he was called nor will he ever forget while he lives; nor will he be at ease before he knows why he was called thus" *(Queste*, pp. 65-66). A different view of this passage and of Malory's attitude towards Lancelot is detailed by Sandra Ness Ihle, *Malory's Grail Quest: Invention and Adaptation in Medieval Prose Romance* (Madison: University of Wisconsin Press, 1983), pp. 143-52. Ihle is in the Vinaver tradition and approaches Malory's tale in isolation from other portions of his history (see p. 172, n. 6).

[13] See *Queste*, pp. 61-62. The distinction Lancelot draws here between the two classes of "aduentures" must qualify the claim of Mary Hynes-Berry that in Malory's account of the Grail Quest there is "only one chivalry" in evidence; see "Malory's Translation of Meaning: The Tale of the Sankgreall," *Studies in Philology*, 74 (1977), 245.

[14] *Queste*, pp. 65-66.

[15] Vinaver notes the difference, though he appears to see it as another instance of Malory's misunderstanding his source (*Works*, p. 1553). P. E. Tucker, in "The Place of the 'Quest of the Holy Grail' in the *Morte Darthur*," *Modern Language Review*, 48 (1953), 391-92, and "Chivalry in the Morte," *Essays on Malory*, ed. J. A. W. Bennett (Oxford: Oxford University Press, 1963), p. 85, sees Lancelot's confession, and his Grail Quest in general, as Malory's means of coping with the embarrassment of his hero's courtly attachment to Guenevere. The evidence for such embarrassment is not convincing.

[16] Malory omits from Nacien's speech (433.28-32) the requirement that the knights confess before setting out (*Queste*, p. 19), but retains the demand that each knight be "clene of his synnes." Thus, Malory leaves it to the knights themselves to seek out confession and penance. Melyas fails to do so, and Malory's hermit, unlike the *Queste*'s, blames this failure for Melyas' misfortunes (886.9-12; see *Queste*, pp. 42-44).

[17] *Queste*, pp. 143-45.

[18] C. S. Lewis cites this passage in particular in arguing that the praise of Lancelot as the best of worldly knights serves not to diminish the impact of Lancelot's humiliation in the Quest but actually to increase it ("The English Prose *Morte*," *Essays on Malory*, pp. 18-19).

[19] This passage has been frequently commented on. Two noteworthy views are those of Tucker, "The Place of 'The Quest of the Holy Grail' in the *Morte Darthur*," pp. 393-94, and Benson, pp. 220-21. Both see the passage more as Malory's attempt to cope with his source than as part of an overall adaptation and development of his own version of the history. See also Hynes-Berry, pp. 248-49.

[20] This expression has of course been used throughout Malory's work, and while we may have been struck by it initially, with repetition it has come to mean no more than "he took his chances." In the context of the Grail Quest, however, where God's agency in sending adventures is extremely clear and in which the adventures are arranged as allegorical *ensamples*, the expression suddenly resumes its literal meaning. Indeed, its use here reminds us of what, had Arthurian chivalry aspired to the heavenly chivalry enjoined in the Grail Quest, it should have meant all along.

[21] *Queste*, p. 252.

[22] This is, of course, the same point that C. S. Lewis made some fifty years ago: that Malory had a "three-storeyed mind" which could see the moral hierarchy of his tale as either good-bad-worst or bad-good-best, depending on the starting point of the list; Lancelot, representing the middle term, can thus be seen in two very different lights. (See his review of *Sir Thomas Wyatt and Some Collected Studies* by E. K. Chambers, *Medium Aevum*, 3 [Oct. 1934], 238-39.)

[23] The command, "flee. . . and entre not" (496.21) cannot mean depart, since Lancelot is allowed to look his fill through the open door.

[24] *Queste*, p. 255.

[25] See, in addition to Vinaver, who was the first to articulate such a position, Benson, pp. 220-22. Hynes-Berry offers a more balanced view; see pp. 250-51.

[26] *Queste*, p. 259. See Ihle, p. 153.

[27] *Works*, p. xci.

[28] An exception is Ihle, p. 156, whose reading is very different from mine.

[29] For a full discussion of my reading of the Urry episode, see "Malory's 'Healing of Sir Urry': Lancelot, the Earthly Fellowship, and the World of the Grail," *Studies in Philology*, 79 (1981), 341-52.

Tunc se Coeperunt non Intelligere: The Image of Language in Malory's Last Books

John F. Plummer

The Arthurian world, from Chrétien de Troyes onward, was a logocentric one in which speech counted for as much as action, and sometimes more. The knight errant, engaged in a quest (from *quaerere* to seek, ask, inquire), is properly both searcher and inquirer, actor and speaker, as Perceval, whose quest is necessitated by a failure to question, discovers. In the final tales of Malory's *Morte Darthur,* as the Arthurian world slides towards dissolution, human language assumes increasing importance, coming forward as a central concern of Malory's story. To be sure, adultery, the shadow of incest, conflicting loyalties, anger, and accident all play a role in the court's destruction, and failures in love, in chivalry, and in spirituality offer themselves as causes of the court's demise. But to these we should add another: from the implicit and explicit questioning of the court's values in the Grail Quest, through the divisive slander and strife of the closing books, and culminating in the destructive vengeance of Sir Gawain, runs a progressive degeneration and ultimate failure of language. What one might then call the image of language serves to clarify and to enlarge the meaning of Malory's final tales.[1]

Galahad and the Grail come to Camelot on the feast of

Pentecost. Though Pentecost is a commonplace date for the commencement of Arthurian adventure, the moment seems here to have particular importance, for the date is noted by the Queen (427),[2] Lancelot (428), and Arthur (432).[3] Most significant, though, in signalling the importance of Pentecost is the imagery surrounding the appearance of the Grail itself in the midst of the assembled court:

> Thenne anone they herd crakynge and cryenge of thonder that hem thought the palace shold alle todryue. In the myddes of this blast entred a sonne beaume more clerer by seuen tymes than euer they sawe daye, and al they were alyghted of the grace of the Holy Ghoost. Thenne beganne euery knyghte to behold other, and eyther sawe other by theire semynge fayrer than euer they sawe afore.   (432.20-25)[4]

The scene is clearly modeled upon the Acts of the Apostles 2:1-4:

> And when the days of Pentecost were drawing to a close, they were all together in one place. And suddenly there came a sound from heaven, as of a violent wind coming, and it filled the whole house where they were sitting. And there appeared to them parted tongues as of fire, and settled upon each of them. And they were all filled with the Holy Spirit and began to speak in foreign tongues, even as the Holy Spirit prompted them to speak.

Why, one may ask, this insistence upon Pentecost here as the Tale of the Quest opens? The grace of Pentecost brought to the disciples eloquence, the gift of tongues, which allowed them to be understood by the speakers of any language. Pentecost also brought a new sense of community and social harmony, both symbolized and effectuated by their miraculous linguistic facilities. Ominously for Camelot, neither eloquence nor unity accompanies the appearance of the Grail. Far from receiving the gift of tongues, the court is bereft of language entirely, for while the Grail is in their midst "there was no knyght myghte speke one word a grete whyle, and soo they loked euery man on other as they had ben dome" (432.25-26). Only after the Grail has departed "had they alle brethe to speke" (432.31). Similarly, Arthur senses that the Round Table is to experience not a new sense of communion but rather dissolution. He plans a tournament, for, he says to his men,

> neuer shalle I see yow ageyne hole togyders. Therfor I wille see yow alle hole togyders in the medowe of Camelot to iuste and to

torneye, that after your dethe men maye speke of hit, that suche
good knyghtes were holy togyders suche a day. (431.32-35)

The notion of a final communal joust is present in the *Queste del
Saint Graal*,[5] but the poignancy, the three-fold repetition of "hole
togyders" is new in Malory. Malory also bears down hard on the
sorrow of Arthur as he realizes that his fellowship, following
Gawain's lead in taking the oath of the Grail Quest, is indeed
dissolving. To Gawain, Arthur says,

ye haue nyghe slayne me with the auowe and promesse that ye
haue made, for thorugh you ye haue berafte me the fayrest
felaushyp and the truest of knyghthode that euer were sene
togyders in ony royalme of the world. For whan they departe
from hens I am sure they alle shal neuer mete more in thys
world . . . I haue loued them as wel as my lyf, wherfore hit shal
greue me ryght sore, the departycyon of thys felaushyp, for I
haue had an olde custome to haue them in my felaushyp.
(433.5-12; see also 433.24, 434.6-8 ff.)

In sum, the effect of the Pentecostal appearance of Galahad and
the Grail upon Camelot is to deprive the court of those very things,
speech and fellowship, which the original Pentecost had amplified.
Arthur's accusation here that Gawain has destroyed the fellowship
is of course a powerful foreshadowing of the role Gawain will play
in the last books. But in a sense the unprepared and apparently
unworthy court, on whom fall the gifts of Pentecost only in an
inverted form, is already well along the road of dissolution.

This inversion suggests not merely a Pentecost which fails, but
also another Biblical story, that of the Tower of Babel. Pentecost
was customarily understood in medieval exegetical writings to be
the anti-type of Babel, signifying a reunion of language and faith
which the dissolution at the Tower had destroyed.[6] Babel itself was
seen as an image of heresy, bad faith, pride, and spiritual and social
dissolution resulting from the sinful use of the gift of language.
According to Origen, Christ's statement in John 10:30 that "I and
the Father are one" betokened a reunion between God and man, a
reunion accomplished at Pentecost, which brought together in one
language and one faith what the Tower of Babel had sundered.[7]
Origen's understanding of Babel as a symbol of disharmony
between God and man, and man and man, the image of which is
mutual linguistic incomprehensibility, and Pentecost as a symbol

of mutual comprehension symbolizing social and cosmic harmony, is echoed and amplified in Augustine. In a sermon for Pentecost Augustine wrote that Pentecost not only united in humility the tongues separated by pride at Babel, but signified the ability of the Church to speak to all men:

> Linguae illae quibus loquebantur a Spiritu sancto impleti, per omnium gentium linguas futuram Ecclesiam praesignabant. Sic humilis fidelium pietas earum linguarum diversitatem Ecclesiae contulit unitati; ut quod discordia dissipaverat, colligeret charitas.[8]

In *The City of God*, Augustine emphasized the appropriateness of the punishment to the crime at Babel: "Quoniam dominatio imperantis in lingua est, ibi damnata est superbia, ut non intelligeretur jubens homini, qui noluit intelligere ut obediret Deo jubenti."[9] This pride and its linguistic punishment is overcome at Pentecost:

> Turrem illam recordare superborum factam post diluvium: quid dixerunt superbi? Ne pereamus diluvio, faciamus altam turrem (Gen. xi, 4). Superbia se munitos esse arbitrabantur, exstruxerunt altam turrem; et Dominus divisit linguas ipsorum. Tunc se coeperunt non intelligere, . . . ne se intelligendo perniciosam faceret unitatem. Per superbos homines divisae sunt linguae, per humiles Apostolos congregatae sunt linguae: spiritus superbiae dispersit linguas, Spiritus sanctus congregavit linguas. . . . Ergo si adhuc saeviunt et gentiles sunt, expedit eis divisas habere linguas. Volunt unam linguam, veniant ad Ecclesiam; quia et in diversitate linguarum carnis, una est lingua in fide cordis.[10]

The conception of Babel and Pentecost as an opposed pair is found in medieval plastic arts as well, as for example in an illustrated *Speculum humanae salvationis* of 1330-40 which shows the descent of the Holy Ghost upon the apostles in the top, and the crumbling Tower at the bottom, of a single page.[11] A miniature of Jacopo Butinone of about 1500 opposes the old heresies of Babel to the true speech of the Church in depicting the young Christ seated upon a tiny zigarrut while speaking to the elders in the temple.[12] The same notion is alluded to even later in architectural symbolism in a church of Borromini in which the zigarrut motif is "conquered" by incorporation into a tower suggestive of the triumph of the apostles and the Church at Pentecost.[13]

That Arthur's court is struck dumb by the Pentecostal apparition of the Grail and, to Arthur's dramatized dismay, scatters in a quest that is soon shown to be marked by confusion, suggests powerfully the relevance to Malory's story of the tension between Babel and Pentecost. If the curse of Babel has indeed come upon Camelot, then we may expect that divisive language will divide permanently the members of the court, shattering their fellowship and enterprise, as at Babel itself. A final division does, of course, come to pass, and in destructive language we may mark both its progress and one of its prime causes. The court moves, as it were, backwards from Pentecostal communion to the chaos of Babel.

Though fewer than half of the knights who seek the Grail reassemble at Camelot after the quest (499.7), the reunion is happy enough to erase for a moment the thought of dissolution: "thenne was there grete ioye in the courte, and in especyal Kynge Arthur and Quene Gueneuer made grete ioye of the remenaunt that were comen home" (506.3-5), Malory tells us. But the moment is very brief, for by the next paragraph Lancelot has begun to resort to the queen, and the joy of reunion is drowned in the dissonance of slander over the affair: "many in the courte spak of hit, and in especial Sir Agrauayne . . . for he was euer open-mouthed" (506.14-15). This compact introduction to the story of Lancelot and Guenevere juxtaposes the values of the Grail Quest with the court's flawed nature and, like an enthymeme, moves through premises to conclusion, cause to effect: "*Thenne* . . . Launcelot . . . forgat the promyse . . . For . . . *had not* Sire Launcelot ben . . . *But* euer his thoughtes were pryuely . . . *and so* they loued . . . *that* many in the courte spak." Lancelot's broken vow is in itself a failure of speech. The hermit to whom the promise was given had admonished him, "Loke that your herte and your mouthe accorde" (446.18).[14] The eventual lack of accord between heart and mouth, fact and speech, makes Lancelot false to his God and to himself. But false speech and the suspicion of falseness ripple outward immediately from Lancelot's relationship with his promises to himself, to his relationship with his lover, and to her relationship to her court.

As the story of the Poisoned Apple opens, Lancelot withdraws from Guenevere "for to eschewe the sklaunder and noyse" (506.20), a withdrawal she interprets as a rejection. His explanation is dismissed: though "the quene stood stylle and lete Sir Launcelot saye what he wold" (507.24), his language strikes her as false, and she dismisses him from the court. Her heated words in turn leave Guenevere helpless in the face of Mador's words accusing her of poisoning Sir Patrise. Though the accusation is misinformed, it is credited by a court already suspicious of its queen. As the knights hear Mador's words, "stode they all stylle that none wold speke a word ageynst hym" (509.11-12). The accusation ("noyse and crye") attracts the attention of Arthur (exactly as will a later public accusation) who understands the seriousness of Lancelot's absence and the linguistic dimensions of Guenevere's problem: "none of these foure and twenty knyghtes . . . wille doo batail for yow, nor none of hem wille saye well of you, and that shalle be a grete sklaunder for yow in thys courte" (510.12-14).

The statement links "doo batail" and "saye well" in parallel, as is fitting, for in the judicial combat here, as later in the Knight of the Cart episode, the outcome of the battle, the nature of the action, is theoretically determined by the truth of the "saying," the nature of the speech. One measure of the degeneration of speech in the court is, to anticipate, Arthur's eventual rejection of trial by combat for Guenevere. Though Gawain will argue that Agravain's entrapment of Lancelot in Guenevere's chambers does not conclusively prove guilt, and add that Lancelot would "make hit good" in battle for the queen, Arthur will reply "That I byleue wel . . . but I wil not that way worke with Sir Launcelot, for he trusteth soo moche vpon his handes and his myghte that he doubteth no man. And therfore for my quene he shalle neuer fyghte more, for she shall haue the lawe" (563.17-20). The opposition of "fyghte" to "haue the lawe" shows that action and language eventually separate, with the result that judicial combat, and therefore law itself, loses its theoretical underpinning.

How, Arthur may wonder, can one credit the speech of a physically invincible man? In the story of the Poisoned Apple, though, Lancelot's victory is rightly taken as establishing truth, and the queen is cleared of the charge. Lancelot insists further, however, on a linguistic affirmation of Guenevere's innocence. He stipulates that "no mencyon be made vpon Sir Patryces tombe that euer Quene Gueneuer consented to that treason" (513.34-35); nor does Malory fail to give us the exact words engraved, which tell the truth of the poisoning, and tell too of the false accusation and successful defense: "Alle this was wryten vpon the tombe of Syr Patryce in excusyng of the quene" (514.39).[15] The story moves, then, from a broken vow to slander,[16] to a lover's quarrel, to a false accusation and more slander, to an eventual "unsaying" of falsehood and the engraving of true words on a tomb, so that the narrative tension and resolution of the tale result directly from acts of speech.

The residue of slander remains in the court, and surfaces again briefly in the story of the Fair Maid of Astolat, and it is this time Guenevere who raises the issue, chiding Lancelot for remaining with her after Arthur has left for the tournament: "What will youre enemyes and myne saye and deme?" (515.24-25). Again in the Knight of the Cart story Guenevere shows a concern for slander, preferring to leave her abduction by Melyagaunt unavenged rather than encourage more talk of the matter. When Melyagaunt shamelessly throws himself on her mercy to avoid facing the enraged Lancelot, the queen says, agreeing to calm her lover, "better is pees than euer werre, and the lesse noyse, the more is my worship" (543.4-5). She tells Lancelot she does not seek peace out of any favor towards her abductor, but in order "to laye doune euery shameful noyse" (543.22-23). Lancelot grudgingly acquiesces, saying he "was neuer willynge nor gladde of shameful sklaunder nor noyse." The battle does come eventually, of course, but the issue is not abduction but rather Melyagaunt's accusation of Guenevere of sleeping with some one of the wounded knights. This accusation recapitulates in a new key that of the earlier Poisoned Apple episode, with the difference that this accusation is only technically incorrect. Guenevere is guilty of adultery in the time and place specified, but not, of course, with one of her wounded knights. The careless wording of the accusation—rather than its true substance—allows Lancelot to defend Guenevere even in a judicial battle in which "God wil haue a stroke." The hapless wording of the accusation is further proof of Melyagaunt's essentially ignoble character.

Even leaving aside the abduction, the attack on the unarmed knights, the ambush of Lancelot, the destruction of his horse by archers (as opposed to a chivalrous confrontation of Lancelot himself), and the entrapment of Lancelot in the dungeon,

Melyagaunt seems not to understand how noble people act or speak. When Lancelot accuses him of an unchivalrous act in opening the queen's bed, Melyagaunt replies "I wote not what ye mene" (545.29), and one must believe he does not. When the wounded knights speak "al in one voys" to defend the queen, he responds impatiently, "away with your proud langage" (545.15-19). Lancelot gives Melyagaunt fair warning to watch his words: "Beware what ye do . . . for and ye say so and ye will preue it, it wil be taken at your handes" (545.32-33), even specifying in advance what he is prepared to deny: "but *as to that* I saye nay playnly, that this nyghte there lay none of these ten wounded knyghtes wyth my lady Quene Gueneuer, and *that wil I preue* with my handes, that ye say vntruly *in that*" (545.37-39, emphases mine). Melyagaunt cannot succeed precisely because, as he has said, God will have His stroke, and the battle will be determined by the language of the judicial oaths. Melyagaunt makes an opposed pair with Mador, who was morally neutral but quite incorrect in his accusation of the queen, while Melyagaunt is morally base, yet substantially correct in his accusation. But because he is base, Melyagaunt lacks the comprehension, acumen, and language to penetrate to or speak the truth.

The pattern of accusation is completed by open-mouthed Agravain,[17] who, though morally repugnant, is sufficiently well informed to hit the truth by firing at it incessantly. Or perhaps it would be more accurate to say Agravain manages, unlike Melyagaunt, simply to get his facts straight. Even without entering into a consideration of the obviously complex feelings of Malory toward his adulterous lovers, one does not feel Agravain manages to articulate from his facts a statement sufficiently subtle or complex to be called truth. His nevertheless pivotal and verbal role in the destruction of the court is unambiguously announced in the closing lines of the story of healing Sir Urry. Malory concludes this narrative with an ominous statement: "But euery nyghte and day Sire Agrauayne . . . awayted Quene Gueneuer and Sir Launcelot du Lake to putte them to a rebuke and shame" (554.10-12). The final two paragraphs, in which Malory skips over much of the French story of Lancelot, conclude with "and here I goo vnto the morte of Kynge Arthur, and that caused Syre Agrauayne" (554.22-23). This statement, which rather startlingly adduces only one cause for Arthur's fall, can be understood as an oversimplification, a substitution of the proximate cause for such ultimate ones as Guenevere's and Lancelot's love affair and Mordred's hatred and treachery. But it can also be seen as an insistence[18] on the role of disruptive speech in the court's last days. For it is open speaking of the adultery, not the adultery itself, which is new in the Morte.

Mark Lambert has signalled the importance of noise, loud sounds, in this tale, especially the noise of shouting, angry men, and the contrasting quiet of the life of Lancelot and Bors which concludes the tale.[19] I would follow Lambert in seeing importance in "that high volume of sound . . . which not only marks but brings about the ruin of Arthur's kingdom."[20] But I would add that the noise is all of human voices, destructive language. Agravain begins the din by accusing Guenevere and Lancelot, and he "sayd thus openly, and not in no counceylle, that many knyghtes myghte here it" (555.12-13). Gawain, in turn, asks for circumspection, telling Agravain to "meue no suche maters no more afore me. For wete ye wel . . . I wylle not be of your counceylle" (555.17-18). The quarrel between open-mouthed Agravain and tight-lipped Gawain is not over the facts of the case, whether or not Guenevere is faithful to Arthur, but over whether to speak of it. Gawain would work by "counceylle," a word, suggestive of judicious speech informed by thought, which hovers over his debates with Agravain:

> Falle of hit what falle may, sayd Syr Agrauayne, I wille disclose it to the kyng.
>   Not by my counceylle, sayd Syr Gawayne . . . Now broder, stynte your noyse, sayd Sir Gawayne . . . for I wil not here your tales ne be of your counceyll."   (556.2-19)

After Lancelot and Guenevere are trapped, Gawain continues to speak for peace: "my lord Arthur, I wold counceylle yow not to be ouer hasty" (563.1-2). Reminded of Agravain's death, Gawain replies that "in soo moche they wold not doo by my counceyll, I wyl not medle me therof" (563.28-29). He cannot agree to condemn the queen: "it shalle neuer be sayd that euer I was of youre counceylle of her dethe" (563.40-41). But speech has already turned from counsel to noise. As Arthur overhears the argument between Agravain and Gawain he asks what "noyse" they are making. He is unhappy to have the rumor publically proclaimed: "the kynge was ful lothe therto that ony noyse shold be vpon Syr Launcelot and his quene, for the kynge had a demynge, but he wold not here of hit" (556.36-38). Lancelot's entrapment in Guenevere's chambers is accompanied by choruses of accusations, threats, and taunts, "noyse," "cryeng," "sklaunder," "a loude voys that alle the courte myghte here hit," and "more noyse" (557-59).

That Gareth's death turns Gawain against Lancelot rings true psychologically, for Gareth is as beautiful as Agravain is repulsive. It is ironic that Lancelot kills his truest friend, and ironic too that Gareth dies because he would not arm himself against Lancelot. But Gareth's death at Lancelot's hand also represents a stage in the degeneration of communication in the court; though Gareth does not speak to Lancelot, he nevertheless sends him an unambiguous message of friendship, which Lancelot fails to heed. For Gareth, wearing armor to the field of judgment would be a sign of acquiescence in Arthur's condemnation of the queen. Gaheris and Gareth thus say that, though they must obey Arthur's command to appear, "we wyl be there in peasyble wyse and bere none harneis of warre vpon vs" (564.7-8). This understanding is apparently shared by the court as a whole, for Malory says that "there were but fewe in comparyson that wold bere ony armour *for to strengthe the dethe of the quene*" (564.15-16, emphasis mine). But in the "rassynge and hurlyng" of the battle, his anger, and his passion, Lancelot misses this sign; he fails or refuses to heed the message. The battlefield in whose din Lancelot cannot understand his friends is a fitting metaphor for both his inner turmoil and the unintelligible babble of the court.

Gawain's incredible heat in pursuing Lancelot for Gareth's death is emphasized by its contrast to his cool-headedness and judiciousness during the strife which precedes the death. The contrast is made more pointed in that his physical fury against Lancelot is matched by an equal verbal fury. I would argue, in fact, that Gawain loses not only his calm and his counseling ways but all patience with language itself. To clarify this point we might look at Gawain's reaction to Lancelot's elaborate speech of self-justification given as he returns Guenevere to Arthur during the Papal truce. Lambert has shown how this speech demonstrates not that Lancelot is a hypocrite engaged in "lying, sophistry, and

162

blasphemy," as some readers have felt,[21] but a knight for whom shame, and not guilt, is the issue in question. I agree fully, but I would add that as important as the content of the speech is the very fact that Lancelot, not customarily a rhetorician, is giving a speech at all, in fact a long and complex one. Lancelot gives voice to several speeches in the Morte proper, in fact. The roots of these speeches lie by and large in the sources of the tale, but as Vinaver has shown, their exfoliation and prominance is found only in Malory.[22]

If we do not at first notice that Lancelot has become very verbal, certainly Gawain and Arthur do: Gawain interrupts the speech, which has brought the court and king to tears, to say "Sire Launcelot . . . I haue ryghte wel herd thy speche and thy grete profers. But . . . I will neuer forgyue my broders dethe" (574.32-34). And again, after Lancelot has moved even himself to tears with his words, Gawain blurts out, "Make thow no more langage . . . but delyuer the quene from the and pyke the lyghtely oute of this courte" (575.29-30), just as he has earlier rejected, before Joyous Garde, conciliatory words from Lancelot with "Fy on thy proude wordes" (568.21). Arthur, it should be added, has swung with Gawain to an anti-rhetorical position, responding to another of Lancelot's speeches during a lull in the siege at Joyous Garde, "Fy vpon thy fayre langage . . . For . . . I am thy mortal fo and euer wylle to my deth daye" (567.25-26).

Gawain does use language, but only as a weapon, spurring on Arthur in his moments of weakening resolve—in obvious opposition to his earlier counselling of restraint—and goading Lancelot to fight, calling him "false traytour knyght" in all available permutations, even taking the remarkable step of orchestrating group taunts: "Syre Gawayne made many men to blowe vpon Syr Launcelot, and all at ones they called hym fals recreaunt knyght" (569.9-11). These verbal assaults wound deeply: "Alle this langage herd Sir Launcelot euery dele" (580.5-6); "I am ryghte heuy of Sire Gawayns wordes" (580.10); "Alle thys langage Sir Launcelot herde, and than he sayd thus: Sir Gawayn, me repentys of your foule sayeng, that ye wyll not sease of your langage" (582.6-7). The challenge that finally provokes Lancelot into action is perhaps the most symbolically appropriate of all: "Thenne Sir Gawayne sayd, Sir Launcelot, and thou darst doo batail, leue thy babblynge and come of, and lete vs ease our hertes" (580.23-24). To Gawain, Lancelot's language is so much unintelligible babble. Not only do they seem not to speak the same language, not only does language fail to unify the two friends, it is in Gawain's mouth an engine of war, and in the end the once verbal Gawain cannot express himself through language at all. Whereas in the story of the Poisoned Apple to do battle and to speak were congruent with one another, action shaped by language, here, at the full extension of Babel's curse where rage is literally inarticulate, action and language diverge, radically and permanently. Where language has no meaning, its product, action, is likewise meaningless, and both are socially entropic. The linguistic and political severance of Arthur and Gawain from Lancelot thus leads inexorably to the destruction of the society of which the three are the chief pillars.

From this point to Arthur's death, action springs (awry) from broken, lying, unheard, or unheeded language. As the story shifts from the French battlefield to England, it demonstrates abundantly the effects of language's breakdown on the society at large. Mordred "dyd do make letters as though that they came from beyonde the see, and the letters specefyed that Kynge Arthur was slayn in bataylle wyth Syr Launcelot" (584.1-3). When Guenevere learns of Mordred's intention to marry her, we are told that she "durst not dyscouer hyr herte, but spake fayre and agreyd to Syr Mordredes wylle," but she begs leave to go to London, and "bycause of hyr fayre speche, Syr Mordred trusted hyr wel ynough and gaf hyr leue" (584.9-13). Once she is secure in the Tower, the queen refuses, "for fayre speche nor for foule" (584.20) to come out again. Even the Bishop of Canterbury's threat to curse Mordred cannot alter events at this point, suggesting that the secular efficacy of the Church's strongest language has evaporated, though not, presumably, its spiritual power. The bishop does curse Mordred "in the moost orgulist wyse that myght be doon" and then flees to Glastonbury, to become a "preest eremyte in a chapel and [lyue] in pouerte and in holy prayers. For wel he vnderstode that myscheuous warre was at honde" (585.11-15). In his flight from the social to the solitary the bishop re-affirms the nullity of England as a community. The bishopric of Canterbury, a visible, political, and social as well as spiritual entity, has ceased to exist. Mordred attempts to validate his ersatz community by sending "wryttes to al the barownry"; the content of the writs is not specified, but they have the effect that the "comyn voys" among the people is against Arthur, who is "depraued and euyl sayd of, and many ther were . . . myght not than say hym a good worde" (585.22-27).

The lies, impotent curse, inflammatory writs, and seditious grumblings set the linguistic scene of collapse, and events now move very rapidly; within a few pages Arthur has landed in England; Gawain has been mortally wounded, has sent a death-bed letter of apology to Lancelot, and has appeared to Arthur in a dream; a treaty has been made and broken; and Arthur has received his own death wound. Gawain's death-bed letter returns him, too late, to the role of wise user of language. He implicitly forgives Lancelot for his faults, confesses his own, and urges Lancelot to speed to Arthur's side. This role is continued in his appearance to Arthur in a dream the night before the final battle, warning against the battle and counseling a treaty. This series of texts (letter, dream-counsel, treaty) is curiously prominent and yet plays no role in shaping events in the narrative, for none of the texts takes effect. The letter arrives too late; the dream-counsel is heeded only temporarily; and the treaty does not outlast its own toasting. The function of these failed texts, then, is not to shape action but to signal action's moral significance. Each is a reminder of an earlier failure to use similar language in a timely fashion. Gawain's letter points to his earlier inability to confess error and to forgive Lancelot; his counsel in Arthur's dream reminds us of his bellicose goading of Arthur in France, and the treaty, likewise, of the refusal to make peace earlier. Those failures in language had removed events from the control, linguistic or otherwise, of the central characters; their language now serves not as shaper of action but rather as ironic commentary upon their linguistic impotence. The fate, spiritual and physical, of a Round Table whose members are mutually unintelligible was foreseen by John of Salisbury in his twelfth century *Metalogicon*:

> Deprived of their gift of speech, men would degenerate to the condition of brute animals, and cities would seem like corrals for livestock, rather than communities composed of human

beings united by a common bond for the purpose of living in society, serving one another, and cooperating as friends. If verbal intercommunication were withdrawn, what contract could be duly concluded, what instruction could be given in faith and morals, and what agreement and mutual understanding could subsist among men?[23]

Disasters of such scope provoke us to search for causes. If one assumes, as a medieval reader might, that a moral problem had caused the linguistic one, and not vice-versa, then pride would be the sin most eligible for blame in the court's self-destruction. Indeed, as Augustine had argued, pride caused the dispersal at Babel, and only the humble charity of the Apostles at Pentecost rectified the loss. The punishment of pride, though, is most commonly associated in late medieval narrative with the image of Fortune's Wheel. The appropriateness of this image to the fall of Arthur is seen in its prominence in the alliterative *Morte Arthure*.[24] By way of contrast, in Malory's version the image of Fortune's Wheel is reduced to a few lines, is not identified as Fortune's Wheel, and shares space in Arthur's dream with Gawain's prophecies. The substitution, if I may provisionally so term it, of the myth of Babel for the image of Fortune's Wheel leads to several shifts in emphasis.

First, the story of Babel is about social rather than personal catastrophe. Arthur's dream of Fortune's Wheel, as all such dreams, places him alone on the Wheel, and shows only his fall. As king his fall implies the fall of others, but in fact the fall of a prince may lead simply to his replacement by another and certainly does not imply, as the story of Babel does, the absolute cessation of the community of which he is the head.[25] Second, the story of Babel emphasizes that tragic quality so many readers find peculiar to Malory, a quality which makes Boethian thought (the source of the image of Fortuna) seem somehow inadequate in searching to understand Malory's tale of Arthur. The great number of people destroyed at Salisbury makes its own contribution to the sense of tragedy, of course, but the loss of the fellowship itself perhaps goes beyond even the loss of lives. The number of the dead emphasizes the scope of the disaster, but its quality is to be measured in the loss of the intangible and essential *communitas* which Arthur repeatedly laments. At Babel likewise it is the loss of community, not the loss of life, or even prosperity or power (as in Boethian narrative) that is central. Furthermore there is in the pattern of Babel a sense of the inexorable, and that for two reasons: the building of Camelot, as of the Tower of Babel, involved many people; the impossibility of isolating one character or pinpointing one action which might be singly blamed for the eventual calamity creates a feeling of momentum; one can imagine no single change which could reverse the direction of events. Second, Babel is a story about language, and while we all participate in linguistic change, and are all partially responsible for the nature of our shared language, the individual speaker of a language can do little to alter the directions in which it moves. This feeling of inexorability naturally increases the pathos of Malory's version of Arthur's story, buffering it at least partially against any merely reflexive Boethian reading and simultaneously deepening the ethical and moral complexity of the tale.

Finally, the pattern of Babel lends pathos to the Arthurian story because of the inescapable paradox that Babel and Camelot were destroyed by success. Though the same would seem to be true of the protagonist of a Boethian fall, there is an essential difference. The Boethian figure may achieve what looks like success in wealth or power, but the conventions of the genre and of medieval Christian thought define wealth and power as trivialities, or worse, impediments to true success. By contrast, it is axiomatic that a society is successful insofar as it is stable and cohesive, in a word, social. It is the very success in these terms that precipitates Babel's destruction, "ne se intelligendo perniciosam faceret unitatem," leading to the paradoxical notion that the only way to avoid anarchy is to be anarchic to begin with. Of course the medieval exegetical position was that the cohesiveness of Babel was, like the fortune of the Boethian protagonist, misused. It was no doubt just such an understanding of the story that led to its original assimilation, apparently at the hands of the monastic author of the *Queste,* into the Arthurian material. Thus understood, Camelot's social cohesiveness is misspent on such frivolities as quests, jousts, and the pursuit of lovers' favors. In fact, though, there is no way such social cohesiveness can not be misspent.

Social activities (the relations of men to each other, rather than to God) are by their very nature secular, at least in structure. The theoretical impossibility of a moral society is suggested even in the fact that all of the holy personages of the *Queste* (and Malory's story of the Sankgreal) are recluses, asocial, or at least non-social, solitaries, including the holy knight Galahad, a pattern reconfirmed in the flight of the bishop of Canterbury to his wilderness hermitage, and, finally, in the hermetic lives of Lancelot, Bors, and the others at the end of the story. The paradox of success equalling destruction is built into the Babel story, and the exegesis of it as a parable of pride does not remove the paradox, except to suggest that the only possible (moral) society is the metaphorical community of the church: "Volunt unam linguam, veniant ad Ecclesiam." Whereas the Boethian protagonist may be saved by directing his energies towards spiritual ends and yet still remain who he is, the story of Babel suggests that literal, historical society may not be saved and remain what it is, social.

It is this paradox lying within medieval ideas about Babel, language, and society, that Malory seems to have found in his source materials and developed, not, as in the *Queste*, in purely otherworldly condemnation of secular society, but more complexly. Rather than suppressing paradox Malory focuses upon it. He could not argue that the City of Man was equal in value to the City of God, but he seems to have taken no pleasure in rejecting that earthly city. The Pentecostal vision of the Grail, suggestive of Apostolic unity, brings only pain to Camelot. The monastic *Queste* author no doubt saw this pain as a side effect of a lesson to be learned, for his text implies that Camelot must be dissolved, cede place to the non-localized, purely symbolic community of the Grail recluses and succesful Grail questors. Camelot in such a vision cannot be salvaged and reshaped into an Apostolic community, for Camelot like Babel is defined as local, physical, and social. Few of Malory's readers fail to be moved by the sense of loss in his last books, the loss of something earthly, man made, linguistic and (like Babel) great. But whether we or Malory like it, the political and linguistic edifice is doomed to impermanence. Only, apparently, outside what one thinks of as society can language be permanent and redeemed: Lancelot ends his life by entering the priesthood and singing Mass. Here finally the curse of Babel is lifted, for here again language and action are one.

Vanderbilt University

NOTES

[1] Though I have compared those passages in Malory on which I focus to their apparent sources, and I have indicated in notes those passages where Malory seems to be diverging from his sources in interesting ways, I make no claim to have isolated what is Malory's from what is at least suggested in the Arthurian tradition as he received it. What I would claim is that the late medieval Arthurian tradition, as exemplified best, even crystallized, in Malory, exhibits a deep concern for the effects, creative and destructive, of language among men.

[2] All references to Malory's text are to *Caxton's Malory*, ed. James W. Spisak (Berkeley and Los Angeles: University of California Press, 1983) and will hereafter be given, as here, in parentheses.

[3] The insistence on the date is heard even later: in explicating Lancelot's experience in the tournament of black and white knights, a recluse says that "The daye of Pentecost, whan Kynge Arthur helde his court, it befelle that erthely kynges and knyghtes toke a turnement togyders, that is to say, the quest of the Sancgreal" (463.7-9). Percival's aunt, another recluse, likewise refers to Galahad's sitting in the Sege Perelous "at his mete on Whytsonday last past" (449.28-29). It is also worth noting, in this Pentecostal vein, that when Lancelot first sees Galahad, the young man seems to him "semely and demure as a douue" (428.12).

[4] The French *Queste* is less definite on the presence of the Holy Ghost: "*Comme s'il feussent* en lumiere de la grace du Saint Esprit," *La Queste del Saint Graal*, ed. Albert Pauphilet (Paris: H. Champion, 1975), p. 15.

[5] *Queste*, p. 13.

[6] Louis Réau, *Iconographie de l'art chrétien* (Paris: PUDF, 1956), II, 1, p. 121. "Dans l'art typologique du Moyen-âge, la *Confusion des langues* (Confusio Babylonica) . . . s'oppose à la Pentecôte ou Descente du Saint Esprit sur les Apôtres qui reçoivent le don des langues."

[7] *In Genesim Scholia*, PG XII, 109-12; cited in Arno Borst, *Der Turmbau von Babel: Geschichte der Meinungen über Ursprung und Vielfalt der Sprachen und Völker*, 4 vols. in 6 (Stuttgart: A. Hiersemann, 1957-63), p. 236. See also Chrysostom, *In epist. I Cor. Homilia* 35, I *PG* I, 296.

[8] "The languages spoken by those filled with the Holy Spirit signified the future Church. . . . The humble piety of the faithful brought together their diverse languages in the Church. Thus what discord dispersed charity unified." *Sermo cclxxi, in die Pentecostes*, v; *PL* XXXVIII, 1245.

[9] "The power of the imperious is seated in their language, and therein pride was punished, so that he who would not understand in order to obey God was himself not understood." *De Civitate Dei* XVI, iv; *PL* XXXXI, 483.

[10] "Remember that tower made by the pride-filled after the deluge; what did they say? 'Lest we perish by flood, let us build a tall tower' (Gen. xi, 4).

In their pride, they believed themselves to be fortified, and they built a high tower, and the Lord divided their tongues. Then they began to misunderstand one another . . . lest understanding each other they form a pernicious union. By proud men tongues were divided, and by the humble Apostles tongues were unified: the spirit of pride dispersed languages, and the Holy Spirit unified them. . . . Therefore if even now some rage and remain Gentiles, it is fitting that they have several tongues. If they wish one tongue, let them come into the Church; because while many are the tongues of the flesh, the language of the faith is one." *Enarratio in Psalmum* LIV, 11; *PL* XXXVI, 636.

[11] Karlsruhe, Badische Landesbibliothek, Cod. H 78, fol. 20r, reproduced in Gertrud Schiller, *Ikonographie der Christlichen Kunst* (Gutersloh: Gutersloher Verlag, Gerd Mohn, 1976), vol. 4, pt. 1, p. 221, pl. 50.

[12] Reproduced in H. Ost, "Borrominis rom. Universitätskirche S. Ivo all Sapienza," *Zeitschrift für Kunstgeschichte*, 30 (1967), 101-42.

[13] *Ibid.*

[14] I must disagree with Larry Benson's understanding of Lancelot's promise. Benson argues that the hermit extracts the promise to avoid the queen's company "as moche as ye may forbere" (446.17), which is "curiously equivocal compared to the unqualified and stern words of the hermit in the French version," *Malory's Morte Darthur* (Cambridge, Mass.: Harvard University Press, 1976), p. 200. But to say as Benson does that "Malory's Lancelot keeps his vow; he does avoid the queen's company as much as he can," and that "Lancelot . . . does his best, and that is all that Malory's hermit requires" seems to me to go too far. Malory says, after all, that Lancelot "forgat the promyse" (506.9); he surely could not be trying his best to keep it if he had forgotten it. Furthermore, Lancelot promises the hermit that "he nold," which can only refer to "come in that quenes felaushy." I admit to belaboring a small point, but I do not believe Malory would cast back so many pages to the promise if he did not see it as binding and its betrayal as important.

[15] In neither the *Mort Artu* nor *Le Morte Arthur* does Lancelot dictate the words for the tomb. In those texts, in fact, the tombstone is inscribed before Lancelot even hears of the troubles. Malory omitted this first tomb, presumably in the process of disentangling the interwoven plots of the stories of the Poisoned Apple and the Fair Maid of Astolat as he found them in his source(s). That he then returned to "revise" the tomb though his version did not require it suggests his interest in the role of language in the tale.

[16] The querulous quality of Lancelot and Guenevere's conversations here and in the opening scene of the Fair Maid story is Malory's doing. Vinaver has shown that the two scenes are almost entirely new (*Works*, pp. 1588-89).

[17] According to Vinaver (*Works*, p. 1596, note to 1045.21), Malory's "for he was euer open-mouthed" (506.15) represents an error, a mistaking of French *beer à* (to aim or aspire) for *beer* (to gape, be wide open) in the *Queste* statement "pour çou k'il beast le roi vengier de sa honte." The slip is actually fortunate stylistically and is evidence that Malory conceived of Agravain as a loud-mouth. Vinaver says, in *Malory* (Oxford: Oxford University Press, 1929), p. 151, that Agravain's motivation, as "given in the French *Mort Artu* is distinctly preferable," translating the French lines as "because he intended to revenge the king's dishonour." Whether this is preferable depends on whether one sees Agravain as emblematic of revengefulness or, as I believe Malory did, of linguistic disruptiveness.

[18] The whole passage is of course Malory's invention.

[19] *Malory: Style and Vision in Le Morte Darthur* (New Haven: Yale University Press, 1975), pp. 176-94.

[20] Lambert, pp. 193-94.

[21] Lambert, p. 177.

[22] *Works*, p. 1618.

[23] *The Metalogicon of John of Salisbury*, trans. Daniel D. McGarry (Berkeley and Los Angeles: University of California Press, 1955), p. 11; *PL* CXCIX, 827.

[24] *The Alliterative Morte Arthure*, ed. Valerie Krishna (New York: Burt Franklin, 1976), pp. 127-34, ll. 3218-3455.

[25] See Howard R. Patch, *The Goddess Fortuna in Medieval Literature* (New York: Octagon Books, 1967), pp. 147-77; and Benson, pp. 236-41.

Wounds, Healing, and Knighthood in Malory's Tale of Lancelot and Guenevere

Robert L. Kelly

Eugène Vinaver showed that the sequence of five episodes in Malory's Tale of Lancelot and Guenevere (Caxton's Books XVIII and XIX) is highly original, but neither he nor any of the book's more recent critics[1] has noticed the curious turn Malory's inventiveness takes in his two most original tales: he opens the third episode (the Winchester tournament) with Lancelot's being wounded by a "lady huntresse," while he focuses the fifth (the healing of Sir Urry) on Lancelot's miraculous ability to heal. What is even more striking is that Malory selects and orders materials in such a way as to produce a series of four episodes in which Lancelot is wounded—he is gashed in the thighs by Mador de la Porte (513), speared in the side by Bors (518), shot in the buttocks by the huntress (532), and cut severely in the hand as he tears out the bars of a window to Guenevere's bedroom (544)—climaxed by one in which he "searches" and heals wounds, thereby proving himself "the best knyghte of the world" (550.1).[2] Unquestionably the intent of the Urry story is, as Vinaver has observed, to show Lancelot at "the height of his glory" on the eve of "the catastrophe that was to put an end to Arthurian knighthood" *(Works,* p. 1591). But if Malory selected healing as the symbol of superior knighthood, did he

173

intend for Lancelot's four wounds to signify that his knighthood is wanting? That does indeed seem to be the implication of Lancelot's cut hand in the episode of the Cart. Blood from his hand discovered on Guenevere's sheets leads to Melyagaunt's charge that the queen had committed adultery with one of the wounded knights sleeping in her room; when Lancelot agrees to champion her despite his knowledge that the charge is essentially true, he is false to his vow to "take noo batails in a wrongful quarel" (92.35).[3]

Malory's purposeful use of what seems to be a conflicting pattern of symbolic imagery is understandable in the light of the texts from which he derived the imagery of wounds and healing. Despite the originality of the Urry story, Malory borrowed the association of healing with true knighthood, as well as other features of the tale, from the account of Lancelot's initiation as a knight in the French prose *Lancelot*.[4] Another influence making itself felt on the entire Tale of Lancelot and Guenevere is Malory's own Tale of the Sankgreal, in which true knights are associated with humility and healing and false ones with pride and being wounded. While the symbolic imagery thus strengthens one's impression of continuity between Malory's Grail story and its sequel, its principal effect is to point up an important discontinuity in the characterization of Lancelot, arising from two conflicting estimates of Lancelot's knightliness.

- I -

That Malory knew the prose *Lancelot* version of the knighting of Lancelot is clear from an allusion to it in his tale of the Poisoned Apple. After Lancelot's successful defense of Guenevere, Arthur thanks him for his service to himself and the queen, and Lancelot replies that he is obligated to serve them both because Arthur gave him the "hyghe ordre of knyghthode" and Guenevere on that same day sent him his sword, which he had lost (514.7-12). Vinaver notes that the speech has no parallel in the corresponding place in the *Mort Artu,* but that "the incident to which it refers is found in the first part of the *Lancelot* proper which Malory must have read, even though he did not use it as a model for any of his works." He goes on to summarize the relevant part of the knighting of Lancelot

(*Works*, p. 1599). Vinaver's considerable authority notwithstanding, there is solid evidence that the prose *Lancelot* episode was the model of Malory's tale of Urry. Malory made use of three features: a desperately wounded knight is brought to Arthur's court as the only possible source of help; Lancelot provides the succour requested; and Lancelot embodies a religious conception of knighthood.

The most important idea Malory borrowed is the demonstration of Lancelot's Christian knighthood through his ability to heal. In the French work, when Lancelot announces at age eighteen that he wishes to become a knight, the Lady of the Lake instructs him in the origin, nature, and purposes of knighthood and describes the moral symbolism of the knight's armor. The instruction is standard, corresponding closely, for example, with the ideas in Raymon Lull's perennial treatise, *Libro del orde de cavalleria* (ca. 1300), translated from a French version by Caxton as *The Book of the Ordre of Chyualry* (1484).[5] The author of the prose *Lancelot* stresses the religious nature of knighthood in several ways. The chief purpose of the knight is to defend Holy Church: "cheualiers fu establis outreement por sainte eglize garandir."[6] The knight's armor and even his steed symbolize this commitment.[7] The chief moral requisites for knighthood, expressed in the Lady of the Lake's doctrine of the knight's "two hearts," reflect Christian values:

> Cheualiers doit avoir . ij . cuers . lun dur & serei autresi com aimant . & lautre mol & ploiant autresi comme cyre caude . Chil qui est durs com aymans . doit estre encontre les desloiaus & les felons . Car autresi com li aymans ne sueffre nul polissement . autresi doit estre li cheualiers fel & cruex vers les felons qui droiture depechent & empirent a lor pooirs . Et autresi com la cyre mole & caude puet estre flequie & menee la ou on le veut mener . Autresi doiuent les boines gens & les pitex mener le cheualier a tous les poins qui apartienent a debonna[i]rete & a douchor.[8]

It is important to see Lancelot's act of healing in the French source as an expression of the compassion (the "soft" heart) of the true Christian knight. The circumstances are as follows: just prior to Lancelot's own arrival at Arthur's court, a knight with two lance heads in his body and a sword embedded in his skull is brought before Arthur as he is hunting in the forest. He declares that if he is to find aid anywhere it will be at the court of Arthur, "le millor roi que soit" (Sommer, III, 120). He requires someone capable not only of removing the weapons from his body but also of avenging him against all who love his attacker better than they do him. Arthur regards the request as foolish and dissuades all his knights from attempting to aid him, as the task could not be accomplished even by thirty knights (Sommer, III, 120). The king does allow the knight to be installed in his palace. Lancelot spies him there on the eve of the day appointed for his being knighted, St. John's Day, and, upon hearing of his need, immediately vows to aid him. Ywain cautions him that he has vowed to undertake what twenty knights could not perform; he adds that Lancelot, not yet a knight, should not dream of undertaking a task even an experienced knight would not attempt (Sommer, III, 126-27). After receiving the accolade the next day, Lancelot leaves the church, goes directly to the knight, swears to revenge him according to his request, and removes the weapons from his body. Rebuked for his folly by Ywain, Lancelot replies that he did what he did "car ien avoie si grant pitie que plus ne pooie souffrir sa grant mesaise."[9] The point of the healing, then, is to manifest a major virtue of knighthood, compassion. Lancelot subsequently shows he has the "hard" heart of justice in volunteering to rescue the Lady of Nohaut from the King of Northumberland (Sommer, III, 129-30).

The religious quality of Lancelot's knightliness is heightened by the French author's foreshadowing of Galahad, who as healer of the Maimed King is analogous to Christ as the Divine Physician.[10] Lancelot is knighted on St. John's Day because he is analogous to John the Baptist,[11] as the Lady of the Lake explains:

Et diex que de la viergene nasqui por son peuple rachater . autresi com messires saint Iehans fu li plus haus hons de gueredon & de merite qui onques en feme fu concheus par carnel assamblement . que autresi vous doinst il le don que vous puisies trespasser de bonte & de cheualerie tous les cheualiers que ore sont.[12]

The implication is that one is to come later (as Christ followed the Baptist) who is to surpass even Lancelot, and that could only be Galahad.[13]

In transferring the healing scene from a point prior to Galahad's birth to a point after his death, Malory eliminated the typological link. Lancelot approximates his son as healer, rather than foreshadowing him. Malory actually heightens Lancelot's eminence in a religious sense, in giving him the power of direct healing by "searching" wounds. In the *Lancelot*, the removal of lance heads and sword is not a miraculous act in itself. Lancelot removes the weapons with great delicacy and skill, "si douchement . . . que li cheualiers nen sent se moult poi non" (Sommer, III, 127), but the knight still requires the aid of a physician.

The circumstances of the healing are different as well, although Malory keeps the basic plot. Urry, a knight of Hungary, had been wounded in single combat by Alpheus, a Spanish knight slain by Urry. In revenge for his death, his enchantress mother had cast a spell so that Urry would not be whole until "the best knyghte of the world had serched his woundes" (549.24-25). Malory eliminates the complication of the vow to fight all the friends of the knight who had inflicted the wounds, and in so doing simplifies the nature of the test. In the *Lancelot*, it is partially a test of courage, and there is an element of self-sacrifice as well; in reply to Ywain's ridicule, Lancelot replies that "moult est ore miex que ie mure en cheste besoigne se morir i doi. que chis cheualiers qui est espoir de grant proece."[14] Malory also makes the "best knight of the world" motif explicit; the closest the French work comes to Malory's formula is Ywain's assertion that Lancelot is a fool "car il a chaiens des millors cheualiers del monde qui entremetre ne sen voloient."[15]

Malory's most significant change is to focus on humility, rather than compassion, as Lancelot's primary virtue. Arriving at court after all the other knights have failed to heal Urry, Lancelot initially refuses to "presume vpon me to encheue that alle ye, my lordes, myghte not encheue" (552.39-40). Lancelot avoids vainglory as well as presumption; when Arthur commands him to make the attempt, he replies that he cannot refuse his lord's command but adds: "wete yow wel, I wold not take vpon me to touche that wounded knyghte in that entente that I shold passe alle other knyghtes. Ihesu defende me from that shame" (553.3-4). Arthur makes it easier for Lancelot by saying that he is to do it not for presumption but for fellowship. Lancelot's humility appears again when he prays that he may be able to help Urry, adding that "neuer was I able in worthynes to doo so hyghe a thynge." When he finally kneels to make the attempt, he prays silently to the Trinity that "Thow mayst yeue power to hele this seke knyghte by Thy grete vertu and grace of The, but good Lord, neuer of myself" (553.19-21). Having healed Urry, Lancelot "wepte as he had ben a child that had ben beten" (553.29), apparently overwhelmed that he had been graced beyond what he considers to be his merit.[16]

Lancelot's humility might be viewed as being apart from or transcendent of his knighthood, but the pattern of the prose *Lancelot*, in which the act of healing symbolizes his possession of a central virtue of knighthood, suggests otherwise. Malory substitutes humility for compassion, but we are to understand Lancelot's act of healing as a confirmation of his *knightly* virtue, as in the source. He is "the best knight of the world" in part because of his humility. Lancelot's standing as a knight is the focus of the entire episode.

The catalogue of knights bears on Lancelot's worship as a knight just as directly as does his act of healing. It cannot be simply a list of those who attempt to heal Urry and fail, for many of those mentioned are not present, and some are dead. Nor is Malory's main purpose narrative recapitulation, a recollection of the "halcyon days" of the Round Table, as Edmund Reiss has suggested.[17] Mark Lambert has seen that the list mainly conveys the objective fact and "measurability" of knightliness.[18] I would add only that the chief standard or measure is the familiar "order of worship," which Malory brings to mind here through references to Gareth, Lamerok, and Tristram—the fourth, third, and second best knights:

> Thenne cam in Syr Agrauayne, Syr Gaherys, Syr Mordred, and the good knyght Sir Gareth, that was of veray knyghthode worth al the brethren.
> . . . Syre Lamorak, the moost noblest knyght one that euer was in Arthurs dayes . . .
> . . . There was neuer none so bewailed as was Syre Tristram and syr Lamorak. . . .   (550-51)

A few pages earlier, Malory writes that Lancelot fought Gareth without recognizing him and thought, "for and Syr Tristram de Lyones outher Syr Lamorak de Galys had been alyue, Syr Launcelot wold haue demed he had ben one of them tweyne" (535.25-26). In the Tale of Sir Gareth, Lancelot had fought Gareth to a draw before knighting him; in the tournament at the end of the tale, Lamerok overcame thirty knights the first day to win the honors; on the second day, Tristram defeated forty, and on the third day, Lancelot defeated fifty. The list, then, is intended to suggest Lancelot's traditional standing as the supreme knight. Even though absent, he is mentioned four times (550-51), and when he arrives, it is obvious that the healing of Urry has been reserved for him.

Evidently, for Malory healing, humility, and supremacy as a knight are all associated. The prose *Lancelot* explains everything but Malory's emphasis upon humility, rather than compassion, as the chief virtue of the knight. Malory would have found a strong recommendation of humility as a knightly virtue in Lull's treatise, assuming that he knew it.[19] Or, if one assumes that Malory associated the healing motif with St. Augustine's "Christus Medicus" image, he would have found support there for a connection between healing and humility, as humility is the principal moral lesson behind the metaphor.[20] However, one need not look beyond Malory's own Tale of the Sankgreal to understand why healing, humility, and true knighthood had for him an almost necessary connection.

- II -

In Malory's Sankgreal, humility and healing are repeatedly associated with true knighthood, and pride and wounding (or being wounded) with false knighthood.[21] Malory's two categories of knights correspond to the distinction between *cheualerie celestiale* and *cheualerie terrien* in his source, the *Queste del Saint Graal*. The author of the *Queste*, like the author of the *Lancelot*, portrays knighthood as a fully religious calling; for him the "celestial" knight is one who practices the virtues of knighthood, whereas the "earthly" knight does not.[22] Because Malory greatly reduced the doctrinal commentary he found in the *Queste*, thereby lessening the allegorical tendency of the Grail story, he seems much more concerned than the French author with literal knighthood. He distinguishes the two classes of knights most directly through hermits' comments on false knights—especially Melyas, Gawain, and Ector—and on Lancelot, who seen from different aspects falls into both classes.

The episode of Melyas is normative because it illustrates both the false knight, wounded for his pride, and the true knight, who heals. That the episode is intended to focus on knighthood is evident from Galahad's comment to the newly made knight, Melyas: "sythe that ye be come of kynges and quenes, now loketh that knyghthode be wel sette in yow, for ye oughte to be a myrrour vnto all chyualry" (438.16-18). Melyas, however, against Galahad's advice, presumes to undertake a path at a fork in the road forbidden except to "A GOOD MAN AND A WORTHY KNYGHTE" (438.28-29), and he is soon wounded severely by another knight. Galahad removes the truncheon of a spear from his side and carries him to "an olde monke whiche somtyme had ben a knyghte," who both heals Melyas and gives him the medicine of spiritual counsel:

> And I merueylle . . . how ye durst take vpon yow soo ryche a thynge as the hyghe ordre of knyghthode withoute clene confession, and that was the cause ye were bytterly wounded. For the way on the ryght hand betokeneth the hyghe way of our Lord Ihesu Cryste, and the way of a true good lyuer, and the other wey betokeneth the way of synners and of mysbyleuers. And whanne the deuylle sawe your pryde and presumpcyon for to take yow in the quest of the Sancgreal, that made you to be ouerthrowen, for hit may not be encheued but by vertuous lyuynge. (439.37-440.4)

The hermit clearly understands knighthood itself to be sacred. Melyas is called proud and sinful for entering the "hyghe ordre of knyghthode" without confession as well as for entering the Quest in a sinful state.

Of the major characters in the *Morte Darthur*, Gawain is the chief examplar of the proud knight. Like Melyas, he is presumptuous in attempting to withdraw the sword of Balin intended for "THE BEST KNYGHT OF THE WORLD" (429.11). As Lancelot warns, he is severely wounded for that offense later, when Galahad "smote hym soo hard that he claf his helme and the coyfe of yron vnto his hede" (481.16-17), effectively eliminating Gawain from the Quest.

Wounding others inadvertently is another indicator of the false knight, and Gawain is punished with such an act when he kills his cousin and sworn brother Uwayne les Avoutres (466). The hermit Nacyen makes it clear that Uwayne's death is a divine judgment upon Gawain. Interpreting Gawain's vision of the 150 black and white bulls, he explains that the three white bulls who remained grazing in the meadow of "humylyte and pacyence" were the Grail knights, adding that the Round Table was founded that these two virtues might prosper. The black bulls which departed from the pasture are those who, like Gawain, entered the Quest without confession. The waste land into which they wander represents death, *"Eueryche of them shalle slee other for synne"* (467.30; my italics). Nacyen chastises Gawain and Ector for being "knyghtes of poure feythe and of wycked byleue," and he calls Gawain "an vntrue knyghte and a grete murtherer" (468.19, 27-28).

If in Melyas and Gawain we see the association of false knighthood with pride and wounds in opposition to the three true Grail knights, Lancelot, paradoxically, falls into both categories. Lancelot is humble in refusing to attempt Balin's sword, but once the Quest is underway he appears as the vainglorious and presumptuous knight. In his first adventure Lancelot finds himself unable to enter a richly furnished chapel; he lies down to rest, and half-waking and half-asleep sees a sick knight carried in a litter into the chapel to the altar. When the knight expresses his longing to be cured, the Grail Vessel appears, the knight touches and kisses the Vessel, and he is made "hole." Lancelot tries to approach the Vessel, but he is "ouertaken with synne" and cannot rise (444.35). The healed knight and his squire observe that Lancelot must have unconfessed sins on his soul, and they take his helmet, sword, and horse with them. When fully awake, Lancelot says:

> my synne and my wyckednes haue brought me vnto grete dishonour. For whanne I soughte worldly aduentures for worldly desyres, I euer encheued them and had the better in euery place, and neuer was I dicomfyt in no quarel, were it ryght or wronge. And now I take vpon me the aduentures of holy thynges, and now I see and vnderstande that myn olde synne hyndereth me and shameth me.   (445.18-23)

This might sound as if Malory is distinguishing between "secular" and "celestial" chivalry, but he is not. "Worldly aduentures for worldly desyres" is not "secular" knighthood, but false knighthood, equatable with a condition of pride. An old hermit explains to Lancelot that he is guilty of the same error as Melyas: "presumpcyon to take vpon you in dedely synne for to be in His presence" (implying that Christ was present in the Grail Vessel).

Lancelot is then moved to confess his long-concealed adultery, but his chief sin is vainglory, not adultery:[23]

> and alle my grete dedes of armes that I haue done I dyd for the moost party for the quenes sake, and for her sake wold I doo batail, were hit ryght or wronge. And neuer dyd I bataille alle only for Goddes sake, but for to wynne worshyp and to cause me to be the better biloued, and lytel or noughte thanked God of hit.   (446.11-15)

He has not violated any special requirement of "heavenly" chivalry, but the first requirement of all knights, that they serve God and the right. Significantly, the hermit enjoins him to "ensure me" that he will refrain as much as he can from the queen's company (446.16); and Lancelot, in taking leave, promises "neuer to be so wycked as I haue ben, but as to folowe knyghthode and to do fetys of armes." The hermit then "ioyned Syr Launcelot suche penaunce as he myghte doo, and to sewe knyghthode" (447.8-10). The close verbal association of penance and knighthood implies that they are complementary means to salvation. Since penance is an expression of humility, the scene implies the same close affinity between humility and knighthood which appears in the Urry episode.

Pride is a motif in later adventures of Lancelot—in his vision of Galahad, himself, and their forbears[24]—and in the tournament of the black and white knights. In the latter, Malory emphasizes Lancelot's vainglory more than does the author of the *Queste*. In both versions, Lancelot joins the black knights because they are getting the worst of the battle; Malory adds that Lancelot joined them "for to helpe there the weyker party in encrecynge of his chyualry" (462.5-6). In the hermit's allegorical commentary on Lancelot's behavior in the French version, Lancelot is said to have joined the black knights because he, like them, was in mortal sin (Sommer, VI, 102-03). Malory's hermit says he did so for "bobaunce and pryde of the world." He adds a comment not in the *Queste*, that the adventure was intended "that thow sholdest knowe good from euylle and vayne glory of the world, the whiche is not worth a pere. And for grete pryde thou madest grete sorow that thou haddest not ouercome alle the whyte knyghtes" (463.20-22). As Lancelot is leaving, the hermit reminds him to beware "of thy vayne glory and of thy pryde" (463.27).

For having previously been a proud, false, knight, Lancelot is stricken into a coma-like sleep after he charges into the Grail chamber, having been warned not to enter (496). The coma is the equivalent of the symbolic wounds Gawain and Melyas experience; it is clearly retributive, as it lasts twenty-four days—one day, we are told, for each year he had lived in unconfessed adultery with Guenevere.[25]

But Lancelot also appears as the true knight insofar as he confesses his sins and does penance. The hermit, Nacyen, comments on his humility in interpreting Ector's vision. In that vision, Lancelot alights out of a chair and leaps upon two horses, one of which says to the other, "go we seke that we shal not fynde" (465.17). Then a man despoils Lancelot of his armor, clothes him in garments full of knots, seats him upon an ass, and takes him to the fairest well ever seen. When Lancelot alights and tries to drink from the well, the water sinks away from him, whereupon he returns to the place he had been when the adventures of the vision began. Ector dreams further of himself coming to a "ryche mans hows" where a wedding feast was in progress, but in which he was not permitted to join (465). Nacyen interprets the vision as follows: Lancelot and Ector both came from one chair, which signifies "maistership and lordshyp" (i.e., by virtue of their being brothers and of noble birth). But the horses represent Gawain and Ector, who "seke that [they] shalle neuer fynde," that is, the Holy Grail. Lancelot's fall from the horse means that he "hath left pryde and taken hym to humylyte. For he hath cryed mercy lowde for his synne and sore repented hym, and our Lorde hath clothed hym in his clothyng whiche is ful of knottes, that is the hayre that he weryth dayly" (467.37-40). The ass he rides on "betokeneth mekenes" (468.2). Nacyen goes on to contrast Lancelot with Ector and Gawain. As sinful as Lancelot had formerly been, he has not killed anyone during the Quest, whereas Gawain has; the reason is that Lancelot "hath taken vpon hym for to forsake synne. And nere were that he nys not stable, but by his thoughte he is lykely to torne ageyne, he shold be nexte to encheue it, sauf Galahad, his sone" (468.31-33).

While Lancelot's present humility and repentance place him among the true knights (along with Galahad, Percival, and Bors), we have also seen the appropriateness of the "wound" he receives as punishment for his former vainglory and presumption. The ultimate development of this dual view of Lancelot appears in the Tale of Lancelot and Guenevere.

- III -

Although the Sankgreal may be Malory's earliest and least polished tale,[26] it appears to have shaped definitively his conception of Lancelot. Consistent with the pattern of the Sankgreal, Malory intends the succession of wounds Lancelot receives in the first four episodes of the Lancelot and Guenevere to mark a gradual falling off from the true knightliness he had attained during the Quest through confession and repentance. In the beginning of the first episode, that of the Poisoned Apple, we learn that Lancelot had forgotten "the promyse and the perfectyon that he made in the quest," and that he and the queen now "loued togyder more hotter" than ever previously (506.9-13). Lancelot recognizes that the standards of Christian knighthood are still binding, as he observes them in everything but his relation to Guenevere. We are reminded that he would have surpassed all others in the Quest had he not been "so sette inwardly to the quene as he was in semyng outeward to God" (506.10-11). The same duality is evident now. He answers the bequests of many ladies and damsels "for the pleasyr of oure Lord Ihesu Crist," but he withdraws from Guenevere's company as much as possible only to avoid "sklaunder and noyse" (506.18-20). Lancelot has reserved this one area of his life apart from his obligations to God and knighthood.[27] Eventually his integrity as a knight suffers, as if by a malignancy spreading through the body.

In his first defense of Guenevere against Mador de la Porte's accusation of murder, Lancelot, objectively considered, serves the cause of justice and appears as the true knight, for the queen is not guilty. Even here Lancelot's motivation is called into question by his reply to Arthur's expression of gratitude for Lancelot's extraordinary devotion to both himself and his queen. Lancelot states that he had undertaken to serve the queen from the time that he was first made knight "in ryghte outher in wronge" (514.12), implying that he had defended Guenevere without regard to the justice of her cause. In the Sankgreal Lancelot had confessed this absolute commitment to Guenevere as his chief offense against knighthood and as an example of vainglory: "and for her sake wold I doo batail, were hit ryght or wronge. And neuer dyd I bataille alle only for Goddes sake, but for to wynne worshyp and to cause me to be the better biloued" (446.12-14). In view of the symbolism of wounds in the Quest, the severe wound in the thighs Lancelot suffers in judicial combat with Mador de la Porte (513) can readily be seen as a judgment upon the impurity of his motive.

The wound Lancelot receives in the second episode, that of the Fair Maid of Astolat, is explicitly interpreted as a result of pride. The pride motif, together with the presence of this tale of a former knight turned healer and hermit, carries with it an echo of the Grail Quest. For the tournament at Winchester Lancelot wears the red sleeve of the Maid of Astolat in order that he not be identified by his kinsmen, as it was well known that Lancelot never wore the love token of any woman. In the melee, Bors smites through Lancelot's shield and strikes a grievous wound in his side; his spear breaks, leaving the "truncheon" in the wound. He is "so sore yhurte that he wende there to haue had his dethe" (519.6). Despite his pain, Lancelot manages later to unhorse Bors and comes near to slaying him, until he recognizes him, and he goes on to do "the merueyloust dedes of armes that euer man sawe or herde speke of" (519.20). His companion, Lavayne, plays the role Lancelot himself had played in the prose *Lancelot*; he extracts the truncheon from Lancelot's side, and he takes him, near death, to "a gentyl heremyte that somtyme was a fulle noble knyghte and a grete lord of possessions." This is Bawdwyn of Bretayne, "a ful noble surgeon and a good leche" (520.11-14).

Bawdwyn, recognizing Lancelot from an old wound on his cheek, salutes him as "the moost noblest knyghte of the world" (521.5), but this is not Malory's own judgment. Guenevere, hearing of Lancelot's wound, scoffs at his suffering at Bors' hands a rebuke to his "pryde and bobaunce" (523.38), repeating a verbal formula of the Sankgreal. Although Guenevere is speaking from her jealousy of the Maid of Astolat and probably hiding her true feelings, Lancelot nevertheless later confesses the same fault. Bors seeks him out to apologize for wounding him, but Lancelot takes the blame upon himself. Bors would never have injured him had Lancelot not deliberately kept his identity secret by wearing the Maid's sleeve; and he had disguised his identity so as to be able to fight against the Round Table, thereby winning the greater honor:

> I wold with pryde haue ouercome yow alle. And there in my pryde I was nere slayne, and that was in myn own defaute, for I myghte haue gyue yow warnyng of my beynge there, and thenne had I had noo hurte.   (525.21-23)

While Malory's next episode, the Assumption Day tournament at Winchester, is original, he takes care to fit it into the sequence of his Tale of Lancelot and Guenevere. R. M. Lumiansky has noted the careful attention to chronological development.[28] A sense of continuity is gained also by the repetition of the love-token motif; when Arthur announces the tournament at Winchester, Guenevere orders Lancelot to wear *her* golden sleeve so that he will not be mistaken by his kinsmen, a clear allusion to the tournament in the previous episode, when Lancelot wore the red sleeve of the Maid of Astolat. While the wound Lancelot receives in this episode is less serious in itself than the previous one, there is a sense of development in that he shows less moral awareness than he did previously. He has no idea that this wound has moral significance, although it clearly does. Reiss observes that the lady huntress who shoots an arrow into Lancelot's buttocks as he sleeps beside a well is a Diana figure. Malory states that she lives in a forest and is never accompanied by men, but only by women. Since Diana is a goddess of chastity, the "barayne hynde" she is hunting when her arrow by accident hits Lancelot stands for Guenevere, with a glance at the fact that her love for Lancelot violates the medieval subordination of love to procreation. The wound "acts as an *exemplum* to Lancelot who had been spiritually sleeping. Lancelot, failing to see any *sententia*, however, curses the lady: 'The devyll made you a shoter!'"[29]

In Reiss's view the episode implies that Lancelot is to be punished for Guenevere's sins, as the hind and not Lancelot was the huntress's target, but one can also see the wound as a judgment upon and warning to Lancelot. The parallels with the previous episode highlight Lancelot's growing moral blindness. Lavayne repeats his role in the episode of the Maid of Astolat—he extracts the arrow from Lancelot's wound and carries him to "the hermytage" (probably Bawdwyn's) to be healed. Whereas formerly Lancelot had blamed himself for pride, he sees no lesson here; he only exclaims: "A, mercy, Ihesu . . . I may calle myself the moost vnhappyest man that lyueth, for euer whan I wold faynest haue worshyp, there falleth me euer somme vnhappy thyng" (533.12-14). Another difference is that, while Lancelot takes the honors in this tournament as in the previous one, it is Gareth and not Lancelot who is singled out as the ideal knight. Lancelot fights against the Round Table, presumably for the same motive as he had in the first tournament, to win the greater honor. Arthur's praise of Gareth contains an implicit judgment of Lancelot. Gareth had fought on Lancelot's side, but not to win honor; rather, so as not to see "a worshipful man shamed." His actions also manifest charity: "always a good man wille doo euer to another man as he wold ben done to hymself" (537.4).[30] Malory has Lancelot appear at the tournament in the guise of a Saracen (533), a possible symbol of his falling away from the standards of Christian chivalry. The Winchester tournament leads naturally into the episode of the Cart.

Vinaver did not appreciate that Malory had deliberately modified the *sen* of Chrétien's tribute to courtly love to fit the pattern he develops from the beginning of Book XVIII. The entire sequence is focused on Lancelot's decline from true knighthood, and Malory uses all the important details of the episode toward that end.

Melyagaunt is no longer significant only because his abduction of Guenevere motivates Lancelot's cart ride; Malory uses him to reiterate the theme of fallen knighthood. Although because of his treachery we initially recognize him as Lancelot's opposite, by the end of the tale we perceive an important resemblance.[31] Melyagaunt's abduction of the queen is contrary to everything he pretends to believe in as a knight:

> Traytoure knyghte, sayd Quene Gueneuer, what cast thou for to doo? Wolte thow shame thyself? Bethynke the how thou arte a kynges sone, and knyghte of the Table Round, and thou to be aboute to dishonoure the noble kynge that made the knyghte; thow shamest alle knyghthode and thyselfe.   (539.23-26)

Eventually we understand that these same charges are appropriate to Lancelot as well: as an adulterer with Arthur's queen, he shames both knighthood and himself, and he further shames knighthood when he defends Guenevere in a cause known to be bad. It is ironic that even Melyagaunt can give Lancelot good advice about a knight's duty:

> I rede yow beware what ye do, for though ye are neuer so good a knyght, as ye wote wel ye ar renomed the best knyght of the world, yet shold ye be aduysed to do batail in a wrong quarel, for God wil haue a stroke in euery batail.   (545.34-36).

Of course, God's stroke has already fallen in the form of the torn hand which exposed the adultery to Melyagaunt and revealed Lancelot's fallen knighthood to the reader.

The tribute to Lancelot as "beste knyghte of the worlde," together with the humility motif evident in Lancelot's cart ride, might suggest that Malory intends to parallel Lancelot's humility in love with the religious humility he exhibits in the Urry episode. But this is not the case. The cart ride is an appropriate shaming of Lancelot, not a sign of his humility. The appropriateness is clear from the circumstances giving rise to the cart ride. Having abducted Guenevere, Melyagaunt learns of her sending a messenger to Lancelot and sets an ambush for him. Lancelot of course answers Guenevere's call for help, and the ambushers succeed in wounding his horse so severely that he must go on foot. He takes refuge in a forest, where he encounters two of Melyagaunt's carters who have been sent to gather wood.[32] When Lancelot demands that the carters convey him immediately to the castle, one refuses. Lancelot strikes him with a backward blow of his gauntlet and *kills him*. The other carter is frightened into compliance (542). The scene shifts to the castle, where Guenevere's companion, peering out a window, spies a cart carrying a knight. She surmises that he "rydeth vnto hangyng." Guenevere, recognizing her lover, angrily rebukes her: "Hit was fowle mouthed . . . and euylle lykened, soo for to lyken *the moost noble knyght of the world* vnto suche a shameful dethe. O Ihesu defende hym and kepe hym . . . from alle mescheuous ende" (542.19-27; italics mine). Having just read of Lancelot's rash slaying of the carter, the reader does not see him as "the moost noble knyght of the world." In the Sankgreal, inadvertent manslaughter was one means of identifying false knights, and so it is here. Malory's point is that once Melyagaunt and Lancelot allow themselves to be led by appetite and corrupted will, such unknightly behavior is inevitable.

The cart ride, then, with its associations of criminality and shameful death, reflects the condition of Lancelot's knighthood. Lancelot's wounded horse, which follows the cart treading "his guttes and his paunche vnder his feet" (542.21), may be a parallel symbol to the cart ride itself. (The wounded horse is another of Malory's inventions, as in the prose *Lancelot* the horse is killed in the ambush.) Malory may have remembered the symbolism of the horse from the Lady of the Lake's explanation to Lancelot of the symbols of knighthood; the knight's steed represents the people, to whom the knight is to be guide and father (Sommer, III, 115). The gutted horse would represent Lancelot's violation of that duty in his rash killing of the unarmed carter.

The question, finally, is why Malory sets up a sequence of episodes united by the motif of Lancelot's wounds as a means of depicting Lancelot's deterioration as a knight, only to follow that sequence with an episode in which Lancelot appears as the ideal Christian knight/physician. Lumiansky, E. M. Bradstock, and Beverly Kennedy find ways of reconciling the episode of the Cart with the healing of Urry. Lumiansky's solution is to interpret the phrase "the best knight of the world" to mean "the best of all worldly knights," as distinct from the "spiritual" knights of the Grail; there is thus no inconsistency between Lancelot's healing of Urry and his "limitations as a spiritual knight" by reason of the recommenced adultery.[33] But the idea of a secular knighthood distinct from a religious one is not valid, as has been shown above; the conception of knighthood in the Urry episode is essentially religious, as it is in the source, the prose *Lancelot* account of Lancelot's initiation into knighthood, and in Malory's own Sankgreal.

Bradstock follows Lumiansky in believing that the episode of the Cart indicates Lancelot's resumption of his adulterous relationship with the queen, but argues that the healing of Urry reveals a conversion:

> In the juxtaposition of these two episodes . . . we have in fact a juxtaposition of the two loyalties which dominate Lancelot's life. It is an externalization of the two forces at war within him, and a reminder that his old love has the power to revive itself and destroy Lancelot's efforts towards salvation. There is no further evidence of adultery following the grace bestowed upon

Lancelot in "The Healing of Sir Urry." The quality of his love appears to change. But Malory's inclusion of "The Knight of the Cart" demonstrates forcibly that Lancelot's rejection of Guenevere was not an easy or instantaneously effected decision.[34]

Bradstock's interpretation avoids Lumiansky's error of ignoring the religious implications of Lancelot's healing of Urry, but it lacks adequate textual support. One might infer from Lancelot's humility and from the divine favor he receives that he has sincerely repented of the adultery with the queen, but the text of the tale says nothing at all about his relationship with Guenevere. One must therefore look to the subsequent narrative for evidence of Lancelot's supposed repentance, and I cannot agree that there is "no further evidence of adultery following the grace bestowed upon Lancelot."

Immediately following the Urry episode, the Morte proper begins with Agravain charging that "Sire Launcelot lyeth dayly and nyghtly by the quene" (555.14). Gawain will not countenance Agravain's detraction, but significantly he does not deny the truth of his charges. In narrating the scene in which the lovers are trapped in Guenevere's bedroom, Malory could have said flatly that the lovers were not in bed together, but he says rather that he does not know whether they were. The implication is that he would like to have said the meeting was innocent, but that he could not do so given that it was arranged after Arthur's absence from the court was announced, it is a secret meeting, and it is held at night in the queen's bedroom. Furthermore, even if one were to accept Kennedy's argument that the meeting is sexually innocent,[35] that is not enough to bring Lancelot back to the religious heights of the Urry episode. Lancelot is not simply required to avoid acts of physical adultery. What he must do as a knight is "fyrst reserue the honour to God, and secondly the quarel must come of thy lady" (537.26-27). He had confessed during the Grail Quest his inability to do that: he had served Guenevere "in ryghte outher in wronge," and it was this failing that marked him as an untrue knight. He makes the same commitment in the bedroom scene, even as Agravain and Mordred pound on the door of the queen's room: "I neuer fayled yow in ryghte nor in wrong sythen the fyrst day Kynge Arthur made me knyghte" (558.18-19). The defense of Guenevere has always been an absolute good, and remains so. He is in effect saying that he would defend her now even if she were in the wrong—as, indeed, I believe the text shows her to be. This, then, is the fallen Lancelot of the Cart episode, not the ideal Christian knight who heals Urry. To argue that it is the same Lancelot throughout is to make his "repentance" so short-lived as to imply that he is ridiculously inconstant. Thus, as desirable as it would be to reconcile the episode of the Cart with the healing of Urry, the text does not support doing so. The Urry episode cannot be understood as part of a pattern of cause-and-effect development.[36]

The pattern of four wounds followed by a miraculous healing corresponds to and restates the double view of Lancelot developed in the Sankgreal, but without resolving it in a way that makes sense according to modern conceptions of character. Malory leaves us with two Lancelots. Committed to Guenevere in right or wrong, Lancelot perverts his gifts as a knight and is not only a false knight, but in some sense the worst of knights, given his potential for good. Insofar as, apart from that destructive relationship, Lancelot was the true knight originally, was again temporarily during the Quest, and will be again after his final renunciation of Guenevere, he is "the best knight of the world." Even at the end, the double view of Lancelot appears: he confesses to have "layed ful lowe" both Arthur and Guenevere through "my defaute and myn orgule and my pryde" (597.26-27); yet he was for Ector the "hede of al Crysten knyghtes" (599.5).

Malory does not blench from Lancelot's failings as a knight; if anything, he even exaggerates them through his modifications of the *Mort Artu* in his Tale of Lancelot and Guenevere. But he seems to insist that the real and essential Lancelot is the ideal one. The vindication of his knighthood in Urry is especially important because this tale leads directly into the events from which the final calamity flows. Malory suggests that whatever part Lancelot has in the disaster, his knightly character remains intact. Essence and existence, character and deeds, seem to be separable and discontinuous.[37]

The disjunction between the two Lancelots calls into question the traditional understanding of Malory's vision as being essentially tragic. The pathos of tragedy can result only from a conception of character and deeds as being aspects of the same reality, as with Tennyson's Lancelot:

> "But in me lived a sin
> So strange, of such a kind, that all of pure,
> Noble, and knightly in me twined and clung
> Round that one sin, until the wholesome flower
> And poisonous grew together, each as each,
> Not to be plucked asunder."
>
> ("The Holy Grail," ll. 769-774)

But Malory plucks asunder the sin and the nobility in his Tale of Lancelot and Guenevere, and the pathos arising from the perception of wasted goodness is considerably lessened. Malory's vision is revealed as being didactic, rather than tragic. He seems to share Caxton's view, that the *Morte Darthur*'s purpose is that

> noble men may see and lerne the noble actes of chyualrye, the ientyl and vertuous dedes that somme knyghtes vsed in tho dayes, by whyche they came to honour, and how they that were vycious were punysshed and ofte put to shame and rebuke.
>
> (2.36-39)

Having decided that Lancelot was to be "the hede of al Crysten knightes," Malory felt the need to show him in possession of the virtues of knighthood even when his actions reveal that he is not. If Malory's moral purpose required sacrificing his story's finer tragic implications, he was prepared to do so.

University of North Carolina
at Greensboro

NOTES

[1] Eugène Vinaver, ed., *The Works of Sir Thomas Malory*, 3 vols., 2nd ed. (Oxford: Oxford University Press, 1967; rpt. 1973), 1585-94. Also see Larry D. Benson, *Malory's Morte Darthur* (Cambridge, Mass.: Harvard University Press, 1976), pp. 223-34; E. M. Bradstock, "The Juxtaposition of the 'Knight of the Cart' and 'The Healing of Sir Urry,'" *Journal of the Australasian Universities Language and Literature Association*, 50 (1978), 208-23; D. S. Brewer, ed., *Malory: The Morte Darthur Parts Seven and Eight* (Evanston: Northwestern University Press, 1974), pp. 20-35; R. T. Davies, "The Worshipful Way in Malory," *Patterns of Love and Courtesy*, ed. John Lawlor (London: Edward Arnold, 1966), pp. 157-77; Beverly Kennedy, "Malory's Lancelot: 'Trewest Lover, of a Synful Man,'" *Viator*, 12 (1981),

411-56; Mark Lambert, *Malory: Style and Vision in Le Morte Darthur* (New Haven and London: Yale University Press, 1975), pp. 56-66; R. M. Lumiansky, "'The Tale of Lancelot and Guenevere': Suspense," *Malory's Originality: A Critical Study of Le Morte Darthur* (Baltimore: Johns Hopkins Press, 1964), pp. 222-32; Edmund Reiss, *Sir Thomas Malory* (New York: Twayne Publishers, Inc., 1966), pp. 165-72; Janet Wilson, "Lancelot and the Concept of Honor in the *Morte Darthur*, Parts VII and VIII," *Parergon*, 14 (1976), 23-31.

[2]All references to Malory's text are to *Caxton's Malory*, ed. James W. Spisak (Berkeley and Los Angeles: University of California Press, 1983).

[3]As Janet Wilson observes, "Lancelot," p. 26. She notes that later in the same episode Lancelot also violates the spirit of his vow to "gyue mercy vnto hym that asketh mercy" (92.32-33), when, at Guenevere's veiled hint, he refuses to grant Melyagaunt's plea for mercy, but instead encourages him to fight to his death by offering to continue partially disarmed and encumbered.

[4]H. Oskar Sommer, *The Vulgate Version of the Arthurian Romances*, 7 vols. (Washington: Carnegie Institute, 1909-13; rpt. New York: AMS Press, 1969), III, 112-32. Lancelot appears as healer in other episodes of the prose *Lancelot*, but the knighting episode is the *locus classicus* of the motif. P. E. Tucker, "A Source for the Healing of Sir Urry," *Modern Language Review*, 50 (1955), 490-92, argued that the source of the story was an episode in the Agravain section of *Lancelot* (Sommer's vol. V. pp. 224-28, 231, 254, 268-69, 275). A knight is wounded in the thigh by a damsel when he interrupts her as she is bathing at a fountain. Another damsel passing by tells the wounded knight he can only be healed by "the best knight of the world." Bradstock, "Juxtaposition," pp. 213-14, notes two earlier instances in the *Lancelot* of the same motif. In the first (Sommer's vol. IV, pp. 93-96), Lancelot succeeds in rescuing a knight from a coffer, a deed that only "*li mieldres cheauliers del monde*" could perform. The knight in question, Trahans, reveals to Lancelot that he is the knight from whom Lancelot had removed two spear-heads from his wounds at Arthur's court in his youth. Later in the same volume (pp. 279-82), Bors is told that a maimed knight he meets can only be healed by the best knight of the world, meaning Lancelot. Bradstock is unaware of the healing motif in the knighting of Lancelot episode; the knight, Trahans, whom Bradstock mentions, is the person Lancelot aids on the occasion of the knighting ceremony.

[5]Ed. Alfred T. P. Byles, E.E.T.S. O.S. 168 (London: Humphrey Milford, 1926).

[6]Sommer, III, 114. "Knighthood was established expressly to safeguard Holy Church." Compare Caxton, *Ordre*: "The office of a knyght is to mayntene and deffende the holy feyth catholyque" (p. 24).

[7]As the shield protects the knight from his foes, the knight must stand between Holy Church and the "robeur ou mescreant." The helmet, hauberk, and lancehead have a similar significance. The double-edged

sword signifies that the knight must fight off the enemies of God and his people. The sword's point represents obedience, and all must obey the knight. The horse which the knight rides represents his intimate relationship to the people. As the knight directs his horse, so the knight must be guide and even father to the people, defending the clergy, widows, orphans, tithes, and alms. In return, the people must maintain the knight materially, as the clergy must maintain him spiritually (Sommer, III, 113-15). Caxton's *Ordre*, pp. 76-89, provides a more imaginative and detailed symbolic commentary on the knight's armor.

[8] Sommer, III, 115-16. "The knight must have two hearts, the one hard and dense as a diamond, the other soft and pliant as softened wax. The one which is hard as a diamond must be set against the treacherous and false, because as the diamond cannot be worn smooth, so must the knight be fierce and harsh toward the caitiffs who destroy and tear down rectitude to the best of their ability. And as the soft and pliable wax is able to be bent and shaped as one wishes to shape it, so must the knight be to good persons and those in need in all particulars pertaining to graciousness and gentleness."

[9] Sommer, III, 128. "Because I have such great pity for him I am no longer able to tolerate his great suffering."

[10] Rudolph Arbesmann discusses this popular image of Christ in the writings of the Fathers, especially St. Augustine, in "The Concept of 'Christus Medicus' in St. Augustine," *Traditio*, 10 (1954), 1-28. The metaphor seems to have been well-known in England; it appears in *Piers Plowman: The B Version*, ed. George Kane and E. Talbot Donaldson (London: Athlone Press, 1975), XVI, 100-20, and in Caxton's account of Advent in *The Golden Legend*, ed. F. S. Ellis (London: J. M. Dent, 1900), I, 9-11.

[11] Pauline Matarasso, *The Redemption of Chivalry: A Study of the Queste del Saint Graal* (Geneva: Librarie Droz, 1979), p. 115, takes note of this analogy, but does not comment on it.

[12] Sommer, III, 118. "And God—who was born of a virgin in order to redeem his people, just as Saint John was the most highly favored and meritorious man ever conceived carnally—may He now likewise give you the gift that you shall surpass in goodness and in chivalry all the knights now alive."

[13] The position of St. John's feast within the Church and seasonal calendar is suggestive of his role as a type of Christ. S. Baring-Gould cites a sermon by St. Augustine on the Nativity of St. John, June 24, in which Augustine notes that John is one of few saints whose principal feast is celebrated on his nativity rather than his death because he was sanctified while still in his mother's womb. Augustine sees the Nativity of John and the Nativity of Christ as having a symbolic connection within the yearly cycle. As John was born near the summer solstice, Christ was born at the winter solstice. Augustine interprets the Baptist's words, "He must increase,

but I must decrease" (John iii. 30), as a mystical reference to the seasonal relationship: "At the nativity of Christ the days increase in length, on that of John they decrease. When the Saviour of the world is born, the days lengthen; but when the last prophet comes into the world, the days suffer curtailment"—*The Lives of the Saints*, 3rd ed. (Edinburgh: John Grant, 1914), vol. 16, 332.

[14]Sommer, III, 128. "It is much better that I die now in this one's need, if die I must, than this knight who is capable of great prowess."

[15]Sommer, III, 128. "For there are here some of the best knights of the world who do not wish to involve themselves in it."

[16]For a summary of differing views of the significance of Lancelot's weeping, see Benson, *Malory's Morte Darthur*, p. 229.

[17]Reiss *(Malory*, pp. 170-71) says "This recounting is in effect a curtain call; and, by looking back Malory suggests that the great days are over."

[18]Lambert, *Malory*, p. 57.

[19]Lull, as translated by Caxton, writes: "And thenne yf a knyght in as moche as he is prowd mayntened chyualry / he corrupteth his ordre whiche was begonne by Iustyce and humylyte for to susteyne the humble ayenst the prowde / For yf hit were so knyghtes that now ben / shold not ben in that ordre in whiche they were fyrst knyghtes / But all the knyghtes now Iniuryous and prowd ful of wyckednesse be not worthy to Chyualrye / but oughten to be reputed for nought" (Caxton, *Ordre*, pp. 44-45).

[20]Arbesmann writes: "In ever-changing sketches he [Augustine] depicts Christ in the role of the Divine Physician, who by the medicine of His humility heals man from the festering wound of pride, which had caused humanity's fall, thus accomplishing the Redemption and inviting man to imitate Him in this virtue" ("Christus Medicus," p. 11).

[21]The dichotomy also appears in a major structural pattern Malory begins in the Tale of Balin. Balin, in his attempt to heal the rich man's wounded son, only wounds King Pellam (the "Maimed King") and brings about the Wasteland; Galahad, in the course of the Grail Quest, heals the Maimed King, thus appearing as the ideal knight/physician (502). The same contrast is brought out in the failure of Balin's female companion to cure a certain woman by the sacrifice of her own blood. Malory prophesies that Perceval's sister would provide the needed succour (73), a prophecy later fulfilled (491-93). Balin is not explicitly said to fail because of pride, but I believe that to be a valid inference; see my article, "Malory's 'Tale of Balin' Reconsidered," *Speculum*, 54 (1979), 90, 94-95.

[22]Vinaver prompted a major scholarly debate by suggesting that Malory kept the two chivalries of the *Queste*, but favored "secular" (Lancelot) over "heavenly" (Galahad). For a review of the resulting controversy see Charles G. Whitworth, "The Sacred and the Secular in Malory's 'Tale of the Sankgreall,'" *Yearbook of English Studies*, 5 (1975), 19-29; see also: G. R. Symes, "Chivalry and Malory's Quest of the Holy

Grail," *Parergon*, 17 (1977), 37-42, and Mary Hynes-Berry, "A Tale 'Brefly Drawne Oute of Freynshe,'" *Aspects of Malory*, ed. Toshiyuki Takamiya and Derek Brewer (Totowa, N.J.; Brewer and Rowman and Littlefield, 1981), pp. 93-116. All parties to the dispute err, I believe, in assuming that the author of the *Queste* meant to condemn regular knighthood under the category of "secular" knighthood. Careful reading will show that by a "secular" knight he means a sinful knight. Lancelot was a "celestial" (good) knight as long as he remained true to his original vows. See, for example, the anchoress's interpretation of Lancelot's tourneying with some black and white knights (Sommer, VI, 102-3) and the instructions a hermit gives Bors (Sommer, VI, 117). The problem in recognizing "celestial" knighthood as simply true knighthood is that the author of the *Queste* has slightly skewed the definition of knighthood as a religious calling which appears in the *Lancelot*, by adding monastic virtues, especially celibacy, to the virtues of knighthood, possibly under the influence of the Templar ideal (see Pauline Matarasso's preface to her translation, *The Quest of the Holy Grail* [London: Cox and Wykman, Ltd., 1969], pp. 20-21.) The unlikelihood that a medieval author would consciously formulate a conception of knighthood as a non-religious calling is clear from Carl Erdmann's discussion of the essentially religious nature of knighthood from the eleventh century onwards, in *The Origin of the Idea of the Crusade*, trans. Marshall W. Baldwin and Walter Gofart (Princeton: Princeton University Press, 1977), pp. 3-34.

[23] As Kennedy observes, "Malory's Lancelot," pp. 431-32.

[24] God, represented as an "old man," descends through the heavens in the company of angels and addresses the person in the vision who represents Lancelot: "I haue lost alle that I haue sette in the, for thou hast rulyd the ageynste me as a warryour and vsed wrong werres with vayne glory, more for the pleasyr of the world than to please me" (460.22-24).

[25] Earlier, the number of years is put at fourteen (446.8).

[26] As argued by Terence McCarthy, "Order of Composition in the 'Morte Darthur,'" *Yearbook of English Studies*, 1 (1971), 18-29, and "The Sequence of Malory's Tales," *Aspects of Malory*, pp. 107-24.

[27] Davies, "The Worshipful Way," p. 167, writes that "worldly and holy values appear to be confused" in the episode, but what we actually see are values in conflict: Lancelot has chosen to act contrary to his commitment to knighthood; Malory is quite clear on this point.

[28] *Malory's Originality*, p. 224.

[29] Reiss, *Malory*, pp. 166-68.

[30] I am indebted to Reiss, *Malory*, pp. 166-67, for this analysis of the tournament itself.

[31] As Reiss observes, *Malory*, p. 168.

[32] The carters are entirely Malory's invention, as are most of the other details of the episode; see Vinaver, *Works*, pp. 1592-96.

[33] Lumiansky, *Malory's Originality*, p. 231.

[34] Bradstock, "Juxtaposition," pp. 212-13. Kennedy ("Malory's Lancelot," pp. 439-41) argues similarly. She sees signs of repentance in Lancelot following the night he spent with Guenevere in Melyagaunt's castle; thus the divine favor that allows Lancelot to heal Urry is merited. But however pious Lancelot may act, he is defending Guenevere in a cause that is fundamentally bad, as Wilson argues (see note 3, above). He persists in this intention right up to the end of the Cart episode, when he fights and kills Melyagaunt. If the issue is Lancelot's integrity as a knight, what he must repent is his willingness to defend Guenevere "in right or wrong."

[35] Kennedy, "Malory's Lancelot," p. 442.

[36] This is an example to the contrary of Brewer's observation, which I believe is generally correct, that "the distinguishing mark of Malory's narrative . . . is its sequaciousness, its connectedness. One sentence leads to the next, one event to the next" *(Malory*, p. 21).

[37] Jill Mann sees a similar discontinuity in Malory's Balin; see "Taking the Adventure: Malory and the Suite du Merlin," *Aspects of Malory*, pp. 71-91. While Mann's description of this type of disjunctive characterization is insightful, I happen not to agree that Balin exemplifies it.

Malory's "Very Mater of La Cheualer du Charyot": Characterization and Structure

John Michael Walsh

For the last part of *Le Morte Darthur,* the section comprising Books XVIII to XXI in Caxton's version and designated in Eugène Vinaver's edition as the seventh and eighth tales,[1] Malory's chief sources were the Old French prose *La Mort le Roi Artu*[2] and the Middle English stanzaic *Le Morte Arthur.*[3] Book XIX, however, opens with an episode based instead on material from the *Lancelot.* This is the central part of the prose cycle of which *La Mort le Roi Artu* is the conclusion, and the whole cycle, the Vulgate or prose *Lancelot,* is named for this central part.[4] The interpolated episode is that of the Knight of the Cart.[5] It is followed in Malory's version by the story of Lancelot's miraculous healing of the wounded Sir Urry, for which there is no known source. It was at one time believed that Malory was not himself responsible for placing the Cart episode in this last phase of the story but was working from some version of *La Mort le Roi Artu* that already included it.[6] However, later studies have revised this uncomplimentary view of Malory's originality, and it is no longer assumed that he was incapable of anything more sophisticated than abridgement.[7] There is, in fact, no reason to believe that Malory is indebted to any source for the position that the Cart episode occupies in his version.

The episode deals, of course, with Sir Melyagaunt's abduction of Guenevere while she is out Maying with ten of her knights, Lancelot's coming to her rescue (making part of the journey in a cart), the assignation between the lovers in which Lancelot leaves blood on the queen's bed, Melyagaunt's accusation of adultery, and the judicial combat in which Lancelot slays Melyagaunt and thus vindicates the honor of the queen. Vinaver held that the most significant differences between Malory's version and that in the prose *Lancelot* occur in the earlier part of the episode (covering the abduction and Lancelot's arrival at Melyagaunt's castle), while in the later part his version is closer to that in the extant source. This raises another possibility about the nature of the source Malory drew on. Granted that he himself is responsible for relocating the story in the last part of the book, is it possible that the differences between the early part of his version and the corresponding parts of the prose *Lancelot* derive from some other version of the story that has not come down to us? Vinaver thinks so and draws attention to a curious rubric that occurs in Malory's text at just about the point where, as Vinaver sees it, his version begins to agree more closely with the extant prose *Lancelot*:

> Thenne as the Frenssh book sayth, Syr Launcelot was called many a day after Le Cheualer du Charyot, and dyd many dedes, and grete aduentures he had. And soo leue we of this tale, Le Cheualer du Charyot, and torne we to this tale. (543.38-41)

Concerning the section following this rubric, Vinaver writes:

> From p. 1130 to p. 1140 parallels [between the prose *Lancelot* and Malory's version] are frequent, especially in the scene of Lancelot's meeting with the Queen and in the description of the fight between Lancelot and Meleagant. But in the earlier section (pp. 1120-29) the bare outlines of the story remain recognizable. The first division ends with the remark: *And so we leve of here of La Shyvalere le Charyote*, and it seems that at this point Malory simply substituted for the still undiscovered *Shyvalere le Charyote* a work very similar to the extant Prose *Lancelot*. The *Shyvalere le Charyote* probably contained, in addition to traits only known through Chrétien, a version of the story of the abduction of Guinevere not otherwise extant.
> (*Works*, p. 1592)

Vinaver has done a great deal, especially in connection with his last two tales, to discourage the proliferation of hypothetical sources in

Malory criticism in favor of a broader assessment of his inventive capabilities.[8] When he does posit a lost source, then, one can be sure that he finds the evidence for it compelling. I believe, however, that careful scrutiny of the plot of Malory's version of the Cart episode renders the hypothesis of a lost source unnecessary and, further, that a close study of the characterization of Guenevere makes it unlikely.

The differences between the extant source and Malory's version in the first half of the episode do not constitute proof that Malory worked from a source other than the prose *Lancelot*. The revisions he makes are major ones, to be sure, but they are not really very surprising. One surely does not need to posit an intermediate source to account for the difference between the way in which Guenevere falls into Melyagaunt's hands in Malory and the corresponding events in the prose *Lancelot*. It would be strange if Malory had *not* departed from his source here. First of all, Melyagaunt comes to Arthur's court to deny a report that at a certain tournament he wounded Lancelot by treachery. The account of that tournament appears over one hundred pages earlier.[9] This is a connection with the rest of the *Lancelot* that, of course, had to be erased if the episode was to be lifted out of its original context. Lancelot is not present when Melyagaunt arrives, for reasons which again would have involved Malory in lengthy explanations of earlier episodes of the French. Lancelot not being there to answer him, Melyagaunt issues a general challenge to the court to put up a champion to fight with him. If he wins he is to take away Guenevere; if he loses he will free the people he has been holding captive in his kingdom of Gorre. Now, even allowing for the fairy-tale atmosphere that marks many parts of the French romances, Melyagaunt's challenge is ridiculous. Arthur has no intention of gambling the safety of his queen on the prowess of one of his knights, and the narrator comments that everyone regards Melyagaunt's proposition as "grant folie."[10] The combat comes about only because Kay is piqued that he has not been delegated to answer Melyagaunt. He complains that he is not properly appreciated, and, in order to mollify him, the king and the queen say that they will give him anything he asks. He asks to be allowed to accept Melyagaunt's challenge. Malory could hardly have failed to realize how creaky this machinery was, and it is not surprising that he should have preferred to jettison it all and have Melyagaunt simply kidnap Guenevere.

It should also be mentioned that Vinaver himself points out an episode in the prose *Lancelot* that "bears some resemblance" (*Works*, p. 1606) to the abduction in Malory. It occurs, significantly, just after the account of the reaction of Melyagaunt's father, King Baudemagus, to the news of the death of Melyagaunt.[11] The French author makes much of Baudemagus's high regard for Lancelot, and it does not seem unlikely that as Malory meditated his version of the Cart story he became curious about how his source handled the effect on Baudemagus of the death of his son at the hands of his friend. In examining this passage, then, his attention could well have been drawn to the curious episode that immediately follows it, in which Bors (of all people), in fulfillment of a rash vow,[12] attempts to claim the queen as his captive while she is riding in the forest with a party of knights. The resemblance is indeed faint, but it deserves notice as another point against the necessity of positing a lost source.

Baudemagus's absence from Malory's version is another change that seems natural, even inevitable. For one thing, Malory has earlier reported him killed in the Grail Quest.[13] More important, his chief function in the source has been obviated in Malory. In the French, there is a duel between Melyagaunt and Lancelot when the latter first arrives in Gorre. The old king asks Guenevere to stop the fight when his son is getting the worst of it. In Malory, this combat does not take place. To the brave though treacherous Melyagaunt of the French source Malory has given the rank cowardice appropriate to a kidnapper, so that on hearing of Lancelot's arrival Melyagaunt does his own pleading to the queen. The solicitous father is thus superfluous.

Like Baudemagus, Gawain too has been written out of Malory's version. In the original, Gawain follows Lancelot to Gorre and his adventures on the journey thither take up almost as much room as Lancelot's own, without significantly affecting the main plot. The omission of Gawain can readily be credited to Malory. It is no more than a simple abridgement that is a consistent feature of his method of adaptation.

Also missing from Malory's version are the numerous adventures encountered by Lancelot on the way to Gorre, including a lance that comes out of nowhere and—rather anticlimactically—

202

misses him, and a tomb from which the voice of the nephew of Joseph of Arimathea predicts the coming of Galahad. Such omissions, obviously, are dictated partly by the fact that Malory's version of the story is placed after the Grail Quest, when the adventures of Logres have come to an end. His usual tendency toward condensation is at work also, of course, but mainly these omissions seem the result of Malory's realistic cast of mind. He always tends to reduce the proliferating marvels of his sources,[14] and I doubt that even before the Grail Quest he would have had much interest in anything so difficult (or at least so ludicrous) to visualize as the sword-bridge which Lancelot had to cross by straddling it and pulling himself along at the cost of severe cuts on the hands, knees, and feet.

Like the French author's machinery for getting Guenevere into Melyagaunt's power, the French explanation for Guenevere's coldness toward Lancelot upon his arrival at Melyagaunt's castle was unsuited to Malory's needs because it hangs on events that precede the episode of the Cart by many pages and are not represented in Malory. About sixty-five pages before the beginning of the *Charrette* episode, Gawain is suddenly captured and Lancelot immediately sets out to rescue him without informing the queen of his departure.[15] During his quest he is captured in his turn by Morgan le Fay, who manages to take from him a ring the queen had given him. She sends a messenger to court to report that Lancelot has confessed to his treasonous adultery and repudiated the queen and to present the ring as proof of the truth of what she says.[16] It would have been extremely uneconomical for Malory to reproduce the scenes of Lancelot's departure from court without the queen's congé and the arrival of the scandalous message from Morgan merely for their importance as motivation for Guenevere's attitude to Lancelot in the Cart episode. Thus the excision of the episode from its original context made some kind of change in Guenevere's reception of Lancelot inevitable.

The changes in Malory's version at this point are, however, more radical than we might have expected. They cannot be wholly accounted for by the displacement of the story from its original context. We find more than only a different motivation for Guenevere's behavior; we find entirely different behavior. She frustrates Lancelot in a way for which the extant source provides no precedent. Here if anywhere the possibility of a lost source must be seriously considered. It is just after this scene that Malory makes the remark about the "many dedes and grete aduentures" of Lancelot as "Le Cheualer du Charyot," and it is, in Vinaver's view, just after that remark that the closer correspondence between Malory and the extant prose *Lancelot* begins. However, the hypothesis of a lost source which Malory abandoned at this point to follow instead the prose *Lancelot*, omitting the "grete aduentures" that he mentions here, would imply a version in which Lancelot left the queen at Melyagaunt's castle while he went off to have those adventures. The only conceivable reason for Lancelot's not taking Guenevere away with him at this point would be some such refusal on her part to speak with him as is present in the prose *Lancelot* but not in Malory. There is in Malory, as we shall see, a disagreement between them that raises some bitterness in Lancelot, but, far from driving him away, it is not even serious enough to keep him from going to her bed that night. Certainly in the French tradition, where the perfect lover accepts the whim of his lady without question, such a disagreement could not possibly cause Lancelot to depart. In order to account for his leaving the queen at Melyagaunt's castle, then, the lost source would have to contain a scene in which Guenevere actually turns Lancelot away—in other words, one that would bear a much closer resemblance to the prose *Lancelot* than to Malory. But in that case we would still be left without a precedent for what happens between the lovers in Malory's version upon Lancelot's arrival. With the exception of the way in which Guenevere gets to Melyagaunt's castle in the first place, the other peculiarities of Malory's account are the result of omission only, and we need no lost source to explain those. It is to account for Malory's unique version of the queen's reception of Lancelot and her protection of Melyagaunt that one is inclined to take the rubric as indicating that Malory used a source distinct from the prose *Lancelot*. Since the same rubric seems to imply a source that at just this point would bear a closer resemblance to the *Lancelot* than to Malory, the hypothesis turns out to be useless.

A weightier argument against the hypothesis of the lost source is that the revisions in the scene of Guenevere's reception of

Lancelot here in Book XIX give a picture of the queen that is strikingly consistent with that in the preceding book, where Malory is adapting *La Mort le Roi Artu* and the English stanzaic *Morte*. After Lancelot's return from the Grail Quest at the end of Book XVII, Guenevere grows jealously possessive of him. In the opening chapter of Book XVIII, we learn that Lancelot has redoubled his exertions in the service of distressed damsels in order to avoid giving rise to gossip by being too much in the company of the queen. In the first of several confrontations that mark the varying course of their relationship throughout Book XVIII, Guenevere accuses him of neglecting her for other women. He defends himself by saying, first, that he would have been more successful in the Grail Quest but for his liaison with her and that his experience in that Quest "maye not be yet lyghtely forgeten" (507.11), and, second, that his services to other women serve as a blind. Malory draws attention to her silence during this long speech. Then after a fit of weeping she accuses him of philandering and banishes him from the court. (She attempts no response to his point about the Grail Quest.) During his absence she gives the dinner at which Sir Patrise dies after eating a poisoned apple. A tender reconciliation follows the trial by combat in which Lancelot's victory acquits her of the poisioning charge, but at the start of the very next episode, the story of Elaine of Astolat, the queen is being difficult again. Assuming a discretion which, as Lancelot pointedly remarks, is new with her, she sends him to the tournament at Winchester rather than allowing him to stay behind with her. Since he is not fully recovered from the trial by combat, her sending him to Winchester leads to his sustaining a serious wound there. It also leads to his sojourn with Elaine, which causes Guenevere intense jealous anguish. Once Elaine is dead, the changeable queen reproaches Lancelot for not having been kinder to the girl. When she apologizes for her jealousy, his answer expresses weary sadness tinged with resentment: "This is not the fyrste tyme . . . that ye haue ben displeasyd with me causeles. But madame, euer I must suffre yow, but what sorowe I endure [ye] take no force" (531.23-25).[17] At Winchester, Lancelot had carried a sleeve of Elaine's as part of his disguise, and when another tournament is announced, to be held at Westminster on Candlemas Day, Guenevere requires him to wear a favor of hers in the lists. Of all these scenes, only the one in which she sends him to Winchester has a prototype in the sources, and the resemblance is faint.

Throughout Book XVIII, then, Malory highlights the queen's temperamental nature, her insecurity, and her desire to assert authority over Lancelot. These traits are, as we shall see below, so thoroughly consistent with the characterization of Guenevere in the Cart episode of Book XIX that it is very hard to believe the revisions in the Cart story are not entirely Malory's own. A lost version of the Cart episode in which Guenevere's behavior was much like it is in Malory would seem to entail the necessity of our believing that it was the main inspiration for his treatment of the queen in Book XVIII as well, and that Malory's revisions of *La Mort le Roi Artu* and the stanzaic *Morte* were made with the specific purpose of bringing them into conformity with the picture of Guenevere in the hypothetical lost source. That source would then take on an importance much greater than one cares to attribute to something for whose actual existence there is no real proof.

Malory's version of Guenevere's reception of Lancelot can now be examined as largely original material. When Melyagaunt learns of Lancelot's arrival he runs to the queen to ask her protection. She is at first unmoved. "What eyleth yow now?" she says coldly. "Forsothe I myghte wel wete somme good knyght wold reuenge me, though my lord Arthur wyste not of this youre werke" (542.36-38). It was shortsighted of Melyagaunt to think he would get away with it, and she displays not the slightest inclination to stand between him and what is coming to him. He promises to make amends, and she answers, "What wold ye that I dyd?" Malory's dialogue is rarely supported by pointers from the narrator to indicate the tone of it. It rarely needs them, being so fully expressive in itself. But there is perhaps some ambiguity about this line. It might, I suppose, be read as implying willingness to do something for him, but the brevity of it (as compared with the longer statement she makes later when she clearly is agreeing to protect him) suggests terseness rather than clemency. Its import seems to be not "What shall I do for you?" but rather "What do you expect me to do about it?" Yet after only a few more words from Melyagaunt she has changed her mind and agrees to intercede for him. "Ye saye wel," she says, "and better is pees than euer werre, and the lesse noyse, the more is my worship" (543.4-5).

Why this abrupt volte-face? The statement itself contains one answer to this question, but it rings rather hollow. Can we really believe that Guenevere has suddenly been struck with a conviction of the ugliness of violence? And what reason has she to fear scandal in the present circumstances, when she has done nothing but is herself the wronged party, having been abducted by Melyagaunt against her will? These are mere rationalizations, then, though we recognize the touch of the master psychologist in the fact that one of the justifications that occur to her should be the avoidance of scandal—its cropping up in a context where it is actually irrelevant indicates the extent to which it has become a constant concern in her life. However, the real ground of her reversal becomes apparent only when we look back to the terms in which Melyagaunt has formulated the plea that wins her over. What he has said is, "I wold no more . . . but that ye wold take alle in your owne handes, and that ye wille rule my lord Sir Launcelot" (542.40-543.1). He has by sheer chance hit upon an expression of the situation that we might well expect would appeal to Guenevere. When she realizes that her preventing the fight that she had been looking forward to with evident satisfaction a moment ago will constitute a manifestation of her power over Lancelot, she is immediately attracted to the idea. Melyagaunt has here provided her with an occasion from which she can draw the same kind of satisfaction as she got from making Lancelot wear her sleeve at Westminster.

The queen goes to Lancelot, who is shouting for Melyagaunt to come forth, and asks with deflating aplomb, "Syre Launcelot, why be ye soo moeued?" Lancelot asks what she means by the question, for it seems to him that she ought to be even angrier than he. She does not attempt to dispute this, but says soothingly, as to a child who will not brook contradiction, "Truly . . . ye saye trouth. But hertely I thanke yow . . . but ye muste come in with me peasyble, for al thynge is put in my hand"—Melyagaunt's phrase, and the pleasure she takes in it is evident—"and alle that is euylle shalle be for the best, for the knyghte ful sore repenteth hym of the mysauenture that is befallen hym" (543.13-16). Lancelot submits to his unpredictable mistress, as he must, but his bitterness is obvious when he adds, "and I had wyst ye wold haue ben soo soone accorded with hym, I wold not haue made suche haste vnto yow" (543.19-20).

At this the queen reprovingly asks him if he regrets his good deed and, realizing the depth of his anger at Melyagaunt and seeing that she may by her arbitrary clemency be attracting some of it to herself, she makes her first and only attempt at justifying it. She points out the necessity of avoiding scandal that she had mentioned in talking to Melyagaunt, and it reminds us now of her assumption of discretion in the dialogue at the beginning of the Elaine episode. Lancelot is as unimpressed by it here as he was then. He must submit, but he repeats that it is against his will and no one but Arthur or herself could prevent him from killing Melyagaunt. "That wote I wel, said the quene, but what wille ye more? Ye shall haue alle thynge rulyd as ye lyst to haue it" (543.27-28). Balked of his purpose, Lancelot cannot miss the irony of this statement, and it is underscored for us because we recognize the echo of Melyagaunt's words to the queen, "and that ye wille rule my lord Sir Launcelot" (543.1). Lancelot replies, "Madame . . . soo ye be pleasyd, I care not; as for my parte ye shal soone please" (543.28-29). This is by the book, but its brevity gives it a perfunctory ring. It is apparent that he is still not reconciled, as is further shown by a remark he shortly afterwards makes to Sir Lavayne, who has followed him to Melyagaunt's castle: "lete ye this passe, and we shalle ryghte hit another tyme when we beste may" (544.9-10). The tone of Lancelot's last words to Guenevere recalls the trace of resentment we noticed in him at the end of the Elaine episode.[18]

It is at this point that the puzzling rubric quoted at the beginning of this essay occurs. As we noticed, Vinaver took it as a reference to a lost source because, in his view, there are greater differences between Malory and the extant source in the section preceding the rubric than in the section following it. But we have seen that the changes that occur in the section preceding it are either structurally inevitable (as the results of the episode's excision from its original context) or notably consistent with earlier changes in the characterization of Guenevere. Moreover, comparison will show that, Vinaver notwithstanding, there are important differences between Malory and the extant source in the section *following* the rubric as well. The scene in which Melyagaunt discovers the blood on the queen's bed and the account of the combat between him and

Lancelot are both heavily reworked, yet Vinaver does not doubt that all of the latter part of the episode is drawn from the extant *Lancelot*. Two readers may reasonably differ on the comparative importance of the revisions in the first and second parts. However, it is certainly important to recognize that Vinaver's assertion—that in the last part of the episode "parallels are frequent," while in the early part "the bare outlines of the story remain recognizable"—is debatable.[19]

The parallels between Malory and the French are admittedly quite close in the scene immediately following the rubric, which tells of Lancelot's nocturnal visit to the queen, his cutting his hands in the process of tearing out the bars of her window, and his leaving bloodstains in her bed. The next scene, however, in which Melyagaunt discovers the bloodstains, is notable for several touches that sharply dramatize his cowardliness and demonstrate how fully Malory has realized his new conception of him. When he sees the blood he accuses Guenevere of infidelity with some of the ten knights who were wounded in the ambush which he laid for the queen and who have been sleeping nearby. They immediately want to vindicate her honor by combat. Melyagaunt's reply evidences his aversion to fair fights and manifests his frustration and anger at the chance of the damning evidence's being contradicted and set aside by the outcome of a judicial combat: "Ye shal not . . . away with your proud langage. For here ye may alle see . . . that by the quene this nyghte a wounded knyghte hath layne" (545.18-20). This is the voice of a small man who feels that he is being taken advantage of by his betters.[20] Nor has Malory forgotten to adjust the details of Melyagaunt's private feelings. In the source he is full of the angry resentment of the rejected lover and reproaches Guenevere for having refused him only to accept Kay, a man to whom he has proven himself superior in combat. By contrast, Malory explains that the worm is secretly pleased at what has happened: "And wete you wel, Syr Mellyagraunce was passynge glad that he had the quene at suche an auauntage, for he demed by that to hyde his treson" (545.21-22).

Malory's handling of Lancelot's entrance is one of those remarkable passages where a surface simplicity that refuses to draw attention to itself gives way upon close examination to reveal a great

deal of dramatic and psychological sophistication. The scene is
indebted to the French only in its broadest outlines; the details I am
about to consider are Malory's own work.

> What araye is this? sayd Sir Launcelot. Thenne Syr
> Mellyagraunce told hem what he had fonde and shewed hem
> the quenes bed. Truly, said Syr Launcelot, ye dyd not your part
> nor knyghtly to touche a quenes bedde whyle it was drawen and
> she lyeng therin. For I dar say my lord Arthur hymself wold not
> haue displayed her courteyns, she beyng within her bed, onles
> that it had pleasyd hym to haue layne doune by her; and therfor
> ye haue done vnworshipfully and shamefully to yourselfe.
>
> (545.24-29)

It is absolutely right that Lancelot should at first not respond to the
actual charge at all. One is reminded of Guenevere in the dialogue
at the beginning of Book XVIII, evading the main issue of
Lancelot's speech, his experience in the Grail Quest, by fastening
on the question of his relations with other women. With a true
dramatist's insight, Malory here presents Lancelot as too taken
aback at the evidence of his and Guenevere's guilt—the rumpled
bloodied bed in the morning light with all these people staring at
it—to be able to speak anything to the purpose at once. So, needing
time and knowing that attack is the best defense, he attempts to put
Melyagaunt in the wrong. Fortunately what he says strikes directly
at the satisfaction Melyagaunt was feeling a moment ago, the
satisfaction that the queen's crime would divert attention from his
own. Frustrated, as at the challenge of the wounded knights, at
everyone's apparent determination to ignore the conclusive
evidence in pursuit of secondary considerations, and threatened
now, as well, with the prospect of their managing to turn his
discovery against him, Melyagaunt petulantly reiterates the charge
and adds that he is willing to prove it by combat:

> I wote not what ye mene . . . but well I am sure ther hath one of
> her wounded knyghtes layne by her this nyghte, and therfor I
> wil proue with my handes that she is a traytresse vnto my lord
> Arthur. (545.29-32)

Now Lancelot sees his loophole and warns Melyagaunt that the
challenge will not go unanswered. His conviction of the queen's
guilt, however, gives the coward courage to warn Lancelot in his
turn against trusting to his prowess in a wrong quarrel, "for God

wil haue a stroke in euery batail" (546.36). But at the close of the
dialogue there is a clever touch that clearly indicates that
Melyagaunt does not intend to trust the outcome to God and also
shows how the base man judges others by himself: "But now," he
says to Lancelot, "sythen it is so that we must fyghte togyders, I pray
yow, as ye be a noble knyght, awayte me with no treason nor none
vylony the meane whyle, nor none for yow" (546.4-6). Clearly, he
has already formed his intent to imprison Lancelot, and if the latter
were a little less noble he would have realized it: "For euer a man of
worshyp and of prowesse dredeth lest alwayes perils, for they wene
euery man be as they ben" (546.14-16).

In the French, Lancelot is delivered from prison for the final
battle with Melyagaunt by the latter's sister, who hates her brother.
In Malory, the girl who brings Lancelot his food while he is in
prison becomes enamored of him and volunteers to help him escape
on the condition that he sleep with her. In making this change,
Malory is drawing on a section of the French story that he has
already passed over. The French prototype of this forward young
lady is the wife of the seneschal of Gorre, but the incident is handled
much more lightly in the French. First of all there is not in the
French the same necessity that Lancelot should escape. There has
already been a fight over Melyagaunt's accusation. It was
interrupted by Baudemagus and is not to be continued for about a
year yet.[21] Lancelot wants the seneschal's wife to let him out so that
he can attend a tournament, after which, he promises her, he will
return to prison. Moreover the lady does not lay siege to him over
the course of several days as she does in Malory, nor does Lancelot
have to make such an emphatic resistance. We have the device
(common in the French) of an unspecified favor asked and granted,
whereupon the lady informs him that what he has granted her is his
love. He thinks for a moment and then says that he will not refuse
her anything he has, because she has well deserved it. She asks him
if, then, she has his love and he repeats that he grants her as much as
he can "sans contredit."[22] She sees that he is troubled, understands
that in good faith he can concede no more, and decides to help him
anyway.

In Malory, Lancelot's easy sophistry has disappeared, and the
scene is treated much more heavily. The lady attempts to use

Guenevere's danger of being burnt to pressure Lancelot into complying with her demand, but he expresses his confidence that someone else will champion her if he cannot be there and reiterates his refusal. Finally, the lady gives up and reduces her price to one kiss. Lancelot pays it only after pronouncing a careful justification of his capitualtion: "As for to kysse yow . . . I maye doo that and lese no worshyp. And wete ye wel, and I vnderstood there were ony disworship for to kysse yow, I wold not doo hit" (547.16-18). Thus, in arranging Lancelot's escape from prison, Malory has rejected the delivery by the sister of Melyagaunt and instead turned back several pages to write a scene modelled on the incident of the seneschal's wife. He has developed that incident into a sober and fairly heavy-handed demonstration of Lancelot's fidelity, unshakeable even by fear for his lady's safety. It seems appropriate that we be strongly reminded just here of the chief virtue of the otherwise guilty pair,[23] for what immediately follows has an undeniably ugly side to it. The ugliness, as we shall see, is largely of Malory's own making, but though it is intentional, he apparently wants to prevent our being completely alienated by it, for he prefaces it with this emphatic dramatization of the redeeming factor in their relationship.

Lancelot reaches the court on the appointed day. The antagonists engage, and Melyagaunt is quickly bested and cries for mercy.

> Thenne Sir Launcelot wyste not what to doo, for he had leuer than all the good of the world he myghte haue ben reuenged vpon Syr Mellyagraunce. And Sir Launcelot loked vp to the Quene Gueneuer, yf he myghte aspye by ony sygne or countenaunce what she wold haue done. And thenne the quene wagged her hede vpon Sir Launcelot, as though she wold saye, slee hym. Ful wel knewe Sir Launcelot by the waggynge of her hede that she wold haue hym dede.   (548.23-28)

At this, Lancelot tells his opponent to rise and continue the fight, but Melyagaunt refuses. Lancelot is stymied.

> I shalle profer yow large profers, sayd Sir Launcelot; that is for to say, I shall vnarme my hede and my lyfte quarter of my body alle that may be vnarmed, and lete bynde my lyfte hand behynde me, soo that it shalle not helpe me, and ryghte so I shall doo bataille with yow. Thenne Sir Mellyagraunce starte vp vpon his legges and sayd on hyghe, my lord Arthur, take

> hede to this profer, for I wille take hit, and lete hym be
> dysarmed and bounden accordynge to his profer. (548.30-36)

With all these concessions, Lancelot soon cuts Melyagaunt's head in two. Lancelot's unprecedented handicapping of himself has given his opponent the greatest conceivable advantage and has provided a spectacular demonstration of his own prowess. The quickness with which Melyagaunt seized the advantage offered him by one who had already proven himself a better man has surely eliminated any remnant of sympathy for him that might have been left in the reader when the fight began.[24] Yet, for all that, the scene remains distasteful. When the queen signals for Melyagaunt's death in the source, Lancelot simply lets him up to renew the fight and kills him when he loses a second time.[25] Lancelot's voluntary disarming is Malory's own invention. He gives us a vivid indication of the intensity of the lovers' desire for vengeance by making Lancelot go to such spectacular lengths to secure it. We realize that what we have witnessed is no better than a kind of legalized murder. Guenevere feels no inclination to oppose Lancelot's wishes now. The abduction could be forgiven when it suited her, but the near-exposure of the adultery must be punished. The scene is a powerful dramatization of the destructive potential of guilt and of the way in which the adultery is mining their characters. In the preceding episodes the queen has sometimes appeared in a less than flattering light, but her earlier lapses are minor in comparison with what she sinks to here. And as for Lancelot, when the threat of exposure can bring the embodiment of the knightly ethic to an action that runs so sharply counter to the spirit of chivalry, whatever its relation to the letter, we realize that we are watching the first real eruption of the long-dormant conflict of loyalties which will ultimately prove one of the main factors in the destruction of the Table. Melyagaunt is a knight of the Round Table (another detail in which Malory differs from his source). Lancelot has tilted against his fellows in tournaments, and on one occasion—at Winchester—Guenevere was indirectly the cause of it. But here the conflict is mortal and the queen is implicated directly. The episode concludes without the sense of elation that closed each of the three chief phases of Book XVIII. The Westminster tournament concluded in a unanimous celebration of the virtue of loyalty to a worthy comrade; Elaine's

story, though a sad one, ended with a description of the pleasures of
winter sports; and the queen's acquittal of the charge of poisoning
in her previous trial by combat was greeted by a general jubilation
that contrasts sharply with the subdued tone in which the case of the
bloodstained bed is closed.

Close analysis of Malory's version of the episode of the Knight
of the Cart, then, reveals considerable variations from the extant
prose *Lancelot* but no evidence that justifies our crediting them to a
lost intermediary between that source and Malory. Indeed, much of
the most dramatically effective revision occurs in the second half of
the episode, *after* the point at which, according to Vinaver's reading
of the rubric, Malory has turned away from the supposed lost source
and begun to draw upon the extant prose *Lancelot*. But if there is no
lost source, what are we to make of Malory's remark about leaving
off the "Cheualer du Charyot"? I suggest that Vinaver's assumption
that the phrase is the title of a separate work is questionable. It
might equally well be a designation for that section of the extant
prose *Lancelot* which recounts the hero's journey to Gorre and his
adventures there. In this case, Malory's remark about leaving off
may mean simply that he does not intend to recount how Lancelot,
after Guenevere refused to receive him upon his arrival, went in
search of Gawain, was taken prisoner by the citizens of Gorre, and
then was reported dead, but intends, instead, to pass directly to what
follows all these complications in the source, namely the episode of
the bloodstained bed.

There is, however, one other passage in Book XIX that looks
like a reference to a source other than the prose *Lancelot*. It occurs at
the very end, in the conclusion to the episode of the healing of Sir
Urry, for which there is no known source.

> And soo I leue here of this tale and ouerhyp grete bookes of
> Sir Launcelot du Lake, what grete aduentures he dyd whan he
> was called Le Cheualer du Charyot. For as the Frensshe booke
> sayth, bycause of despyte that knyghtes and ladyes called hym
> the knyghte that rode in the charyot, lyke as he were iuged to
> the galhous, therfor in despyte of all them that named hym soo,
> he was caryed in a charyot a tweluemoneth. For but lityl after
> that he had slayne Sir Mellyagraunce in the quenes quarel, he
> neuer in a tweluemoneth came on horsbak. And as the Frensshe
> book sayth, he dyd that tweluemoneth more than XL batails.

> And bycause I haue lost the very mater of La Cheualer du
> Charyot, I departe from the tale of Sir Launcelot, and here I goo
> vnto the morte of Kynge Arthur, and that caused Syre
> Agrauayne.   (554.13-23)

Unlike the previous passage, this one can hardly be taken as a
reference to the prose *Lancelot*. Though Vinaver's note on this
passage asserts that Malory means "the portion of the prose
Lancelot which comes immediately after the *Charrette* episode"
(*Works*, p. 1614),[26] the description given here of the contents of the
book does not tally with the Vulgate Cycle as it has come down to
us. I can find no authority in the extant source for the statement that
Lancelot rode in a cart for a year. Nor does the tone of a remark the
French Lancelot later makes about having been in a cart before
suggest that he would have elected to enter one again.[27] Does it not
begin to seem that there must indeed have been a volume of
adventures of the Knight of the Cart that has since been lost and that
it included not only the peculiar version of the central story reflected
in Malory, but the story of the healing of Urry as well? However, if
such were in fact the case, we should expect that in Malory's version
of the healing there would be some reference to Lancelot's riding in
a chariot and being known as the Knight of the Cart. Yet there is
none. Quite the contrary, the description of Lancelot's entrance in
the episode of the healing includes an explicit reference to his
dismounting "from his hors" (552.30). It seems to me possible, then,
that the present passage is a hoax designed to conceal the fact that
the story of the healing of Urry is actually Malory's own creation. As
an authority for the episode he invents a mythical French book—
one, moreover, of a very impressive size. Then to excuse his not
giving us more of it, he explains that he has lost it. The earlier
passage, then, if it is not simply a declaration that he is radically
abridging the prose *Lancelot*, as I suggested above, but is, rather, as
Vinaver takes it to be, a reference to a wholly different source, may
well be part of the same device. It would certainly not be the first
time in Malory's book that an explicit reference to a source marked a
passage of his own invention.[28] Admittedly the passage in question
is an unusually long one, incorporating as it does the substantial
revision of the Cart story and the unprecedented Urry episode, but
that very fact might, to him, have seemed reason for inventing a

mythical source rather than simply prevaricating about the content of the actual one, as he does with smaller changes.

Of course, in the absence of even a disputed source with which to compare the episode of the healing of Urry, we cannot approach it in quite the same way as we did the episode of the Cart. It has been argued that the Urry episode was within Malory's powers of invention insofar as it consists of one of those roll calls of knights of which Malory was clearly fond and of which the description of the Westminster tournament (533-35) provides an almost surely original instance.[29] As for the miraculous healing itself, it has been suggested that Malory developed it from a mere kernel in the prose *Lancelot*.[30] But even if the episode does derive from some lost book of Lancelot's adventures, as the concluding rubric claims, what matters most in Malory is the audacity of the story's placement. Even granting the existence of "grete bookes" now lost that Malory chose to "ouerhyp," his selecting this episode to follow the Cart story is a masterstroke. After the slaughter of Melyagaunt, the only point in the whole book where Lancelot appears in an undeniably bad light, he is allowed to perform a miracle. The only thing that keeps the episode from being downright blasphemous is Lancelot's sharp awareness of his own unworthiness. But the episode is very complex and must be examined in some detail if we are to assess its effect with any accuracy.

Sir Urry's wounds will never close until "the best knyghte of the world" (549.24-25) has searched them. R. M. Lumiansky resolves the contradiction implicit in the episode by saying that Lancelot's success indicates that the phrase "best knyghte" is to be taken in a restrictedly worldly, physical sense.[31] The French *Queste* seems to be grounded in a similar distinction between celestial and worldly chivalry, but P. E. Tucker has argued very persuasively that such a distinction was foreign to Malory and that the English author saw no necessary conflict between the two.[32] For him true earthly chivalry was a way of life in which it was possible to save one's soul. Not everyone is called to follow Galahad, nor is anyone automatically damned for not being thus favored. Moreover, the present episode itself would seem to forbid our restricting the phrase to an exclusively worldly application, for the prayer Lancelot makes before touching Urry clearly places the whole scene on a spiritual plane and makes what follows a miracle rather than a mere secular feat of disenchantment by virtue of physical superiority.

It is clear, then, that for Lancelot there is a religious dimension to the episode, and it seems unsatisfactory to conclude that his success must mean he was mistaken. Such a reading makes the resolution an anticlimax that retrospectively renders the whole episode trivial. Yet the questions that Lumiansky raises are central to the scene. When Arthur commands Lancelot to take his turn he answers, "Ihesu defende me . . . whan soo many kynges and knyghtes haue assayed and fayled, that I shold presume vpon me to encheue that alle ye, my lordes, myghte not encheue" (552.38-40). Though Vinaver disagrees,[33] Lumiansky is surely right in saying that the ground of Lancelot's reluctance is his awareness of his spiritual ill-health, but here we part company. His view of Lancelot's state of mind at this point is that he fears failure because it will expose him as a sinner. Lumiansky believes that Arthur suspects Lancelot of having fallen back into the adultery that, according to Lumiansky, he confessed to Arthur at the end of the Grail Quest. Arthur is using Urry as a test to learn whether or not his suspicions are true, and Lancelot realizes it.[34] His view is slightly qualified by Stephen C. B. Atkinson, who rejects the idea that Arthur is seeking proof of his suspicions about the adultery but agrees that Lancelot fears exposure of "his carefully guarded secret."[35] This approach to the episode strikes me as questionable.

Even leaving aside the objection that Lancelot's confession to Arthur is an invention that the text does not support, I cannot accept Lumiansky's view of the king as happily deluded by Lancelot's ultimate success in healing Urry. I do not believe Malory would put his Arthur in such a foolish position. As for Lancelot, the main fact about his state of mind is undeniably that he does not believe that he can heal Urry, but it does not follow that he fears the consequences of failure, as Atkinson argues. What is expressed in the lines quoted above is the fear of appearing to act in the expectation of success, the fear of the sin of presumption. That is what he says, and there is no good reason not to take him at his word. Only upon the compulsion of Arthur's command does he submit, and even then he reiterates his reluctance:

My most renoumed lord, said Sir Launcelot, ye knowe wel I dar

not nor may not disobeye your commaundement; but and I
myghte or durste, wete yow wel, I wold not take vpon me to
touche that wounded knyghte in that entente that I shold passe
alle other knyghtes. Ihesu defende me from that shame.

(553.1-4)

Arthur reassures him, saying "ye shal not do it for no presumpcyon,
but for to bere vs felaushyp," and the bystanders, and Urry too, urge
Lancelot to make the attempt. Still he protests: "I shame me sore
that I shold be thus rebuked, for neuer was I able in worthynes to
doo so hyghe a thynge" (553.13-15). It seems perverse to read these
simple expressions of humility as indicating that Lancelot fears the
construction the king will put upon his failure. Lancelot is not even
much concerned with any such merely social embarrassment as
might attend failure—which would be minimal anyway when no
one else, not even the king, has succeeded. Such a concern would be
a manifestation of pride. He does pray at the last moment "that my
symple worshyp and honeste be saued," but he adds immediately
that the grace can only come from God and not from himself. We
may notice, also, that there is no mention of Guenevere's "worshyp
and honeste." If Lumiansky and Atkinson were right, this would be
most ungallantly self-centered of Lancelot.

Compounding his belief that his sin with the queen has
debarred him from the title of "best knyghte of the world" and
incapacitates him for such an achievement as the healing of Urry is
a different though related shame. He has only recently been led by
his love for Guenevere to kill a man who, but for that entanglement
with the queen, would have been beneath his notice, incapable of
posing a threat to him. He is, after all, the paragon of knightly
virtue, and, after the threat had been eliminated and his anger had
cooled, he can have taken little satisfaction in the merciless slaying
of Melyagaunt. It was the first time he had knowingly put his
prowess in the service of a wrong quarrel, and he had been driven by
a vengeful thirst for his opponent's blood. With the ruse of
handicapping himself he lured the already defeated plaintiff to his
death. It was the ultimate display of the kind of spectacular skill for
which people had long regarded him as the greatest of knights, only
it has spoiled his taste for the title. The prowess that everyone
applauds, after what it enabled him to do in the previous episode,
has become for him an occasion of self-reproach that is much more

immediate than the long-standing adultery. It seems to me that of the two, this is the primary reason for his reluctance to search Urry. The "best knyghte of the world" would not have done what he did to Melyagaunt.

When Guenevere heard from Bors how the latter had wounded Lancelot at Winchester, she said, "yet for all his pryde and bobaunce, there ye proued yourself his better" (523.38-39). Shortly thereafter, Lancelot said of the same tournament, "there in my pryde I was nere slayne" (525.21-22). D. S. Brewer says that Lancelot's "chief sins are pride and unchastity" and that the healing of Urry demonstrates that he has purged his pride.[36] There is an episode during the Grail Quest in which Lancelot comes upon two parties of knights fighting, and decides to aid the weaker "in encrecynge of his chyualry" (462.6). To his chagrin he is overcome and captured. After being released he laments that "neuer or now was I neuer at turnement nor iustes but I had the best, and now I am shamed . . . now I am sure that I am more synfuller than euer I was" (462.20-22). The experience is expounded for him by a recluse, who explains that he joined the weaker side for the wrong reasons: "thow enclynest to that party for bobaunce and pryde of the world, and alle that must be lefte in that quest" (463.13-14). His only consideration in choosing the smaller party was that it would provide occasion for the greater display of strength and skill; "therfor God was wroth with yow, for God loueth no suche dedes in this quest" (463.23-24). The episode of the healing of Urry presents a Lancelot who has risen above "bobaunce and pryde of the world"—disillusioned, in fact, with distinguished knightly achievement—and its placement immediately after the Melyagaunt story implies a reason for this new development. The misuse of his prowess in that affair is analogous to his fighting on the wrong side in the symbolic tournament, though in the latter instance his choice, however misguided, was comparatively innocent. There were no evil consequences, not even to himself, since he was undergoing a monitory experience rather than committing a sin. The fight with Melyagaunt is the sin against which the Quest episode was only a warning. As such, it carries with it real guilt which constitutes a direct personal experience of the vanity of prowess. The fact that he has at last really learned this lesson, and not any limitation of the application of the phrase "best knyghte" to the merely physical, explains why it is granted to Lancelot to perform a miracle. The physical is not an irrelevant factor, for if the "best knyghte" would not have done what Lancelot did to Melyagaunt, the fact remains that only the "best knyghte," physically speaking, could have done it. But the remorse consequent upon the slaughter of Melyagaunt has made him more than the nonpareil of prowess. It has brought him to the point where that prowess has ceased to be an occasion of the sin of pride.[37]

So great is his new humility that when the miracle he has prayed for occurs he feels it, ironically, not as a reward but as a reproach.[38] The manifestation of the infinite mercy of God in the face of his profound sense of unworthiness brings home to him, in a way that simply failing the test could never have done, the magnitude of that love he has turned his back on for the love of Guenevere. Books XVIII and XIX have shown a decline in Lancelot from "the promyse and the perfectyon" (506.9) of the Grail Quest. His speech to the queen at the opening of Book XVIII revealed the conflict in him between the claims of that higher life that could "not be yet lyghtely forgeten" (507.11) and his renewed attraction to Guenevere, and if there was even in the renewal of the liaison an element of remorse that prompted him to withdraw from her "as moche as he myghte" (506.19), we may suppose that since the duel with Melyagaunt he feels himself both more strongly tied to the queen and more than ever aware of the part of himself that resents and resists the captivity. To this issue of the conflict between his religious aspirations and his love for Guenevere he has not specifically alluded since the quarrel at the beginning of Book XVIII, and there are, as Malory insists, interludes when they are happy together; but the main episodes have given us glimpses of a Lancelot weary of the strain of loving Guenevere, and at such times the thought of what he has lost for her must give him pause. Admittedly, the spiritual claims on Lancelot are not so strongly dramatized in these episodes as the tensions with which Guenevere's insecurities are burdening their relationship—partly precisely because as he becomes more and more involved with her the call to spiritual perfection becomes more and more distant—but it seems that the main reason for those insecurities is her recognition of the vitality of Lancelot's spiritual life and her fear that it may eventually overwhelm his love for her.[39] When in the opening scene of Book XVIII she fails to answer Lancelot's statement about his experience in the Grail Quest, it is surely not because she dismisses it as unimportant but because it is unanswerable. It is the opening point in a speech of unusual length, and when she lets it go by we feel the gathering tension in her silence, a silence of which Malory takes explicit notice when Lancelot finishes speaking.[40] When she fastens instead on Lancelot's activities in aid of other women, for which he has given a perfectly reasonable justification, we perceive that her abuse is a mask for the fear and, no doubt, guilt that have been generated by his remark about his spiritual life.[41]

With the episode of the miraculous healing, Malory again brings to the fore the conflict in Lancelot that he showed us at the beginning of Book XVIII so that we should understand the reactions of Guenevere, to which it then yielded center stage. It is surely significant that Guenevere is almost wholly absent from the Urry episode. For both the characters and the narrator, the event is a state occasion: everybody congregates in the meadow; a cushion is placed for the king to kneel on; and the extremely full catalogue of knights includes much recapitulation of earlier adventures. Yet the queen's name is not even mentioned in the course of the episode proper. The miracle takes us back to the world of the Grail Quest, a world Guenevere never actually entered, although there, as here, her influence was crucial for her lover. To be once more in the presence of the miraculous makes Lancelot acutely conscious of his failure to live out "the promyse and the perfectyon" of the Quest. His sense of what he has thereby lost explains why, in the midst of general rejoicing, "euer Syre Launcelot wepte as he had ben a child that had ben beten" (553.28-29).

The healing is followed by a tournament. Its festive character is suggested by the prize—a diamond—and by the fact that "none of the daungerous knyghtes" (553.39-40) take part. Malory gives us one last, bright picture of the court "alle hole togyders," as Arthur expressed it on the eve of the Grail Quest (431.33). The young knights joust; Lavayne and Urry distinguish themselves and are admitted to the fellowship of the Table; and there is even a wedding, between Lavayne and Urry's sister. Only at the very last does the shadow that hangs over them all cast its chill upon the scene, as Guenevere is mentioned for the first time in the episode: "But euery nyghte and day Sire Agrauayne, Syr Gawayns broder, awayted Quene Gueneuer and Sir Launcelot du Lake to putte them to a rebuke and shame" (554.10-12).

The placement of the Urry episode is thus beautifully appropriate. It forms a bright contrasting bridge between the near-exposure of the adultery by Melyagaunt and the actual exposure by Agravain which immediately follows at the beginning of Book XX and which leads to the queen's being put on trial for the third time. It also enriches the characterization of Lancelot by reasserting the spiritual element in him that conflicts with his love for Guenevere. Most important, the audacious juxtaposition of this exalted scene with the sordid killing of Melyagaunt gives special point to Lancelot's tears. His conviction that he is unworthy to serve as God's instrument in the healing is grounded not only in the old sin of adultery but also, and perhaps chiefly, in the recent slaughter of Melyagaunt. As for the Cart story, because it is placed after the episodes of the Poisoned Apple and Elaine, which likewise emphasize Guenevere's contrary temperament, it deepens our understanding of the ironic conflict in the queen between love for Lancelot and the refractory impulses, rooted in insecurity, that often threaten to alienate him. Whatever one makes of Malory's references to the "Cheualer du Charyot," then, they should not be allowed to obscure his achievement in Book XIX. Even taken simply at their face value, they imply that Malory isolated the episodes of the Cart and the healing of Urry from a much more diffuse and prolix context in which they could not possibly have had the structural prominence that they so effectively assume in Malory's taut narrative. And if the rubrics are in fact the prevarications that I have suggested they are, then Malory must be credited with a thorough and highly successful revision. Through extensive recasting of dialogue and situations he has deftly freed the Cart material from its original context and fitted it neatly into its new setting, and he has created in the episode of the healing a strong climax for the unified sequence of events that stretches through Books XVIII and XIX both.

St. Peter's College

NOTES

[1] *Caxton's Malory,* ed. James W. Spisak (Berkeley and Los Angeles: University of California Press, 1983); *The Works of Sir Thomas Malory,* ed. Eugène Vinaver, 3 vols., 2nd ed. (Oxford: Oxford University Press, 1967; rpt. 1973), cited hereafter as *Works.* All references to Malory's text are to Spisak's edition, unless otherwise noted.

[2] *La Mort le Roi Artu,* ed. Jean Frappier, 3rd ed. (Geneva: Droz, Paris: Minard, 1964).

[3] *Le Morte Arthur,* ed. J. Douglas Bruce, E.E.T.S. E.S. 88 (London: Kegan Paul, Trench, Trübner, 1903).

[4] Published as *The Vulgate Version of the Arthurian Romances,* ed. H. Oskar Sommer, 7 vols. (Washington: Carnegie Institution, 1908-16). The *Lancelot* proper, recounting the hero's life from birth to the eve of the Grail Quest, occupies Volumes III-V. This has now been published as *Lancelot: Roman en prose du XIIIe siecle,* ed. Alexandre Micha, 8 vols. (Geneva: Droz, 1978-82). My references are to the older edition, still perhaps the more widely accessible.

[5] *Vulgate Version,* IV, 156-226. The source of this part of the *Lancelot* proper is the poem by Chrétien de Troyes known as *Lancelot* or *Le Chevalier de la Charrete,* to which Malory is not directly indebted.

[6] H. Oskar Sommer, *Studies on the Sources,* Vol. III of *Le Morte Darthur by Syr Thomas Malory* (London: David Nutt, 1891), pp. 248 and 272-78. Sommer dubbed this hypothetical source the *Suite de Lancelot* and assumed it accounted for all the details in which Malory differs from the extant prose *Lancelot.*

[7] See especially Robert H. Wilson, "The Prose *Lancelot* in Malory," *University of Texas Studies in English,* 32 (1953), 1-13. Wilson believes Malory worked only from normal texts of the *Lancelot* both in Book VI and in Books XVIII and XIX. Malory's creativity throughout his work is stressed in the essays in *Malory's Originality: A Critical Study of Le Morte Darthur,* ed. R. M. Lumiansky (Baltimore: Johns Hopkins Press, 1964).

[8] See *Works,* pp. 1585-91 and 1615-26.

[9] *Vulgate Version,* IV, 43.

[10] *Ibid.,* 158.

[11] *Ibid.,* 300-01.

[12] *Ibid.,* 267.

[13] However, it is not unusual to find a character taking part in the action after he has been reported dead, and, although this is more common in the long middle section of the book than in the later part, Bagdemagus does in fact reappear in Book XX (578).

[14] See *Works,* pp. 1278-79, and C. S. Lewis, "The English Prose *Morte,*" *Essays on Malory,* ed. J. A. W. Bennett (Oxford: Oxford University Press, 1963), pp. 11-13.

[15] *Vulgate Version*, IV, 88.

[16] *Ibid.*, 140 ff.

[17] Caxton here reads "I take no force." Wynkyn de Worde and Vinaver have *ye* in place of *I*. This reading, which obviously heightens the tone of resentment in Lancelot's words, also seems to make better sense after the *but*. To move from "ever I must suffer you" to "what sorrow I endure *I* do not care," the likely conjunction would seem to be *and*. Malory's *but* is more appropriate to a contrast between Lancelot's pain and Guenevere's alleged indifference to it.

[18] For a more favorable view of Guenevere in this episode (more favorable, I believe, than the text warrants), see Janet Jesmok, "Malory's 'Knight of the Cart,'" *Michigan Academician*, 13 (Summer, 1980-Spring, 1981), 107-15. She maintains that "the queen graciously welcomes her rescuer, without anger or reproach" (p. 107), and sees the whole episode as "a tribute to Guenevere as queen and paramour" (p. 109).

[19] Wilson is also skeptical of the lost source hypothesis, but he suggests that the rubric means that Malory "composed the first part of his 'Charrette' freely, from memory, then shifted to closer following of the *Lancelot*" ("The Prose *Lancelot* in Malory," p. 12). In addition to resting on the questionable premise that the first part of Malory's version shows more significant revision than the second, this theory fails to take account of the fact that the revisions in the early part seem structurally inevitable. As it appears impossible that Malory could have used the same mechanics as the *Lancelot* does for introducing the episode, it is beside the point to suggest that he had forgotten them.

[20] T. H. White, in *The Once and Future King* (New York: G. P. Putnam's Sons, 1958), pp. 524 ff., presents Melyagaunt as a cockney. While this picture is rather too broadly comic, it is grounded in a sharp appreciation of the shadings of Malory's characterization. White's version of the Melyagaunt episode is notably different from Malory's in several significant particulars, such as the tone of the dialogue between Guenevere and Lancelot upon the latter's arrival at Melyagaunt's castle and the attitude of Lancelot in the trial by combat; but his treatment of Melyagaunt is a development of suggestions which are actually present in Malory's text, and which White appears to have been the first to appreciate.

[21] This is the second combat in the French between Lancelot and Melyagaunt, and the second to be interrupted by the queen at the behest of Bagdemagus. When it is resumed at Arthur's court, there is no mention of the bloodstained bed as being at issue. Apparently that is taken as settled even though the duel was interrupted, and there is, in distinct contrast to Malory's version, no indication that word of it ever reaches Arthur.

[22] *Vulgate Version*, IV, 219.

[23] Their fidelity I take to be, likewise, the main point of the controversial passage on the "lusty moneth of May" (537) which immediately precedes the Cart episode.

24 T. H. White at this point presents Melyagaunt as shouting to the spectators that they have all heard the offer and that Lancelot must not be allowed to go back on his word (*The Once and Future King*, p. 538), and it seems to me that once again the presentation is apt.

25 According to Vinaver's note on this passage, the French manuscripts differ among themselves. Some of them "make it clear that in reply to Arthur's request Lancelot merely permitted Meleagant to stand while he beheaded him with one blow" (*Works*, p. 1611).

26 There is a discrepancy between this statement of Vinaver's and that on p. 1592 in which he takes "Shyvalere le Charyote" to refer to a lost source distinct from the prose *Lancelot*. The statement on p. 1614 was not in the first edition, and perhaps Vinaver added it to the second without noticing its inconsistency with his earlier position.

27 See *Vulgate Version*, V, 105.

28 See Robert H. Wilson, "Malory's 'French Book' Again," *Comparative Literature*, 2 (1950), 172-81. Wilson writes: "Most of the references without known source authority must certainly have been made for camouflage. Increasing use of this device is indicated by the fact that, while the second half of Malory's work contains approximately half the references supported by source texts, it contains three-fourths of the unsupported ones" (p. 176).

29 See *Works*, p. 1591, and Wilson, "The Prose *Lancelot* in Malory," pp. 11-12.

30 See P. E. Tucker, "A Source for 'The Healing of Sir Urry' in the *Morte Darthur*," *Modern Language Review*, 50 (1955), 490-92. The parallels between Urry and the knight in the passages Tucker cites seem slight. However, in addition to Tucker's candidate, there are in the French two other wounded knights whom Lancelot heals. See *Vulgate Version*, III, 119-27, and IV, 92-94.

31 "'The Tale of Lancelot and Guenevere': Suspense," *Malory's Originality*, p. 231.

32 "Chivalry in the *Morte*," *Essays on Malory*, p. 84.

33 *Works*, p. 1613.

34 "'The Tale of Lancelot and Guenevere': Suspense," pp. 229-31. Lumiansky's reading of Lancelot's attitude to this test resembles that presented by T. H. White (*The Once and Future King*, pp. 541-42). As for Arthur's motivation, Lumiansky's view of that is wholly original.

35 "Malory's 'Healing of Sir Urry': Lancelot, the Earthly Fellowship, and the World of the Grail," *Studies in Philology*, 79 (1981). 348.

36 "Form in the *Morte Darthur*," *Medium Aevum*, 21 (1952), 22.

37 For another view, see E. M. Bradstock, "The Juxtaposition of 'The Knight of the Cart' and 'The Healing of Sir Urry,'" *Journal of the Australasian Universities Language and Literature Association*, no. 50 (November, 1978), pp. 208-23. Bradstock sees the juxtaposition of the

episodes as "an externalization of the two forces at war within [Lancelot], and a reminder that his old love has the power to revive itself and destroy [his] efforts towards salvation" (p. 213). Bradstock does not discuss Lancelot's pride or the manner of his slaying of Melyagaunt.

[38] My view here is close to Atkinson's, but I find at best unhelpful his comparison of Lancelot to the Absolon of the *Miller's Tale*, to whom Chaucer applies the simile of the beaten child, but in a situation very different from Lancelot's ("Malory's 'Healing of Sir Urry': Lancelot, the Earthly Fellowship, and the World of the Grail," p. 349).

[39] My reading of Guenevere's motivation here is indebted to Vida D. Scudder, *Le Morte Darthur of Sir Thomas Malory and its Sources* (New York: E. P. Dutton, 1917), p. 316.

[40] Caxton's edition, with its frequent chapter breaks, nicely heightens Malory's effect by opening a new chapter with the remark about Guenevere's silence.

[41] It may be objected that this view of Guenevere is inconsistent with her later fear of a human rival in the person of Elaine of Astolat. But it seems that, though Guenevere's insecurity originates in her fear that Lancelot is being drawn toward God, this insecurity, once established, can be aggravated by anything that exerts a claim on her lover, and this is surely credible. Moreover, as is suggested by her abusive retort in the scene discussed above, she may actually prefer to believe that her rival is another woman or other women. It is easier to compete with Elaine than with God.

Malory's "Lost" Source

James W. Spisak

At the end of his tale of Sir Urry, Malory provides a transitional statement that links the Lancelot and Guenevere section with that of the death of Arthur: "And bycause I haue lost the very mater of La Cheualer du Charyot, I departe from the tale of Sir Launcelot, and here I goo vnto the morte of Kynge Arthur, and that caused Syre Agrauayne" (554.21-23).[1] Scholars have always interpreted this as meaning that Malory misplaced his source or that it was incomplete; but a close look at his use of "lost" in this and other contexts makes it unnecessary to assume anything but a whole, accessible French prose *Lancelot* as Malory's source for his Knight of the Cart episode.

Scholarly attention was first called to this statement by Eugène Vinaver, who initially suggested that Malory had "lost his way" among the many "heterogeneous episodes" contained in his source and that this transitional passage is a translation of a similar one in his French anthology.[2] Vinaver later modified his opinion and yielded to that of R. H. Wilson, who reads Malory's conclusion as a "definite indication of disconnected source materials" and an "apparent reference to lost *Lancelot* volumes."[3] Other editors of the *Morte,* such as D. S. Brewer and P. J. C. Field, have suggested that

Malory misplaced the copy of the prose *Lancelot* he was working from. But if Malory used "lost" here in the sense of "give up" or "let go," as other writers of his time did,[4] there is no need to assume that his source was disconnected or that he misplaced it.

In the "Castle of Love," when Mercy asks that Man be saved, she is rebuked by Soothfastness. This rebuke is reiterated by Righteousness, who feels such virtues should not be bestowed on those who have deliberately abandoned them: "Mercy ne pite is non worthi,/ ffor that he lost thaim wilfully."[5] In an English version of the later *Speculum Christiani*, Seneca is quoted as an authority on faith: "He holdes ryght noght that loses hys feyth."[6] This statement could as easily have come from Malory's Grail Quest, and the sense of abandonment in this earlier use of "lose" is confirmed by the Latin version from which it was translated: "Nihil retinet, qui perdidit fidem."[7] Finally, in the *Conspiracio* of the Towneley Cycle, Pilate becomes angry at learning that Jesus is in the Temple. In ordering a soldier to go capture him, Pilate rebukes him for having abandoned (i.e., not obeyed) the law: "The dwill, he hang you high to dry!/ whi, wold ye lese oure lay?"[8]

There are four passages other than that containing the crux at hand in which Malory uses "lost" in a way that connotes abandonment or a conscious giving up. When Guenevere dismisses Lancelot and he goes into a mad exile, she is rebuked by her competitor, Elaine: "Madame, ye are gretely to blame for Syr Launcelot. For now haue ye lost hym, for I sawe and herd by his countenaunce that he is mad foreuer" (407.26-27). After Elaine leaves the court, Bors also rebukes Guenevere for her hasty action: "Allas, said Sir Bors, that euer Syr Launcelots kynne sawe yow; for now haue ye lost the best knyght of oure blood and he that was alle oure leder and oure socour" (408.28-30). Guenevere's action is regarded by both Bors and Elaine as deliberate, which makes "let go" a more acceptable sense of "lost" than, say, "ruined" would be.

A clearer example of Malory's use of this sense of the word is to be found in the Grail Quest. When a hermit is explicating one of the miracles to the Grail knights, he compares a hart's transubstantiation into a man with Christ's resurrection:

> Ryght soo cometh ageyne oure Lord from dethe to lyf, for He
> lost erthely flesshe, that was the dedely flesshe whyche He had

> taken in the wombe of the Blessid Vyrgyn Mary, and for that
> cause appiered oure Lord as a whyte herte withoute spot.
>
> (491.16-19)

Malory's last use of "lost" in this sense is perhaps best suited to my purpose, since it comes in a passage which, like the transition statement in question, is addressed directly to his readership. In his famous "Lo ye al Englisshemen" paragraph, which has acquired profound political significance over the years, Malory complains to his countrymen of their persistent trait of not fully supporting the crown. He compares earlier fickle habits with contemporary ones:

> Loo, thus was the olde custome and vsage of this londe, and also men saye that we of thys londe haue not yet loste ne foryeten that custome and vsage. Alas, thys is a grete defaulte of vs Englysshemen, for there may nothynge plese vs noo terme.
>
> (585.31-34)

If we interpret Malory's transitional statement as using "lost" in the above sense, understanding his use of the prose *Lancelot* becomes less complicated.

This interpretation of "lost" also resolves another question, that of the position of the passage in which it appears. If Malory had misplaced or somehow lost access to the prose *Lancelot,* one would expect him to say so at the end of the Knight of the Cart episode, where he stops using it. But his transitional statement comes one tale later, at the end of the tale of Sir Urry, which has no basis in the prose *Lancelot,* and a few lines before the transitional statement quoted, Malory summarizes what he has chosen to omit: "And soo I leue here of this tale and ouerhyp grete bookes of Sir Launcelot du Lake, what grete aduentures he dyd whan he was called Le Cheualer du Charyot" (554.13-14). If we recall T. C. Rumble's distinction between "tale" and "booke,"[9] Malory's concluding paragraphs make perfect sense in their present position. He is leaving the *story* ("tale") of Sir Lancelot, which culminates in the Sir Urry episode, and moving on to the death of Arthur. As he tells us clearly, he has already set aside the "very mater" ("booke") of Le Cheualer du Charyot, the French prose *Lancelot.*

Virginia Polytechnic Institute
and State University

NOTES

[1] The "very mater" here clearly refers to the prose *Lancelot,* not the *Mort Artu.* Wilson, in "The Prose *Lancelot* in Malory," *University of Texas Studies in English,* 32 (1953), 1-13, has already demonstrated that the *Lancelot* was probably the source for the first section of Malory's Knight of the Cart episode (XIX, 1-5) as well as the second (XIX, 5-9). All references to Malory's text are to *Caxton's Malory,* ed. James W. Spisak (Berkeley and Los Angeles: University of California Press, 1983).

[2] *Malory* (Oxford: Oxford University Press, 1929; rpt. 1970), pp. 148-49.

[3] *The Works of Sir Thomas Malory,* 2nd ed., 3 vols. (Oxford: Oxford University Press, 1967; rpt. 1973), p. 1614, and *Comparative Literature,* 2 (1950), 179-80.

[4] See the *Middle English Dictionary* (Ann Arbor: University of Michigan Press, 1956-), *losen, v.* (2), 2(c).

[5] *The Minor Poems of the Vernon MS.,* Part I, ed. Carl Horstmann (London: Kegan Paul, 1892; rpt. New York: Kraus, 1973), E.E.T.S. O.S. 98, 414/223-24.

[6] *Speculum Christiani,* ed. Gustaf Holmstedt (Oxford: Oxford University Press, 1933; rpt. New York: Kraus, 1971), E.E.T.S. O.S. 182, 10/6.

[7] *Speculum Christiani,* 11/5.

[8] *The Towneley Plays,* ed. G. England and A. W. Pollard (Oxford: Oxford University Press, 1897; rpt. 1966), 209/162-63.

[9] In "The First *Explicit* in Malory's *Morte Darthur,*" *Modern Language Notes,* 61 (1956), 564-66, Rumble convincingly shows how Malory uses "tale" to refer to his narrative and "booke," to his source.

Time and Elaine of Astolat

P. J. C. Field

Like many literary masterpieces, Malory's *Morte Darthur* manages to be simultaneously of its age and for all time. Like much of the best mediaeval Arthurian literature, it achieves this partly by being in a sense of no time. Our own century has produced many historical novels about "the real Arthur" and his period, designed to make the differences between past and present as vividly apprehensible as possible.[1] Dates and datable events remind us of precisely when in the distant past the events took place that we are now reading about, and systematic differentation of the minutiae of life shows us, perhaps with considerable skill, that (say) the middle of the fifth century was a time very different not merely from the twentieth century but from the early sixth as well.

Malory works in quite other ways. As narrator, he creates in his story a strong sense that the events he relates are in the past. The very tenses of his verbs insist on it, and many of the occasional comments he makes in his own person about the story reinforce this.[2] He will remind us of this or that which was different in King Arthur's time, or tell us of difficulties with the sources that give him access to his story—and separate him from it. Yet although the events in the *Morte Darthur* seem to happen at some considerable distance in the past, there are very few dates or datable events to give us any sense of precisely how long ago it all took place. More important still, there is very little in the story to suggest that being at a particular distance in time from us has made any systematic difference to the physical or social or intellectual detail of Malory's world. A knight's occupation is war, and warfare changed considerably between the fifth century and the fifteenth, but Malory describes both individual and group combat in terms so general that the reader rarely "sees" anything to make him feel that the fighting is taking place in one part of the millenium rather than another. So too with the construction of castles, the feudal tenure of land, and other features of Malory's world. Even when, as a matter of historical fact, some feature of the world of the *Morte Darthur* flourished in one part of the Middle Ages and not another—tournaments, for instance, were not invented until the middle of the eleventh century[3]—there is nothing in Malory's presentation of that feature to bring its chronological limitations home to the reader's mind. The result is an indefinite pastness very different from the specific pastness characteristic of historical novels.

This indefinite pastness is quite compatible with a strong individuality in the world of the *Morte Darthur*. Indeed, indefinite pastness is one aspect of that individuality, along with what Malory as narrator feels to be a certain enviable (although by no means uniform) simplicity and goodness as compared with the world he lived in.[4] As usual with Malory, there are a few exceptions, when definite dates are asserted or implied, but these are rare enough to be lost in the bulk of the *Morte Darthur*. It is doubly fortunate that they are so lost, because not only would specific dates detract from the book's accessibility, suggestiveness, and symbolic power, but the dates that are actually asserted or implied are incompatible with one another. The only (almost) conventional objective date in the *Morte Darthur* is that of the beginning of the Grail Quest, 454 years after the Passion of Our Lord; but the questers come across white monks, in other words Cistercians, whose order was founded in 1098.[5] Again, Arthur's knights fight both an emperor from Rome (which saw its last emperor in the late fifth century) and Turks in the Holy Land (where the Turkish empire began in the early eleventh).

We wrong Malory's story if we force the inconsistencies between these widely separated and (in every case but one) implicit dates into prominence. The *Morte Darthur* is in every sense big enough for a passage implying a particular date or period to have nearly all its effect in its immediate context. It need not have much effect on the book as a whole. Nevertheless, in its context it may deserve close attention.

One such passage occurs in the story of Elaine of Astolat, perhaps the most sympathetic character in the whole *Morte Darthur*. On her death-bed she tells her confessor that she loved Sir Lancelot "oute of mesure" (529.35). We cannot doubt that she is speaking the truth; but what she is saying is ambiguous. *Oute of mesure* may mean "immeasureably," "more than anyone could measure," "very greatly," or it may mean "beyond what the virtue of *mesure* or moderation would allow," "excessively." The remainder of her speech would fit in with either interpretation. In the wider context, the fact that she is dying of love might perhaps suggest that she is confessing to a fault, but does not prove it. Yet the difference in interpretation will make a considerable difference in tone to an important episode, which in turn will make a small but definite difference to the close of the *Morte Darthur*.

Fortunately, the matter can be decided. A little earlier in the story, Bors and Elaine's brother Lavayne try to help Lancelot ride a horse before he has fully recovered from a wound. Lancelot faints, and Elaine finds him on the ground unconscious. While trying to revive him she turns on Bors and Lavayne and says that if Lancelot should die she would "appele them of hys deth" (526.37).[6] The key word here, *appele*, is generally glossed as "accuse," but in Malory's time it had a more specific meaning, which can throw unsuspected light on the frame of mind that Malory sees in Elaine.

In fifteenth-century England, the appeal was one among several possible kinds of legal accusation. It was typical of late medieval English law in general and of the various kinds of accusation the law allowed in particular in being subject to a large number of restrictions as to who could appeal whom for what crimes and under what circumstances.[7] If a father of sons was murdered, for instance, only the eldest son could appeal the murder, no matter how strongly the younger sons felt about it. Unless every restriction was punctiliously observed, the whole complicated, time-consuming, and expensive process might be invalidated, perhaps at a late stage. It could even happen as a result of a trivial variation in spelling the name of the accused.

Malory's treatment of the appeal elsewhere in the *Morte Darthur* shows a definite awareness that the appeal was a process with rules and limits. In every instance apart from that of Elaine's threat, he envisages the most famous use of the process, the appeal of treason, leading to trial by battle.[8] His awareness of how restrictive the law on appeals was in real life in his own time is shown by a comment he makes as narrator on the law in King Arthur's time. Nearly all those appealed in the *Morte Darthur* were accused of crimes that fifteenth-century English law would have called murder rather than treason,[9] so immediately after the first case has been mentioned, Malory explains that "alle maner of murthers in tho dayes were callid treason" (219.13-14).[10] This narrator's comment is most unusual in emphasising by explicit statement that the world of the *Morte Darthur* was different from that of fifteenth-century England (and indeed from the other medieval centuries) in something other than greater goodness or simplicity or both; and it justifies us in taking the word *appele* in other respects in the full sense it had in law in Malory's day.

What Elaine of Astolat has in mind, however, cannot be the appeal of treason, which was not available to a woman. The law said a woman could only appeal for two crimes.[11] One of them is obviously not in question here: rape. The other must be and is: a woman could appeal if her husband, having been mortally wounded, died in her arms. In practice the king's justices sometimes allowed a woman to appeal for other offences, such as the killing of a son, a brother, or a nephew, or even, on occasion, for robbery; but these were irregular accretions to the two crimes for which this redress was provided by law. To understand how Malory has characterized Elaine, we must set her words against this background. In a moment of acute distress, she is saying much more than that if Lancelot were to die she would tell the world that Bors and her brother were morally responsible for his death. She is saying that she would start proceedings against them for murder, proceedings that the law would only have allowed her to initiate if Lancelot had been her husband. The image of Lancelot as her husband has taken such firm possession of her that an acute emergency, far from dislodging it, reinforces it. Yet it is an illusion: she is living in a world that does not exist. This is surely excess, even if Lancelot's thoughtless behavior is partly responsible for it. With this in mind we must surely interpret her later words on her death-bed as accusing herself of excess. It is characteristic of her that she should lay no blame on Lancelot.

In all this, Malory as narrator is momentarily a man who knows the criminal law of the fifteenth century, which Malory the author knew from bitter experience, and the *Morte Darthur* is momentarily of the fifteenth century rather than timeless.

University College of North Wales

NOTES

[1] See Mary Wildman, "Twentieth-Century Arthurian Literature: An Annotated Bibliography," *Arthurian Literature*, 2 (1982), 127-57, and the "Supplementary Bibliography" by various hands in *Arthurian Literature*, 3 (1983), 129-36.

[2] See my *Romance and Chronicle: A Study of Malory's Prose Style* (London: Barrie and Jenkins, 1971), pp. 144-45.

[3] Noel Denholm-Young, *Collected Papers* (Cardiff: University of Wales Press, 1969), pp. 95-98.

[4] *Romance and Chronicle*, passim.

[5] See 428.28-29, 498.33, and 502.30. A handful of references, all in the Grail story, help to keep the date mentioned in the first of these passages in the reader's mind: 450.15, 450.34, 500.13, 501.25. All references to Malory's text are to *Caxton's Malory*, ed. James W. Spisak (Berkeley and Los Angeles: University of California Press, 1983).

[6] This line is not in the *Mort Artu*, ed. J. Frappier (Geneva: Droz, 1954), § 40-41, or in *Le Morte Arthur*, ed. J. Bruce, E.E.T.S. E.S. 88 (London: Trübner and Co., 1903), ll. 384-91.

[7] John Bellamy, *Crime and Public Order in England in the Later Middle Ages* (London: Routledge and Kegan Paul, 1973), pp. 126-27. The rest of what I say on the law of appeals follows Bellamy, pp. 121-61.

[8] See George Neilson, *Trial by Combat* (Glasgow: Hodge and Co., 1890); Ernest C. York, "The Duel of Chivalry in Malory's Book XIX,"

Philological Quarterly, 48 (1969), 186-91; Nadine R. Eynon, "The Use of Trial by Battle in the Work of Sir Thomas Malory," M.A. diss. (Saskatoon, 1974).

[9] King Angwysshe by Sir Blamour (murder), 219.6; King Mark by Sir Amant (murder), 301.25; Sir Palomides by Sir Archade (murder), 339.16; the Earl de la Planche by Sir Safyr (? rebellion), 341.5; Queen Guenevere by Sir Mador de la Porte (murder), 509.10; Queen Guenevere by Sir Melyagaunt (adultery by the queen as "hyghe treason"), 546.29.

Adultery by the queen had been made treason by a statute of 1352. It was one of the charges on which Anne Boleyn was executed in 1536 (along with incest, poisoning the previous queen, and aiming at the deaths of the king and the Princess Mary), and the sole charge on which Catherine Howard was executed in 1542; *Calendar of State Papers, Spanish*, v, 125-31; *Statutes of the Realm*, iii (London, 1817), 857-58. In the first case the court gave the king the option of having his wife burnt (like Guenevere) or beheaded. He chose beheading, which seems to have set a precedent in the second case.

[10] See also 512.13-16.

[11] Bellamy, p. 126.

Malory's Diptych *Distinctio*:
The Closing Books of his Work

Judson B. Allen

As we learn more about medieval definitions of literature, the character and quality of Malory's art become more visible.[1] It is not enough to notice that he re-compiles sequential narratives from interlaced materials, nor that he is a master of the effects possible to a primitive English parataxis,[2] though these matters are true and important. Now that we know what such medieval structures as compilation properly are,[3] we are justified in looking for large, even architectonic, effects.

The proper understanding of a medieval text begins when one has divided it into its true parts, in order to see these parts, arrayed in the text, as a *distinctio* of whose name or title the text is a treatment, and whose form is the *forma tractandi* of the text.[4] James F. Burke has recently found these notions useful in the analysis of medieval Spanish romance.[5] Jill Mann, writing of Langland and *distinctiones*, says that "the influence of their structure is fundamental to his meditation" on scripture.[6] My purpose in this essay is not to identify any particular surviving *distinctio* as the thematic ground of Malory's text, but rather to show how the form of the *distinctio* can explain the end of his work—that part where it is customary to notice that he best achieves tragic narrative in the

237

modern plotted sense. In part, what I intend is simply to explain Malory's text—how it works and what it means. In part, I attempt an experiment in literary theory. By exhibiting Malory's last tales as a diptych *distinctio*, whose normal end is definition, rather than as a tragic plot, whose end is conclusion, I hope to suggest that there is a medieval "sense of an ending" just as satisfactory as the modern ones which require "tock" after "tick" in a temporal sequence.[7]

In a number of places, Malory's medieval practice of making arrays of parts is simply obvious. It is universally acknowledged that the Tale of Balin, put as parallel to a great deal else, is a microcosm of much of Malory's larger story. The description of Sir Lancelot in Sir Ector's eulogy is schematic in the extreme; in medieval terms, it is a double *distinctio* of knightly actions and knightly virtues (1259).[8] Malory's Roman War episode is another double *distinctio*: of embassies and combats. Malory's displacing the story of the engendering of Galahad to the end of the book of Tristram, where it parallels the love story of Tristram and Isolde with which the book begins, suggests that in that long compilation of treason, love, feud, and matricide there may well be found a *distinctio* on love. Clearly, Malory the compiler has both precedent and skill for the arraying of many parts on large tapestries.

The Roman War episode, where Malory's manipulation of the *distinctio* is especially elegant and clear, can serve as a formal introduction to his more complex strategy in the closing books. In this tale, four embassies alternate with three pairs of battle episodes. In terms of the *distinctio* form, the book is interlaced, even as the narrative follows a straight temporal sequence. Of the four embassies, the first and last are to Arthur from his enemy Rome. The middle ones are to the Romans from Arthur. The first embassy, in which Lucius asks tribute of Arthur, is outrageous in its demands, but all proper forms are observed, and the messengers' personal safety is assured. The second embassy, that of Gawain and others of Arthur's knights to Lucius, is outrageously unformed— there are ambushes and treacheries of all sorts—but the message delivered is a true one, within the economy of the triumphant Arthurian order. The third embassy is decorously formal, but its content is not. Arthur returns the bodies of the Emperor Lucius and his royal allies to Rome with great ceremony; but he uses captured

Roman senators as his messengers, and the message itself—that the bodies are all the tribute Rome is going to get—is declaration of further war. The final embassy, in which Roman senators and cardinals offer Arthur coronation as emperor, is full of propriety both in form and content and establishes peace and good order throughout what amounts to the world.

The three pairs of battle episodes interlaced in this series of embassies are themselves also an array. The first consists of Arthur's dream, followed by his combat with the giant of Gene. The second consists of an escort of prisoners to Paris, much hindered by fighting, and the general battle in which Lucuis is killed. The third consists of city-takings, followed by the combat with Priamus which comes before his conversion and baptism. The pattern which this series of six forms is that of a center in a frame. At the ends are direct transactions with the supernatural—a dream at the beginning, and a baptism at the end. The combat with the giant, which destroys a miraculous evil, balances the city-takings which construct the earthly realm. In the middle is simple war.

Malory, it would seem, agrees with Clausewitz. War is the continuation of diplomacy by other means. Malory's double interlaced *distinctio* of embassies and combats arrays all the possiblities, *realiter* and *formaliter*, of the kinds of diplomacy and the kinds of confrontation, in a text which is also a story line accomplishing the imperial dignity for whose accomplishment and preservation the various activities of diplomacy and war are chief instruments. The formal parts of Malory's text exhibit and, by arraying in exhibit, analyze the logical topics of which the story is an example and an enactment. The story tells us what happened. The *distincto* tells us the *quidditas*—tells us what it was that happened. The *distinctio*, to use the medieval terminology, exhibits the *forma tractandi* of the story. Arthur's imperial history, like all imperial histories, is an interlace of conflict and negotiation.

Malory's two-part conclusion is more subtle than this, but it works in the same formally sophisticated way. This part of Malory's work occupies Caxton's Books XVIII through XXI, which is found in Eugène Vinaver's version as Books Seven and Eight. My analysis depends on the plots to be found in the text as it divides wherever a major section of narrative is completed. Thus the episode of the

Poisoned Apple is the first part, the story of the Fair Maid of Astolat is the second part, and so on. These are generally the divisions Vinaver makes, but without much help from the rubrication of his manuscript.[9] Caxton's divisions make the same sort of diptych point which I intend to argue, but with less clarity; in effect, he groups the two sets of five narrative parts into two sets of two, each of which makes one part of the first three narratives, and another of the last two. Caxton thus balances chivalric war with real war in his first parts, and treason and holiness with treason and holiness in his concluding parts. For convenience I refer to the two major units as Books Seven and Eight.

Malory's text, then, concludes with two units of five parts each. The parts of Book Seven form a five part *distinctio* of *exempla,* which array the defining activities of the good knight: defense of the innocent, love, combat, defeat of treason, and the work of holiness. The parts of Book Eight repeat, part by part and topic by topic, in the same order, this same *distinctio.* In both parts the chief actor is Lancelot; in both, his paradigmatic actions are good and honorably motivated. He is the definitive good knight. But his presence in the story makes no consistent, definitive difference. In the first book, the society of the Round Table is stable and secure and, if not totally good, then in control of internal and external evil, and able, in the end, to be the social context of Lancelot's holy miracle of healing. In the second, by contrast, Lancelot, though just as good and upright as before, is present in the society of the Round Table as pretext, even cause, of its destruction, and the holiness achieved at the end of the book is achieved by the sacrifice of society and finally of life itself. Malory's point in this maneuver of parallelism is that the good knight is not enough.

The tragedy of Malory's great work is precisely this, that the goodness and continuing life of society is not guaranteed by the presence in it of good and noble knights. In all times and places, this is a tragic question—why can good people not make life work? It is manifestly true that they cannot, and never could, for long. For Malory, the question is particularly poignant because his knights, and especially Lancelot, are admirable not just as human beings but also as people of worship, as nobles, as aristocrats. Their goodness is not just personal; it is ontological, rhetorical, typical. The failure of the ideal society which their goodness, real as it is, cannot sustain, is therefore an even more radical failure. What is pitiable in the meanest wretch is past speaking of in a noble gentleman as well as in a king.

Intuitively, this tragedy is obviously central to Malory's thought and to his story. Neither Lancelot nor Arthur can save the Round Table from its doom, and Galahad does not try. Both religious idealism and the idealism of love impinge in ways which are ultimately destructive on the real society which must live out real history. The story that Malory tells is the story of the death of Arthur's ideal society. But what the story tells, the form also says, and says with a clarity of articulation and definition which is, even more than story as such, the central achievement of Malory's art.

The parallels between Books Seven and Eight are precise and detailed beyond all possibility of coincidence. In most cases the parallels involve a simple repeating—the same things happen in the same places in both books. In both first parts, for instance, Lancelot rescues Guenevere from death by fire. Sometimes, however, the parallels involve precise opposites, or inverses. Thus, at the beginning of the episode of the Poisoned Apple Lancelot's love is spoken of as "in his prevy thoughtes and in hys myndis so sette inwardly to the quene" (1045.13-14).[10] By contrast, at the beginning of Book Eight "sir Aggravayne and sir Mordred had ever a prevy hate unto the quene" (1161.11-12). Further, there is at the beginning of both these parts a separation: in the first, Lancelot goes away from Guenevere, and "depaited with grete hevynes, that unneth he myght susteyne hymselff for grete dole-makynge" (1047.10-11). In the second, Gawain, Gaheris, and Gareth separate from Agravain and Mordred: "And therewythall they three departed makynge grete dole" (1162.30). As departures, the two incidents are exactly congruent; the difference, that the one is a parting of lovers and the other of brothers, evokes by its existence that complex awareness of the family values so destructive to the Round Table society. The sense of parallel is doubtless reinforced by Malory's formulaic prose, which makes all incidents sound, in their telling, similar, but behind the words are actions, which would be what they are however described. The repeating of major actions, so that the five parts of each unit say the same definition of knighthood twice, thus receives contrapuntal commentary when details contrast or when, as in the example I have just proposed, the same action (a separation) happens to different people.

In both parts one, as I have said, Lancelot rescues Guenevere from death by fire. In both parts she is innocent of the charge upon which she has been condemned. At least Malory wished to believe so, in what might be considered the teeth of the evidence, for he comments:

> For, as the Freynshhe booke seyth, the quene and sir Launcelot were togydirs. And whether they were abed other at other maner of disportis, me lyste nat thereof make no mencion, for love that tyme was nat as love ys nowadayes.   (1165.10-13)

In both parts, Lancelot is hidden and reveals himself as deliverer at the last moment. In both parts Bors is Lancelot's counselor. In both parts the innocent are killed by mistake.

In both parts two, the Fair Maid of Astolat and Lancelot's final rescue of Guenevere, the fundamental parallel is that Lancelot's household includes a loving woman, whom in both he gives up. In both, for the sake of making his renunciation of the woman perfect, Lancelot offers a money endowment. Both conclude with a mournful departure by boat. In both, Lancelot cannot press his victories in combat to their mortal conclusion, because of the pity and love he feels for those he has vanquished. In both, Arthur and Gawain are especially singled out: in the first they do not participate in the combat (1069); in the second they should not (1191). As far as definitions are concerned, what is centrally at stake in both parts is the nature of Lancelot's potential consort, if he is to have one, and the ground of his renunciation.

Malory underlines this focus at the beginning of Book Eight, as Lancelot and Bors plan their appropriate courses of action if Guenevere is to be rescued:

> "Sir, that shall be the leste care of us all," seyde sir Bors, "for how ded the moste noble knyght sir Trystram? By youre good wyll, kept nat he with hym La Beall Isode nere three yere in Joyous Garde, the whych was done by youre althers avyce? And that same place ys youre owne, and in lyke wyse may ye do, and ye lyst, and take the quene knyghtly away with you, if so be that the kynge woll jouge her to be brente. And in Joyous Garde may ye kepe her longe inowe untyll the hete be paste of

the kynge, and than hit may fortune you to brynge the quene
agayne to the kynge with grete worshyp, and peradventure ye
shall have than thanke for youre bryngyng home where othir
may happyn to have magré."

"That ys hard for to do," seyde sir Launcelot, "for by sir
Trystram I may have a warnynge: for whan by meanys of tretyse
sir Trystram brought agayne La Beall Isode unto kynge Marke
from Joyous Garde, loke ye now what felle on the ende, how
shamefully that false traytour kyng Marke slew hym as he sate
harpynge afore hys lady, La Beall Isode. Wyth a grounden
glayve he threste hym in behynde to the harte, whych grevyth
sore me," seyde sir Launcelot, "to speke of his dethe, for all the
worlde may nat fynde such another knyght." (1172.34-1173.20)

Throughout the whole tradition of Arthurian storytelling, it is the
love story of Tristan and Isolt that is the paradigm, in that it is this
one which is most often adduced as exemplum when other loves are
being contemplated, consummated, or evaluated. Tristram and
Isolde commit the paradigmatic courtly adultery; Lancelot's
relation to Guenevere exists, at least for Malory, as a part of an
exercise of worshipful knighthood whose center is courtly honor
rather than sexual passion. But Malory's reference to Tristram and
Isolde raises the question of the consort, and defines Lancelot's
taking of Guenevere to Joyous Garde as analogous to Tristram's
keeping of Isolde, even while the conclusion drawn from the
reference is that King Arthur, unlike King Mark, is "trew of hys
promyse" (1173.25). Lancelot, however, chooses to have no consort.
He says to the Fair Maid of Astolat: "'I myght have bene maryed and
I had wolde, but I never applyed me yett to be maryed'" (1089.26-27).
When he delivers Guenevere at Carleil, he says to Gawain: "'For and
the quene had be so dere unto me as ye noyse her, I durste have kepte
her frome the felyshyp of the beste knyghtes undir hevyn'" (1202.6-
8). Both statements, of course, put the point they deny—Lancelot
could have had a consort had he wanted one. But his real love is the
society of the Round Table:

> "Moste nobelyst Crysten realme, whom I have loved aboven all
> othir realmys! And in the I have gotyn a grete parte of my
> worshyp, and now that I shall departe in thys wyse, truly me
> repentis that ever I cam in thys realme, that I shulde be thus
> shamefully banysshyd, undeserved and causeles!" (1201.9-14)

And this frustrated lament corresponds to the sorrow of Elaine of

Astolat, both in its theme and in the fact that it comes, as does hers, just before the departure by boat.

At the center of both major sections there is ritual combat: the Candelmas Day tournament at Westminster and the battle at Benwick. The first of these is a tournament and the second a war, but both are decorous. The first is, in fact, more warlike than the second, in that it involves general melee, while the fighting at Benwick consists largely of single combats. A sense of ritual form, including Gawain's magical increase in power, dominates in the real war—Malory's obvious purpose is to draw these events as far as possible within the decorum of worshipful combat in tournament. In both conflicts the principal opponents are Lancelot and Gawain; in both cases a central concern, on Lancelot's side at least, is for honorable behavior. Family concerns are chiastically balanced. In the Candelmas Day tournament it is Lancelot who must be identified, so that his family will know him, and not repeat the mistake made in the previous tournament, when Bors wounded Lancelot so grievously. In the battle of Benwick Arthur is not so much king and sovereign of the Round Table as he is simply Gawain's uncle, waging war as family feud. In both parts personal relations predominate. In the tournament, Gareth's love for Lancelot takes precedence even over his relation to his brothers, "And he that was curteyse, trew, and faythefull to hys frynde was that tyme cherysshed" (1114.31-32). In the siege there would have been no war at all had not Gawain pursued so relentlessly his personal hatred of Lancelot.

In both parts four, the central theme is treason; the event which enacts it, the abduction of Guenevere. Near the beginning of both, Malory puts a lament over the fickleness and instability of the people of modern times. Just before the Knight of the Cart episode:

> For, lyke as wynter rasure dothe allway arace and deface grene summer, so faryth hit by unstable love in man and woman, for in many persones there ys no stabylité . . . But nowadayes men can nat love sevennyght but they muste have all their desyres. That love may nat endure by reson, for where they bethe sone accorded and hasty, heete sone keelyth. And ryght so faryth the love nowadayes, sone hote sone colde. Thys ys no stabylité. (1119.14-1120.2)

And before Arthur's final battle with Mordred:

244

> Lo ye all Englysshemen, se ye nat what a myschyff here
> was? For he that was the moste kynge and nobelyst knyght of
> the worlde, and moste loved the felyshyp of noble knyghtes,
> and by hym they all were upholdyn, and yet myght nat thes
> Englyshemen holde them contente with hym. Lo thus was the
> olde custom and usayges of thys londe, and men say that we of
> thys londe have nat yet loste that custom. Alas! thys ys a greate
> defaughte of us Englysshemen, for there may no thynge us
> please no terme.   (1229.6-14)

Since the abduction by Melyagaunt happens within the sovereignty
of Arthur, and the abduction by Mordred leads to the end of that
sovereignty, the later episode does not so much balance the first as
fulfill it. In both, a happy outcome depends on the presence of
Lancelot, but only in the first does Lancelot actually come in time.
The society of the Round Table rejects Lancelot, but cannot survive
Lancelot's absence from it. Moreover, a similar atmosphere of evil
broods over both parts. The ambushes and trap-door tricks of
Melyagaunt, and the spectacle of a faithful horse walking on its
own entrails, are more trivial than the slaughter of a hundred
thousand, but no less dark and ugly.

The final focus is on the personal and individual holiness of
Lancelot. In Book Seven he performs a miracle of healing, as the
best knight in the world. In Book Eight he gives up knighthood
altogether, obeys the queen's command that he never see her again,
and dies eventually, after seven years of rigorously penitential life,
of an ideal and holy sorrow—"and he laye as he had smyled, and the
swettest savour aboute hym that ever they felte" (1258.16-17). The
renunciation of Book Eight seems to be rehearsed in Book Seven
when Lancelot prays:

> "Now, Blyssed Fadir and Son and Holy Goste, I beseche The of
> Thy mercy that my symple worshyp and honesté be saved, and
> Thou Blyssed Trynyté, Thou mayste yeff me power to hele thys
> syke knyght by the grete vertu and grace of The, but, Good
> Lorde, never of myselff."   (1152.20-25)

And when the healing is accomplished, and the court rejoices, "ever
sir Launcelote wepte, as he had bene a chylde that had bene
beatyn!" (1152.25-26). Children deserve their beatings, but when
they are beaten, their very vulnerability vindicates them. Lancelot is
never more of a sinner than when he is most holy; his achievement

is his punishment and his vindication at the same time. This point may well be taken as the emotional climax of the book.

Books Seven and Eight, then, are elaborately parallel. This diptych effect must be what Malory meant in his rubric, put between the two books, when he said, "And here *on the othir syde* folowyth the Moste Pyteuous Tale of the Morte Arthure" (1154.16-17, italics mine). Each side of the diptych is, as I have said, a *distinctio*: five parts, each containing one paradigmatic action, which as a set of five defines the ideal knight as one who defends the innocent, loves honorably but does not marry, engages in the mannered combat of tournament and honorable war, fights against treason, and accomplishes the works of holiness.

Eques, the knight, is not a popular *distinctio* topic, doubtless because collections of *distinctiones* tended to be made as aids to preachers, not romancers.[11] I have found it only in the *Repertorium morale* of Pierre Bersuire. His outlining introduction is suffucient indication of his concern:

> Cum igitur equites respectu peditum sint, ut communiter, conditione nobiliores, factis bellicis utiliores, ad invadendum audaciores, ad fugiendum agiliores, videtur, quod per equites intelliguntur omnes illi, qui alios virtute et potentia praecellunt, et qui aliis praeeminent et praesunt. Dicam ergo, quod equites, significant animos corpora foventes, praelatos subditos regentes, tyrannos pauperibus nocentes. Primo ergo dico, quod equites possunt dici animi, qui in humanis latent corporibus. Animus enim seu spiritus est quasi eques, corpus vero est sicut equus, . . .[12]

Bersuire's knowledge of knights is obviously practical, rather than chivalric. Malory's knights are not "ad fugiendum agiliores." The superiority which Bersuire picks out for notice soon ceases to relate in more than the most nominal way to knights as such.

For the topic *bellum* or *bellare*, Bersuire assembles the obvious conventions:

> Bellum. Idem est quod guerra, prelium, duellum, controversia, litigium. Et accipitur in scriptura in bono et in malo. In bono quando quis temporaliter iuste bellat, et militat contra malos iustitiam exequendo, vel infideles persequendo. Spiritualiter autem accipitur quando quis contra vitia et tentationes resistit, quando contra ea per penitentiam abstinentiam et castitatem, et caetera opera meritoria preliantur. . . . Item potest accipi in

malo, et hoc temporaliter et spiritualiter. Temporaliter, et sic bellum accipitur pro dissensione, et discordia, divisione, controversia, et murmuratione. . . . Spiritualiter autem accipitur in malo, et sic bellum signat Hostis suggestiones, Carnis tentationes, Mundi vexationes, Inferni turbationes.[13]

The *Distinctiones* of Nicholas Gorham, "cum additionibus," contain under *Bellare*, an article which seems to be outlined with the knight in mind, though *eques* is not mentioned:

Bellare oportet hominem in hac vita contra peccata. Ad quod requiritur primo magnanimitas in agrediendo ut non consentiat sed resistat quia bellator deficiens pre inopia displicet deo. Psal. (17.d.) precinxisti me virtute ad bellum. Secundo sagacitas in progrediendo ut insidias precaveat et occasiones casus fugiat. Prov. 20.e. cogitationes consiliis roborantur et gubernaculis tractanda sunt bella. Et in Psal. (143.a.) benedictus dominus deus meus qui docet manus mea ad prelium et digitos meos ad bellum. Tertio fortitudo ut prevaleat in expugnando et nunquam succumbat. Sap. 8.e. in multitudine videbor bonus in bello fortis. Quarto constantia in perseverando ut nunquam deficiat, sed usque ad finem proficiat. quia tunc amplius insidiatur hostis. Iosue 14.f. hodie septuaginta quinque annorum sum. sic valens ut eo valebam tempore quando ad explorandum terram missus sum. Illius in me temporis fortitudo usque hodie perseverat tam ad bellandum quam ad gaudiendum. Et hanc dat deus. Judith 9.d. tu ipse es deus noster qui conteris bella ab initio et dominus nomen tibi es. Quinto rectitudo intentionis ut propriam vitam eternam faciat et sibi aliis valeat. Mac. 2.e. omnis homo quicumque venerit ad nos in bello in die sabbatorum pugnemus adversus eum et non moriamur. omnes sicut mortui sunt fratres nostri in occultis. Et hanc dat dominus.[14]

Magnanimity, sagacity, fortitude, constancy, and right intention better describe a knight than any other literal combatant, even though the war is a spiritual one, against sin. Lancelot has all of them consistently except "sagacitas in progrediendo ut insidias precaveat et occasiones casus fugiat"—he can cope with anything except, sometimes, treason and enchantment.

Malory's own collected *distinctio*, spoken by Sir Ector, is formally similar; Lancelot is courteous, a true friend and lover, kind, meek, goodly, and stern (1259). The characteristics that Malory chooses are different from those to be found in the Gorham *distinctio*, but they are equally obvious and conventional, and achieve the same effect. The art of such things is very different from that which modern theories of the creative artist would lead us to expect, but it is just as artful in its way, which may be seen in three aspects: as a normative art, as an art of sets, and as an exercise of decorum.

Modern art is an art of particulars—of individuals in uniquely existential situations. Medieval art is an art of universals, which seeks to exhibit, or argue from, definition. Medieval culture is saturated with predictable ideas, values, types, and tropes. Since we already know the definition in question, and since invention ranges within a limited array of topics, it is not the content of a description or an action that makes an author's making of it distinctive. Rather it is his selection and arraying of *groups* of details, each one of which is already likely to be well known. All romance plots are much alike; all knightly battles involve the same strategy of lance and sword. Malory's art is not one of details, nor even of stories and characters, but of sets and sets of sets. An embassy in the Roman War episode is significant not just because it marks a particular stage in the developing relation between Arthur and Lucuis, but because it occurs as one of four embassies, and in relation to one of three double episodes of battle.

Malory's diptych is significant, first of all, because Lancelot occurs twice. We do not have a diptych with Lancelot on one side, and Christ, or Mordred, or the devil on the other. Both sets of five stories, considered as *distinctiones*, define Lancelot. Thus there is no analogy of levels in this diptych, no hierarchy, no demand to read the literal against the spiritual, *in bono* against *in malo*. To realize how unusual this diptych is, we have but to imagine a Doom painting having, not one central Christ enthroned, but two identical ones, one presiding over the heavenly side, and the other over the hellish. The meaning of such a Doom painting would have to be that the presence of Christ does not make the crucial difference between heaven and hell. Theologically, this meaning is manifestly absurd. Ethically and politically, it is profoundly true, and intuitively true of Malory's work. Lancelot is good—he is the best knight that ever was. But his goodness is not enough to alter the fact that the world in which he occurs may be either the society of the Round Table, or the chaos of exile and Salisbury plain.

Malory's twice displayed *distinctio* defines the goodness which thus fails, acting itself out in terms of the kinds of war found in Bersuire's *Repertorium morale*. Besuire tells us that *bellum* includes "guerra, prelium, duellum, controversia, litigium." Three of these are literally military, in a series leading from the more chaotic to the more decorous: war, battle, duel. The second two make a similar progress: controversy in general, and litigation as its most formalized manifestation in due process. Malory's *distinctio* attempts to limit *bellum* to *duellum*. All of Lancelot's fighting seeks the form of single combat, either in its legal form of trial by combat, in its recreational form of tournament, or in the duel form which seeks the punishment of a villain or a criminal. Agravain and Mordred cultivate *controversia*. Lancelot attempts to make it into *duellum*. Arthur insists on *litigium*: "And therefore for my quene he shall nevermore fyght, for she shall have the law" (1175.22-23).[15] Lancelot, in response, turns *duellum* into *guerra*. In so doing he does rescue a queen wrongly condemned and acts, according to his lights, within the essence if not the full decorum of trial by combat. But there is a discrepancy here between the foreground figure of the diptych and the background. Hell—or heaven, if one wishes to admire litigation as more civilized than chivalry—is showing around the edges of the hero. Lancelot's goodness does not quite fit. Accident permits him to kill unarmed friends. And the fit grows more and more imperfect as the society of the Round Table degenerates toward the accidental snake of Salisbury plain, with Lancelot, exiled, present only as a tragic absence.

Lancelot's goodness as a lover fits no better. Malory puts the real paradigm at the end of the Roman War episode, after King Arthur enriches his knights and lords.

> "Sir kynge, we beseche the for to here us all. We ar undir youre lordship well stuffid, blyssed be God, of many thynges; and also we have wyffis weddid. We woll beseche youre good grace to reles us to sporte us with oure wyffis, for, worshyp be Cryste, this journey is well overcom."   (246.6-10)

Lancelot's love is more idealistic than this. He loves the queen, and will not marry at all, because he would give himself and his loyalty totally to the society of worship and knightly combat within which such ideal love is appropriate and all other and more practical loves a distraction. Thus at Joyous Garde Lancelot possesses, for a while, the person of the queen, but the love he professes as he departs is for the "moste nobelyst Crysten realme, whom I have loved aboven all othir realmys!" (1201.9-10).

Lancelot's love of God—the power to be holy which being the best knight in the world gives him—is more ideal still. But within the society of the Round Table, that holiness is a gift, not an achievement. Lancelot's prayer, before the healing of Sir Urry, includes the phrase, "that my symple worshyp and honesté be saved" (1152.21-22). I take seriously here both Vinaver's glosses on "saved"—"to protect" and "to fulfill."[16] On the one hand, Lancelot is asking that his reputation not be compromised by a failure in this crucial test; on the other, he is asking that whatever he is in himself be transformed by the power of God into a greater grace. Both desires are true, and it is the deal of Christian perfection, seldom achieved even within the Pelagian sensibility of English Christianity, that they can both be true at the same time. Even so, however, what happens when Sir Urry is healed is a grace, not an achievement. It is a gift of God. Within the society of the Round Table, holiness is not something that Lancelot achieves, but only something that happens to him by the intervening grace of God. Outside that society, either on the Grail Quest or in the penances of the religious life, holiness may be achieved, and Lancelot, in his way, achieves it. But it is precisely Malory's point that to devote one's self to the achievement of holiness is to leave the society of chivalry—it is an idealism incompatible *in practice* with knighthood. For the knight, love may be believed in, whether love of woman or love of God, but the knight cannot do anything about that love without causing either scandal on the one hand or change of life on the other.

The *distinctio* normally understood as defining all this is the one to be found in the *De regimine principum* of Aegidius Romanus, where the ruler (and by extension, *mutatis mutandis*, any good person) must rightly rule himself, his family, and his realm.[17] Aegidius, of course, is concerned with practical ethics, with *agenda*, not just *intelligenda*. Lancelot's perfection, defined in five paradigmatic actions, is ideal. He is definitively the good knight. Such men are too good to be true—that is, too good to live in the real world. (Galahad did not even try to do so.) Malory does not say this, explicitly. In a sense, he says just the opposite, by claiming so repeatedly that it is the presence of knights such as Lancelot which makes the society of the Round Table worshipful and good. But Malory's structure is also his statement. This ostentation of form, whose focus and referent is Lancelot's knightly perfection and its five defining actions, is also a carrier of meaning.

About this meaning two things can be said. The first is that it is a meaning that contains a "sense of an ending." The second is that, in addition to concluding the story of the Round Table, it also tells us what to conclude about that story. In terms of plot, of course, these last two books are universally understood as the end of the story. But as a diptych *distinctio*, they also contain a definition—of ideal knighthood in the person of Lancelot. The fact that we get the definition twice, in the *distinctio* of Book Seven and again in the *distinctio* of Book Eight, enacts by its very balance a stasis of ending. Further, and still more important, this realization of the definition just as the words stop communicates to Malory's readers a sense of *quod erat demonstrandum*, as if, after vast evidence had been presented, we have just had the summing up. There have been knights and knightly deeds throughout Malory's book; now at the end we find that we have been told what a knight is. Definition has been achieved, and the achievement is conclusive.

It is vitally important, since we live now in an age in which most argument is conducted in terms of cause and effect, that we realize what a different thing it is that Malory has done. Argument from definition is an intrinsically idealist thing to do. It goes with a belief, however lingering and attenuated, in the reality of universals. It goes with belief in natural law instead of only in case law, with the ability to think of right and wrong as ultimately absolute. There is, even as late as Malory, a platonist resonance in it, a hint of static perfection which is even more conclusive, because philosophical, than is the narrative fact that everybody is dead.

The platonic forms of things, of course, never succeed for long in having a real history in the real world. Lancelot functions as an integral part of a society in which God gives a healing miracle in Book Seven; Lancelot is the slandered and disordering outsider whose absent presence explains the chaos of Book Eight. The diptych says what Malory knew, as any idealist who is honest will know, that the ideal is at once most desirable and most destructive. Without its real presence, society is not worth having, but if it is present for long, it causes either chaos or fascism. The dilemma is a diptych, whose two sides are occupied by Lancelot. As narrative, the *Morte* is the story of the fall of the Arthurian society of the Round Table. As logical argument concluding in definition, its focus is Lancelot, and as such, it tells us what it is worth, as human individuals, to be good. Being good is worth infinitely much and, at the same time, nothing at all. The good must always go, like Bors and Ector and Blamour and Bleoberis, "into the Holy Lande, thereas Jesu Cryst was quycke and deed" and there to do "many bataylles upon the myscreantes, or Turkes" and to die "upon a Good Fryday for Goddes sake" (1260.9-15). To be good is to be the necessary alien, living in a society in which one's fellows, by some inevitable accident, misunderstanding, or unexpected snake, turn out to be miscreants and Turks. It is still worth it to be good, but the worth is not of this world, even when the world is Arthur's.

University of Florida

NOTES

[1] The book which best treats with proper seriousness Malory's powers of structural organization is Larry D. Benson, *Malory's Morte Darthur* (Cambridge, Mass.: Harvard University Press, 1976). I especially admire his treatment of the book of Tristram, and of Book One. I have argued for a unity in Malory's book grounded in the *distinctio* of the days of creation week in *The Ethical Poetic of the Later Middle Ages: A Decorum of Convenient Distinction* (Toronto: University of Toronto Press, 1982), pp. 156-66.

[2] P. J. C. Field, *Romance and Chronicle: A Study of Malory's Prose Style* (London: Barrie and Jenkins, 1971).

[3] M. B. Parkes, "The Influence of the Concepts of *Ordinatio* and *Compilatio* on the Development of the Book," *Medieval Learning and Literature: Essays Presented to R. W. Hunt*, ed. J. J. G. Alexander and Margaret Gibson (Oxford: Oxford University Press, 1975), pp. 115-41.

[4] See *The Ethical Poetic*, esp. chapters two and three.

[5] "A New Critical Approach to the Interpretation of Medieval Spanish Literature," *La Corónica*, 9 (1983), 273-79.

[6] "Eating and Drinking in 'Piers Plowman,'" *Essays and Studies*, 32 (1979), 37.

[7] This is the famous image of Frank Kermode, in *The Sense of an Ending* (Oxford: Oxford University Press, 1967), pp. 44-46.

[8] *The Works of Sir Thomas Malory*, 2nd ed., 3 vols., ed. Eugène Vinaver (Oxford: Oxford University Press, 1967). Further references to Malory are cited from this edition by page and line number.

[9] Books seven and eight begin with large initial letters and with their first two lines in larger writing—the decoration indicates that these two points begin parts of equal status. Inferior to these decorations, there are a number of two-line initial letters in the manuscript: on f. 414v, beginning the phrase "than the kynge" (1056.29); on f. 431v, "Than they blew" (1108.3); on f. 435v, "So hit befelle" (1120.14; this a three-line initial); on f.465, "My moste redouted" (1197.4); on f. 475, "As sir Mordred" (1227.1); and on f. 483, "that whan he harde" (1249.4). The three-line initial occurs at the beginning of Caxton's Book XIX; all the others occur at Caxton's chapter breaks. The sentence which Vinaver prints in small capitals on p. 1130, suggesting that it is a rubric of division, is not distinguished in the manuscript by any special handwriting. Vinaver's edition really ignores the *ordinatio* of the manuscript. For a full treatment of this fact, see Murray J. Evans, "The Explicits and Narrative Division in the Winchester MS: A Critique of Vinaver's Malory," *Philological Quarterly*, 58 (1979), 263-81.

The decoration of the manuscript seems to reflect both the eight-book division Vinaver prints, and the twenty-one-book organization of Caxton, with its multitude of chapters. But the manuscript records only a very few of the sixty-nine chapters into which Caxton divides this part of the text. The simplest way to account for this situation is to suppose the manuscript is a revision of Caxton, or at least made under conditions permitting it to be corrupted by contact with Caxton's divisions. Without more manuscripts, it is impossible to tell whether these initial letters represent a tradition of division now not properly understood, or a muddled mixture of two (or more). My reading depends fundamentally on the division between Books Seven and Eight which permits the diptych, but is otherwise made in terms of parallels between incidents, which the presence or absence of initial letters does not change.

[10] The motif of poison in particular, and hiddenness in general, coupled with reference to "prevy thoughtes," suggest that the large question of subjectivity may well be involved here. The same diptych which displays Lancelot as ideal also isolates him as an individual. We can from within the perspective of the twentieth century understand clearly how destructive individualism must be to a society of types, and how private thoughts conduct to solipsism. The incidents Malory records suggest such an individualism *in potentia*. This is not, however, the place for a reading of the unconscious, either of Malory or of his text; I think it highly unlikely that Malory had reached any articulate sense of these matters.

[11] I do not find the entry in the *Summa Abel* (MS. Bodl. 820), nor in the collection of Nicholas Gorham (MS. Hatton 71), Amalric's *Distinctiones ewangeliorum* (MS. Auct. D. 4. 13), the *Rosarium theologicum* (MS. Bodl. 448), the *De vocabulis predicabilibus* of Simon of Bolaston (MS. Bodl. 216), nor in MSS. Bodl. 98, Bodl. 863, Bodl. 627, or Rawl. C. 899. All these are in the Bodleian Library, Oxford.

[12] *Dictionarii seu repertorii moralis Petri Berchorii Pictaviensis ordinis Divi Benedicti* (Venice, 1583), vol. II, p. 41. "Therefore since knights are commonly more noble than foot soldiers, and more useful for war, braver in attack, and more agile in retreat, it appears that knights stand for all those who excel others in strength and power, and are superior and in command. I should say therefore that knights signify souls supporting bodies, prelates ruling subordinates, and tyrants harming paupers. First I say that knights can be called souls, which are concealed in human bodies. The soul or spirit is like a rider, and the body is like a horse."

[13] *Ibid.*, vol. I, p. 248. "It is the same as war, battle, duel, controversy, and litigation. And war is found in scripture in both a good and a bad sense. In a good sense when someone wages war justly in this life, and fights against evil people in defense of justice, or in pursuit of infidels. Spiritually war has a good sense when someone resists vices and temptations, and wages war against them with penitence and abstinence and chastity and other good works . . . . War also has a bad sense, and this both in this world and spiritually. In this world, war means argument, and discord, division, controversy, and grumbling . . . Spiritually war in a bad sense means the suggestions of the enemy, the temptations of the flesh, the vexations of the world, and the disturbances of hell."

[14] Oxford, Bodelian Library MS. Hatton 71, ff. 49v-50r. "A man should fight in this life against sin. For which is required first magnanimity in attempting, so that one resist and not make an armistice, because a warrior who fails because of poverty displeases God. Psalm 17:40, thou hast girded me with strength unto battle. Second is required cleverness as one goes in order to avoid traps and flee occasions of disaster. Proverbs 20:18, designs are strengthened by counsels, and wars are to be managed by governments. And in the Psalter (143:1), blessed be the Lord my God, who teacheth my hands to fight, and my fingers to war. Third is required fortitude that one may fight to win and never fall. Wisdom 8:15, among the multitude I shall be found good, and valiant in war. Fourth is required constancy in persevering that one never fail, but go on to the end, because thus the enemy is more effectively besieged. Joshua 14:10-11, this day I am seventy-five years old, as strong as I was at that time when I was sent to view the land: the strength of that time continueth in me until this day, as well to fight as to rejoice. And God gives this. Judith 9:10, thou art our God, who destroyest wars from the beginning, and the Lord is thy name. Fifth is required rectitude of intention that one make eternal life one's own and strengthen one's self against others. 1 Maccabees 2:41, whosoever shall come up against

us to fight on the sabbath day, we will fight against him, and we will not all die, as our brethren that were slain in the secret places. And the Lord gives this."

[15] For discussion of the fact that legal process is subversive of chivalric values, see R. Howard Bloch, *Medieval French Literature and Law* (Berkeley and Los Angeles: University of California Press, 1977).

[16] Vinaver, *Works,* p. 1739.

[17] See *The Ethical Poetic,* pp. 160-61.

Malory and Caxton's Chivalric Series, 1481-85

J. R. Goodman

Up to the present, the student of Malory has tended to see William Caxton as an interloper rather than as a valuable witness.[1] His testimony as to the fifteenth-century reception of the *Morte Darthur* is, admittedly, complex and scattered. Still, an understanding of Caxton's methods of publication, his patrons, and their political circumstances leads in unexpected ways to the better understanding of Sir Thomas Malory's romances.

It is important to appreciate that Caxton planned his publication of the *Morte Darthur* as one volume in a series of four works of chivalric literature, a series begun in 1480-81 with *Godefroy of Boloyne* and continued through the 1484 *Book of the Ordre of Chyualry* to the *Morte Darthur* and *Charles the Grete* in 1485.[2] The fact that Caxton's series offers a unified political solution to the problems besetting fifteenth-century England has suggested that the printing of these volumes may have been inspired by a single patron.[3] Anthony Wydville, Earl Rivers (1442-83) had been Caxton's main supporter in England.[4] The series reflects Wydville's known interest in the crusade and in chivalric practice.[5] In particular, he shared Caxton's admiration for Burgundian court culture, in Wydville's case inherited from his Burgundian mother,

257

and in Caxton's case the result of thirty years' residence in the Low Countries. While the series' unifying motif of the three Christian Worthies—Arthur, Charlemagne, and Godfrey of Bouillon—was never exclusively Burgundian, the group mirrors its designers' special associations with Burgundian territory.

William Caxton's period of residence in the Low Countries has been dated from around 1444 until 1476. Caxton made Bruges and its environs his base of mercantile operations soon after leaving his apprenticeship. In Flanders, Caxton's distinguished career as a merchant reached its highest point when he served as Governor of the English Nation of Merchant Adventurers in the Low Countries (1462-ca. 1471).[6] In this capacity, Caxton supervised the English trading community in Bruges, Utrecht, and the Low Countries generally, acting as a negotiator in Anglo-Burgundian commercial discussions and as agent for Edward IV. This thirty-year sojourn established Caxton's mature literary taste together with his preeminence as a businessman, diplomat, and administrator.

Beginning in the late fourteenth century, the Valois Dukes of Burgundy had united their French province with Hainaut, Flanders, Brabant, and Zeeland—modern Belgium and the Netherlands.[7] In essence, they had recreated Lotharingia, the Middle Kingdom of the Carolingian period.[8] This unstable chain of territories strung between France and the Holy Roman Empire had parted for a second time by the end of the fifteenth century. Still, when Caxton arrived in Bruges in 1444, he found the Burgundian state at the height of its power. The resplendent court of Duke Philip the Good (1396-1467) has been described in some detail by Otto Cartellieri, Georges Doutrepont, Richard Vaughan, and, most influentially, by Johan Huizinga in *The Waning of the Middle Ages*.[9] This attention has revealed both the familiar and the unexpected. Of the court's attractive power, the most telling example may remain the fact that the Dukes of Burgundy provided later centuries with an ideal picture of the Middle Ages. The costume of our fairy-tale royalty, with their steeple hennins, plate armor, and pointed shoes, testifies to the lasting impact of this Burgundian court on the European imagination.

At least one scholar has described Caxton's program of translation from French into English, begun in 1469 and continued without apparent intermission until his death in 1491, as an attempt to bring Burgundian best-sellers to England.[10] Comparisons of Caxton's list of publications with the catalogues of the library of Philip the Good show how much this was the case. Caxton's first printed books were his own translations of two popular works by one of Philip's chaplains. Caxton states in his epilogue to the *Recuyell of the Histories of Troy* that he was induced to learn printing in order to provide copies for all those who requested them.[11] Analysis of his later chivalric series demonstrates how much Caxton's Westminster printing continued to reflect the taste of the Burgundian court circle he knew in the 1450s and '60s.

Under the Burgundian aegis, Caxton would have been able to attend a large variety of chivalric spectacles.[12] These jousts, pageants, and festivals seem to show real life colliding with fiction. The study of fifteenth-century documents assures the skeptic that the knights of Philip the Good did not consider themselves children amusing themselves with a "make-believe chivalry" or dreamers clinging to an impractical and outmoded ideal of conduct.[13] The conviction of the participants, no less than the pragmatic political goals of their tournaments, conveys their belief in what they were performing. This conviction may also account for the survival of chivalric display and codes of action well into the seventeenth century.[14] The language of the tournament was easily read by Caxton and his contemporaries. It may seem indecipherable now, but often the message can be decoded.

We assume too often that medieval class structure must have been too rigid to allow the prince and the merchant any shared experience. The attempt to define the audience of a literary work strictly by class grows from this frequent supposition.[15] Once again, contemporary witnesses reveal how much the merchant and the knight depended upon one another. In the cities of his domain, the duke brought his court into contact with the mercantile communities that supported his cultural and chivalric enterprises. In fact, these enterprises were often joint ventures. One tournament record of Philippe de Lalaing's 1463 joust, the Bruges *Pas du perron fée,* asserts the necessity of the merchant to such a tournament.

Car Bruges est ungne ville entre les aultres du monde ou l'en rencouvre plus aysement tout ce qu'il fault a faire ungne grant

feste pour tout vivres et marchandissez, a cause qu'elle est si
bien servie de la mer, et pour les grans et riches marchans qui y
sont et qui y viennent de toutes pars.[16]

The merchants of Duke Philip's realm were involved as
spectators and suppliers to court pageants, and also as participants
in ceremonials of their own devising. The innumerable ducal
entries in which the cities of their domain welcomed Philip the
Good and his son Charles the Bold show the citizens' familiarity
with the chivalric mythology of the Burgundian court. Philip the
Good's 1455 Arras entry and the 1466 and 1473 Abbeville and Dijon
entries of Charles the Bold celebrated Gideon, one of the founding
heroes of the Burgundian order of the Golden Fleece.[17] At a 1454
entry to Louvain, Philip the Good was hailed as the conqueror of
the Middle East, anticipating the success of the Duke's newly
announced crusade. The 1463 Mons entry renewed this theme with
its tableaux of past crusades.

Perhaps the most celebrated spectacle of Caxton's years in the
Low Countries would have been the 1454 Feast of the Pheasant held
by Philip the Good at Lille. The duke mounted this elaborate
production in support of his ambition to avenge the Western defeat
at Nicopolis in 1396 and free the Holy Land from the Turks.[18]
Caxton was hardly likely to have attended the feast itself; still, news
of its marvels spread with understandable speed. The event began
with Adolph of Cleves' joust in the character of the Knight of the
Swan (the *Chevalier au cygne* of romance). This elegant *pas d'armes*
paled before the banquet at which Philip announced his
project. The smallest table in the hall bore three *entremets:* a
tropical forest populated by automata to represent wild animals
stalking through it, another of a peddler carrying his pack, and a
third of a lion following his tamer, who was beating a dog to
intimidate the lion.[19] A play of *Jason at Colchis* complimented the
duke's order of the Golden Fleece. These interludes were crowned by
the entrance of a Saracen giant leading an elephant. A tower on the
elephant's back accommodated the chronicler Olivier de la Marche
himself, dressed as a Beguine to impersonate the distressed Holy
Church. Philip the Good offered his crusading vows on a live
pheasant with a collar of gold. He engaged himself to join the King
of France in a new crusade and to face the Sultan in single combat.
His oath was approved by God's Grace, a lady dressed as a white

nun, leading twelve maidens in golden veils to represent the Twelve Virtues.[20] The nobles who attended were encouraged to present similar vows, as were the absent princes collected in Arras, Bruges, Mons, and Holland over the following two months. The feast represented a shocking extravagance, of course, *fort oultrageuse et desraisonnable despense,* but it also harnessed the forces of court theatre and chivalry to accomplish the duke's major goal. Set against the Duke of Burgundy's crusade propaganda, that of William Caxton's series seems modest indeed.

Caxton's residence in Bruges and its environs coincided with the chivalric career of a young man who has always been considered the Burgundian knight *par excellence.* Jacques de Lalaing (1421-53) is celebrated in his chivalric biography, *Le Livre des faits de Jacques de Lalaing.*[21] He carried his own fame as a knight-errant as far as the courts of Portugal and Scotland, where he displayed his skill in jousting matches. His 1450 *pas d'armes,* the *Pas de la fontaine aux pleurs,* required him to defend a chosen piece of land near Châlons-sur-Saône in Burgundy against all comers for an entire year, much as the knight Alexander the Orphan defends the grounds of a ruined castle in Malory's *Tristram.*[22] Before his death in 1453, Jacques de Lalaing was meditating a final expedition to snatch a cup from the Emperor's table and challenge the imperial knights to joust for it. After that exploit, he intended to end his career as a crusader. He was, instead, killed by cannonfire during the revolt of Ghent.[23] This fate has been regarded as dampeningly unchivalric, but Jacques' contemporaries saw nothing incongruous in his life and death. They regarded him from start to finish as a paragon. Jacques de Lalaing, as master of chivalric spectacle, soldier and courtier—the three roles were considered inseparable from one another—fulfilled the ideal of Burgundian knighthood. (Today, he would have been an astronaut.) William Caxton would have been attentive to observe this knight of renown who was also a young man of his own generation.

Jacques' younger brother Philippe de Lalaing emulated him in chivalric endeavor. The records of Philippe's three-day *Pas du perron fée* provided the reference to the foreign merchants of Bruges cited earlier in this essay. The "fiction" on which the joust was based—in effect, a custom-made romance giving the plot of the tournament—imagined Philippe as the captive of an enchantress much like a benevolent Morgan le Fay. The knight was imprisoned in a magic boulder *(le perron fée)*. He might only win release by agreeing to challenge the knights of Philip the Good to joust against him. On the day of the tournament, the marketplace at Bruges had been supplied with an artificial rock, out of which the knight challenger rode at the outset of the day's engagement. Caxton could have attended the *Pas du perron fée*. Indeed, he would have had some difficulty in avoiding it, since it was held in the great market square of the city. The penchant for "justes of pees" Caxton was to display in his epilogue to the *Ordre of Chyualry* would have been founded on his experience as a spectator at events of this kind.

Caxton's presence was indispensable at one chivalric spectacle in particular. This was the *Pas de l'arbre d'or* held by the Great Bastard of Burgundy, Antoine de la Roche (1421-1504), the bibliophile, crusader, and diplomat, perhaps Philip the Good's most distinguished illegitimate son. The tournament celebrated the wedding of the new duke, Charles the Bold, and Edward IV's sister Margaret of York in July 1468. Caxton would have appeared prominently as the English merchants of the Low Countries greeted a duchess of their own nation. The ceremony took place on the third of July. On the fourth, the English merchants joined in a procession to escort the new duchess into Bruges. The nine days that followed were devoted to appropriately magnificent festivities. The market square was requisitioned once more for the tournament, and ornamented this time with a golden fir tree *(l'arbre d'or)* on which the shields of the knights who jousted there were to be hung. The Bastard of Burgundy awaited his opponents in a pavilion of white and gold damask blazoned with golden trees.

Among the most resplendent of the participants was Anthony Wydville, then Lord Scales, the Queen of England's eldest brother. Perhaps significantly, these marriage celebrations united Caxton with his two major patrons, Margaret of York and Anthony Wydville. Margaret was to encourage Caxton's first venture into translation, as his prologue to the *Recuyell* indicates. Upon Caxton's return to England, Wydville began to supply Caxton's press at Westminster with translations and suggestions for projects.

Anthony Wydville's appearance as the principal escort of Margaret of York testified to his position of trust at the court of his brother-in-law. Edward IV's policy of supporting the Wydvilles to counterbalance the less dependent nobility was to end in the ruin of the Wydvilles after the king's death, but in 1468 the scheme was still operating as intended.[24] The Wydvilles recognized their immediate and natural unpopularity; they became targets of disdain from the moment of Edward's unwelcome announcement that he had married Elizabeth Wydville. In fact, Anthony Wydville's bias toward Burgundian elegance and chivalry can be seen as an apposite reaction to his family's notoriety. The Wydvilles were the children of a handsome upstart, Sir Richard Wydville, and Jacquetta de St. Pol, who was the daughter of an illustrious Burgundian house and the widow of Henry V's brother John, Duke of Bedford. Since their mother had once been the second lady in England, her offspring understandably chose to emphasize their maternal lineage as they attempted to demonstrate that they were in every respect worthy of an alliance with the House of York.[25]

Anthony Wydville's memorable joust with the Bastard of Burgundy at Smithfield in 1467 had summoned the Burgundian knight to confront him before an audience of Londoners. The London chroniclers and the *Mirror of Magistrates* of the next century still recall Wydville's feats on this occasion with nostalgia. One major object of this famous performance would have been to display the Wydville coat of arms beside that of the ducal house of Burgundy. Proof of nobility was required as a prerequisite for participation in any tournament of this kind. The joust established Anthony Wydville's good birth and that of his sister the Queen; the Wydville claims of high ancestry were reinforced as the spectators eyed the shared quarterings of the opponents' shields.[26]

To no one's surprise, the Anthony Wydville who graced the proceedings at Bruges in 1648 seemed almost more Burgundian than the Burgundians. Cartellieri singled out the English lord's entourage to exemplify the splendor of the occasion. Even his pages were resplendent in "white hoseaux and bodycoats of black satin; the green velvet surtouts were studded with silver blossoms, yellow feathers waved on the black velvet berets which were lined with crimson gold brocade."[27] Unfortunately, the elegance of Anthony Wydville's arrival in the lists was marred by a mishap. The Bastard of Burgundy, who had sworn friendship with Wydville at the

Smithfield joust, and therefore could not oppose him, accompanied Wydville into the lists as a gesture of courtesy. There the Burgundian prince was kicked in the knee by a horse and injured so severely that he had to abandon his role as challenger in the tournament. Wydville's meeting with Caxton was unlikely to have offset this major embarrassment in the English jouster's mind.

William Caxton returned permanently to England in 1476. He did not arrive in pomp as the Governor of the English Merchant Adventurers, but in a state he may have thought of as eclipse. Caxton's demotion seems to have occurred about 1470, at the time of Edward IV's exile.[28] Caxton retreated to the court of Margaret of York, and from there to Cologne, where he lived for the next year or so, translating Raoul LeFèvre's *Recuiel* and learning the new art of printing.[29] By 1473, Caxton had returned to Bruges, where he began his career as a printer with his translation of LeFèvre's popular Burgundian prose romance.

The political chill that was setting in against the English under Charles the Bold may have hastened Caxton's return to England. The aggressive new Duke of Burgundy, who, as Grafton says, "in hys time could neuer agree with peace and concorde," liked to boast of his own claim to the English throne.[30] Peaceable mercantile relations suffered accordingly. Perhaps by coincidence, Anthony Wydville had also just returned from his succession of Spanish and Italian pilgrimages. Like Caxton, Earl Rivers had suffered a change of fortune, narrowly escaping as Warwick hunted down and executed his father and brother. Over the next seven years, Wydville, governor to his nephew the Prince of Wales, proved an important patron for Caxton's new press at Westminster. Wydville's own translations of the *Dicts and Sayings of the Philosophres* (1477), Christine de Pisan's *Moral Proverbs* (20 February 1478), and the *Cordiale* (February 1479) may bear witness to their translator's escalating high seriousness.[31] Wydville wrote of himself as "subgette and thral vnto the stormes of fortune . . . perplexid with worldly adversitees Of the whiche I, Antoine Wydeuille . . . largely and in many different maners haue had my parte."[32] The gesture reported in Grafton, where Wydville is depicted sending a message of comfort to this nephew Dorset after their arrest in 1483, echoes the same mood of resignation:

> And at dinner the Duke of Gloucester sent a dishe from his awne table to the Lorde Ryvers, praiyng him to be of goode cheere, all should be well enough. And he thanked the Duke, and prayed the Messenger to beare it to his Nephew the Lorde Richard Gray, with the same message for his comfort, as one to whom such aduersitie was straunge: But himselfe had bene in all his dayes inbred therewith, and therefore could beare it the better.[33]

This is the same Earl Rivers who wrote "somewhat musing, and more mourning," the unpredictability of fortune on the eve of his execution later that same year.[34]

The prologue to Wydville's first translation, the *Dicts*, conveys an immediate sense of Caxton's familiar commerce with his patron. Caxton teases the serious Earl for having omitted a string of antifeminist aphorisms from his text:

> But I apperceyue that my sayd lord knoweth veryly that suche defautes ben not had ne founden in the wymen born and dwellyng in these partyes ne Regyons of the world. . . . For I wote wel. of what someuer condicion women ben in Grece. the women of this contre ben right good/ wyse/ playsant/ humble/ discrete/ sobre/ chast/ obedyent to their husbondis/ trewe/ secrete/ stedfast/ euer besy/ and never ydle/ Attemperat in speking/ and vertuous in alle their werkis. or atte leste sholde be so.[35]

Caxton's lively banter with his somber patron establishes the closeness of their collaboration.

In 1481, when Caxton translated and printed a *Godefroy of Boloyne* based on William of Tyre's history of the First Crusade, he evidently had a clear prospect of the chivalric works that were to succeed it. His prologue describes the Nine Worthies, the group of chivalric heroes among whom Godfrey of Bouillon held the final place after Charlemagne and Arthur. The 1481-85 series was to present lives of these three heroes, together with a closely related chivalric manual.

Caxton had printed complementary works in sequence before—LeFèvre's two romances provide one instance—and had envisioned interlocking publications like the 1480 *Chronicles of England* and the *Description of Britain* often bound with it. Still, the 1481-85 group must be accounted his most impressive series. His prologues and epilogues demonstrate that Caxton intended the works to be read together. Their printer returns again and again to his unifying themes—the three Christian Worthies, the need for a reformation of English knighthood, and the attractions of a crusade against the Turks. This is more than Wydville or Yorkist partisan propaganda. The series responds urgently to the political difficulties of fifteenth-century England, presenting its diagnosis and remedy in a chivalric vision of history.

The Nine Worthies were already well established as an iconographic and literary motif by the fourteenth century. The frequent references to this grouping of chivalric heroes in art and literature underscore the importance of their assemblage. In itself, the gathering of these nine figures implies an ordered view of the past. As Caxton explains repeatedly, the Worthies were subdivided into three groups—pagans, Jews, and Christians. The pagan heroes selected were Hector of Troy, Alexander the Great, and Julius Caesar. The Jews of the Old Testament were represented by Joshua, David, and Judas Maccabeus. The Christians were Caxton's triumvirate: Arthur, Charlemagne, and Godfrey of Bouillon.[36] Clearly, the Nine Worthies abbreviated a wide span of chivalric legend. The Trojan conflict, the biblical wars of conquest and rebellion, Arthur's Round Table, Charlemagne's twelve peers, and the First Crusade are all implicit in the representation of their presiding figures. A chivalric history of the world lies behind any reference to the Nine Worthies; under their sway the past becomes a succession of great chivalric movements.

The specter of an unnamed patron hovers around Caxton's series. In Caxton's prologue to *Godefroy of Boloyne* he is suggested in the description of Edward IV's "noble capytayn" who is "to empryse this warre agayn the sayd Turke and hethen peple." In the *Ordre of Chyualry* he returns as the "gentil and noble esquyer" who requested the work's translation.[37] In the prologue to Malory he takes the form of the "noble gentleman" who defends the historical Arthur and insists on the printing of the volume.[38] Perhaps, in the prologue to *Charles the Grete*, he may even be detected as one of "somme persones of noble estate and degree . . . my good synguler lordes and specyal maysters and frendes" who joined with William Daubeny to encourage the publication of that work.[39] Norman Blake, Hilton Kelliher, and George Painter have all suggested that

Anthony Wydville should be identified with this insubstantial being. They adduce some persuasive further evidence. In the case of *Godefroy,* Caxton had expressed a hope that the ten-year-old Prince of Wales would "see and here redde this simple book." The surviving instructions for the education of Edward IV's sons required a period of reading in vernacular texts.[40] Anthony Wydville, the Prince of Wales' governor, could easily ensure that Caxton's printed account of the First Crusade would come to the attention of his nephew. Indeed, the Earl might have had personal reasons for enticing the future Edward V towards a crusade. Edward IV had already crushed Wydville's proposals for a crusade in Portugal, accusing the Earl of cowardice in planning to leave England. *Godefroy of Boloyne*—and perhaps the entire series, with its stress on the knight as defender of the faith—might represent an indirect return to Wydville's original aspiration. Painter and Kelliher also connect Wydville with the "squire" who presented the French *Ordre of Chyualry* manuscript to Caxton and suggest that Wydville might have transmitted the Winchester MS. of the *Morte Darthur* to Caxton in the same way.[41] This possible connection between Wydville and Sir Thomas Malory himself makes the Earl's role as patron to Caxton's series doubly significant.

Caxton's veiled references in the prologues and epilogues of the 1481-85 series seem unsatisfactory and also paradoxical. The patron of any era generally demands public acknowledgement of his assistance. Still, political events of 1483-85 made it impolitic to advertise any association with Earl Rivers, who had been Caxton's most visible patron in England up to that year. Edward IV died unexpectedly on April 9, 1483. The friction between the Queen's party and Richard, Duke of Gloucester, had indicated clearly that only one of the new king's incompatible uncles could flourish under the new regime. On April 30, Gloucester restored the unstable political equilibrium by arresting Wydville. On June 25, 1483, Anthony Wydville was beheaded at Pontefract Castle. Richard III was crowned in London on July 6.

In the face of Richard's known hostility to the Wydville family and to all things Burgundian, Caxton's decision to continue the series may bear witness to the printer's conviction of its importance. It also suggests a continued Wydville influence on Caxton—

perhaps Elizabeth Wydville's presence in sanctuary at Westminster. Most of all, it establishes the extent to which Caxton had already committed his press to the project.

As the volumes in the 1485 series are reexamined individually, their implications for the reading of Malory become clear. *Godefroy of Boloyne,* the first to be printed, also ranks first in historical authenticity. In it, Caxton translated a French version of William of Tyre's history of the First Crusade. The miracles, exotic scenery, battles, and chivalric heroes that fill its pages link this authoritative twelfth-century text with the later romances of the series. The main emphasis of the volume falls on the crusade as the supreme endeavor of Western knighthood. The same insistence on the defense of the faith as the knight's first responsibility may be implicit in the concept of the three Christian Worthies. This insistence is echoed in the second volume of the series, *The Book of the Ordre of Chyualry* (1484), Caxton's translation of Ramón Lull's *Libre del orde de cavayleria.* This chivalric manual provides a key to the theory of knighthood behind Caxton's reading of romance. Caxton commended the *Ordre* to "noble gentylmen that by their vertu entende to come and entre in to the noble ordre of chyualry." Lull's treatise is remarkable among chivalric manuals for its theoretical and secular point of view. As Lull enumerates the physical and spiritual qualities necessary to a knight, he repeats his demand that the defense of the faith stand as a primary duty.

Of the three works, *Charles the Grete* may prove the most enlightening companion volume to Malory. At a first glance, this seems unlikely. *Godefroy of Boloyne* is the work of one of the great historians of the Middle Ages, the *Ordre of Chyualry* of one of its most influential visionary philosophers. By contrast, *Charles the Grete* seems a clumsy patchwork of legends of Charlemagne from the Pseudo-Turpin Chronicle and a minor Charlemagne romance. Jean Bagnyon's fifteenth-century prose compilation parallels Malory's in collecting a national legend in one compact volume. In retelling the story of Charlemagne's career, from the rise of the kings of France through the Spanish campaigns against the infidel to the great king's death, the romance repeats the theme of the crusade. More than this, *Charles the Grete*'s principle of construction, presenting the rise, triumph, and fall of

Charlemagne's chivalric order, confirms and parallels the tripartite structure that has been postulated for the *Morte Darthur*.

Caxton's prologue to *Godefroy of Boloyne* indicates that Malory's publisher regarded the story of King Arthur, from the first, as a corporate biography:

> Kyng Arthur, Kyng of the Brytons, that tyme regnyng in this royamme, of whos retenue were many noble kynges, prynces, lordes and knyghtes, of which the noblest were knyghtes of the Round Table of whos actes and historyes there be large volumes and bookes grete plente and many.[42]

The history of King Arthur is also the narrative of the Round Table. This view may be necessary to any description of Malory's work; how else can its contents be classified? Still, Caxton's repetition of the statement in the epilogue to the *Ordre of Chyualry* and in his colophon to the *Morte Darthur* holds the reader's attention. It seems that Caxton cannot mention "that noble Kynge of Brytayne, Kynge Arthur" without including "al the noble knyghtes of the Round Table." He sums up Malory's work, similarly, as

> thys noble and ioyous book entytled Le Morte Darthur, notwythstondyng it treateth of the byrth, lyf, and actes of the sayd Kyng Arthur, of his noble knyghtes of the Rounde Table, theyr meruayllous enquestes and aduentures, th'achyeuyng of the Sangreal, and in th'ende the dolorous deth and departyng out of thys world of them al. Whiche book was reduced into Englysshe by Syr Thomas Malory, knyght.   (600. 4-9)

This interest in the exploits of an order of chivalry links the *Morte Darthur* with *Charles the Grete* no less than with *Godefroy of Boloyne*.

The effect of Bagnyon's compilation of history and romance was to reassert the importance of Charlemagne as the central figure of the volume. The image of the emperor is brought before the reader in a series of portraits, ranging from Charlemagne the man— or, perhaps, superman—to Charlemagne the icon atop his tomb. The romance material functions as the central panel in a literary triptych; the two historical books direct the attention of the reader to the presiding figure, that of Charlemagne. Roland, Oliver, the giant Fierabras, and the rest of Charles' peers deflect the eye successively; their disparate experiences are focused by the central theme of Charles and his order. Without the twelve peers, the medieval reader would have little interest in Charlemagne; without Charlemagne, the twelve peers mean nothing.

The critical reader may ask whether a similar biographical preoccupation can be found in Malory. Caxton certainly seems to think so; his colophon describes the contents of the volume comprehensively. The events of the three books of *Charles the Grete* are mirrored in those of the three major divisions of Malory's volume; the picture of the Round Table in the central Tale of Sir Tristram de Lyones corresponds nicely to the depiction of the Peers of France in the second book of *Charles the Grete*. Both volumes place the portrait of an order of knighthood in action between the scenes of the birth of its founder and of his "dolorous death and departing out of this world."[43]

The student of Arthurian literature has never found it difficult to see how thoroughly Malory's portrait of Arthur depends upon its sources. *Le Morte Darthur* may be most characteristic of its century in its propensity to reorder older material within a compact biographical form. Malory must be given credit for devising the pattern that his printer detected. Both *Charles the Grete* and the *Morte Darthur* reflect a renewed interest in Arthur and Charlemagne as historical figures and leaders of orders of Christian knighthood. Each chivalric fellowship comprises a world of individual knights, each with his own story. Still, the overriding scheme continually reminds the reader of the central image of Arthur, Charles, or Godfrey of Bouillon, the single man whose lifetime sets bounds to the history of his order, the giant on whose shoulders the dwarves stand.

Caxton's prologues and epilogues show how thoroughly he sympathized with the crusading ambitions of his age. His residence in Burgundian territory would have made the English merchant all too aware of the crusading vows pronounced by Philip the Good in 1454. The two subordinate Christian Worthies, Godfrey and Charlemagne, achieve their renown in combat against infidel opponents. It almost seems as though some form of crusade is a prerequisite for admission to the order of Christian Worthies; in his prologue to *Godefroy of Boloyne* Caxton urged his own sovereign and his sons to become candidates for a tenth position by some such activity. Caxton reads Malory's Tale of the Sankgreal, in defiance of its original purpose as a criticism of secular chivalry, very much to the credit of King Arthur. Indeed, the mystery of the Grail Quest overshadows the Christian marvels of both *Godefroy of Boloyne* and *Charles the Grete*. Arthur stands in first place in Caxton's chivalric pantheon, presiding over the highest Christian adventure of all. Anthony Wydville, the frustrated crusader, might have been particularly pleased that the English hero should hold the chief position.

The contrast between Caxton's chivalric series of 1481-85 and the printer's later publications is notable. Caxton did print a second chivalric manual, his translation of Christine de Pisan's *Livre des faits d'armes et de chevalerie* (1489), and three prose romances, *Blanchardyn and Eglantine* (1489), *The Four Sons of Aymon* (1488-89), and his *Eneydos* (1490). These later volumes represent a striking change of outlook. Where the 1484 *Ordre of Chyualry* addressed a knightly audience on a theoretical plane, the 1489 *Fayttes of Armes* is requisite, says Caxton, for any man in need of a pragmatic handbook of war. *The Four Sons of Aymon* jars against *Charles the Grete*; Caxton's second Charlemagne romance chronicles Renaut de Montauban's rebellion against an unsympathetic, senile Charlemagne. Here, Charles the Great hardly shines as a Christian Worthy. Combat against the Saracens is still valued in these works, but it is not linked to any unified program of action or vision of history. The cohesiveness of the earlier series becomes manifest when it is set against the isolated volumes of Caxton's last years. Malory's *Morte Darthur* and its companion volumes appealed urgently to the knights of England to conform to a standard of conduct marked out in Lull's work. They demand that the "noble gentlemen" of York and Lancaster forget their parties and unite in an assault on the threatening forces of the Turks. *Godefroy of Boloyne, Charles the Grete* and the *Morte Darthur* depict the aspirations of the High Order of Knighthood with all the allurements of art. After 1485 the appeal is not repeated, since, for William Caxton, English chivalry died in that year.

Texas A&M University

NOTES

[1] See Eugène Vinaver, ed., *The Works of Sir Thomas Malory*, 2nd ed. (Oxford: Oxford University Press, 1967), pp. xxxv-xli.

[2] William of Tyre, *Godefroy of Boloyne, or the Siege of Jerusalem*, trans. William Caxton, ed. M. N. Colvin, E.E.T.S. e.s. 64 (London: Oxford University Press, 1893); Ramón Lull, *The Book of the Ordre of Chyualry*, trans. William Caxton, ed. A. T. P. Byles, E.E.T.S. o.s. 168 (London: Oxford University Press, 1926); James W. Spisak, ed., *Caxton's Malory* (Berkeley and Los Angeles: University of California Press, 1983); William Caxton, trans., *The Lyf of the Noble and Crysten Prynce Charles the Grete*, ed. S. J. H. Herrtage, *The English Charlemagne Romances*, parts 3-4, E.E.T.S. e.s. 36-37 (London: Oxford University Press, 1881).

[3] See Hilton Kelliher, "The Early History of the Malory Manuscript," in *Aspects of Malory*, ed. Toshiyuki Takamiya and Derek Brewer, (Cambridge: D. S. Brewer, 1981), pp. 153-56; George Painter, *William Caxton: A Quincentenary Biography of England's First Printer* (London: Chatto and Windus, 1976), pp. 84-91, 112-16, 121-23, 147.

[4] See N. F. Blake, *Caxton and his World* (London: Andre Deutsch, 1969), pp. 47, 68, 71-72, 84-87, 89-91; N. F. Blake, *Caxton: England's First Publisher* (New York: Barnes and Noble, 1976), pp. 45-47, 49-50; Grant Uden, *The Knight and the Merchant* (London: Faber and Faber, 1965).

[5] See Uden; P. M. Kendall, *The Yorkist Age* (1962; rpt. New York: Norton, 1962), p. 190.

[6] Blake, *Caxton and his World*, pp. 26-45; Painter, pp. 16-42.

[7] See Georges Doutrepont, *La Littérature française à la cour des ducs de Bourgogne* (Paris: Champion, 1909); Otto Cartellieri, *The Court of Burgundy: Studies in the History of Civilization*, trans. Malcolm Letts (1929; rpt. New York: Barnes and Noble, 1970); Richard Vaughan, *Philip the Good: The Apogee of Burgundy* (New York: Barnes and Noble, 1970); Richard Vaughan, *Philip the Bold* (Cambridge, Mass.: Harvard University Press, 1962).

[8] Cartellieri, p. 1.

[9] See Cartellieri; Doutrepont; Vaughan, *Philip the Good*; Johan Huizinga, *The Waning of the Middle Ages* (New York: Doubleday, 1954).

[10] Painter, p. 64; also see Blake, *Caxton and his World*, pp. 67-70.

[11] W. J. B. Crotch, ed., *Prologues and Epilogues of William Caxton*, E.E.T.S. o.s. 176 (1928; rpt. London: Oxford University Press, 1956), p. 7.

[12] See Cartellieri, pp. 119-34.

[13] Painter, p. 142. Also see Larry D. Benson, *Malory's Morte Darthur* (Cambridge, Mass.: Harvard University Press, 1976), pp. 137-85, on fifteenth-century chivalry.

[14] Benson, pp. 141, 176-77, 186, 191-95.

[15] An instance of this might be the controversy over the social origins of the *fabliau*.

[16] British Library MS. Harley 48, fol. 61r, from the *Pas du perron fée* of Philippe de Lalaing. "For Bruges is the one city among all the others of this world where one finds most easily everything necessary to make a great feast, with regard to all kinds of food and merchandise, since it is so well supplied by sea, and on account of the great and rich merchants who are there and who come there from all regions." The transcription and translation are both my own. I am grateful to the British Library Board for permission to quote from this MS.

[17] Doutrepont, pp. 157-58, 257.

[18] William R. Tyler, *Dijon and the Valois Dukes of Burgundy* (Norman: University of Oklahoma Press, 1971), pp. 132-47. See also A. S. Atiya, *The Crusade in the Later Middle Ages*, 2nd ed. (1938; rpt. New York: Kraus, 1965).

[19] Tyler, p. 139.

[20] Cartellieri, pp. 145-49.

[21] *Livre des Faits de Jacques de Lalaing*, in Georges Chastellain, *Works*, ed. Kervyn de Lettenhove, 8 vols. (Brussels: Heussner, 1866).

[22] See Spisak, pp. 334-36. All citations to Malory's text are to this edition.

[23] *Livre des faits*, p. 254. For the *pas de l'arbre d'or*, see Cartellieri, pp. 124-33.

[24] See J. R. Lander, "Marriage and Politics in the Fifteenth Century: the Nevilles and the Wydevilles," *Bulletin of the Institute of Historical Research*, 36 (November, 1963), 119-52.

[25] See Lander, pp. 130-31.

[26] See Benson, pp. 172-73.

[27] Cartellieri, p. 129.

[28] See Crotch, p. lxxvii; Painter, pp. 43-44.

[29] Blake, *Caxton and his World*, p. 46.

[30] Richard Grafton, *Chronicle* (London, 1568), on the 1477 death of Charles the Bold. See Painter, *William Caxton*, p. 68, on Charles' English claim.

[31] Kendall, *Yorkist Age*, p. 190.

[32] Crotch, p. 111.

[33] Grafton, *Chronicle*, under the year 1483.

[34] John Allen Giles, ed., *Chronicles of the White Rose of York* (London: Bohn, 1845), p. 209.

[35] Crotch, p. 23. See also Painter, p. 88.

[36] See N. F. Blake, ed., *Caxton's Own Prose* (London: Andre Deutsch, 1973), pp. 138-39 and notes; Bruce Dickins, "The Nine Unworthies," in

Medieval Literature and Civilization: Studies in Memory of G. N. Garmonsway, ed. D. A. Pearsall and R. A. Waldron (London: Athlone, 1969), pp. 228-32.

[37] Blake, *Caxton's Own Prose*, pp. 140-41; Crotch, p. 82.

[38] See Spisak, 1.25.

[39] Crotch, p. 96.

[40] Kelliher, pp. 153-56. See also P. M. Kendall, *Richard III* (London: George Allen, 1955), pp. 183-84.

[41] Kelliher, pp. 143-56.

[42] Blake, *Caxton's Own Prose*, pp. 138-39.

[43] For the tripartite construction of the *Morte Darthur*, see Benson, p. 35. See also James M. Gibson, "The Book of Sir Tristram and the Chronology of Malory's *Le Morte Darthur*," *Tristania*, 5 (1979), 23-38; Georgianna Ziegler, "The Hunt as Structural Device in Malory's *Morte Darthur*," *Tristania*, 5 (1979), 15-22.

"Clerkes, Poetes and Historiographs": The *Morte Darthur* and Caxton's "Poetics" of Fiction

Elizabeth Kirk

That Caxton put the *Morte Darthur* into print, and that he presented it as he did, is an event in its own right, quite distinct from, though highly illuminating of, the character of the *Morte* itself.[1] Some of the implications of this event are obvious. Caxton's edition is a revealing example of how a late medieval text was transformed by the change from manuscript to print. Caxton's text and his formatting make an independent contribution to the development of the Arthurian legend. More important still, however, is that, for Caxton, printing the *Morte* was part of a larger project, that of bringing to as wide a readership as possible an appropriate selection of works he considered valuable, accessible, and salable. In doing this, he was performing a pragmatic but highly revealing retrospective analysis of the literature and learning available in his time. The way in which Caxton classified Malory's work with other works and the way his prologue to the *Morte* relates to his other prologues display a system of assumptions about narrative, about genre, and about the function of literature within which Malory's achievement can best be understood.

It is often difficult to decipher the rationale for Caxton's comments, since he was, of course, writing with the primary intention of attracting readers and buyers to particular books. For that reason, the prologues and epilogues he incorporated into his editions shed light on the attitudes toward literature held, not by the erudite, and not by the exceptional minds of artists and philosophers, but by more common readers. Thus they deserve more critical attention than they have received. Apart from that, the prologues are especially helpful to modern students of Malory because a comparison of Caxton's prologue to the *Morte* with his others reveals that many of the aspects of Malory's work which have been of most concern to critics since the discovery of the Winchester manuscript were already the very ones that Caxton, on behalf of his readers, felt he needed to address. However different the conclusions he drew are from those of any modern critic, the fact that he identified the questions to be asked about Malory as he did sheds light both on Malory's achievement and on the state of narrative in the late fifteenth century. Caxton and his press stand at a watershed in the history of narrative, when the printed book begins to distance author, reader, and text from each other in ways that raise new and troubling questions.

Crucial to Caxton's thinking, as to Malory's book, are assumptions he makes about the relationship between history and poetry.[2] In the period between 1481, when he published *Reynard the Fox*, and 1485, when the *Morte* appeared, Caxton kept returning to the question of what distinguished history from fable and poetry. Three major prologues, to a history, Higden's *Polychronicon* (1482), to the *Canterbury Tales* (1484), and to the *Morte* itself are especially revealing of Caxton's underlying attitude toward narrative.[3] In these essays criteria based on authorial intent and criteria based on reader response recur in kaleidescopic patterns, defeating modern generic expectations and implying a new definition of the experience provided by reading.

Caxton's early prologues and epilogues, such as those to *The Recuyell of the Histories of Troy* and *The Game and Playe of the Chesse* (both 1475), remain close to the terms used in Caxton's French originals. Caxton's own comments are of interest in two respects. First, he characteristically places the works he has chosen in multiple generic categories. For example, he recommends de Cessolis' moralization of the chess pieces because there "I fynde thauctorites. dictees. and stories of auncient Doctours philosophes poetes and of other wyse men whiche been recounted and applied vnto the moralite of the publique wele . . . ."[4] He also justifies the work because it conduces directly to some moral benefit, public or private, as in this comment on the *Recuyell:*

> but alle [auctorities] acorde in conclusion the generall destruccion of that noble cyte of Troye/ And the deth of so many noble prynces as kynges dukes Erles barons. knyghtes and comyn peple and the ruyne irreperable of that Cyte that neuer syn was reedefyed whiche may be ensample to all men duryng the world how dredefull and Ieopardous it is to begynne a warre and what hormes. losses. and deth foloweth.
>
> (p. 8)

Secondly, he tends to cut through the problems of historical accuracy and authorial intention by turning to the Pauline tag to which Chaucer too had recourse in times of stress: *all that is written is written for our doctrine* (Rom. 15.4). Sometimes Caxton uses it, as in the 1483 edition of the *Chesse,* as if he were speaking of the author's intent in writing the book:

> The holy appostle and doctour of the peple saynt Poule sayth in his epystle. Alle that is wryten is wryten vnto our doctryne and for our lernyng. Wherfore many noble clerkes haue endeuoyred them to wryte and compyle many notable werkys
> . . . .   (p. 10)

At other times, he uses it to exhort the reader to draw a moral in marked contrast to the book's expressed value system, as with the pacifist moral which, as we have seen, he hopes the reader will extract from the *Recuyell,* and to which he adds:

> Terfore thapostle saith all that is wreton is wreton to our doctryne/ whiche doctryne for the comyn wele I beseche god maye be taken in suche place and tyme as shall be most nedefull in encrecygn of peas loue and charyte.   (p. 8)

In other words, sometimes he speaks as if St. Paul were commenting on the properties of texts and sometimes as if he were admonishing readers how to make valuable use of texts whose intrinsic qualities are irrelevant.

Whether Caxton already realized the problems implicit in his divergent use of this text in 1475, he certainly did by 1481 when he published *Reynard the Fox*. Caxton's close familiarity with Chaucer dates at least from 1478, the year in which he published his first edition of *The Canterbury Tales*, an edition which was superseded by the 1484 edition whose prologue we will be examining, on the (ostensible) grounds that he had subsequently acquired a better manuscript. Caxton reveals a sophisticated awareness of Chaucer's use of St. Paul, a matter that has presented perennial problems to Chaucerians. On the one hand, *The Nun's Priest's Tale* radically undercuts the authority of the narrator, as when he first attributes Chauntecleer's misfortunes (inaccurately) to taking his wife's advice, only to add, "Thise been the cokkes wordes and nat myne;/ I kan noon harm of no womman divyne."[5] Yet he concludes:

> But ye that holden this tale a folye,
> As of a fox, or of a cok and hen,
> Taketh the moralite, goode men.
> For Seint Paul seith that al that writen is,
> To oure doctrine it is ywrite, ywis.
> Taketh the fruyt and lat the chaff be stille.
>
> (VII, 3438-43)

But, on the other hand, the Retraction cites the same text in a tone of agonized sincerity: "For oure book seith, 'Al that is writen is writen for our doctrine,' and that is mine entente." It certainly is curious to find this assertion used to defend the excellence of the author's intention since St. Paul's point is that all texts are beneficial whatever the intention behind them. Furthermore, Chaucer goes on to confess that, St. Paul or no St. Paul, the works he has produced throughout a lifetime do not benefit the reader and must be rejected as "enditynges of worldly vanitees" and "tales . . . that sownen into synne" (X, 1084, 1086). He does not even ask, as he asked "moral Gower" and "philosophical Strode" to do with the *Troilus*, that the readers "vouchen sauf ther nede is to corecte/ Of youre benygnites and zeles goode" (V, 1858-59). Caxton's appreciation of this Chaucerian play with St. Paul is suggested by the epilogue to *Reynard the Fox*, which seems to allude to both of Chaucer's conflicting uses of Paul:

> And yf ony thyng be said or wreton herin/ that may greue or dysplease ony man/ blame not me/ but the foxe/ for they be his

wordes and not myne/ Prayeng alle them that shal see this lytyl
treatis/ to correcte and amende/ Where they shal fynde faute.
(p. 62)

Perhaps the most interesting and suggestive—certainly the
most ambitious—of Caxton's major prologues is the first, the 1482
Prohemye to John of Trevisa's translation of Higden's
Polychronicon, in which Caxton gives history an astonishingly
crucial role for the individual and for society.[6] The Polychronicon,
though the least familiar today of the three works, enjoyed great
popularity and respect through the later fourteenth and fifteenth
centuries. As its name suggests, it interweaves the chronicle histories
of many countries, giving primacy to biblical history, but including
that of the Greek, Roman, Egyptian, and Assyrian-Babylonian
states, and continuing to the author's own time with continental as
well as English history. The history of philosophy is included as
well as political and biblical history. In view of the stress which
Caxton, as we will see, lays on the value of the Polychronicon as a
teacher of character and culture, it should be noted that, like many
chronicles, the Polychronicon does not present history from an
eschatological perspective, or, indeed, in such a way as to suggest
any teleological pattern, but merely organizes the material for
convenience into seven books and surveys the events with the same
kind of interest as that displayed in the survey of world geography
which forms the first, introductory and prefatory book. While
Higden does not resist any typological or teleological patterns
inherent in the biblical part of his material, his approach is not
overtly interpretive or hortatory. The first chapter of Book One of
the Polychronicon is a defense of the value of history as memory of
deeds,[7] in which St. Paul's dictum is treated quite differently than in
Chaucer and Caxton: "For the apostel seith nought, 'All that is i-
write to oure lore is sooth,' but he seith 'All that is i-write to oure
lore it is i-write'" (I, 19).

Caxton's response to Higden's strategy reveals his awareness of
problems about the difference between history and fiction that were
beginning to define themselves at the end of the fifteenth century.[8]
Caxton begins in high style: "Grete thankynges lawde and honoure
we merytoryously ben bounde to yelde and offre vnto wryters of
hystoryes/ which gretely haue prouffyted oure mortal lyf . . . "(p.

64). The profit does not come, however, from knowing the historical truth as such, for its own sake, but from something histories teach readers to do in the present about new events as they arise: "[histories] shewe vnto the reders and herers by the ensamples of thynges passyd/ what thynge is to be desyred/ And what is to be eschewed" (p. 64). This touching faith that historic events confirm present morality is not peculiar to Caxton; like his medieval predecessors he sees no need to face the difficulties Sir Philip Sidney was to raise almost a century later about the historian:

> the historian . . . is so tied, not to what should be but to what is, to the particular truth of things and not to the general reason of things, that his example draweth no necessary consequence, and therefore a less fruitful doctrine.[9]

But even if history does accord with morality, why should we need the past to tell us what is desirable and undesirable in the present? Why can we not simply form our own opinion directly? Caxton argues that living through an experience confers one kind of wisdom, whereas the right kind of second-hand knowledge transmits an altogether different and in some respects more privileged kind of wisdom, and that both kinds differ qualitatively from judgment based on reason or opinion. History's special contribution is that it presents: "those thynges whiche oure progenytours by the taste of bytternes and experyment of grete jeopardyes haue enseygned/ admonested and enformed vs excluded fro suche peryllys . . . " (p. 64). Readers seek to know what those who have suffered through history know. But we want to learn it without paying the price exacted of those who experienced the events at first hand:

> For in hym [the man of experience] is presupposed the lore of wysedome and polycye/ by the experyment of Jeopardyes and peryllys whiche haue growen of folye in dyuerse partyes and contrayes/ yet he is more fortunat/ and may be reputed as wyse yf he gyue attendaunce without tastynge of the stormes of aduersyte. (p. 64)

Histories excel the memories even of the most ancient not only because they cover more than the memory of the longest-lived individual can tell us, though that is important. For Caxton, history possesses a power that neither events themselves nor individual memory has: the power to confer vicariously "the taste of bytternes and experyment of grete Jeopardyes." As he says, marvelling over the phenomenon he describes, "For certayne it is a greete beneurte vnto a man that can be reformed by other and straunge mennes hurtes and scathes" (p. 64). Through history, we can apprehend something about reality that is both retrievable and transferable. This seems so important to Caxton that he assigns history a crucial role in human life: "And thus the pryncipal laude/ and cause of delectable and amyable thynges/ in whiche mannes felycyte stondeth and resteth ought and maye wel be attributed to hystoryes . . . "(p. 65).This happens because history, unlike personal memory or doctrinal teaching, has a double character: "Hystorye is a perpetuel conseruatryce of thoos thynges/ that haue be doone before this presente tyme/ and also a cotydyan wytnesse of bienfayttes of malefaytes/ grete Actes/ and tryumphal vyctoryes of all maner peple" (p. 65). In its role of "perpetual conseruatryce" history is valuable to the extent that the information it offers about the past is true. The second element—that of being a "cotydyan witnesse"—is quite a separate matter, however, and has nothing directly to do with the degree of accuracy with which the past has been discerned. Caxton acknowledges this when he adds that the latter function is shared by poetry, in kind if not in degree:

> yf the terryble feyned Fables of Poetes haue moche styred and moeued men to pyte/ and conseruynge of Justyce/ How moche more is to be supposed/ that Historye assertryce of veryte/ and as moder of alle philosophye/ moeuynge our maners to vertue/ reformeth and reconcyleth . . . . (p. 65)[10]

In other words, history and poetry share the power to move through language. But history excels poetry because of the congruity which history creates between the events it recounts and the language in which it recounts them. This gives history its privileged position among the human arts: "historye representynge the thynges lyke vnto the wordes/ enbraceth al vtylyte and prouffite . . . " (p. 66). The special efficacy of history depends not only on the reality of its content, which it shares with mere record-keeping or chronicle, but on the character of its language. Caxton's analysis of history causes him to devote considerable attention to the subject of eloquence:

> eloquence is soo precious and noble/ that almooste noo thyng can be founden more precious than it/ By Eloquence the grekes

> ben preferryd in contynuel honour to fore the rude barbares/
> Oratours and lerned clerkes in like wise excelle vnlerned and
> brutyssh peple/ Syth this eloquence is suche that causeth men
> emonge them self somme texcelle other . . . .   (p. 66)

Caxton contrasts this civilizing effect of eloquence with two other
ways by which men have attempted to inculcate civilization, poetry,
and the legal system:

> other haue taken another waye for tenflamme more the
> courages of men by fables of poesye/ than to prouffyte And by
> the lawes and Institutes more to punysshe than to teche Soo
> that of thyse thynges the vtylyte is myxt with harme. (p. 66)

Clearly Caxton means more by "hystorye" than at first appears.
He seems to be trying to define a mode of communication which
offers more than simply a civilizing force (since poetry and law
share that intent), more than the power to move through language
(since poetry does that too), but also more than events themselves.
He seems to be arguing that because the events recounted are real—
paid for by "other and straunge mennes hurtes"—and because they
have been put into language which is fully fitting to their nature
and fully moving to others, they have the power to communicate by
experiment, to speak to the whole person as experience itself does.
How these selected and transmitted events have an efficacy that
unselected reality does not have, Caxton does not say; nor does he
explain in what way the historian's perfectly fitting words "causeth
men . . . texcelle" (a good thing) rather than "enflamme" as do the
"terrible feyned fables of Poetes" (a bad, or at least mixed, thing).
The curious order of Caxton's sentence—"historye representynge
the thynges lyke vnto the wordes"—has significant implications.
Clearly, Caxton is saying that "historye" offers both "wordes" and
"thynges," while poetry offers only words. But there is more to it
than that. He does not say, as one would expect, that the historian
chooses words similar to the things. What he actually says is that
history "represents" (makes present again?) the things that are like
the words.[11] This way of putting it suggests that a given form of
words could occur in either a history or a "feyned fable." Since the
two do not differ in the kinds of events and themes they treat of, the
difference between them would seem to be, for Caxton, that in
history, the power of the words would be backed up or

authenticated by a reality to which they mediate our awareness, some "other and straunge mennes hurtes."

Thus Caxton's analysis places a special primacy on the re-creation of reality through language: "The fruytes of vertue ben Inmortall/ Specially whanne they ben wrapped in the benefyce of historyes" (p. 66). Thus Caxton offers a striking reversal of the common image of fruit and chaff, or veil and reality, used to describe the relation of form and content. It would seem that *experiment* kind of language, and that such language, in turn, can transmit *experiment*. Furthermore, *experiment* is quite a different matter from mere accurate factual information about the real world, past or present. When real events are embodied in language, language creates a connection between the consciousness of the reader encountering a text in the present and that of another human being encountering the real world in the past. Caxton's criteria for making a generic distinction are, then, quite extra-literary. But, by implication, they also assert a privileged status for one kind of language, the kind—however it ought to be defined—that has the power to give access to *experiment*.

Caxton's prologue to the *Canterbury Tales*, written two years later, is much more familiar. When we look at it in its entirety, however, rather than in the selections commonly quoted, we see much that relates to the *Polychronicon* prologue and carries Caxton's view of language a step further. The prologue begins with the very same words as that of the *Polychronicon* and, as we have seen Caxton do before, links together achievements in diverse disciplines: "Grete thankes laude and honour/ ought to be gyuen vnto the clerkes/ poetes/ and historiographs that haue wreton many noble bokes of wysedom . . . " (p. 90). These works he specifies as of three types: "of the lyues/ passions/ and myracles of holy sayntes of hystoryes/ of noble and famous Actes/ and faittes/ And of the cronycles sith the begynnyng of the creacion of the world/ vnto thys present tyme" (p. 90). (Note the distinction he now makes between "hystoryes" and "cronycles.") He then goes on: "Emong whom and inespecial to fore alle other we ought to gyue a synguler laude vnto that noble and grete philosopher Gefferey chaucer" (p. 90). This classification of Chaucer as a philosopher is one which Caxton had already made in his prologue to Chaucer's translation of Boethius in 1478. But the matter becomes more complicated as Caxton continues: "the whiche for his ornate wrytyng in our tongue may wel haue the name of laureate poete" (p. 90). Then, as if that were not enough, he both shocks the modern reader's generic assumptions and departs from his own recent distinction between poetry and history by describing Chaucer's "bokes and treatyces" as "many a noble historye as wel in metre as in ryme and prose." The *Canterbury Tales* in particular are "many a noble hystorye/ of every astate and degre . . . ." Caxton is far from making the naive error of assuming that the Canterbury pilgrimage itself really took place, so that Chaucer the Pilgrim is simply a journalist, since he says that the stories the pilgrims tell, apart from the pilgrimage frame, are "historye." Rather, he seems, in radical contradiction to the criteria for history he had enunciated in the *Polychronicon* prologue, to find some self-evident "realness" in the experience Chaucer's poetry portrays, as if Chaucer's language stood in the same relationship to authenticating "experiments of dyuerse thynges" as narratives that recount "real" events.

Caxton seems to be resting his view of Chaucer's achievements to a considerable extent on the particular characteristics he finds in Chaucer's language. He calls him laureate "For to fore that he by hys labour enbelysshed/ ornated/ and made faire our englisshe/ in thys Royame was had rude speche and Incongrue" (p. 90). Chaucer's works are noble histories at least in part because they are "so craftly made/ that he comprehended hys maters in short/ quyck and hye sentences/ eschewyng prolyxyte/ castyng away the chaf of superfluyte/ and shewyng the pyked grayn of sentence/ vtteryd by crafty and sugred eloquence" (p. 90). It is significant that the phrase "short/ quyck and hye" comes from Chaucer's own description not of a poet but of a spare-spoken philosopher, the Clerk. What Caxton calls "crafty" language and "sugred eloquence" is not, as the Renaissance association of these terms would misleadingly suggest, decorated and lavish. Indeed, Caxton himself dismisses such styles elsewhere as "rhetorike" or "subtle [or] new eloquence" (p. 96). Caxton firmly identifies Chaucer's style as spare and intense, focused directly on essentials, especially essentials of meaning. "Crafty" language is indeed heightened; but what differentiates it from the "rude speche and Incongrue" which, he tells us, preceded Chaucer is that it is denser, more ordered, so chosen and arranged as to be more powerful and effective than ordinary speech, not more diffuse and decorated. Indeed, "ornate" and "ornament" in earlier rhetoric denoted a functional, rather than a merely—in the modern sense—"ornamental" use of language.[12] In short, Caxton approached Chaucer in terms of an analysis of literature that created a tension between two different criteria: criteria about content (did the event really happen in the past?) and criteria about language (does the language move the reader to examine his own life and his world in the present?). Both qualities must be there if the work is to move the reader to mold his own experience in the future so that it will reflect "delectable and amyable thynges/ in whiche mannes felicity stondeth and resteth." In that case the work is a "hystorye." By placing Chaucer, in the teeth of ordinary logic, in the category of an historian, Caxton seems implicitly to approach the position Sidney was to take a century later when he dignified poetry over history and philosophy. Lurking behind Caxton's confusing terminology is an intuitive sense that great fiction addresses, and rests on, the authentic in human experience as much as, if not more than, narratives that accurately report real events.

One would expect, therefore, that Caxton would find in the *Morte Darthur,* which he published in the next year (1485), a story to meet all his demands, a story which combined the credentials of history with the narrative force of "poetry." In fact, in the very year of the Chaucer prologue (1484), Caxton had argued that the story of King Arthur was uniquely precious to the English and that it epitomized the virtues we have seen him praise as those of "historye." To *The Book of the Ordre of Chyualry* he had appended an epilogue singling out King Arthur in particular as the model who reveals to the English the lost glory of knighthood:

> And syth the Jncarnacion of oure lord/ byhold that noble kyng of Brytayne kyng Arthur with al the noble knyghtes of the round table/ whos noble actes and noble chyualry of his knyghtes/ occupye soo many large volumes/ that is a world/ or as thyng incredyble to byleue/ O ye knyghtes of Englond where is the custome and vsage of noble chyualry that was vsed in tho dayes/ what do ye now/ but go to the baynes and playe atte dyse And some not wel aduysed vse not honest and good rule ageyn

> alle ordre of knyghthode/ leue this/ leue it and rede the noble
> volumes of saynt graal of lancelot/ of galaad/ of Trystram/ of
> perse forest/ of percyual/ of gawayn/ and many mo/ Ther
> shalle ye see manhode/ curtosye and gentylnesse. (pp. 82-83)

This praise is the more striking in that it does not, like most of
Caxton's observations, fall within the functions of a blurb, since it
is not praise of a book that Caxton has for sale; and if it indicates
that Caxton was already planning to publish a book of Arthuriana,
that only makes more surprising the fact that, when he actually did
publish a book that seems designed to meet the very need he had just
articulated, we find a prologue whose tone is completely different
from those to the *Polychronicon* and Chaucer.

The prologue to Malory does not begin, like the other two,
"Grete thankynges/ lawde and honoure . . . ." Rather, it begins in a
low key with yet another schema classifying Caxton's various
publications: "dyuers hystoryes as wel of contemplacyon as of other
hystoryal and worldly actes of grete conquerers and princes, and
also certeyn bookes of ensaumples and doctryne" (1.1-3).[13] (Note
that accounts of contemplation, unlike the saints' lives mentioned
earlier, are now under history, not under doctrine and example,
presumably because they transmit "experiment.") Furthermore, the
bulk of the prologue deals not with the merits of the work but with
Caxton's reluctance—whether ostensible or real—to publish
anything about King Arthur on the grounds that "dyuers men holde
oppynyon that there was no suche Arthur, and that alle suche
bookes as been maad of hym ben but fayned and fables" (1.31-33).
Caxton pictures himself as having been persuaded by "many noble
and dyuers gentylmen of thys royame of Englond" that there is
enough evidence in the way of historical monuments and relics to
suggest that Arthur existed.[14] Caxton does call the *Morte* a "noble
and ioyous book" in his colophon. But the prologue continues to
express reservations of a kind he shows no sign of feeling about
other comparable works: "And for to passe the tyme thys book shal
be plesaunte to rede in, but for to gyue fayth and byleue that al is
trewe that is conteyned herin, ye be at your lyberte" (3.5-6).

Why should Caxton, who had printed comparable
compilations of semi-mythological material without a murmur and
who had called Chaucer an historian without qualification or
disclaimer, speak in this way of the hero he had so eloquently

evoked the year before? One possible explanation is political. *The Book of the Ordre of Chyualry* had been dedicated to Richard III; the *Morte* was printed, Caxton's colophon tells us, on July 31, 1485; on August 7 the future Henry VII landed at Milford Haven; by August 22 Richard was dead at Bosworth. Caxton could not know that Henry was to make the Arthurian legend a conspicuous feature of his kingship. But even if uncertainties of this kind played a role in Caxton's attitude toward the *Morte,* they are not an adequate explanation for all of its peculiarities.

Furthermore, it is not just Arthur's historicity that worried Caxton. He seems to have been equally uneasy about whether Malory offers any easily abstractable *moralitee.* When he published the life of Godfrey of Bouillon, for example, Caxton could readily point out the edification that awaited its reader.[15] Godfrey's story, Caxton had asserted in his 1481 prologue, was

> translated and reduced out of ffrensshe in to englysshe by me symple persone Wylliam Caxton to thende that euery cristen man may be the better encoraged tenterprise warre for the defense of Cristendom. and to recouer the sayd Cyte of Jherusalem . . . . (p. 48)

The beneficial effects of "history," for Caxton, depend not only on a real-world referent for the story but on its ability to convey the nature and the desirability of personal and civil morality, and to do so no less clearly, though perhaps more subtly, than the Life of Godfrey. He has trouble finding anything comparable in the *Morte.* He does his best to present Malory's work in terms of a moral intention, his own if not the author's:

> I, accordyng to my copye, haue doon sette it in enprynte, to the entente that noble men may see and lerne the noble actes of chyualrye, the ientyl and vertuous dedes that somme knyghtes vsed in tho dayes, by whyche they came to honour, and how they that were vycious were punysshed and ofte put to shame and rebuke. (2.35-39)

But even here we see several qualifiers—"somme" knights, but not all, "ofte" but not always; Caxton's knowledge of a work he edited with such pervasive attention and far-reaching effect cannot let him omit them. In the same way, the best-known sentence of the prologue begins as if the work were exemplary in the traditional way and gradually acknowledges what does not fit:

> wherin they shalle fynde many ioyous and playsaunt hystoryes
> and noble and renomed actes of humanyte, gentylnes, and
> chyualryes. For herein may be seen noble chyualrye, curtosye,
> humanyte, frendlynesse, hardynesse, loue, frendshyp,
> cowardyse, murdre, hate, vertue, and synne.   (2.42-3.3)

It is a far cry from humanity and gentleness to cowardice, murder
and sin. (Note how this sentence at first closely parallels the list of
virtues associated with Arthur in the prologue to *The Book of the
Ordre of Chyualry,* then gradually introduces vices Caxton had
argued stories of King Arthur would help to cure.) The worth of the
book must be left to the creative action of the reader: "Doo after the
good and leue the euyl, and it shal brynge you to good fame and
renommee" (3.3-4). We recall that Roger Ascham, three generations
later, was to single out these less ennobling aspects of the *Morte*
when he summed up its contents scathingly:

> the whole pleasure of which book standeth in two special
> points—in open manslaughter and bold bawdry; in which
> book those be counted the noblest knights that do kill most
> men without any quarrel and commit foulest adulteries by
> subtlest shifts: as Sir Lancelot with the wife of King Arthur his
> master, Sir Tristram with the wife of King Mark, his uncle, Sir
> Lamorak with the wife of King Lot that was his own aunt.[16]

Nor did Ascham think the reader's ability to turn everything to
doctrine could be counted on as an adequate protection: "What toys
the daily reading of such a book may work in the will of a young
gentleman or a young maid that liveth wealthily and idly, wise men
can judge and honest men pity" (p. 69).

Caxton's slippery transition from the properties of the book to
the responsibilities of the reader is especially perceptible in the final
lines of the prologue. Here Caxton turns from the acknowledgment
that the *Morte* is not reliable history to the Pauline tag he has not so
far employed in the major prologues:

> But al is wryton for our doctryne and for to beware that we falle
> not to vyce ne synne, but t'excercyse and folowe vertu, by
> whyche we may come and atteyne to good fame and renomme
> in thys lyf, and after thys shorte and transytorye lyf to come
> vnto euerlastyng blysse in heuen, the whyche He graunte vs
> that reygneth in heuen, the Blessyd Trynyte. Amen. (3.6-11)

Somewhere in this sentence Caxton stops describing what texts do
and begins exhorting the reader to do what the text does not do, to

take the final step that gives the work meaning and value. The syntax is too slippery to let us say where the shift comes—with "beware" perhaps?—and reflects Caxton's uneasy but definite recognition of how crucial a role the reader's subjectivity must inevitably play.

This prologue can only be explained on the assumption that Malory's text had troubled Caxton in a way no comparable text had done, and that Caxton was a much more astute and perceptive—if also unhappier—reader of Malory than is generally supposed. Malory's narrative stance is one which places conflicting incentives on the reader, incentives that focus on the two elements of a "history" that were important to Caxton, morality and historicity. The paradox of Malory's method lies in its combination of surface simplicity with underlying complexity. His surface involves a well-known story which he claims to be "reducing" from his sources as naively and dutifully as any "Me symple person William Caxton," and its narrative units are largely variations on a limited number of type-scenes. Its surface analysis gives the impression of confining itself to the liberal sprinkling of an equally limited number of favorable adjectives, of which "good" and "best" and Caxton's favorite "noble" and "gentyl" predominate. The complexity emerges from the juxtaposition of these units in cumulative structures.

Moral complexity emerges as Malory's characters find themselves faced with a decision under conditions in which it is impossible to know enough about the situation to make valid moral choices, and where good intentions are no protection whatever against committing acts with tragic and irreversible consequences. Hence the crucial role of the Tale of Balin in the larger dynamics of the *Morte*. Characters are presented with situations in which there is no good thing to be done that does not conflict with some manifest obligation or loyalty; no sooner have Arthur and his court taken the Pentecostal oath with its commitment never to fight in a wrong cause than Arthur finds himself, in his battle with Accolon, confronted with a situation in which the least of several evils is to fight in a wrong cause. We find our empathy and even affection enlisted on behalf of characters whose moral status we are made to see is problematical. Side by side with overt adulterers like Sir

Tristram, we find characters like Sir Lancelot who find themselves carried by a momentum partly arising within them but partly driving them from without towards positions of moral ambiguity of which they themselves do not always seem fully cognizant. Characters who do more than could have been expected but less than they conceivably might have done are responsible for more hurt and damage, and blame themselves more for it, than those with worse motives. The *Morte* is a work in which Sir Lancelot finds the knowledge that he is indeed the best knight in the world forced upon him by the healing of Sir Urry, and yet greets that knowledge with despair and shame: "And euer Syre Launcelot wepte as he had ben a child that had ben beten" (553.28-29).

Malory's narrative exerts the same contradictory pressure on the reader about the validity of its historical witness. On the one hand, Malory's story demands assent to major claims of truth for itself; on the other, he calls attention to the fragmentary basis for his narrative and to the limited authority of its teller. Furthermore, the narrative fluctuates between sober self-definition as chronicle and manifest violation of the verisimilitude suggested by some of its more realistic detail—topographical, financial, psychological, or dramatic. Malory's narrative is no more incredible and no less supported by cultural tradition than are the accounts of Charles the Grete or Godfrey which gave Caxton no pause. But his narration constantly directs our attention to the problem. It is as continually preoccupied as *Troilus and Criseyde* with the factitious character of history itself. This is perhaps most poignantly revealed in Malory's own final comment on the historicity of the legend he is recounting, with its eloquent shift from objective fact to personal transformation:

> More of the deth of Kyng Arthur coude I neuer fynde, but that ladyes brought hym to his buryellys, and suche one was buryed there that the hermyte bare wytnesse that somtyme was Bysshop of Caunterburye. But yet the heremyte knewe not in certayn that he was veraly the body of Kyng Arthur. For thys tale, Syr Bedwer, knyght of the Table Rounde, made it to be wryton.
>
> Yet somme men say in many partyes of Englond that Kyng Arthur is not deed, but had by the wylle of our Lord Ihesu into another place. And men say that he shal come ageyn and he shal wynne the Holy Crosse. I wyl not say that it shal be so, but rather I wyl say here in thys world he chaunged his lyf.
>
> (592.28-37)

The *Morte Darthur* confronted Caxton with a work which clearly had an authentic role to play in his own culture's definition of itself. Yet, at the same time, he could not but see that it eluded the categories in terms of which he construed the value of narrative. More disturbingly still, it persisted in calling attention to its own nature and limitations in ways that could not be ignored. Malory's historical status is too complex for definition; the intent of the work is far from clear, at least in the usual didactic terms; the book asks us to remember, and yet at the same time to set aside, the constraints of the real world in which we must come to terms with questions of value, purpose, and causality. Its knights exist neither in Froissart's ostensibly contemporary arena, nor in the *Polychronicon*'s historical continuum, nor in the "faerielond" which Spenser was to bring into being to accommodate their descendants. Yet Malory places the responsibility for interpretation squarely on the reader.

As we have seen, Caxton has been moving, in his pragmatic and intuitive way, towards a view of narrative based—far more radically than traditional theory—on its effect on the reader. His view of literature attempts to explain its capacity to teach us not conceptually, like philosophy or ethics, but experientially, as experience does, yet even better. He had been groping for a definition of the way in which a special kind of language can give access to the experience that illuminates instead of to some doctrine that can be abstracted from the illumination. He has tried to articulate how consciousness of experience is heightened by that language. Being not only a pragmatist and a merchant but a fundamentally non-innovative thinker, he tried to contain this view within the existing generic categories, feeling free to use them almost metaphorically when necessary, as when he calls a *laureate poete* an historian, as if that fell within the acceptable limits of hyperbole. The *Morte* forces him into an uncomfortable encounter with the implications of a theory he is happy enough to apply so long as he can do so without self-consciousness. Malory's narrative mode forces him to think about the implications of a literary theory that places central emphasis on the reader's responsibility to interpret the text and to use it to come to terms with his own experience, unprotected by authorial intention or privileged subject matter.

Malory confronts Caxton with a text that really works according to the dynamic implied in St. Paul's tag, which comes to look less comforting when seen in this light. The moral value of a work, and ultimately the "experiment," the "hurtes and scathes" that authenticate moral and civil teaching, are the reader's. The writer may do everything he can to create a context in which the reader's response will be channelled in the intended direction; nevertheless, what ultimately happens to his text happens when and if the reader does his job in responding to it. What St. Paul's formula and Malory's practice have in common is that they make the exigencies with which a text presents us much more like those presented to us by life itself than most literary theory will accomodate. Certainly the *Morte* presented Caxton with something too disturbingly like what some of his speculations about narrative had suggested, while, at the same time, being too uncomfortably unlike his idea of culture and education. From then on, apparently, he backed away from these difficult questions entirely, and his remaining prologues avoid any further exploration of them.[17]

Caxton thus presents us with an invaluable witness to the extent to which features of the *Morte* that have been of special concern to modern critics not only could be but actually were perceived by a contemporary—a contemporary, furthermore, whose basic critical ideas were neither unique nor anomalous, and who sought to follow in his work not the exceptional views of the atypical few but the best culmulative wisdom of a culture available generally to the aristocracy and the upper middle class. Caxton's simultaneous responsiveness to, and discomfort at, the *Morte* shows something of the assumptions and responses of that audience which Malory thought he was addressing, and, at the same time, of the extent to which the originality and force of Malory's vision went beyond those expectations.

Brown University

NOTES

[1] The original version of this essay was written for a panel on Malory and his readers organized by Bonnie Wheeler for the 1982 International

Congress on Medieval Studies, and is much indebted to the papers which she and Robert Sturges presented there. I also owe much to the comments of Judith Anderson and to the suggestions of participants in two National Endowment for the Humanities Summer Seminars which I taught in 1981 and in 1983, especially Gail Berkeley, David Harrington, and Elizabeth Russell.

[2] Behind all medieval thought on this subject lies the distinction made by Cicero between three kinds of narrative, "fabula," a manifestly invented story, "historia," an account of real events, and "argumentum," a plausible story, which is in keeping with reality and could well be true although it is not. See Cicero, *De Inventione*, I, xix, on *narratio*. Medieval discussion of the subject treated this distinction as a commonplace, but disagreed on how to classify poetry, which was most generally treated as a subdivision of rhetoric, but was sometimes classed with grammar, sometimes with logic, or sometimes, depending on the subject matter treated, with philosophy or theology. The criteria behind these distinctions are extra-literary. Caxton's working assumptions are thoroughly conventional, and any efforts he makes to go beyond them remain conditioned by his acceptance of the traditional terminology. For an extremely useful survey of attitudes to history among medieval English writers of what we consider history, see Bryce Lyon, "From Hengist and Horsa to Edward of Caernavon: Recent Writing on English History" and Margaret Hastings, "High History or Hack History: England in the Later Middle Ages," *Changing Views on British History: Essays on Historical Writing since 1939*, ed. Elizabeth Chapin Furber (Cambridge, Mass.: Harvard University Press, 1966), pp. 1-57 and 58-100.

[3] In several additional prologues Caxton makes an even less systematic attempt to distinguish romance from these genres, which seems to suggest that he found romance closer to overtly didactic discourse. This aspect of his thought, however, is too complex to include in the present discussion.

[4] John Blyth Crotch, ed., *The Prologues and Epilogues of William Caxton*, E.E.T.S. o.s. 176 (London: Oxford University Press, 1928), pp. 10-12. All Caxton quotations follow this edition unless otherwise noted. I have not reproduced Crotch's italics for expanded contractions, and all remaining abbreviations, as well as thorn and yogh, have been expanded.

[5] VII, 3265-66. All citations from Chaucer are to *The Complete Poetry and Prose of Geoffrey Chaucer*, ed. John H. Fisher (New York: Holt, Rinehart and Winston, 1977).

[6] *Polychronicon Ranulphi Higden Monachi Cestrensis together with the English Translations of John Trevisa and of an Unknown Writer of the Fifteenth Century*, ed. Churchill Babington, 8 vols. (London, 1865).

[7] This preface occupies I, 1-21. Note that John of Trevisa consistently translates Higden's "historia" as "storie."

[8] The shift seems to have been concurrent with the emergence of printing, but it is much harder to say whether the two processes are related.

It is difficult to believe that Caxton's attempt to discuss these matters in a new way is not a function of the changed perception of the relationship between author, book, and reader which results once the printing press separates them further than the scriptorium had and standardizes the finished product. As a result the printer can envisage his responsibility for bringing the text to diverse readers simultaneously but under very different conditions, and to see the reading process as more separate from writing. On the other hand, as we will see in the case of Malory, there come to be new elements in the text for the perhaps sensitized printer to react to.

[9] *An Apology for Poetry*, ed. Forrest G. Robinson (Indianapolis: Bobbs-Merrill Co., 1970), p. 27.

[10] See *OED*, *s.v. terrible*. In view of the parallel Caxton draws next between law and poetry as sanctions of public morality, it is clear that "terryble" here carries its earlier, less pejorative meaning, "exciting or fitted to excite terror." Probably not intended is the later (apparently late sixteenth century) meaning, "very violent, severe, painful or bad, hence, colloq., as a mere intensive."

[11] *OED*, *s.v. represent*, especially sense 2, "to bring clearly before the mind, esp. (to another) by description or (to oneself) by an act of imagination." Also see sense 4, "To show, exhibit or display to the eye; to make visible or manifest."

[12] See *OED*, *s.v. ornament*, sense 1, and *ornate*, verb and adj.; and Lewis and Short, *s.v. ornamentum* and *orno*. Perhaps at the most striking illustration of the functional meaning of "ornament" is in Robert of Basevorn's early fourteenth-century *Forma Praedicandi*, in which the "ornaments" of a sermon are its structural features *(Artes Praedicandi*, ed. Thomas M. Charland [Ottawa: Institut d'Etudes Médiévales, 1936]). See also P. M. Kean, *Chaucer and the Making of English Poetry* (London and Boston: Routledge and Kegan Paul, 1972), II, 234-36.

[13] All citations to Caxton's edition of Malory are to *Caxton's Malory*, ed. James W. Spisak (Berkeley and Los Angeles: University of California Press, 1983).

[14] Skepticism about whether Arthur was a real historical character is not an uncommon topos of chroniclers. Higden expressed such doubts in the *Polychronicon*, but when John of Trevisa translated this passage he added a vigorous rebuttal, and his version is, of course, what Caxton himself had just published. See *Polychronicon*, V, 336-39.

[15] We recall that Caxton's prologue to *The Book of the Ordre of Chyualry* specifically links Godfrey and Arthur.

[16] *The Schoolmaster*, ed. Laurence V. Ryan, Folger Documents of Tudor and Stuart History (Ithaca, N.Y.: Cornell University Press, 1967), pp. 68-69.

[17] The one surviving copy of the second edition of *Reynard the Fox* (1489) has lost the page containing the epilogue, but has an authentic-

sounding one copied in a seventeenth-century hand which Crotch prints. If it is authentic, it shows Caxton backing further away from the problematic relationship between fiction and morality, since he replaces the wit and irony of the first edition with a heavy-handed moral in which he assures us the fox got his just deserts.

Illustrating Caxton's Malory

Muriel Whitaker

Almost from the beginning, the texts of Arthurian romance have been accompanied by illustrations[1] because, as William Morris rather verbosely expressed it, the illustrated book

> is not perhaps absolutely necessary to man's life, but it gives us such endless pleasure and is so intimately connected with the other absolutely necessary art of imaginative literature that it must remain one of the very worthiest things towards the production of which reasonable man should strive.[2]

The elegance and charm of such late thirteenth-century illuminated Arthurian manuscripts as London, British Library, Add. MSS. 10292-10294 and Royal 14EIII; Manchester, John Rylands Library, MSS. Fr. 1 & 2; New York, Morgan MS. 805; and Oxford, Bodleian MS. Digby 223 evoke the kind of fairy-tale atmosphere that Victorians like William Morris, Dante Gabriel Rossetti, and Edward Burne-Jones found so beguiling. By the fifteenth century, illustration had become more realistic, with the late Gothic rediscovery of perspective and the use of landscape backgrounds rather than architectural frames and gold leaf or diapering. The appearance of block books in Western Europe ca. 1430 and Johann Gutenberg's perfecting of the printing process in the early 1450s made it possible to produce books more rapidly, more consistently, and in greater numbers than had been possible in the manuscript workshops. For a time illuminating and printing proceeded side by side, as the printers deliberately attempted to reproduce the effects of manuscripts. The leading Parisian publisher, Antoine Verard, who established his business in 1485, printed on vellum books that were then illuminated by hand.[3] However, the woodcut which, like the printed text, could be easily reduplicated, soon replaced hand-painted illustrations.[4]

When William Caxton (ca. 1422-91) introduced printing to England in 1476, his object was to make available to the reading public important Middle English works, such as Chaucer's *Canterbury Tales* which he printed in 1478, and vernacular versions, often in his own translation, of classical and continental works, such as *Ovid's Metamorphoses* (1480) and *The History of Reynard the Fox* (1481). But, according to the British Library's catalogue for the quincentenary Caxton exhibition, his "finest and most enterprising service to English literature"[5] was the printing in 1485 of Sir Thomas Malory's *Morte Darthur*.[6] The fact that this first edition was unembellished probably reflects the publisher's disinterest in illustration *per se*. Of his hundred surviving productions, only nineteen have woodcuts. In the earliest, *The Mirror of the World* (1481), the woodblocks have been crudely cut by inexperienced English artisans from drawings that apparently imitate the illuminations of a Bruges manuscript.[7] After 1486, Caxton imported blocks from the continent, blocks that were inherited by his successor, the Alsatian Wynkyn de Worde,[8] on Caxton's death in 1491.

Unlike his employer, de Worde seldom published a book without illustrations,[9] though he was not particularly concerned with achieving uniformity of effect through consistency of design and relevancy of content. As a businessman, he no doubt appreciated the fact that pictures brightened up a work, making it more saleable. When he reissued the *Morte Darthur* in 1498, Caxton's text was enlivened by twenty-one woodcuts, each of which takes up the full width of the folio page and half its length.[10] Critics have usually taken a rather denigratory tone when describing these woodcuts. Pollard calls them "very ambitious but badly executed;"[11] A. M. Hind says they are "crudely cut in thick line, with regular patches of parallel shading . . . remarkable and somewhat bizarre."[12] Equally equivocal was T. F. Dibden, the cataloguer of the Spencerian library which formerly contained the Rylands copy:

> They are very little superior to the clumsiest embellishments which distinguish the volumes of the two Coplands; yet to the curious antiquary they have a certain degree of value, and to the bibliographer such a volume, remarkable for the beauty of its execution, as well as the rarity of its appearance, cannot fail to be held in very considerable consideration.[13]

At least two illustrators are involved in the design of this edition, and of these the less important is unimaginative and imitative. His double cut for Book X was almost certainly devised by reducing the miniatures of an illuminated manuscript to their outlines and omitting details which would have been beyond the competence of the carver. The picture on the right showing a tournament *mêlée* closely resembles a miniature in the fifteenth-century French manuscript *Tristan et Yseult* by Maître Lucès.[14] The protagonists charging towards one another in the foreground (Arthur and Tristram) wear plate armor and the kind of hinged helmet known as an armet, a type which appeared in the second half of the fifteenth century. There is the same pattern of raised swords and horizontal spears, the same background of diagonal spears. The dismembered hand and head and the torso of the supine knight in the lower foreground reproduce an iconographical device that can be traced back to the earliest romance manuscripts. Omitted in the woodcut is the representation of Iseult and her five ladies who in the miniature watch from a stand in the upper center. This illustration for Book X was not repeated in de Worde's 1529 Malory, perhaps because in the interval it had also been used to illustrate Raoul LeFèvre's *Hystoryes of Troye* (1502 and 1503); *King Ponthus* (1505?); *Kynge Ponthus* (1511); and *Cronycles of Englonde* (1515 and 1528).[15]

A second illustration attributable to the minor artist accompanies Book IX, "How Syre Launcelot rode on his adventure." The left hand cut is relevant to the text in so far as it shows a king (designated by crown, large sceptre, and ermine collar) seated at a round table so small that there is room for only two courtiers. On it are placed a goblet and what appears to be a leg of lamb—rather meager fare for a Pentecostal feast. In the foreground an admonitory hermit raises his forefinger in a gesture familiar from illuminated manuscripts. Pushed against the back wall is the Siege Perilous. The right hand cut shows a mounted Lancelot wearing a court dress consisting of a very short doublet with bulky sleeves. Following late fifteenth-century style, it is opened so widely across the chest that a *pièce* has been inserted to fill the gap. His form-fitting hose are thrust into knee-high boots, and he also wears a peculiarly shaped cap that is tied under his chin. If the absence of armor strikes us as strange, even stranger is the substitution of a swagger stick for his sword. Though this illustration has little to do with knight-errantry, it was sufficiently popular to be reproduced in the two editions of LeFèvre's Troy book and in *Olyuer of Castylle* (1518).[16]

The major illustrator is far more original and entertaining. Says Edward Hodnett:

> Of all the hands that come under our eyes in English books, the *Arthur* cutter is the most markedly individual and the most amusing. His heavy "mourning" borders, his diving black birds, the heavy-lidded eyes of his narrow-chested women and long-legged men, and particularly his heavy outlines and habitual use of white line in fur, hair, foliage and in the patchy, enlarged thumb-print shading trimmed at the edges as though by shears—his idiosyncracies are as good as a signature.[17]

He is evidently familiar with the specific text that he is illustrating, and he takes care to devise illustrations that are faithful to the titles which Caxton attached to each book. Merlin slinks into a formidably rocky cave, urged on by a towering Nimue, the malignity of whose expression may be partly the result of the engraver's inability to cut facial details gracefully. A long-haired Gareth supports himself on the shoulders of two men, as indicated by the text. In one of the most elaborately composed scenes, two gentlewomen (not one, as in the text) attend to the new-born Tristram beside the body of his mother who is already dead, as the arms crossed at the wrist indicate. Beyond the stylized trees of the forest can be seen the realistic architectural detail of a parish church, its tower surmounted by a steeple in the English perpendicular style. However, this illustrator does not always confine himself to the subject indicated by the title. La Cote Male Tayle is shown fighting a horrible lion, as described in the first chapter of Book IX.

For Book XVII, the illustrator declines to depict the tournament of the first chapter, drawing instead the subject of the second, "How Sir Galahad rode with a damsel, and came to the ship whereas Sir Bors and Sir Percival were in." For Book XIX the conventional knight-in-the cart illustration is used instead of Malory's original addition, Guenevere's maying.

This artist cares not only for literal representation but also for historical authenticity. In the illustration of Mordred's attack on the Tower of London, he is careful to include cannons which emit flames and cannonballs. His source, if he is the originator of this cut, may have been the late fifteenth-century *Chroniques d'Angleterre* (London, British Library MS. Royal, 14EIV, f. 281) in which the seige of a castle is conducted by archers and a group of spear-carrying foot soldiers supported by cannon. In the matter of armor and costume, he is scrupulously up-to-date. Gawain and Ector (Book XVI) wear the fluted armor associated with the Emperor Maximilian (1493-1519), splendidly Gothic in its elaboration of gardes-de-bras, demi-greaves and lamboys (a steel skirt hanging from the waist over the thighs). One of them wears a sallet, a type of helmet popular between 1450 and 1510 (see also Books XIX and XXI). Separate from the body armor, it rested entirely on the head, its ridge sweeping down into a longer brim at the back.

The "Decline of the Gothic World," to use the phraseology of a social historian, Margaret Scott,[18] was marked by a loss of that elegant sophistication of dress which is nowhere better depicted than in the Limbourg brothers' calendar paintings for the Duc de Berry's *Très Riches Heures*. Now at the end of the fifteenth century, the "bulky look" is in, accompanied by a deliberate effect of untidiness achieved by the wearing of shaggy hats, wrinkled hose, fluffy shoulder-length hair and short, bulky doublets. The stubby shoes worn by Mordred and his cannoneer, Balin, Galahad, La Cote Male Tayle, Gareth's supporters, and Lancelot are the complete antithesis of the impractically elongated pointed footwear that only began to disappear in the 1480s.

While the ladies' dresses still feature trains (a sign of aristocratic rank since they imply the presence of servants to carry them), the headdresses have changed from spiring steeples and wide banner types held out by wires to hoods so long that they now have to be split vertically so that the pieces can fall before and behind the shoulders. The ladies standing sideways on the far left in the illustrations of Book I and Book III perfectly illustrate this effect (Fig. 1). That the ladies were still more elegantly constrained than the men is evident in the first woodcut where the courtier on the left (the Duke of Cornwall) achieves the chunky effect by wearing a ridiculously short, wide-sleeved doublet with exaggerated lapels. Above, a large hat like the "luggit" bonnet acquired by James IV of Scotland in 1489 is set rather tipsily on his head.

So far as I am aware, no one has previously noticed the authenticity of the *Arthur* cutter's pictures in terms of late fifteenth-century social history. He has added to the romance's credibility in such a way that readers would be encouraged to accept the text as historically true. It's as if he were saying, "Look, these people wear the same clothes as you wear, live in the kind of castles that you can see, and worship in parish churches like those that you attend." The emphasis is on the real and tangible; the magical and mystical are largely ignored.

Wynkyn de Worde reprinted his illustrated *Morte* in 1529,[19] using the same woodcuts with the exception of those for Books VI, X, XVI, and XXI. Each of the reused blocks is marred by wormholes. In 1557, William Copland printed *The Story of Kyng Arthur, and also of his noble and Valiante Knyghtes of the Rounde Table*[20] using de Worde's text.

William (fl. 1556-69) was probably the brother of Robert Copland (fl. 1508-47), a London printer, bookseller, and stationer whose illustrated books depended almost entirely on de Worde cuts. William looked to the same source, though it is impossible to determine whether the blocks were legitimately borrowed or plagiarized by tracing the illustrations in de Worde's Malory and having them cut onto blocks. In any case, those for Books II, IV, V, VII, IX, XI (where de Worde's right hand cut is used on the left), XII, XIII, XIV, XVII, and XIX reduplicate the 1498 edition, while X, XX, and XXI reproduce the 1529 variations. While not identical, the wedding scene for Book III resembles de Worde's in composition, though the number of attendants is reduced and the architectural background features pillars.

Some cuts are far removed from the text; for example, that for Book XVI shows a wolf devouring a child while a troop of soldiers lurks behind a mountain. Outside the picture plain is a Romanesque castle. In Book IX Lancelot's dragon has become a monster with three human heads whose mouths spew forth the kind of scrolls that in illuminated manuscripts had been filled with words as aids to identification. The elaborate floral and faunal borders surrounding the pictures may suggest a desire for aesthetic sophistication, but the effect of quality is sacrificed to convenience and cheapness. Many woodcuts are placed at the bottom of the page to fill up the space, double cuts differ in size, and the de Worde cuts are heavy and smudged, giving an effect of darkness and imprecision.

The last of the Tudor Malorys was Thomas East's *The Story of Kynge Arthur, and also of his Knyghtes of the Round Table* (1585). The text of this edition was based on Copland. Here, too, is the St. George-and-the-dragon frontispiece showing a knight in sixteenth-century armor, holding a red cross shield, and with two excessively long plumes attached to his helmet. In his eagerness to provide as many illustrations as possible at minimal expense, East has evidently used whatever cuts he could get his hands on, with no regard for consistency of size or style. The blocks are of thirteen different sizes, ranging from those for Books I and II which are one column wide to those for Books XX and XXI (b) which take up half a page. Though many of the cuts are modelled on the de Worde Malory illustrations, adaptations have occurred. Gareth now wears peasant dress—a kirtle with a hood. Balin wears cuisses, greaves, and solerets rather than hose and chunky shoes. The Protestant religion having been firmly established, Percival's aunt stands outside a castle, not a priory, accompanied by ladies who are clearly not nuns. The wedding of Arthur and Guenevere (Book III) is illustrated by a copy of Richard Pynson's *Traduction & marriage of the princess (Catherine)* (1501) and Book XX by a cut from de Worde's *Boke of hawkyne* (1496). The vicissitudes which a block might undergo are evident from J. Payne Collier's comment on the cut associated with Book XV (Fig. 2):

> A few of the woodcuts of East's edition are considerably older
> than the date when he printed; one of them was used by W. de
> Worde in 1520 before Christopher Goodwyn's poem "The

Chaunces of a Dolorous Lover." The block then came into the hands of W. Copland and having been used by him in his reprint of the "Morte Darthur" it was subsequently in the possession of East, who applied it to the same purpose in his reprint preceding the 16th (sic) book. Thus W. de Worde's "Dolorous Lover" served the turn, in the hands of Copland and East to represent a dead man in a white shirt an hundred winters old.[21]

These later editions are often technically superior in their cutting to those of de Worde. The faces show a greater range of expression and the physiognomy is less likely to be marred by skewed mouths and drooping eyes. The fantastical landscape features of the *Arthur* cutter are smoothed, and the perspective is more realistic, but the adaptations are not necessarily improvements, as the print of the incarceration of Merlin attests. Without the lowering rocks, the diving birds, the sharp points of mountain, castle, and steeple, and the towering fay's malevolent features, the mood of evil and doom is quite removed. The energy of the early woodcuts has been dissipated—one reason, perhaps, that Thomas East's *Kynge Arthur* was the last illustrated Malory for almost three hundred years.

After W. Stansby's unillustrated 1634 Malory, *The History of the Renowned Prince Arthur, King of Britaine. As also, all the Noble acts and Heroicke Deeds of his valiant knights of the Round Table,* an edition based on East's folio, Puritanism and the Age of Reason made chivalry, courtesy, mystical religion, and magic uncongenial. A revival of interest came in the early nineteenth century as an aspect of romanticism.[22] Two poorly edited *Morte Darthur*s appeared in 1816, followed in 1817 by Robert Southey's annotated republication of Caxton's original text. It was the discovery of this book that so excited two young Oxford students, William Morris and Edward Jones. In her memoir of her husband, Georgiana Burne-Jones later described the effect of the discovery:

> I think that the book never can have been loved as it was by those two men. With Edward it became literally a part of himself. Its strength and beauty, its mystical religion and noble chivalry of action, the world of lost history and romance in the names of people and places—it was his own birthright upon which he entered.[23]

Their interest was shared by their friend and sometime mentor

Dante Gabriel Rossetti, with momentous results, as far as Arthurian illustration is concerned.[24]

Unlike the anonymous early illustrators, those of the nineteenth and twentieth centuries are individuals with consciously formulated opinions about the relationship of literature and art. Many Victorian artists were firmly committed to the story-telling function of art, using as their inspiration historical events of earlier centuries or literary texts. When "history" and literature were combined, as in the *Morte Darthur*, the artist had a passport into a fertile romantic world where he could imaginatively experience what J. Mordaunt Crook has called "The High Victorian Dream."[25] For Rossetti and his followers, the essence of the dream was beauty—the beauty of landscapes faithfully created with due attention to botanical accuracy,[26] of tapestries, jewels, "medieval" furniture, the heraldic panoply of arms and armor, opulently coloured dress, and above all the beauty of women whose sensuality was celebrated as Love.[27] Decoration was paramount, an indulgence which Walter Crane justified on the grounds that "we have in the world of ornament a language not only of extraordinary beauty, but of deep symbolical, historical, constructive, and racial meaning."[28] Though the Pre-Raphaelites wished to emulate the consistent iconographic programs of the early Netherlandish artists in whose paintings every object could be read both naturally and allegorically,[29] they had to limit themselves to images that the Victorian viewers would understand—lilies, doves, chalices, angels with splendid wings, enclosed gardens, knights in armor, and beautiful women in trailing gowns.

Another important Victorian influence on Malorian illustration was William Morris's Kelmscott Press. Morris[30] had devoted a lifetime to promoting his own version of the dream, having found in the Middle Ages ideal social relationships and, in artifacts, the combination of beauty and utility that he attempted to emulate in the products of his factories and workshops. The Kelmscott Press, established in 1891, was the culmination of his search for beauty and truth. His view of the ideal book was described in a paper read to the Bibliographical Society in 1893: "A book ornamented with pictures that are suitable for that book, and that book, only, may become a work of art second to none, save a fine binding duly ornamented or a fine piece of literature."[31] For Morris, the most beautiful printed books were the fifteenth-century productions of Schoeffer at Mainz, Mentelin at Strasbourg, and Caxton in London[32] because all the visual elements—type, illustration, border, page layout, and book materials—were harmonized into an aesthetically satisfying unity. The most significant production of the press, *The Kelmscott Chaucer* (1896),[33] with its hand-made paper, special ink imported from Germany, woodcut illustrations by Edward Burne-Jones, and initials, marginal ornaments, and decorative borders by Morris, set a standard of book decoration that subsequent Malorian publishers and artists would emulate.

An immediate response to the Kelmscott Press came from the English publisher J. M. Dent, who in 1892 conceived the idea of publishing the classics in a style apparently similar to that of Morris[34] but much less expensive, since the line-block illustrations would be reproduced by a photo-mechanical method rather than from hand-engraved wood blocks. Enquiring of his bookseller friend, F. H. Evans, whether he knew of a likely artist to illustrate the *Morte Darthur*,[35] with which he would begin his series, he was introduced to a nineteen-year old insurance clerk, Aubrey Beardsley.[36] Having approved the sample drawing, "The Achieving of the Sangreal," an expression of soulful medievalism in the Burne-Jones style, Evans commissioned Beardsley to produce twenty-one full page illustrations and 585 chapter headings, borders, initials, and ornaments. Although at first enthusiastic— and tempted, no doubt by the £250 fee—Beardsley soon changed his attitude.

In 1896 Edward Burne-Jones recalled for his studio assistant a visit he had had from the young artist:

> I asked him how he was getting on with the book he was decorating—King Arthur that was—and he said he'd be precious glad when it was done, he hated it so. So I asked him, why did he do it, and he said because, he'd been asked. He hated the story and he hated all medieval things. . . . I wondered why he took the trouble to come and see me, unless it was to show off and let me know my influence with him was over.[37]

The Morris and Burne-Jones influence is obvious in the earlier illustrations such as "The Lady of the Lake Telleth Arthur of the

Sword Excalibur" (Fig. 3), with the long loose clothing of the fée
and Merlin, Arthur's bat's-wing armor, the briars, lily pads, realistic
flowers, the trees crowding the picture plain, and the decorative
border in the proportions that Morris approved. Later, the
extravagant and inhibiting *entrelacement* of naturalistic foliage is
replaced by the energy of the whiplash line, the abstraction of floral
motifs, as in Art Nouveau, and a more dramatic use of starkly
contrasted black and white.

So great is the discrepancy between the text and its illustrations
that one wonders whether Beardsley had even bothered to read any
more than the opening books. Certainly his attitude to chivalric life
is the antithesis of Malory's. Malory's knights are the embodiment
of energy. They rush about the tournament ground like lions, wild
bulls, and rams; they are ambushed in the forest by evil knights,
attacked at fords, soused in wells, ejected from castles, gored by
boars, and run away with, when their horses get out of control.
Beardsley's knights, in contrast, are wan and spiritless, moping
about in flowery meadows, using their swords as walking-sticks,
gazing at phallic floral arrangements, and even, as in "Sir
Launcelot and the Witch Hellawes," directing the sword's point at
themselves in a gesture of castration. Malory's assertively masculine
knights dominate the text; Beardsley's effeminate perversions must
share the interest with angels, satyrs, androgynous nudes, and fatal
women. Of the fifteen full-page illustrations depicting Round
Table heroes, seven show knights in recumbent positions and none
shows anything but passive contemplation.

It is the women, not the men, who are the sources of power, in a
role-reversal that Malory would have found difficult to understand.
As Mario Praz has pointed out, "The Romantics made of the Fatal
Woman an archetype which united in itself all forms of seduction,
all vices, and all delights."[38] In Beardsley's illustrations sin is
fascinating, provocative, irresistible, or boring, and its basis is not,
as in Malory, lack of fellowship, disloyalty, and instability but
simply sex. The blousy, aggressive females with their bulging
breasts and the Medusa-locked enchantresses, heavy-lidded, bored,
and contemptuous, have the males at their mercy. The promise of
joy symbolized by Tristram's raised goblet is countered by the
premonition of pain and death that Isolde's Medusa hair

symbolises. Earlier, La Beale Isolde had crouched beside the dying Tristram like a vampire. Guenevere in her habit, with her strange beaked hood and unholy expression, is more witch than nun. Nimue with a mere flourish of her hand directs the slinking Merlin into his prison.

In illustrating Malory, Beardsley is doubly perverse, attacking both Victorian romanticism and Victorian respectability. His castles are towered and pinnacled Neo-Gothic railway hotels. In the garden of the Joyous Gard (Fig. 4) the flowering branches are tied onto the trees to point out the artificiality of the *hortus conclusus* convention and, by implication, of romantic love; the border consists of pears that are unmistakably female torsos, with lop-sided breasts and pubic hair. Courtly love becomes weary and destructive sex, and the chivalric virtues of courage, loyalty, religious devotion, and the defense of helpless women—virtues which the Victorians associated particularly with Malorian chivalry—are shown to be negligible. In an essay first published in 1898, Arthur Symons tried to justify Beardsley's perversity by proposing that "he expresses evil with an intensity which lifted it into a region almost of asceticism, though attempting, not seldom, little more than a joke or a caprice of line."[39] The *Morte Darthur* illustrations are technically skillful, aesthetically appealing, wittily ironic—but they are not Malory.

Of all *Morte Darthurs* the most extensively illustrated (as opposed to decorated) is that published by Philip Lee Warner for the Medici Society (London, 1910-11).[40] Sir William Russell Flint, R.A., P.R.W.S., R.S.W. (1880-1969) was commissioned to provide forty-eight water-colors, twelve for each of four volumes, a commission which won him the Silver Medal at the Paris Salon of 1913. Percy Bradshaw, the admiring author of the Flint monograph in "The Art of the Illustrator" series, extolls the artist's "appreciation of period and sense of romance . . . there is something of the monkish art which beautified the old missals here—a reverence for the author's outlook, and a love for the period when the work was produced."[41]

An examination of the paintings makes clear that what we have here is not the true Middle Ages but the Pre-Raphaelite view, complete with the tapestries, religious objects, stained glass windows, and painted and pointed furniture that Burges, Morris *et al.* were producing, with "everywhere device and symbolism."[42]

Flint's subversion of Malory is more subtle than Beardsley's, for he does not consciously satirize chivalric romance. Yet by focusing on the ladies rather than on the knights, he distracts the viewer's attention from Malory's chief concern. Of forty-eight paintings only half a dozen (and most of those Grail Quest subjects) lack a seductive female, in gorgeous clothes, generally displaying a good deal of bare flesh. One critic regretted that the merits of Flint's landscapes were overlooked "in the contemplation of the banal if technically brilliant breastscapes."[43] Bearing in mind that Guenevere, Lyoness, Isolde, and Alice represent the rewards earned by the heroes' prowess, and remembering, too, that the medieval fée's chief desire was the acquisition of a mortal lover, there is justification in the text for the luscious females, though in Flint's paintings they seem to spend rather too much time stretched out seductively along castle walls (VIII, 31) or beside a lake with a lover, a female harpist and a swan, all of dazzling beauty (X, 39). And there is certainly an abundance of those nameless females whom Malory calls "damosels," but a paucity of knights and squires. All this we may accept, beguiled by Pre-Raphaelite beauty. But Flint goes too far when an erotically depicted half-naked lady turns out to be Percival's saintly sister (XVII, 7; Fig. 5).

One is also disturbed by Flint's eclecticism. While the early woodcut designers, having no sense of historical perspective, dressed their subjects in English contemporary style, Flint flaunts his awareness of various cultures. The pagan knight Segwarides wears a Moorish gown and pointed helmet. Arthur swears his coronation oath by placing his hand on a splendidly illuminated gospel in a sanctuary furnished with Victorian versions of a Baptism window, an altar crucifix, a screen carved with apostles, and an elaborate candelabrum decorated with gilded representations of the evangelists and their signs flanking an obviously symbolic dragon. Isolde's signs include Celtic interlace, an Irish harp with dragon decorations, gold torques, and an ancient cup straight out of the Dublin Museum. The armor, too, is fantastically eclectic.

It is intersting to compare the enthusiasm of Percy Bradshaw and, no doubt, of most of his contemporaries, with the reviews in the *Burlington Magazine*. The critic of Volume I had nothing but praise for the text, but protested against

> spoiling so perfect a piece of typography by coloured
> illustrations so grotesquely inconsistent with the style of the
> book as a whole . . . surely those who can afford ten guineas for
> a reprint of Sir Thomas Malory do not need to have their
> imagination prompted by the romantic clap-trap of a
> provincial theatre.[44]

The critic of Volume II, Roger Fry, was equally vitriolic:

> Alas! the illustrations are of the same distressing Lyceum-stage
> kind as heretofore and completely dispel the visions which the
> perusal of Malory in a beautifully printed edition might be
> expected to arouse. Woodcut, whether plain or coloured, is the
> only possible accompaniment to such type.[45]

When the final volumes appeared, Fry announced that "nothing
taxes the invention of an artist more than the illustration of a long
and well-worn theme, and the 'Morte Darthur' is one of the worst
worn; it is worn out."[46]

As if in defiance of Fry, another opulently produced Malory
was about to appear, a 504 page folio limited edition printed in
Chelsea at the Ashendene Press and decorated with the wood
engravings of Charles and Margaret Gere.[47] The books printed by
this private press, which operated from 1894 to 1935, expressed the
ideals of its owner, C. H. St. John Hornby (1867-1946), who made it
the "hobby of a lifetime." Greatly influenced by Morris, whom he
had visited in 1895,[48] Hornby determined that his publications
would represent "what is best in craftsmanship and indeed in life
itself."[49] That best in life itself was found in the *Morte Darthur*,
which he associated with the qualities of a gentleman.

By now wood-engraving[50] had become almost a cult for the
artist who, in the words of Eric Gill, wanted freedom "to satisfy his
own conscience and not be a mere tool in the hands of others."[51]
Charles Gere (1867-1957), a portrait painter, decorator, designer of
stained glass, and illustrator, had been associated with Morris at the
Kelmscott Press, a fact that is all too evident in the loose dresses,
paved floors, Victorian-medieval furnishings, stone walls, and
Romanesque arches of his cuts. The confined flat back wall, gently
curved vault, and wide floor on which Tristram and Isolde are set
(Fig. 6) clearly derive from Burne-Jones' treatment of space in the
Kelmscott Chaucer. But Gere has the virtue of restoring Lancelot to
his paramount position, including him in ten of his twenty-seven

cuts. He also restores the traditional male-female relationships. One has only to look at his clinging Isolde to realise that she is no Beardsleyan Medusa but an "angel in the house" type. Furthermore, he occasionally provides an original perspective, as in the woodcut of Lancelot's journey to knight his son. The miniscule humans are dwarfed by towering mountains and the enormous Gothic monastery surrounded by its lake-like moat, a scene more Swiss than English. Though his picture of Elaine dreaming over Lancelot's shield is as crowded and confining as Rossetti's "The Tune of the Seven Towers" or Morris's "Queen Guenevere," his depiction of the dying Arthur departing with the three queens makes effective use of empty space, light, and a flight of swans to suggest the king's apotheosis (Fig. 7). The Ashendene *Malory* is technically and iconographically derivative, yet in spirit it is closer to the author than any of the versions so far.

The next Malory illustrations to be discussed are the work of the most technically proficient and the most original artist to turn his attention to this classic. Arthur Rackham (1867-1939), like Beardsley, began his working life as a clerk in an insurance office. In 1892 he joined the *Westminister Budget* where his drawings of contemporary politicians attracted attention. From the following year until his death he was chiefly occupied with book illustration, his whole output being "a consistent protest against the exploitation of sterile realism."[52] Better than any other artist he recreates the milieu of medieval romance where the "historical" world of time and space is penetrated by the otherworldly.[53] This "faerie" effect he produces by the use of line drawing delicately tinted with watercolors and by mingling elements from different genres so that the twisted roots, grasping branches, and rough bark of his trees seem to incorporate human features while the caricatured physiognomies of his humans take on animal characteristics. The possibility of metamorphosis is ever present.

His *Morte Darthur*, published by Macmillan in 1917,[54] contains sixteen full-page illustrations in color, mounted on white paper, and seventy black-and-white drawings, most of them decorated initials in the Beardsley style. Alfred J. Pollard's preface is interesting as an expression of contemporary attitudes which Rackham probably shared. (The American artist, Robert Lawson, in an obituary tribute, remarked, "Rackham was in his work a Gentleman."[55]) Though Pollard disapproved of courtly love, he nevertheless saw Lancelot as "much finer stuff than Arthur. . .the most splendid study of a great gentleman in all literature." Arthur himself was described as "a typical sportsman."

That Rackham is not averse to creating the sensuous, decorative effects of Victorian medievalism may be seen in his glowing Grail Maiden (reminiscent of Rossetti and Burne-Jones) and in the opulent, fifteenth-century clothing of Tristram and Isolde. But his strength is his ability to capture the Malorian sense of forest, a place of danger and mystery, where a knight-errant might encounter evil knights and damsels in distress; the strange questing beast at a murky stream where the gnarled root of a tree reproduces the beast's serpentine shape and cold eye (Fig. 8); and the bodies of the Red Knight's victims dangling like straw men from the trees. The forest diminishes the humans who venture into it. The about-to-be rescued damsel of "How Sir Launcelot slew the knight Sir Peris de Forest Savage" is almost absorbed by the tree protecting her.

Rackham shares Beardsley's ability to powerfully evoke a sense of evil. In the picture of Eliot the harper performing at King Mark's feast, a witty iconographic parody of numerous Marriage at Cana scenes,[56] the rapacious expression of the half-starved dog gnawing on a bone is reproduced on the foxy face of the king with his sharp nose, pointed ears, and clawlike hands. These details, contrasting with the sensuosity of full blown roses, ripe fruit, and the King's splendid crown, effect what Derek Hudson describes as "the ironies of incongruous juxtaposition."[57] Rackham's Arthurian society is not limited to the knights and ladies of the text; overfed merchants and their beady-eyed wives stare disapprovingly at the doings of the upper class in "How King Arthur and Queen Guenever went to see the barge that bore the corpse of Elain the Fair Maiden of Astolat." No picture better illustrates his combination of the real and the fantastic, the noble and the demonic, than that of Lancelot's fight with a "friendly dragon," the archetypal heroic activity (Fig. 9). From the fourteenth-century doorway and the protective cover of a flying buttress the townspeople—anybody's neighbors—peek out, while in the foreground the mailed hero thrusts at the mailed monster. Conflict is created by the use of diagonals: the shield parallels the outstretched right leg and the flames spewing from the dragon's mouth; the sword provides a right angle cross; the dragon assumes a zig-zag pose that gives a sense of crumbling. Form and content are brilliantly unified.

Finally, Rackham shares the tragic sense of alienation that pervades Malory's last books. "How Mordred was slain by Arthur and how by him Arthur was hurt to the death," with its dark foreground and light sky, absence of color, bat-like creatures in silhouette, explosive lines of lance and swords, and devastating fragmentation of horses, arms, and armor, makes visual reference to Goya's disasters of war iconography.[58] But it may also embody Rackham's own depression in 1916 as he contemplated the destruction of that peaceful, prosperous late Victorian and Edwardian world in which he had grown up and created his best work.

The artist most recently associated with a deluxe edition of the *Morte*[59] might be termed a decorator rather than an illustrator. For Robert Gibbings (1889-1958) and the group of wood engravers who worked with him, the literary text was not to be used as a source of naturalistic representations with sentimental values. If the artist successfully overcame the obduracy of the wood, his work would have a value that was absolute. Gibbings' acquisition of the Golden Cockerel Press in 1924 enabled him to be both designer and publisher.[60] Though with a few exceptions he does not allow the text to dictate specific subjects, he is in some ways an admirable illustrator of the *Morte Darthur*, for in his black-and-white prints he captures as did no other illustrator the vigor and joyful urgency of Malory's jousts and tournaments:

> So when they had rested them a while they gede to battle again, tracyng, racyng, foyning as two boars. And at some time they took their run as it had been two rams, and hurtled together that sometime they fell grovelling to earth.   (VII, 17)

Gibbings brilliantly evokes this delight in rollicking action.

He uses botanical forms, as Malory used the forest, to provide a continuum for his human figures while relying on heraldry, armor, and weapons to convey a chivalric ethos. To an extent never approached by other illustrators, he transcends the limits of time and space. That, perhaps, is the weakness of his edition. Containing only a few scenes specifically based on the text—the giant of St. Michael's Mount engaged in his macabre barbecue, a naked Lancelot threatening a naked Elaine with his sword, Lancelot flailing about in his madness, Lancelot in the cart hurtling towards Melyagaunt's castle—the work is decorative rather than illustrative. There is little transition between black and white, a simplification which flattens the designs. Nevertheless, he does approach the absolute at which he aims. In the illustration of Mordred and Arthur exchanging death blows (Fig. 10), visual tension is built up between the battlers and the plant motif which ties them together. The human shapes echo the curving line of the plant while the horizontal spear formally provides a right angle connection with the stem. The duplicated iconographic motif of the crown further unites them in a uniquely momentous act. In this case, only a knowledge of the text enables the viewer to determine which is the true king.

The mystical satisfaction that Gibbings derived from his chosen art form is described in his *Sermons for Artists*:

> When out of the riot of forms and colours in nature the artificier is able to co-ordinate the elements of a more comprehensible design, then it is that for brief moments he reaches harmony with the universal spirit. Sometimes in those seconds of insight time stands still, events past, present, and future remain stationary like resting cattle spotted on the surface of a field.[61]

More pertinent to the desired relationship between an author and his illustrator are Rackham's comments to the Authors' Club of London when they entertained him at Whitehall Court, January 31, 1910:

> An illustration may legitimately give the artist's view of the author's ideas; or it may give his view, his independent view, of the author's subject. But it must be the artist's view; any attempt to coerce him into a mere tool in the author's hands can only result in the most dismal failure. Illustration is as capable of varied appeal as is literature itself; and the only real essential is an association that shall not be at variance or unsympathetic. The illustrator is sometimes expected to say what the author ought to have said or failed to say clearly. . . . Sometimes he is wanted to add some fresh aspect of interest to a subject which the author has already treated interestingly from his point of view. . . . But the most fascinating form of

illustration consists of the expression by the artist of an individual sense of delight or emotion aroused by the accompanying passage of literature.[62]

The fifteenth-century knight-prisoner could never have imagined what varieties of delight his *Morte Darthur* would inspire over a period of five hundred years.

University of Alberta

NOTES

[1] See Alison Stones, "The Earliest Illustrated Prose Lancelot Manuscript," *Reading Medieval Studies*, 3 (1977), 3-44.

[2] Quoted by David Bland, *A History of Book Illustration* (Berkeley and Los Angeles: University of California Press, 1969), p. 19.

[3] Janet Backhouse, *The Illuminatred Manuscript* (Oxford: Phaidon, 1979), p. 80.

[4] The woodcut was made by cutting the wood on both sides of the lines drawn on the block and removing the bare areas with a gouge.

[5] Janet Backhouse, Mirjam Foot, and John Barr, *William Caxton* (London: British Library, 1976).

[6] Two copies of the original printing survive, one in the Pierpont Morgan Library, New York, the other in the John Rylands University Library of Manchester.

[7] *William Caxton*, p. 49.

[8] See Aldred W. Pollard, *Early Illustrated Books: a History of the Decoration and Illustration of Books in the Fifteenth and Sixteenth Centuries*, 2nd ed. (New York: Dutton, 1917); Henry R. Plomer, *Wynkyn de Worde and His Contemporaries from the death of Caxton to 1535* (London: Grafton, 1925); and James Moran, *Wynkyn de Worde, Father of Fleet Street* (London: Wynkyn de Worde Society, 1960).

[9] Moran, p. 23.

[10] The unique copy is in the John Rylands Library, Manchester. A facsimile was published by Basil Blackwell, Oxford, and Houghton, Mifflin, Boston and New York, 1934. For a description of the woodcut series, see Edward Hodnett, *English Woodcuts 1480-1535* (1934; rpt. Oxford: Oxford University Press, 1973), pp. 309-12.

[11] Pollard, p. 23.

[12] Arthur M. Hind, *An Introduction to a History of Woodcut, with a Detailed Survey of Work Done in the Fifteenth Century*, 2 vols. (1935; rpt. New York: Dover, 1963), p. 728.

[13] *Bibliotheca Spenceriana, or a Descriptive Catalogue of the Books Printed in the Fifteenth Century, in the Library of George John, Earl Spencer* (London: Lngman, 1815), VI, 403; quoted by H. Oskar Sommer, ed., *Malory's Morte Darthur*, 3 vols. (London: David Nutt, 1889), II, 5.

[14] Reproduced in H. W. Koch, *Medieval Warfare* (London: Bison, 1978), p. 146.

[15] Hodnett, p. 310.

[16] Hodnett, p. 311.

[17] Hodnett, p. 14.

[18] Margaret Scott, *Late Gothic Europe, 1400-1500. The History of Dress* (London: Bell and Hyman, 1980).

[19] The single surviving copy is in the British Library.

[20] Three copies are in the British Library, two of them imperfect.

[21] Quoted by Sommer, II, 8, n. 3, from J. Payne Collier, *A Bibliographical and Critical account of the Rarest Books in the English Language*, 2 vols. (1865; rpt. New York: AMS Press, 1966), p. 31.

[22] See Kenneth Clark, *The Gothic Revival*, 3rd ed. (London: Constable, 1973) and Mark Girouard, *The Return to Camelot: Chivalry and the English Gentleman* (New Haven: Yale University Press, 1981).

[23] Georgiana Burne-Jones, *Memorials of Edward Burne-Jones*, 2 vols. (London: Macmillan, 1904), I, 116.

[24] Although the Pre-Raphaelites were more interested in painting than in book illustration, D. G. Rossetti and Holman Hunt contributed Arthurian woodcuts to the edition of Tennyson's poems published in 1857 by Edward Moxon. See G. S. Layard, *Tennyson and His Pre-Raphaelite Illustrators* (London: Stock, 1894).

[25] J. Mordaunt Crook, *William Burges and the High Victorian Dream* (Chicago: University of Chicago Press, 1981).

[26] Although the Pre-Raphaelites made a great to-do about painting from nature, Ruskin commented re Rossetti's landscapes that "his foliage looked generally fit for nothing but a fire-screen and his landscape distances like the furniture of a Noah's ark from the nearest toy shop" ("Lectures on the Art of England").

[27] See Girouard, pp. 193-94.

[28] "Of Ornament and its Meaning" in *Ideals in Art. Papers theoretical, practical, critical* (London: George Bell and Sons, 1905), p. 108. In another paper, "Thoughts on House-Decoration," the necessity of ornament is related to the condition of an industrial society; it is "a sort of aesthetic compensation for the increased artificiality, complexity, and restraint of civilized life" (p. 110).

[29] See Erwin Panofsky, *Early Netherlandish Painting, its Origins and Character*, 2 vols. (Cambridge, Mass.: Harvard University Press, 1953), I, 131-48.

[30] See May Morris, ed., *William Morris, Artist, Writer, Socialist,* 2 vols. (1936; rpt. New York: Russell and Russell, 1966) and Philip Henderson, ed., *The Letters of William Morris to his Family and Friends* (1950; rpt. New York: AMS Press, 1978), *passim.*

[31] May Morris, I, 318.

[32] Morris had a considerable collection of illuminated manuscripts and early printed books, including Wynkyn de Worde's *The Golden Legend* (1527); he borrowed from Quaritch de Worde's *Recuyell of the Histories of Troy* when he was looking for sample types. See J. R. Dunlap, *William Caxton and William Morris* (London: William Morris Society, 1964).

[33] See the two-volume Basilisk Press edition (London, 1975) with commentary by Duncan Robertson.

[34] Morris was so annoyed by the imitation of his style that he threatened a lawsuit. See Beardsley's letter to G. F. Scotson Clark, ca. Feb. 15, 1893, in Henry Mass *et al.,* eds., *The Letters of Aubrey Beardsley* (Rutherford, PA: Fairleigh Dickinson University Press, 1970), p. 43.

[35] *Le Morte Darthur* (London: Dent, 1893-94) based on Southey's edition of Caxton's text with modernized spelling. There were 300 copies on Dutch hand-made paper and 1500 ordinary copies.

[36] For a more extensive discussion see my article, "'Flat Blasphemies' — Beardsley's Illustrations for Malory's Morte Darthur," *Mosaic,* 8/2 (1975), 67-75.

[37] Mary Lago, ed., *Burne-Jones Talking; His Conversations 1895-1898,* preserved by his studio assistant Thomas Rooke (Columbia: University of Missouri Press, 1981), pp. 174-75.

[38] *The Romantic Agony,* 2nd ed., trans. Angus Davidson (London: Oxford University Press, 1951), pp. 209-10.

[39] *Aubrey Beardsley* (1898; rev. and rpt. London: Baker, 1967), p. 36.

[40] Five hundred copies were printed on handmade Riccardi paper and twelve on vellum. Each painting was reproduced separately, then attached to the page and covered with a translucent leaf giving the relevant Malorian quotation. Later the edition was republished for general sale in a two-volume set (1920) with 36 illustrations and a one-volume edition (1927) with 24.

[41] Press Art School, London (1918), p. 4.

[42] Crook, p. 319.

[43] H. L. Mallalieu, *The Dictionary of British Watercolour Artists up to 1920,* 2 vols. (London: Antique Collectors' Club, 1976), p. 101.

[44] *Burlington Magazine,* 18 (Oct.-Apr. 1910-11), 358.

[45] *Burlington Magazine,* 19 (Apr.-Sept. 1911), 365.

[46] *Burlington Magazine,* 21 (Apr.-Sept. 1912), 121.

[47] In his *A Descriptive Bibliography of the Books Printed at the Ashendene Press MDCCCXCV-MCMXXXV* (London: Ashendene, 1935),

C. H. St. John Hornby indicates that the pictures of III,5, IX,17, and X,59 were drawn by Margaret Gere, the others by her brother Charles M. Gere. They were cut in wood by W. H. Hooper, who had been Morris's cutter, and J. B. Swain. The text was Southey's 1817 edition of Caxton. 145 copies were printed on paper and eight on vellum. There are two full-page woodcuts and 27 smaller cuts.

[48] Sir Sidney Cockerell, in *The Spectator* (10 May 1946), wrote that on 13 March 1895 Hornby "came to Hammersmith to see the Kelmscott Press of which I was then secretary and stayed to tea at Kelmscott House with William Morris. . . . Hornby parted with his host in a state of elation and high resolve."

[49] Will Ransom, *Kelmscott, Doves and Ashendene* (San Francisco: Book Club of California, 1952), p. 17.

[50] The wood engraver used his graver as a drawing instrument; hence he was an artist rather than merely a craftsman.

[51] Foreward to R. John Beedham, *Wood Engraving*, reprinted as *Foreward to a Treatise Upon the Craft of Wood Engraving* (Vancouver: University of British Columbia Press, 1967), p. 3.

[52] Martin Birnbaum, in *Jacovleff and Other Artists* (New York: Struck, 1946), cited by Roland Baughman, *The Centenary of Arthur Rackham's Birth* (New York: Columbia University Press, 1967), p. 8.

[53] Derek Hudson in *Arthur Rackham, His Life and Work* (1960; rpt. New York: Scribner, 1975), p. 154, writes: "A.S. Hartrick has seen him as a descendant of the English medieval mural painters who decorated our country churches and brought a touch of humour to the portrayal of the 'Harrowings of Hell' and the Seven Deadly Sins."

[54] The work has been abridged by Alfred W. Pollard. The limited edition consisted of 500 signed copies, bound in vellum with pictorial stamping in gold on the cover and spine. There was also a trade edition.

[55] Robert Lawson, "The Genius of Arthur Rackham," *The Horn Book*, 16 (1940), 149.

[56] See, for example, The Marriage at Cana of Hieronymus Bosch.

[57] Hudson, p. 44.

[58] In a letter to Frank Redway (28 May 1914), Rackham attributes his success as an illustrator to his thorough knowledge of the texts. He is one of those rare artists who does not stick to literal realization but expands the meaning by providing iconographical references that are both historical and aesthetic.

[59] The title page reads "Le Morte Darthur. The Story of King Arthur & of his noble knights of the Round Table written by Sir Thomas Malory, first printed by William Caxton, now modernized by A. W. Pollard, illustrated with wood engravings by Robert Gibbings & printed at the Golden Cockerel Press, London, for the Limited Editions Club, New York,

1936." 3 vol. Many of the illustrations are reproduced in Patience Empson, ed., *The Wood Engravings of Robert Gibbings,* introd. Thomas Balston (London: Dent, 1959), pp. 181-97.

[60] Thus he returned to the concept of the artist-designer and produced book that had first been realized in Albrecht Dürer's *Apocalypse.* See Albert Garrett, *A History of British Wood Engravings* (Tunbridge Wells: Midas Books, 1978), p. 204.

[61] Empson, p. xxi.

[62] Hudson, pp. 87-88.

The Illustrations

Fig. 1. Uther, Igraine and the Duke of Cornwall

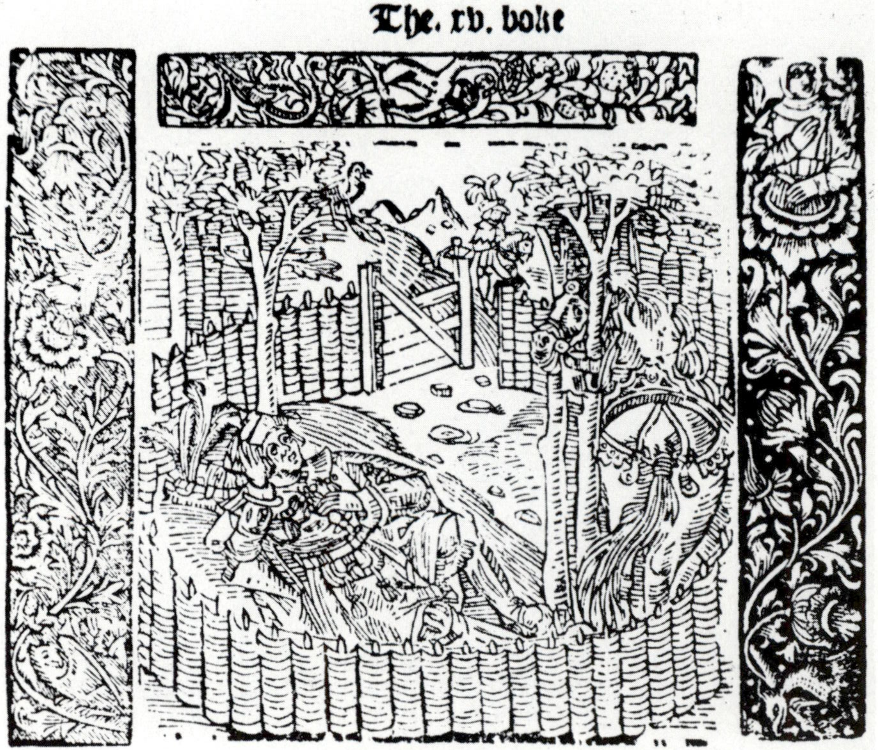

Fig. 2. The Dolorous Lover

THE LADY OF THE LAKE
TELLETH ARTHVR OF THE
SWORD EXCALIBVR

Fig. 3. Arthur and the Lady of the Lake

Fig. 4. Isolde at the Joyous Garde

Fig. 5. Percival's Sister

Fig. 6. Tristram and Isolde

AND THERE RECEYVED HYM THREE QUENES WYTH GRETE MOURNYNG, AND SOO THEY SETTE THEM DOUN, AND IN ONE OF THEIR LAPPES KYNG ARTHUR LAYD HYS HEED, AND SOO THAN THEY ROWED FROM THE LONDE.

Fig. 7. Arthur's Departure for Avalon

Fig. 8. The Questing Beast

Fig. 9. Lancelot and the Fiendly Dragon

Fig. 10. The Last Battle